THE
INNER
LIFE OF
RACE

Duke University Press   *Durham and London*   2024

THE INNER LIFE OF RACE

SOULS, BODIES &
THE HISTORY OF
RACIAL POWER

Leerom
Medovoi

Project Editor: Livia Tenzer
Designed by Courtney Leigh Richardson
Typeset in Garamond Premier Pro by Westchester Publishing Services

Library of Congress Cataloging-in-Publication Data
Names: Medovoi, Leerom, [date] author.
Title: The inner life of race : souls, bodies, and the history
of racial power / Leerom Medovoi.
Description: Durham : Duke University Press, 2024. | Includes
bibliographical references and index.
Identifiers: LCCN 2023053858 (print)
LCCN 2023053859 (ebook)
ISBN 9781478030805 (paperback)
ISBN 9781478026563 (hardcover)
ISBN 9781478059790 (ebook)
Subjects: LCSH: Race—Philosophy. | Racism—History. | Critical
theory. | Other (Philosophy)—Religious aspects. | Passing (Identity) |
Religion and politics. | Religious discrimination—History. | BISAC:
SOCIAL SCIENCE / Sociology / Social Theory | RELIGION / General |
SOCIAL SCIENCE / Race & Ethnic Relations
Classification: LCC HT1521 .M38 2024 (print) | LCC HT1521 (ebook) |
DDC 305.8001—dc23/eng/20240416
LC record available at https://lccn.loc.gov/2023053858
LC ebook record available at https://lccn.loc.gov/2023053859

Cover art: Richard Newton, "A Real San-Culotte!!" (detail), 1792.
Hand-colored etching. British Museum.

For Marcia, Samara, Jacob, Ro,
and for a better world

Contents

ACKNOWLEDGMENTS ix

INTRODUCTION
Ensoulment: A Strategy of Racial Power 1

1
RACE BEFORE RACE
The Flock and the Wolf 31

2
THE RACIAL TURN
Frayed Fabric and Dissimulating Danger 59

3
WESTPHALIAN REASON
The Political Theology of Sedition 97

4
RACIAL LIBERALISM, RACIAL CAPITALISM
Ensouling Property's Adversaries 133

CONCLUSION
The Many-Headed Hydra 191

NOTES 217   REFERENCES 243   INDEX 265

Acknowledgments

I've learned the hard way that there is no reason to save the best for last. My life partner, Marcia Klotz, has patiently lived with this project for more years than I care to admit. She has talked to me about it, suggested ideas, read chapters, encouraged me when I was down, and now she is here to share my joy that it is complete. Marcia, I can't thank you enough for being there for me throughout, especially during those dark COVID years when I didn't know if I would make it.

Some of the earliest work on this book took place while I was an English professor at Portland State University. At that time, I was doing my best to run a small Humanities Center on less than a $10,000 budget. For all its challenges, I look back at that time as one of my most satisfying. We were raising three little kids, which brought me much joy, yet at the same time my life at work was intellectually productive and stimulating, It was the foment of those years that eventually energized me to imagine this book. Looking back, I would like to thank Elizabeth Ceppi, Michael Clark, Paul Collins, Katja Garloff, Kambiz GhaneaBassiri, Amy Greenstadt, Avram Hiller, Alastair Hunt, Bill Knight, Oren Kosansky, Renee Lertzman, Bishupal Limbu, Sarah Lincoln, Marie Lo, Jan Mieszkowski, John Parry, Jennifer Ruth, Paul Silverstein, John Vignaux Smyth, Elliot Young, and many others for the intellectual community they shared with me in the formative years of conceptualizing this book.

At the University of Arizona, I have also been fortunate enough to find a community with whom I can think together. My special thanks go to Elizabeth Bentley, Anna Reynolds Cooper, Luciana Chamorro Elizondo, David Gibbs, Brooke Hotez, Paul Hurh, Miranda Joseph, Mark Kear, Adela Licona, Eithne Luibheid, John Melillo, Kaitlin Murphy, Peter Ore, Hai Ren, Karen Seat, Brian

Silverstein, and Albert Welter. We worked together on a number of collaborative research projects that have found their way into this book.

Along the way, many people read parts of this manuscript and gave me advice that has made this a better book. Among those individuals, I owe special thanks to the late Leo Bersani and Kathleen Woodward for urging me to move the project forward at critical junctures when I wasn't sure that I should. I also owe thanks to David Kyuman Kim and John L. Jackson Jr. for early and inspiring discussions that helped me land on the eventual title. Donald Pease has always been a tremendous supporter of my work, and I cannot thank him enough for his help with this book and with everything else. Eva Cherniavsky has been a gracious and brilliant collaborator, and much of my closing thoughts in this book are indebted to the Simpson Center program we ran together in fall 2019. I also want to single out my deep appreciation for my writing group mates over the last few years: Steph Brown, Scott Selisker, and Ragini Tharoor Srinivasan—you folks are the best, and your encouragement was critical. Faith Harden's careful reading of chapter 2 led to several crucial revisions that have made this a much better book. I also would like to thank Keith Feldman, not only for engaging with the project in profound ways, but also for giving me the glorious opportunity to spend a year in the Ethnic Studies Department at UC Berkeley, where I found renewed energy to finish the manuscript. Mohamad Jarada and Colleen Lye: thank you for your hospitality during that year. Finally, Anoop Mirpuri and Zahid Chaudhary were the best interlocutors one could hope for when I finished the introduction to this book and needed help thinking through the stakes of my frame.

I owe a debt to my dear friend Benjamin Robinson, as well as to Sara Guyer, Catrin Gersdorf, David Watson, Rosi Braidotti, Wang Jianping, Debdatta Chowhury, Lajwanti Chatani, Joe Ramsey, Vanessa Rosa, and April Anson for giving me the opportunity to present portions of this book at Indiana University, the University of Wisconsin, the University of Uppsala, Würzburg University, Utrecht University, Shanghai Normal University, the Centre for Studies in Social Sciences Calcutta, the Forum on Critical Theory in Baroda, the University of Massachusetts Boston, Mt. Holyoke College, and the University of Connecticut. Those presentations were immensely helpful along the way. Raef Zreik, Shaul Setter, Mohamad Mustafa, Ernst van den Hemel, Ori Goldberg, Eva Midden, Mu-chou Pu, Ingrid Diran, Rafael Perez-Torrez, Lynn Itagaki, Christian Haines, Antoine Traissnel, Iyko Day, David Kazanjian, Hylton White, Sarika Chandra, Chris Chen, Nikhil Singh, Ann Pellegrini, Benjamin Arditi, Lajwanti Chatani, and Naminata Diabate are all people with whom I have had the good fortune to engage as I was working on this project. I have learned much from them and appreciate their warmth and comradeship.

My siblings, Amir and Ornah Medovoi, are bone of my bone, flesh of my flesh. I count on you to keep this world a loving and familiar one. Thank you! The love and support of my parents made me who I am. While they are not here to enjoy this book, they are still its foundation. Few members of their families survived the Holocaust. The spirits of the lost ones infuse these pages. Finally, I'd like to offer this testimony of love for my kids, Samara Klotz, Jacob Medovoi, and Ro Medovoi Klotz. You three have literally grown up as I wrote this book, and I remember so many moments of treasuring who you were becoming as I worked on it. I hope you enjoy it someday, and get to see what your pops has been busy with all these years.

INTRODUCTION

Ensoulment: A Strategy of Racial Power

On her way to work one morning
Down the path alongside the lake
A tender hearted woman saw a poor half frozen snake
His pretty colored skin had been all frosted with the dew
"Poor thing," she cried, "I'll take you in and I'll take care of you"
"Take me in tender woman
Take me in, for heaven's sake
Take me in, tender woman," sighed the snake.
—OSCAR BROWN JR., "The Snake"

If the language of race can be grounded in color, physiognomy, ancestry, religion, ideology, identification, or even sexual desire, what exactly holds it together? I will hypothesize in the following pages that race is above all a technology of power. From this vantage point, the best way to theorize race is to begin not with an explanation of how it fractionalizes populations (which it can do in many ways) but with the question of why it does so and with what ultimate results. My answers in this book will revolve around the key concepts of enmity and security, an approach that derives in part from the fact that my project originally began as an attempt to explore Islamophobia as a species of racism. What, I wanted to ask, distinguishes Islamophobia from other racisms that have been central to critical ethnic studies in the United States? To what extent does the word "Islamophobia," which implies the pathological fear of a religion, clarify (or not) this distinctive form of racism? If religious affiliation is spiritually rather than corporeally defined, what conception of "race" is even at stake in Islamophobia? And in the long aftermath of the war on terror, these questions raised another: What role do projects of security and the production of populational enemies play in the history of racial power?

In the process of trying to answer these questions, I began to rethink certain working assumptions about the basic features of race and racism, widening in the process both the theoretical and historical scope of this book. I found that the critical study of Islamophobia opens onto a set of major questions about the shared genealogies of race and security that would require writing a different study than the one I had first conceived. I also found that what W. E. B. Du Bois called racisms of the "color line" cannot easily be cordoned off from the study of Islamophobia and antisemitism, nor indeed from the wider politics of populational security that underlay racisms.[1] All of this became especially clear to me in the face of Donald Trump's powerful recombination of race-making practices, which, as this book intends to show, characterize a late-fascist flexible racism with a paradoxically long genealogy.

As a central feature of his 2016 presidential campaign, Trump lambasted a "corrupt political establishment" for admitting two distinct populations entry into the United States: Syrian refugees fleeing a destructive civil war, as well as other refugees from Muslim majority countries; and Latin American immigrants, likewise seeking an escape from violence in their home countries. However much they looked like humanitarian victims, insisted Trump, these groups were twin Trojan horses smuggling across our borders a murderous intent that would eventually be unleashed on Americans. Trump's proposed solutions to both "threats" were virtually identical: erect a barrier against their entry. For Middle Easterners, Trump proposed a blanket travel ban. For Latin Americans, Trump proposed a border wall.

Trump's ongoing hostility toward Mexican and Central American immigrants can be closely identified with his white nationalist sentiments, a key element in his right-wing populist politics that aim to "make America great again" by stemming a rising tide of color and restoring a political culture of white supremacy associated with some glorious yet unspecified past. This account of Trumpian racism seems right as far as it goes. Taking it as our starting point, however, how do we interpret Trump's symmetrical attitudes toward Latin American immigrants and Muslims? Have Arabs and Muslims, as some argue, become reclassified as people of color in the post-9/11 era, such that the immigrant from Syria embodies today the same dreaded dilution of American whiteness as the immigrant from Mexico or Honduras? Or do we need a different order of explanation? Does right-wing populist racism, perhaps, activate a politics of population that renders Muslims as enemies of national greatness on the basis of something not quite explicable through the hierarchy of the white/nonwhite binary? If so, what could that alternate basis be? And might it also turn out to apply to Latin Americans?

To add yet another level of complication, there is also the question of the racialization of Trump's "corrupt political establishment." To that end, how should we introduce into our overarching analysis the striking resurgence of antisemitism? Jews are certainly not people of color, even in Trump's America. Yet the chants of "Jews will not replace us" heard at the 2017 white supremacist Unite the Right rally in Charlottesville clearly drew inspiration from the appeal of Trump's plan to fight the "very bad people" who "want to do great destruction to our country."[2] The antisemitic variation on Trump's extensive cast of "bad people" was on especially vivid display in the final video ad of his 2016 presidential campaign, titled "Donald Trump's Argument for America," which featured Janet Yellen, George Soros, and Lloyd Blankfein as sinister Jewish bankers busily extracting ever more wealth from the American working class (Trump 2016).

It should be clear that Muslims, Mexicans, and Jews represent far from identical dangers in the Trumpian racist model. The respective perils to America around which each threat is articulated—terrorism, criminality, and finance—adopt very different inflections. But what then do they actually share? In certain respects, this is an old and vexing question in the scholarship on race and racism. Color-line racism, Islamophobia, and antisemitism: are they fundamentally different from one another, or does some common political strategy of racism underlie them all?[3] At the end of the day, this book supports the second position. But to extract the common racial kernel at the heart of their disparate but related politics, I will need to revisit certain features of what is conventionally understood to define both race and racism, rereading them in ways that still centrally feature the hierarchizing action of a color line between white and nonwhite, while recognizing that this line serves as just one important rule in a wider and more encompassing game of racial power.

The principal argument of this book is that racial power employs not so much a differential logic consistently grounded in hierarchies of embodiment, as a dialectic of bodies and souls, a dialectic through which those hierarchies are adduced and within which they are enfolded. Because bodies represent the visible moment in a racial dialectic of the seen and unseen, especially in the context of the "color line," this fuller operation is not always on open display. Once the soul enters into the analysis, however, race proves a far more capacious and flexible strategy of power—bearing a far more complex genealogy—than attention to the body alone would suggest.

The soul may seem a strangely old-fashioned concept to invoke. It is a word that whiffs of religious superstition, so unlike its counterpart, the body, which has become a highly fashionable topic of academic study, whether in the name of a new materialist methodology, a biopolitical analysis, or the underlying concerns of antiracist and antisexist scholarship. I should therefore state at the outset that I generally share the materialist outlook (in my case a historical materialist one) of much contemporary antiracist criticism. This book is meant as a critical intervention into the practical political history of how human bodies have been administered by successive regimes of power. Yet I proceed from the assumption that thinking exclusively from the viewpoint of "body politics" will not suffice for the critical analysis of race and racism, precisely because the exercise of racial power has always involved producing the soul (or its various analogs: the mind, the spirit, the conscience, the subject, the inner self) so that it might serve as what Michel Foucault once called, in a brilliant reversal, "the prison of the body" (Foucault 2012, 30). To be sure, racialized populations are administered in part by regimes of classification that employ what materialist critics might call the politics of "embodiment," but this book will argue that racial embodiment finds its greatest effectiveness within strategies of power that pair it with the tactics of what I will call "ensoulment." By "ensoulment" I mean a political effort to know (and, through knowing, an effort to conduct) an inner life that is assumed to be not directly perceivable on the body's surface even if it can only be deciphered and governed through the mediation of bodily symptoms. In this book, therefore, to "ensoul" a person or a population is to perform a biopolitical calculation that associates them with a certain quantity and quality of threat, and which thereby specifies to which technologies of power their bodies should be subjected.

This tactical concept of "ensoulment" as the work of the dialectic under investigation also suggests something about why this introduction adds the phrase "game of racial power" to the more common terminology of the "racial formation" or the regime of "structural racism." The concept of "racial formation" offers a powerful way of thinking about the socially constructed arrangements through which populations are divided, classified, and hierarchized, but also the way in which these divisions are reconstructed over time. "Structural racism" likewise offers a materialist formulation with which to challenge the reduction of racism to a social mentality, a set of collective prejudices, or a discriminatory attitude, redirecting us instead toward the set of material relations (political, social, economic) that produce and reproduce the disparities of racism. What the language of "game" adds is a way of viewing racism as a regulated conflict over the "truth" of a population that conducts itself at both a macrostrategic and microtactical level. While "regimes" simply govern, "games" must be played, necessitating imaginative judgments, speculative predictions, and tactical "moves" that will have outcomes for all those caught up in the game.

From Biopolitics to the Government of Souls

To consider how ensoulment is advanced through the game of racial power, I would like to return briefly to Donald Trump's first presidential campaign. At his 2016 rallies, Trump at some point discovered and began reading aloud to his supporters the lyrics to an old rhythm and blues song titled "The Snake," which he converted into a fable for the overarching racial threat he associated with Latin American immigrants and Muslim refugees. The song tells the story of a "tender-hearted" woman who, finding a half-frozen snake outside, falls in love with its "pretty skin," which she kisses and holds tight. "Take me in, tender woman," sighs the snake, so she takes him home to share a warm comforter, dishes of honey and milk, and a chance to recuperate. On returning from work at the end of the next day, she finds the snake fully recovered. But even though he "might have died" without her intervention, the snake expresses not gratitude but treachery, biting the woman and injecting her with his lethal venom. When she cries in distress, "you know your bite is poisonous and now I'm going to die," the reptile answers with a malicious grin, "Oh shut up you silly woman . . . You knew damn well I was a snake before you took me in."

Trump's choice of this song was more than a little ironic. "The Snake" was written in 1963 by Oscar Brown Jr., a postwar African American musician, civil rights activist, and former communist. Like another of his songs, "Signifying Monkey," "The Snake" grew out of Brown's interest in the folkloric trickster figure that features prominently in both African American and West African culture.[4] The particular version of the song that Trump originally encountered was likely the better-known cover of Brown's song by R&B performer Al Wilson, whose use of an upbeat tempo also reflects a playful trickster narrative.

At Trump's rallies, however, the song took on ominous new meaning as a racial threat of murderous violence. The snake became the "dangerous immigrant," while the woman stood in for an America too soft-hearted and prone to seduction to avoid what should have been a self-evident danger. Trump's public readings of "The Snake" staged a certain drama of body and soul through which he could operationalize his campaign around racial menace. What exactly is a snake? In Trump's story, a snake metaphorically stands in for populations that are naturally predisposed to injure American life. But the snake's aptness as such a figure concerns a meeting ground between its outer and inner racial nature. Outwardly, the snake is readily identified by its colorful skin, but the reptilian nature that really matters here is an inward propensity to poison and kill even those who have treated it well. Insofar as the snake symbolizes danger to the life of the national population, it appears as the archetypical figure of what Foucault once called biopolitical threat. In that well-known formulation, biopolitics is a form of governance designed to ensure the "security of the whole [population] from internal danger" by introducing mechanisms such as "forecasts, statistical estimates and overall measures" that permit interventions at the level of a population's general or aggregate life (Foucault 2003, 245–46). Foucault also famously argued that racism is critical to biopolitics because the category of race is precisely what allows biopolitical power to establish a militarized frontier in the population that divides those whose life must be defended from those who must be targeted in acts of "defense."

What is striking about Trump's politics of racial threat is that he articulates them biopolitically even in this more precise sense of treating the population as a stochastic domain of probabilities. Although the fable of the snake condenses the entire population into a two-character allegory, it nonetheless mobilizes a distinctly macrological and statistical form of state racism. In his speeches, tweets, and diatribes, Trump has consistently advanced a probabilistic language to describe the biopolitical threat of America's racial enemies. About Muslims, for example, he has said, "we have people out there that want to do great destruction to our country . . . whether it's 25 percent or 10 percent or 5 percent, it's too much" (Johnson and Hauslohner 2017). To relate these numbers back to his fable, Trump implies that perhaps 95 percent of Muslims might prove to be nothing like the snake of his song. Still, according to the political thought process behind the so-called Muslim travel ban, the odds are that every nineteen good Muslims who are admitted entry into the United States will smuggle at least one terrorist in with them. Trump has applied this same sort of probabilism to the people of Mexico: "They're not sending their best. They're not sending you. . . . They're sending people that have lots of problems. . . . They're bringing drugs. They're bringing crime. They're rapists. And some, I assume, are good people" (Trump 2015). This declaration, which Trump pioneered for the populist turn in the Republican Party, establishes a classic biopolitical caesura dividing a "you" (the American population) from a "they" (Mexicans making their way into the American population). While "you" names a law-abiding and life-fostering population, "they" differ from "you" by bearing the lethal threats of drugs, crime, and rape. But once again, Trump's final sentence anticipates the statistical exceptions. A few Mexicans will be good people, just as a few Americans will no doubt turn out to be bad people. The law of averages always ensures outliers. Yet the racial differences between us and them are fixed by precisely these statistical certainties about aggregated danger.[5] And for this reason, the lesson of Trump's macrological fable is permitted to stand: in a country of mostly good people, a healthy population, security is compromised by augmenting it with another population that contains a much higher percentage of bad people. How do we know they are likely to have bad people? Presumably because of their colorful skin. The moral? Enemies of life and health should never be invited into the population just because they may be accompanied by some good ones. Or to put this another way, we should know a caravan containing likely snakes when we see it.

There is one final aspect to the "snake" fable deserving of consideration, namely the woman's motive for sheltering a snake in the first place. Her tender heart refers to more than just misplaced generosity: it is literally a spiritual organ that contains her self-destructive desires. The woman is described as doting on the snake, stroking it's "pretty colored skin," calling it "beautiful," kissing it, and even clutching it to her bosom. Her seduction dramatizes precisely the wrong way to respond to the snake's physicality. Instead of finding the snake's colorful skin attractive, she should have recognized in it the "threat of race," a visual warning about the reptile's cold-blooded intentions.[6] Race here is not just a technology for difference-making; it is also a machine for sounding alarms about perilous proximities, menacing attractions, and looming contamination. It possesses and concerns itself with what Sharon Holland has called its "erotic life" (Holland 2012). For this reason, the woman's tender heart proves not entirely unlike the snake; it signals the danger that the woman invites due to the seducible nature of her *own* inner life, a life that is also gendered and sexual. The threat of race lies inside as well as outside, lodged within a certain segment of the population to be sure, but secreted as well within every heart and soul. The inward threat of race sometimes proves to be nothing less than racial desire itself, a desire that indicates the self's perilous internal resonance with racial difference. By secretly wanting the snake, one actually becomes a snake. It is the danger posed by this desire, therefore, that demands the waging of an outward war not only against one's external enemies but also a civil war of the self against one's inner demons.

The religious significance of the soul is far from irrelevant. One wonders, for example, whether Trump's choice of the song had something to do with the snake's inevitable Biblical significance for his evangelical supporters, who would surely hear in the lyrics a strong echo of Genesis 2–3. In a very old Christian tradition, the snake who appears in the Garden of Eden is an avatar of Satan, wickedly bent on destroying humanity's claim on eternal life by seducing Eve into sinful disobedience against God.[7] Because Eve capitulates to the snake's temptation, she in turn entices Adam, bringing the snake's curse upon him as well. Both she and her man are punished with mortality. The life of body and soul will no longer be eternally yoked together. Instead, the body will experience death and the soul will face a perpetual risk of damnation. The snake of Genesis can therefore stand as a religiously inflected metaphor for the biopolitical threat to life. It is a bookend figure in the Christian Bible, connecting Genesis to the final volume, the Revelation of John, where Satan returns as the serpentine Dragon waging a final battle against the Lamb of Christ, while Eve reappears as the "whore of Babylon." In Trump's politicization of this theology, therefore, the wicked soul of the malicious immigrant figures the satanic "axis of evil" against which the security state must always stand guard, an evil against which America apparently requires special governmental vigilance because the tender hearts of its people leave it so vulnerable to seduction.

Karen and Barbara Fields have argued that "racecraft," by which they mean the regime of racism that creates the classificatory schema of "race," finds a sociological precedent in the kind of "witchcraft" that Martin Luther once produced through his hostile pronouncements: Luther built a Protestant world in part by inventing witches as a theological enemy whose threat to the Christian soul became an early modern social fact (Fields and Fields 2012). In this sense, it was Luther, not the witches, who actually engaged in a kind of occult practice, conjuring something into existence through its discursive incantation. Racecraft is a similar kind of conjuring trick, creating the fiction of "race" as an existing fact about each of us and a social fact about our world. The Fields' useful connection between contemporary racecraft and early modern witchcraft is no historical accident. As this book will show, biopolitics when flexibly construed can be shown to predate the statistical demographics and scientific racism of the early nineteenth century. Before there were statistics, there was already the problem of managing the Christian flock of believers. Before there was an evolutionary racial hierarchy that viewed the "higher European races" as further removed from biological animality than the "lower races," one finds a theological gap between those closer to God and those approaching the Devil's wickedness. And finally, before there was regulation of the life of a biological species, there was a government of souls. Biopolitics concerns itself not only with protecting a society's corporeal life in this world, but also with defending its eternal life against its theopolitical enemies. All this is simply to say, at this early point in the book, that the logic of race we find Trump employing reaches back through a surprisingly long history. As I will show in chapter 3, race was also constitutive of the early security state, which from the very start employed what we normally consider antiquated technologies of power concerning the governance of spiritual conduct. Security is rooted in an ancient promise of redemption from evil, and race is rooted in an equally ancient characterization of the evil from which "we" must be redeemed.

Race, Knowledge, and Risk

If racial fables like that of the snake have a moral, it would be the importance of *knowing* how racial knowledge should serve to protect against danger. To borrow David Theo Goldberg's basic insight, race is not only a marker of difference but also a "suggestion of threat," by which he means that the racialization of a group serves to "conjure or condition, raise or rationalize anxieties about insecurity, possible loss, viral infection, even extinction" (Goldberg 2009, 28). But in order for race to signify threat, it must first be formulated as a problem of power/knowledge. Securing oneself against a racial threat means learning when to know "damn well" (i.e., to grasp the exceedingly high probability) something about another's inner life given the color of their skin, the shape of their body, the fact of their ancestry, the loyalties they declare, the beliefs they profess, or even the company they keep. It is also about ascertaining which vulnerabilities in our *own inner life* present a risk of self-annihilation. But none of these things are actually certainties, or if they are, we should think of them as certainties about an uncertainty. If race is a judgment about threat that can only be specified in the actuarial form of aggregate probabilities, then any individual case can only ever take on an aleatory quality ratified by the opacity of inward life. Since it cannot be directly seen, the soul is technically inscrutable. One can never be sure what kind of person someone is on the "inside" until they reveal themselves through their actions. Similarly, unless and until someone has been seduced, the character of their weakness (or perhaps the weakness of their character) may not be observable.

If probabilities hold, however, one can at least venture estimates about such uncertainties. Risk, as the economist Frank Knight once argued, is that which converts uncertainty (what we cannot anticipate at all) into something calculable (Knight 1921). Risk tells us what we can anticipate about what we do not know. If race serves as an epistemological ground for the management of bodies and populations in the name of neutralizing biopolitical threats, then it does so by converting uncertainty about a population's threat into a calculation of risk. Race is the answer yielded, the effect produced, when a biopolitical regime solves for the risk level of a population's threat. It thereby becomes an apparatus of security. In knowing what part of a population disproportionately threatens the rest, or what aspect of inner life disproportionately leaves the entire soul vulnerable, one can at least attempt to "secure" that threat, to manage it as a risk. Race is an apparatus of security for this reason: although the soul cannot be directly perceived, through technologies of race-making it is converted into something that can be made calculable.

How does this work? Properly speaking, the threat of a biopolitical enemy is taken to emanate from their inner life, their intention to harm the population as a structured whole. But it is important to recall that the calculability of that threat relies upon the inspection of the suspect's outer life. Such discernment is always mediated by the body. This is a rather complex operation. If regimes of race are established through the operation of probability machines for the calculation of populational security measures, then, counterintuitively enough, these regimes of race appear to reject the claim of any absolutely consistent one-to-one relationship between body and soul. Racialization derives from the management of security-relevant correlations between body and soul, but it also presupposes a certain instability in the body/soul relationship that becomes aleatory at the level of the individual. Sometimes the body is presumed to provide an indispensable clue regarding the truth of the soul it contains, but just as easily the body can be expected to elide or deflect that inner truth. If race is a shorthand for reading the body so as to forecast the threat of (or to) the soul, then race also presupposes that the inescapably necessary interpretive act may backfire. Hence Trump's probabilistic language. Sometimes an apparent danger proves to be a false alarm. Conversely, a body suggesting low probability of threat may perfectly camouflage a malicious soul. Put another way, race may be seen as a game of power/knowledge that is played by multiple agents with different strategies and for different effects.

Racial Truth and the Politics of Exposure

What game of truth emerges out of these kinds of conditions? I have found useful here Zahid Chaudhary's conjoining of the Lacanian concept of the "subject presumed to know" with the Foucauldian concept of knowledge/power to develop an account of what he calls the "politics of exposure" (Chaudhary 2020, 12). "Exposure," in Chaudhary's analysis, has multiple meanings, including the unmasking or revealing of something that was hidden, but also the abandonment of someone or something to a state of vulnerability or precarity. Race can be construed as just this kind of game, one that consolidates power through the attempted exposure of a subject's inner truth. As Kirstie Ball has pointed out, surveillance presupposes its targets to possess both visible outer surfaces (such as skin) and hidden or secret inner ones (the layerings of its soul). It is these secret inner layers, the ever deeper psychic contours of the subject, that surveillance aims to expose by unsheltering or stripping them bare (Ball 2009). In such games of concealment and exposure there are therefore two subjects who know: a racial enemy presumed to be hiding their malice, but also the subject of racial security whose policing practices work to expose the hidden biopolitical enmity. For the last four centuries, such policing has often been institutionally located in the governmentality of the state.[8] As we shall see in chapter 2, policing was also once conducted by the church. And as chapter 4 will explain, what we mean by "police" today is this project's secular liberal variant. But the key point here is that the subject of security or police must know what it does not know. It recognizes its own uncertainty regarding the precise individuals who bear enemy intentions, or the specific nature of the enemy intent they harbor. Still, to know that one does not know is to stand ready to calculate risks. This self-knowledge facilitates investigations to expose suspected persons and places, forcing into the open the revelations that security requires.

We can also formulate the exercise of racial power through the somewhat different terms of what Paul Ricoeur famously called the "hermeneutics of suspicion," which addresses that special situation when truth takes the form of lying (Ricoeur 1977, 32–36). Because racial power hypothesizes that the body houses an inner secret, the most important feature of its status as corporeal glyph or text becomes what it elides. One therefore must not accept at face value what one sees, but interpret the immediate manifestation instead as a negative symptom of something else. Ricoeur characterizes the maxim of the hermeneutics of suspicion in this way: "guile will be met with double guile" (Ricoeur 1977, 34). Security exercises a hermeneutics of suspicion because it must always ask under what conditions it is safer not to believe but to doubt. Racial knowledge is therefore of a sort that reveals the truth of a threat potentially denied by the body on its surface. Like Freudian analysis of the unconscious, racial power obtains its knowledge of persons and populations through a negative cryptography or symptomology: it decodes signs that manifestly obfuscate their latent meaning. To racialize a population in this sense is to see through them to a security risk that they do not openly acknowledge. This is the logic that in common parlance we often call "racial profiling." It occurs whenever a security regime singles out a population of individuals whose bodily appearance is read suspiciously as "race"—in other words, as a clue to some concealed threat.

Suspicion can be approached as either an affective or an epistemological state of affairs. In its affective register, racial suspicion bears a special relationship to fear. It is fear, of course, that is the emotion most strongly associated with a figure who threatens harms. Sara Ahmed has characterized the affective politics of fear as fundamentally concerned with the "conservation of power" precisely through its effort to ensure security against a perceived threat to life. But where fear is "produced by an object's approach," specific to an object that we recognize at once as dangerous, anxiety is in Ahmed's view a generalized "approach to objects," an expectation—even in the immediate absence of objects—that any future (approaching) object will constitute a threat worthy of fear (Ahmed 2004, 66). Suspicion, I suggest, lies at the threshold between Ahmed's conception of fear and anxiety because it names an affect that has been subjected to a stochastic logic. Suspicion evaluates its objects in terms of greater or lesser risks of harm. Objects of suspicion can be said to be the ones that *we are presumed wise to fear given what we know*. In relation to those specific objects, we must maintain an affective state of high alert and heightened attention. This could be characterized as a circumscribed and controlled form of *anxious reason*, one that produces for racial power the "anti-ness" that is so critical to anti-Blackness, antisemitism, and anti-immigrant xenophobia. This moment when "anti-ness" is produced is also tantamount to the act I am calling "racial ensoulment."

When we describe the objects of suspicion as those whom we know it is wise to fear, we are already observing how suspicion transforms from an affective state into an epistemological regime. Technologies of security that presuppose an epistemology of suspicion operate by means of hermeneutical preemption. They begin by presupposing the possible existence of a threat that cannot yet be seen. They then convert the uncertainty about that threat into a risk by finding ways to calculate its probability of occurring and the intensity of its likely effects. Finally, they hedge against that risk by conducting inquiries, examinations, and surveillance, and generally employing technologies of knowledge/power to gather evidence that can expose a threat wherever it is most likely to be located. The moment of final revelation, the release of the deepest secret, may or may not lead to an exercise of sovereign violence in which the final "exposure" is of a different order: punishment, incarceration, police brutality, assassination, death. This moment could be described as a necropolitical act of sovereign vengeance against the unmasked racial enemy. But until that moment, the game of racial power operates at a governmental register, exercising suspicion in order to administer the social discipline and biopower through which the entire population is conducted to produce security.

Because security is reactive, always responding to a preexisting secret of inner life, it often cultivates its own countersecrecy; by not letting the presumed enemy "know" what it knows, security seeks to trick its enemy into inadvertent self-exposure. This is why regimes of security are often formulated as variants on what Timothy Melley (2012) has called a "covert sphere," a domain of governance-through-secrecy that is typically mustered as a countering force: a *counter*terrorism, an *anti*communism, an *anti*-Blackness, a colonial *counter*insurgency.[9]

Inner Life of the Color Line

This lengthy excursus into race and security may at first glance seem difficult to reconcile with our conventional critical reading of so much American racism as a regime that both presupposes and establishes the hierarchy of power and privileges of a population deemed white over those populations deemed not. But it can in fact explain much about it. No regime of power can survive long without continuous efforts to maintain itself through some principle of self-adjusting reflexivity. This principle of reflexivity can also be characterized as power's redirection of itself in response to knowledge of changing movements and alignments within the field of its operation. If for all its abstraction this begins to sound like a language of battle, there is a reason for it. Foucault once asked (in a reversal of the Clausewitzian formulation) whether politics might actually be war conducted by other means, and if therefore war might not provide the proper analytics of power (Foucault 2003, 15–16).[10] However one might view this general thesis, there is no question that American white supremacy can be characterized, in Nikhil Singh's words, as a "long war" that produces the color line as a military front, mobilizing those located on the "white" side of the line as a population prepared to fight for those forms of privilege, status, wealth, or right that are presumed to be under perpetual siege by those on the other side (Singh 2017, 23–29). This military logic rests on the idea that the best defense is a good offense. Whether through the force of law, money, language, or physical violence, the "long war" continually repositions, resubjectivizes, dispossesses, incarcerates, or sometimes simply massacres populations deemed not-white whenever a perceived shift in the circulation of power is seen to threaten the future supremacy of a whiteness that the enforcement of the color line is presumed to guarantee. What is striking about this long war of race in America for the purposes of this book, then, is its familiar hermeneutic of suspicion: battles are launched against anyone who is even suspected of waging—sometimes suspected even of *wishing* they could wage—a secret attack on the hierarchies of the color line. Slaves planning revolt, native peoples scheming to reclaim their lands, Japanese Americans plotting treason, Latinos and Asians conspiring against the exploitation of their labor: these are the kinds of hidden threats against which the long war of race preemptively declares itself ready to wage battle. These hidden threats, moreover, might also be ensouled by whites who mingle with people of color, who love, live, or transact with them, or who perhaps simply resemble them in some aspects of their life chances. Since such people may be suspected of wanting to blur or erase the color line, they can become, like Trump's "tender-hearted woman," potential racial enemies who must be struggled against. These battles, self-described as defensive actions, are actually preemptive, continuously reconsolidating the very color line that is presumed to be at risk of erasure. White violence in this way envisions itself as a practice of defensive security, even when most obviously on the attack. And if war, like a game, involves both a level of overall strategy and another of multifarious tactics that include feinting, bluffing, spying, camouflaging, and other forms of covert operation, then in addition to open battle, this long war has involved its own games of concealment and exposure. Baring the secrets of inner life, ensouling one's enemies, constitutes a central theater of operation for the racial power of white supremacy.

"Look, a Negro!" is the repeated refrain in Franz Fanon's famous analysis of Blackness as a produced fact of colonial power that relies upon the epidermalization of human difference (Fanon 2008, 89–91).[11] Fanon's formulation is actually more important than it might seem at first glance because it flags Blackness as something whose political force presupposes its observability within a phenomenological regime of the sensorium. As Simone Browne has argued, surveillance has long been critical to the "dark matter" of anti-Blackness (Browne 2015). The color line presupposes that Blackness is something registered within the field of the perceptible, usually (but not always) meaning that it can be seen, and therefore that it specifies where the eye of white power should direct its practices of surveillance.[12] Surveillance is a strategy of populational control, but it can also be viewed as a military tactic, as a form of reconnaissance that aims to discover the maneuvers of an enemy, whether actual, potential, or probable. This is why, as Browne shows, the history of surveillance has been so closely tied to the history of the American color line's militarization, from the surveillance of every aspect of slave life to the contemporary practices of racial profiling and the dangers of "driving while Black" (Browne 2015, 12–13). But it is also important to see that these practices of surveillance also presuppose a permanent endangerment of the color line and its regime of power that is rooted in the presumptive covertness of the Black soul's effort to resist the regime of the color line that subjects it.

Of course, this presumption that a threat to the color line exists on all sides is itself one of the chief products of the game of power, and precisely because of power's redirectable quality as a movement of capacities, it is in fact self-fulfilling. Once a game of power is in play, it will be played from many directions. When white supremacy bifurcates the population into white and nonwhite through its operations of racial ensoulment, counteroffensives in the "long war of race" become inevitable. W. E. B. Du Bois's famous reading of the striving of the "souls of black folk" constitutes precisely such an effort to counterensoul Blacks, to wage war against what he called the "nameless prejudice" that instills an "all-pervading desire to inculcate disdain for everything black, from Toussaint to the devil" (Du Bois 2007, 12). Movements such as Negritude, Black Power, or Black Lives Matter have repeatedly emerged to provide tactics of self-defense (including covert ones) to those threatened by white supremacy. In the process, such movements initiate their own game of racial power, marshalling the biopolitical capacities of a racialized population in its self-defense, and developing on its behalf their own countervailing mechanisms of security.[13] Race becomes the basis for cultivating a political counterlanguage of struggle, power, solidarity, and liberation. It fights against "microaggressions" and the "weaponizing" of power.

Passing and the Dialectics of Body and Soul

Why are the secrets of inner life critical to this biopolitical logic of race war? Perhaps the easiest way to discern this connection, and to grasp in the process how the color line as a caesura exceeds the politics of sheer embodiment, is to consider the threshold case of "passing." Conventionally speaking, passing is understood as a situation in which someone presents themselves as racially other than what they are, self-presenting as white when they are Black, for instance, or the other way around. In the African American literary tradition especially, as Gayle Wald has shown, passing is sometimes narrated as a means for an individual to "transgress the social boundary of race, to 'cross' or thwart the 'line' of racial distinction that has been a basis of racial oppression and exploitation" (Wald 2000, 6).[14] Passing is therefore, in the story of such individuals, a special tactic on the battlefield of racial power that serves the purpose of what in the field of surveillance studies is referred to as "antisurveillance."[15] Understood as antisurveillance, passing can serve as a means of concealing oneself from the eye of white power as it tries to perform its oversight of Blackness.

Passing can only appear to be a transgression of the color line, however, because it is already a technology of power imminent to the regime of color line racism. Because "passing" confirms that the color line is a frontier that *can be crossed*, it shores up its status as a line whose integrity must be surveilled and policed. In the process, passing comes to organize white people's relationships, not just to Black and other nonwhite people, but to other (presumably) white people.[16] It is not white people who create the color line, but rather the color line that creates "white people," investing them with the responsibility to constantly surveil each other, which in turn has historically placed white people (especially but not exclusively lower-class whites) in a constant danger of being "exposed," lest they deviate from accepted behavior and norms that might tarnish or blacken them with the stigma of the race traitor. Like other games of racial power, then, the color line's long war has been directed inwardly as well as outwardly.[17]

Any effort to explicate the subject of passing without addressing these dialectics of body and soul, and that theorizes race purely from the perspective of embodiment, will fail to grasp how passing exploits the interference or dissonance between the dueling interpretive registers of race conveyed respectively by putatively visible bodies and putatively invisible souls. Where, we might ask, is the "Blackness" located in the "Black person" light enough to pass? Not apparently in the body. Any feasible answer provided by the game of racial power would seem to point toward the inner life: in Du Bois's famous "double consciousness," that person's potentially veiled self-awareness, complex psychic attachments, subjective identifications or evaluations as Black, something they paradoxically may seek to advance by surreptitiously passing as white.[18]

Of course, this reading could be subjected to ideological critique in which the inner life is shown to be the illusory product of what Marx once called the "camera obscura" of our experience of material processes (Marx and Engels 2018, 154). One could offer to locate even the "Blackness" of the passing subject materially in the structures and discourses of racial law and their relationship to structures of kinship or descent, whose framing of racial power the subject has "internalized." But even in such a materialist analysis, the moment in which an act of "internalization" occurs remains indispensable for making the narrative of passing intelligible. We could say that it is indeed this moment of "internalization" that a racial regime seeks to control when it intervenes in relation to a person or population's conduct to reach something "deeper." Such efforts represent what I am calling the passing subject's "ensoulment" by a regime of race, which does not merely try to master the subject's act of internalization, but then sweeps up its own footprints, recoding that internalization as the cause rather than the effect of the passing subject's Blackness.

Like the exception to a grammatical rule, the person who passes should not be viewed as violating the ordinary protocols of race but as demonstrating instead, through their exceptionality, how the rule actually works. Passing is a template for the policing of the color line, but that policing process takes the form of playing a game of concealment/exposure that can sometimes be operationalized by a "person of color," who adapts their body and its performances (clothing, vocalization, choices in fraternization) to anticipate and redirect the expectations of white supremacy. This is the game, for example, that Boots Riley stages for the setting of the telemarketing workplace in his brilliant satirical film *Sorry to Bother You*, when his ill-fated protagonist plays to his advantage (at least for a while) the uses of his "white voice" (see Riley 2018). Ironically, the passing self illuminates the regime of truth through which racialization writ large actually gets enforced. This is obscured only by the color line's presumption that racial subjects normally bear visibly marked bodies that serve as determinant signs of their interior life. The color line, in other words, presents the passing subject as a paradoxical exception, a case in which, for example, a Black soul has been concealed within a body failing to so signify. But those exceptional cases are part of its operations of power. Color line racism is prepared for exceptional cases, which it presents as a form of subterfuge in need of revelation: the moment of public exposure in most passing narratives is precisely the moment when the subject finally fails to outmaneuver the power of race.

These observations lead toward a different account of the color line, one that interprets it within a larger racial frame that involves security's probabilistic calculations about the relationship between body and soul. When it comes to the conventions of color-line racism, it is important not to be naïve about the racialization of the body. Color-line racism is a highly complex strategy of power that—its tacit appeal to phenotypical distinctions notwithstanding—actually operates by mobilizing an ever-changing array of social narratives, habits of perception, and performative practices through which populations are distinguished and administered.[19] Nevertheless, a naturalistic reference to differentiated human embodiment remains its ideological kernel. Color-based categories of race proceed on an ideological basis *as if* the divides in the population that they produce either are or should be visibly marked as distinctions between, for example, the white and the Black, brown, or Asian body. The formulation of color-line racism, to paraphrase Slavoj Žižek, might be: I know very well that I cannot always tell when someone is Mexican or African American, but still I behave as if their Blackness or brownness is something I can see.[20] The very *idea* of color registers this presumption of visual perceptibility, while the idea that one "cannot always tell" necessitates a game of concealment/exposure as the color line's backstop.

Racism without Race?

We can now return to a question I raised near the beginning of this introduction: what does the tactic of ensoulment tell us about the relationship of color-line racism to other modes of racialization, such as those associated with Islamophobia since the war on terror, or with contemporary antisemitism? Steven Salaita has insisted that the color line of white supremacy remains the most productive paradigm for understanding "anti-Arab racism," which he has characterized as "a redirection of classic American racism at a non-White ethnic group whose origins lie in an area of the world marked for colonization by the United States and whose residents are therefore dehumanized for the sake of political expediency" (Salaita 2006, 13). There are two difficulties with Salaita's argument that are worth distinguishing. The first stems from a certain ontologization of race that presupposes the "nonwhiteness" of Arabs as the explanation for anti-Arab racism and colonization, rather than recognizing that the reverse must be true: Western colonialism is a race-making practice that produces anti-Arab racism. And insofar as this anti-Arab racism is adapted to the regime of the color line, it must train the eye of power to see Arabs as "nonwhite." But when Salaita admits to the temptation of subsuming Islamophobia under the sign of anti-Arab racism, a deeper conceptual problem emerges, not only because Islamophobia also targets non-Arabs, but also because it proceeds from assumptions about the meaning of adherence to a "religion" rather than about the signification of "color" (Salaita 2006, 11–12). As Moustafa Bayoumi has suggested, the racialization of Arabs in America has never been understood as a matter of the "color of one's skin," but instead as a fluctuating, geopolitically motivated judgment about Islam (Bayoumi 2006). This raises a question that cannot be treated as merely peripheral to the history of racism. As Junaid Rana observes, the problem associated with the "comingling" of race and religion is nothing new, but rather a dynamic that dates back all the way to the "genealogical foundation of the race concept" (Rana 2007, 149).[21]

As modalities of racism, both Islamophobia and antisemitism can be said to invert the approach to the game of racial power found in the presumptively marked bodies of the color line. They follow the dialectic of body and soul along a different pathway that rings alarms about the threat of the *unmarked* body: the person who can slide right past airport security with their shoe bomb, or perhaps the Jew who could "replace you" without anyone even noticing. These practices delineate a mode of racialization whose ideological kernel begins with the potential *invisibility* of the threat posed by the psycho-politically inner life of the population that it represents. It is not that such racisms are different in kind from the racism of the color line (Medovoi 2012a).[22] It is rather that populations can be subjected to an inverted strategy with which to play the same game of racial power, one that runs the hermeneutic of suspicion in the opposite direction. Not because I *can* see something in their body I know to be suspicious, but on the contrary, I am suspicious because I *cannot* see something in their body.

For a revealing example of this hermeneutic at work, one could turn to the quintessential Nazi propaganda film *Der ewige Jude*, or *The Eternal Jew* (Hippler 1940), in which what makes the Jew so dangerous is that, while he or she is *sometimes* identifiable by clothing, noses, beards, and so forth, the Jew is characterized by a distinctive ability to pass or blend in, becoming the perfectly camouflaged enemy within. By contrast to color-line racism, passing is no longer the threshold case or the exception here, but itself the rule. Consider a particularly telling scene in which *Der ewige Jude* depicts the bearded face of a traditional Jew, dressed in yarmulke and orthodox garb, only to dissolve into another image of the same face, now clean-shaven and wearing a modern suit (see figures I.1 and I.2).

Corporeally indistinguishable from genuine German citizens, Jews constituted, in the conspiratorial logic of this Nazi film, what an antiterrorist regime of state security today might call a "sleeper cell" in the national body politic. This antisemitic game of racial truth involves exposing the hidden Jews whose feigned assimilation within the population represents the gravest possible danger to German society. But we could say that this danger is therefore now associated with a novel problem of uncertainty regarding where to locate the

FIGURE I.1. Marked Jew. From *Der ewige Jude* (1940), dir. Fritz Hippler.

FIGURE I.2. Un-marked Jew. From *Der ewige Jude* (1940), dir. Fritz Hippler.

racial subject. The racial truth about Muslims or Jews is known, but it cannot be acted upon if one cannot know with certainty who is a Muslim or Jew. Yet this does not lead to a delimiting of disciplinary power, nor to a reduction in the application of surveillance. On the contrary, they are expanded because the potential scope of who might carry the racial threat becomes limitless. Uncertainty now becomes doubly productive of racial power because it concerns not only who among the racial subpopulation bears a malignant intent, but how one can even identify that subpopulation at all, given its presumed imperceptibility. Surveillance is multiplied by the task of divulging the racial population before it can proceed to assessing the risk that this racial presence represents.

Ensoulment, Antisemitism, Islamophobia

Several efforts have been made to theorize this variety of racial power. Étienne Balibar offers one influential model in the context of his analysis of "neoracisms," which include for him contemporary Islamophobia in Europe. Balibar calls this always potentially unmarked raciality of the Muslim a case of "racism without race," associated with a long history of antisemitism in which, "admittedly, bodily stigmata play a great role in its phantasmatics, but they do so more as signs of a deep psychology, as signs of a spiritual inheritance rather than a biological heredity. These signs are, so to speak, the more revealing for being the less visible and the Jew is more 'truly' a Jew the more indiscernible he is" (Balibar 1991a, 23–24). This notion of indiscernibility also plays a role in how Salman Sayyid and David Tyrer have analyzed Islamophobia's apparent uncertainty about the existence in Muslims of any phenotypical specificity, something they call the problem of "how to spot a Muslim" (Tyrer and Sayyid 2012, 357), and that Tyrer has characterized as the "scandal of the apparently incomplete raciality of Muslims" (Tyrer 2013, 40). Using a Lacanian lens, Tyrer argues that the marking of raciality facilitates the fantasy of national wholeness from which racial "others" can be safely excluded. If the racially marked "other" serves as a special "object of desire" for white supremacist nationalism, then the phenotypically ambiguous Muslim would apparently threaten the "possible loss of the [racial] object of desire" (Tyrer 2013, 40). It is in this operation that Tyrer locates the "phobia" inherent in Islamophobia.

Another important account can be found in Moishe Postone's provocative reading of Nazi antisemitism as a kind of right-wing anticapitalist ideology that converts the Jew into a concrete figure for money as the fetishized image of abstract capital (Postone 1980). For Postone, the antisemitic discourse of the National Socialists conceived Jews as agents possessing an invisible power capable of manipulating the wealth of a society toward purposes alien and hostile to it. Antisemitism therefore presents itself as a liberatory struggle against the foreign aims of finance to manipulate our lives. I will return to Postone's thesis in my analysis of racial capitalism in chapter 4, but at this stage I want simply to focus on what his argument suggests about the antisemitic embodiment of the Jew. On the one hand, Postone's analysis could suggest that for antisemitism the Jews (as a population) function as the racial body of money. But we could just as easily run this reading in reverse to suggest that money serves as the invisible racial soul of the Jew. Postone does not write at all about Islamophobia. If we were to ask whether Islamophobia posits an analogously invisible racial soul of the Muslim, we might conclude that it invests that soul with some kind of terroristic power, one that perhaps functions as a foreign counterpart to the state's abstract claim on the right to violence. But the key point would be that, for Islamophobia and antisemitism respectively, the soul of the Muslim and Jew "embody" something which is abstracted from their particular physical form and therefore remains invisible to the eye of power.

Bringing the Muslim and the Jew together as twin racial figures reminds us that neither is the unique target of this game of power that is premised on racial invisibility. It is not only that the very idea of antisemitism originally served to conjoin Jew and Muslim together into a unitary threat, as both Gil Anidjar (2008) and Ivan Davidson Kalmar (2009) remind us, but also that at certain historical moments other populations have also been singled out for the invisible danger posed by their inward commitments to religious theologies or political ideologies—Catholics, communists, or anarchists—or even to their perverse inner desires—miscegenators, gays, queers, trans people. We can therefore subsume the history of various practices (antipopery, anticommunism, anti-anarchism), along with antisemitism and Islamophobia, and even homophobia and transphobia, into a certain way of managing the body/soul relationship that foregrounds the problem of the soul's corporeal invisibility. Although I have elsewhere called this "dogma-line racism" because my focus at that stage of reflection was on the "religionization" of race that often characterizes antisemitism and Islamophobia, this mode of racialization can be more generically characterized as one that directs its suspicion toward that which *cannot* be discerned in the body, whether it be a heretical dogma, a treasonous loyalty, or even a perverse desire or identification.

It is important to be careful here in specifying what does and does not distinguish this modality of racism from the color line. The issue is not that the color line always produces a racism of marked bodies while Islamophobia and antisemitism traffic instead in unmarked bodies. As I observed above in relation to the exception of "passing," unmarked bodies are in fact a necessary preoccupation for color-line racism. Conversely, it is possible to be misled by Balibar's characterization of antisemitism or Islamophobia as examples of "racism without races" (Balibar 1991a, 21). If "race" may be lodged in the soul rather than located in the body, then corporeal undecidability is hardly evidence for the absence of race, only the apparent absence of its marker at a particular moment. Markings remain important even to the exercise of antisemitic and Islamophobic racism, as the first, Jewishly garbed, image from *Der ewige Jude* demonstrates, or as Jasbir Puar has observed in regard to the exposure of Sikhs to post-9/11 Islamophobic violence through the catalyst of the turban (Puar 2011): clothing, garments, and badges will appear prominently in this book's history of auxiliary racial markers. Antisemitism and Islamophobia therefore join with color-line racisms in trafficking assumptions about the marked body, or at a bare minimum the markable body.[23] What distinguishes this modality of racism, therefore, is only its inverted axiomatic: antisemitism and Islamophobia proceed as if their racial target either was or could be corporeally undetectable. To wit, I know very well that I can sometimes recognize a Jew on sight. Still, they may always be concealing themselves.[24]

The principal problem introduced by *this* hermeneutic of suspicion is whether the threat to a population might turn out to be lodged not in a particular and identifiable sector within it, such as in the presumptively marked bodies of people of color for example, but rather in *any and all* members of the population, among invisible and unknown cells of terrorists or communists for instance, or worse yet, in previously unthreatening members of the population who have been seduced by terrorists or communists (or indeed people of color) to serve as their agents. This latter suspicion conjures up the need for a security regime that treats threat as the endemic and universal self-endangerment of population itself. It is a game of power that formulates a dark counterpart to John Rawls's "veil of ignorance," grounded in the abstraction of security rather than justice (Rawls 2009). Because we cannot know in advance who are actual (or even potential) members of a threatening race within a population, we must approach security as if anybody might belong (including at the limit even ourselves). Ensoulment and embodiment are axiomatically divergent. Like liberal justice, therefore, security in this form seeks to universalize its sphere of application: everyone must take their shoes off at airport security in an age that presupposes the terrorist's potential inscrutability.

The Pincer Action of Racial Power

The two hermeneutics of racial suspicion I have described—one particularizing and the other universalizing—are neither antithetical nor mutually exclusive formations. Rather, they advance simultaneous and coexisting racial hypotheses through which power works upon the population with a pincer-like action.[25] Even the fable of "The Snake" exhibits this dual movement. The snake represents the extreme instance of the particular. We presume to know a snake when we see one; its serpentine body unambiguously signals its venomous evil; there is a fixed population of snakes and we "know damn well" what they are when we see them. But as we have already noted, the tender heart of the woman living inside the home is also a threat, for through it she becomes a person who maliciously leaves the door to the homeland ajar, allowing the snake to enter. The threat she represents cannot be read off her body, except arguably by pointing to the gendered association of women with either tender hearts or the romantic desire that those tender hearts embody. But this means that the actual threat resides in a place that any of us might be hiding within ourselves. If I am a "man" with a tender heart, I may prove to be gay, transgendered, or simply perverse. This is a threat that will always exist for me because it is impossible to say when I might inadvertently discover myself to be attracted to a dangerous person, ideology, or movement, due to aspects of my inner life previously unknown to others, or veiled even from myself. The snake may therefore live within the self as easily as it does in some part of the population designated as "other." We see this racial danger depicted in the Showtime series *Homeland* through the character of Nicholas Brody, a white, Protestant, decorated Marine war hero and rescued POW who is suspected and finally revealed (after much inconclusive surveillance) to be a secret convert to Islam and a terrorist operative.[26] The fact that Brody nearly becomes a vice-presidential candidate, and thus the ultimate terrorist Trojan horse, captures the kind of anxious suspicion with which this variety of racial power invests its figures: they represent the universalizing dimension of racial threat, since one can never know who has been inwardly converted, seduced, infected, or otherwise turned toward a threatening intent. Any figure of biopolitical danger may end up vacillating between the particularizing and the universalizing delineation of the enemy, at times allegorizing a specified group within which the threat can be fixed, particularized, and isolated (communists, Muslims, Blacks), while at other moments signifying a floating risk, tied to the soul's fundamental inscrutability that circulates through the totality of the population. The history of race involves the history of this productive vacillation.

Methodology of This Book

So far in this introduction I have been conceptualizing the operation of racial power at a considerable level of abstraction. Let me therefore take some care to explain this book's aims. This preliminary excursus has sought to elucidate what will appear in the following chapters as family resemblances shared by successive episodes in the history of race and racism. Yet this book ultimately offers less a theory of racism than a genealogy of the dialectic of body and soul that grounds the changing racial politics of security over the *longue durée*. So, for example, chapter 1 focuses on medieval strategies of security that preceded the historic invention of race, but that nonetheless created its conditions of possibility. Chapter 2 specifies the moment in early Iberia when race first emerged as a problem within the field of security, as well as how it was expanded into a principal technology for the early coloniality of power in the Americas. Chapter 3 explores how racialized religiosity was enfolded into the birth of the Westphalian state as the apotheosis of security, while chapter 4 considers how the racial capitalist project of liberal security gradually reconstituted race as the biopolitical threat to bourgeois civil society. Each of these moments changed the game of racial power in striking ways, yet each still recognizably engages with its own politically distinctive dialectic of body and soul. The analytics of race found in this introduction therefore should not be construed as a transhistorical template that allows each moment to be grasped as another instantiation of racial power's sameness. On the contrary, I hope to show that race first had to be created, then at every turn drastically reformulated to serve the changing historical problems of security. In the era of capitalist production that we inhabit, racial power can and must be understood as a key element in capital's social reproduction. But this relationship, I will argue, is mediated through a political logic of security and should not be quickly reduced to an alibi for class. This requires another set of methodological insights, drawn from elements in the Marxist tradition, that seeks a complex reading of the overdetermined relationship of the "economic" to the political and the cultural.

The book is indebted, in other words, to the Marxist insight that any mode of production always involves not only the production of what Marx and Engels called a "definite mode of life," but also a way for that life activity to reproduce itself, politically and socially, as well as economically (Marx and Engels 2018, 150). What Foucault called "governmentality" is, in my view, best read against the grain as a framework for the Marxist problem of capitalist reproduction, albeit one that engages the domain of the political without relying on a reified conception of the state as its unique and necessary agent. Foucault's account of "governmentality" can be interpreted as a specific mode of political reflexivity that came into existence alongside capitalism and has furnished it with the regulatory apparatus through which regimes of accumulation can be reproduced, particularly in societies where populations are growing rapidly and where forms of social organization are constantly "melting into air" under the revolutionary pressures that capitalism itself exerts.[27] "Race," I will argue, was a key mechanism for the rise of governmentality as that kind of political reflexivity.

As theorists of racial capitalism have shown, the production of race has been especially critical to the relationship between governance and the accumulation of capital.[28] Historically speaking, discourses of race and racism preceded the birth of capitalism, but they were not simply accommodated in accidental form by capitalism as it encountered them. Technologies of race collectively represent a part of what Dipesh Chakrabarty (borrowing from Marx's own terminology) has called "History 1" (the past that capitalism posits for itself), as opposed to "History 2" (the antecedents with which capitalism has come to coexist but does not require) (Chakrabarty 2008, 62–71). What Chakrabarty is trying to distinguish here are elements of the past that simply persist in the capitalist era and those that become critical to the social reproduction of capitalism as a mode of production. As I will show in chapter 4, the technologies of racial power form part of the past that capitalism posits for itself in part because they have furnished capitalism with the means of reproducing the social and legal meaning of private property and free labor, two critical preconditions for the establishment of a regime of capital accumulation. But they are also crucial to the reproduction of capital because they have furnished it with the biopolitical means of responding to radical challenges and revolutionary possibilities. From its earliest moments, capitalism has relied on the highly adaptable strategy of government offered by racialization for rapidly and flexibly reclassifying and redirecting populations in response to emergent threats to governance's forms of impersonal domination. Race is therefore not always reducible to a mediation of class. The more general view, instead, is that race mediates a logic of security politics that runs throughout capitalism's regimes of power. It works to constitute a mode of governance that allows the accumulation of bodies and subjection to keep pace with the accumulation of capital.

In addition to the techniques of genealogy and historical materialism, this book relies at times on an etymological method. I consider the origins and changing uses of certain words as they became attached to racial power to see what light they shed on its changing stratagems. I am following the spirit of what Sarah Kofman terms "genealogical etymology," the study of conceptually freighted words, not to uncover the Platonic essence of each of their ideas but rather to foreground the historical "becoming" that inheres in the metaphors embedded in a word, metaphors whose significance is obscured if we posit the word's conceptual unity (Kofman 1994, 85). The historical materialist basis for this method can be easily found in Raymond Williams's classic study *Keywords*, in which he tracked the social struggles embedded in the contradictory meanings of words that have formed the lexical corpus of British society (Williams 2014). Among the keywords figuring prominently in this book's vocabulary of racial power are *race* itself, but also *security, state, population, sedition, statistics, plantation, fanatic, party, faction, cabal*, and *fundamentalist*. Each of these words brings into focus a certain inflection point in the "becoming" of racial power over the *longue durée*.

To the extent that this book is directly in dialogue with a single thinker, it would have to be Michel Foucault. It is Foucault's reflections on power as a kind of political capacity or ability that emerges when knowledge is invested in social relations (a knowledge of the body's location by discipline, a knowledge of the population's regularities by biopower) that most inspire this project. This book thinks primarily alongside two of Foucault's best-known lecture series: the lectures from 1977–78 published as *Security, Territory, Population* (Foucault 2007), from which it derives the centrality of security to the problem of government, and the 1975–76 series published as *Society Must Be Defended* (Foucault 2003), from which it borrows its thematics of war and race. This book's more obvious intimacy is perhaps with the first of these series, in cleaving so closely to the animating question Foucault posed there: How might the state and its history look different if we did not invest them from the start with a primarily juridical conception of sovereign power connected to the exercise of political will, whether the will of the ruler or that of the people? Foucault answered this question by recommending that we rethink the history of the state as simply one episode in a longer history of government—a history concerned with the political problem of how populations should be secured against endemic risks and uncertainties. To this end, he began his inventory of government with the medieval pastorate, an early form of power he considered to be governmentality's predecessor, and whose spiritual aims regarding the population he then traced forward through the history of the state, and eventually to the development of liberal political economy. This book retraces those exact historical footsteps (pastoral power, reason of state, liberalism), yet ends up on a quite different journey that tracks the genealogy of security and race, as well as the itinerary of the body/soul relationship.

In one important respect, however, I break sharply with *Security, Territory, Population*: I depart from the anemic way in which Foucault had come to think about security by the time he wrote those lectures. By contrast to his immediately preceding works (Foucault 1990, 2003, 2012), in his 1977–78 lectures, Foucault (2007) treats security as a glorified macroeconomic problem, a matter of how best to recalibrate the population's conduct away from practices or behaviors that increase the risk of unfavorable aggregate outcomes (high grain prices, destructive epidemics, economic downturns). "Security" thus loses the military dimension that Foucault had so presciently acknowledged in his preceding explorations. Something critically important in those earlier studies had been jettisoned by the time Foucault turned to the problem of government. For reasons that I continue to find enigmatic, he opted to bracket the important question of when, how, and why war sometimes provides the model for political power, and crucially, how that warlike dimension of politics has depended on governmental practices that establish the caesurae of race.

This book is therefore animated in part by the following question: How would we need to reformulate the genealogy of government traced by Foucault in *Security, Territory, Population* if we insistently retained a view of security as a military and not just an economic project? What might the periodization schema and the account of governmentality found there have looked like had they retained Foucault's earlier attentiveness in *Society Must Be Defended* to race (the permanent military division of the population) and to war (the ongoing state of affairs obtained by that division) as integral mechanisms of security? It is not just that the later lectures would have been completely altered; the political genealogy they trace would necessarily have placed the exercise of war against ongoing racial threats at the very heart of the history of government. Trump would not seem like an anomaly in the annals of government but would instead appear as a familiar and recurring figure. This is the book I have here attempted to write.

Itinerary of the Chapters

In the following chapters, I will move chronologically through a long but nevertheless distinctive genealogy of racism as a key stratagem of power. My focus is on a series of Euro-American projects of security that came to produce the truth of "race" as one of their principal effects, though toward its conclusion this book will admittedly take a global turn. Chapter 1 takes up a moment in the European Middle Ages when "race" as an explicit discourse of political security did not yet exist, but when a conception of threat to the population was nonetheless already central to governmental practice. Although feudalism's agrarian relations of fealty and vassalage are often taken as the paradigmatically medieval regime of power, I proceed on the assumption that it was the Roman Church's pastoral "government of souls," its management of the flock of Christendom through a regime of instruction, inspection, confession, and interrogation, that actually provided the governmental tool kit out of which "race" would eventually be assembled.

I argue that medieval pastoral power was not pacific, as Foucault (2007) misleadingly suggests, but grounded in bellicosity. The so-called war on heresy that gained momentum in the High Middle Ages was central to the Roman Church's practices of "pastoral power." Shepherds were necessary because the flock in Christ's sheep pen was menaced by wolves and foxes. In the Middle Ages, the flock was a governing metaphor for church governance constituted around the politico-theological threat of evil to seduce Christians and steal them away from Christ's promise of eternal life. I have already asserted that there was no language of race as such during the Middle Ages, a position that I recognize is subject to lively scholarly debate, and that I will therefore argue in greater detail through the first two chapters. Nevertheless, even though it operated at a historical moment before race, medieval pastoral power evinced a dialectic of body and soul, conducted through a game of concealment and exposure, that looks ahead to the biopolitics of racial power. This theme of concealment and exposure organized itself not only around heretics, but also around the quasi-heretical dangers posed by the infidelity of Jews and Saracens. The war on heresy, even at this early stage, already constituted a politics of ensoulment out of which the threat of race would eventually be assembled.

Chapter 2 seeks to answer the question of where and when a language of race first appeared. Rather than beginning with early representations of populations who are racialized today, I proceed instead by tracing how the word "race" emerged etymologically in relation to the metaphor of a frayed or strained fabric through which the threat of a hidden defect in the population could be imagined. This etymology, which I locate at the Iberian threshold between the medieval and the early modern, would first be associated with the threat of formerly Jewish conversos and ex-Muslim Moriscos, members of the Spanish population whose imputed heretical threat to church, society, and the state could all be tied directly to the defective predisposition of their souls, a form of inherited probability correlating with their non-Christian ancestry. The momentous future importance of "race" derived from how this political concept came to be exported into new settings in the Iberian colonies of the Americas, where it would become a technology for organizing and securing colonial populations against probable threats ensouled within communities or individuals defined by Jewish, Muslim, African, or Native ancestry.

Although "race" began as a political instrument associated first and foremost with the spiritual mission of the church, in chapter 3 I consider how it became integrated into the aims of government at the precise moment when the political project of the "state" emerged as a defining theme of power. The logic of "reason of state," which concerned above all the problem of political stability (maintaining a "state" of affairs), hegemonized political power by promising to negotiate the schism between Catholic and Protestant Christianity on the European continent. In the process, "reason of state" turned the problem of religious threat to government into a form of racial security. Using the case of Elizabethan English statecraft, I show how the birth of the security state relied upon a tacit reconception of race that, while still orbiting around religious threats, was now displaced from the domain of theology per se onto the two bodies of political theology. Although this reconception of race seems only distantly relevant to the color-line racisms that dominated New World contexts, religionized race in the metropole would prove capable of reinvigorating the ensoulment of dangerous populations as the fundamental problem for state security, advancing in the process the "second pincer" of race as universal threat that I earlier connected to the invisibilizing game of racial power that often characterizes practices of antisemitism and Islamophobia.

In chapter 4, I trace the liberal reconstitution of race that would accompany the expansion of capitalism alongside the triangular Atlantic trade. The chapter offers a novel account of racial capitalism consistent with my book's focus on security and the politics of ensoulment. Liberalism refashioned the state in the image of a political association designed for securing the "society" of possessive individuals. Race, at this point, becomes a language for ensouling the free and propertied individual's living antithesis: the one who fundamentally subverts freedom through their criminal or revolutionary threat to the possessive individual. In the settler colonial setting, liberal freedom and whiteness become tautological as the game of race becomes infiltrated by the capitalist logic of private property. It is at this moment, the long dawn of capitalist modernity, that race became generalized as a biopolitical technology for guaranteeing bourgeois white freedom by waging war against those whose inner lives pose a clear and present danger to that liberal freedom: rebellious slaves, revolutionary communists, and revolting colonials.

The book concludes with a sketch of the last century of the inner life of race, from the quilting point of anticommunism during the Cold War to that of antiterrorism under neoliberal globalization, and returning at last to the current moment when the problem of the dangerous inner life no longer attaches centrally to either communism or terrorism but reflects instead a potentially terminal crisis of the neoliberal phase of capitalism. In the reactive and neofascist politics of today's right-wing populism, racial threat has proliferated into a many-headed hydra, inclusive of dangerous people of color, malevolent Islamic terrorists, amoral Jewish financiers, fake news media, and hostile parties, but more generally representing the danger of any secretly contaminated self, any snake who can be suspected of a plot to poison the population and damage the health of the body politic. Perhaps this book's investigation into the long history of ensoulment will offer some tools for teasing out the unstable rules governing the games of racial power we are forced to play today. Insofar as the soul is still central to them, and insofar as I believe we cannot see past racism without conceiving how to dismantle the technologies of ensoulment, I hope this book can make a contribution in the realm of thought to the forms of antiracism we are looking for in these ominous times.

RACE BEFORE RACE

The Flock and the Wolf

So again Jesus said to them . . . "I am the good shepherd. The good shepherd lays down his life for the sheep. The hired hand, who is not the shepherd and does not own the sheep, sees the wolf coming and leaves the sheep and runs away—and the wolf snatches them and scatters them. The hired hand runs away because a hired hand does not care for the sheep. I am the good shepherd. I know my own and my own know me, just as the Father knows me and I know the Father. And I lay down my life for the sheep. I have other sheep that do not belong to this fold. I must bring them also, and they too will listen to my voice. So there will be one flock, one shepherd." —John 10:7–16

Under sheep's clothing lurk ravening wolves, venomous and keen to bite, their eloquence a cancer. Lying hypocrites offer them protection. The hypocrites heap up the fire while they apply the torches . . . Men who prey on souls make their way with guile into the homes of widows and ensnare the simple. Scraping at the Letter's outer bark—not the honeyed core of Scripture—they offer draughts of death, the bitter gall of error . . . Why asleep, my bishops? Why are you the dogs that fail to bark? Foxes stalk the orchard; you have not chased them; with camels all around you, you're straining off midges, you are the willows that bear no fruit, too busy to save men's souls! —PHILIP THE CHANCELLOR, *Dogmatum falsas species*

The *goyim* are a flock of sheep, and we are their wolves. And you know what happens when the wolves get hold of the flock? —*Protocols of the Meetings of the Learned Elders of Zion*

It would be difficult to find a more hotly debated scholarly question than that of when race and racism were invented in human history. For many decades, the most common view, exemplified by scholars such as sociologist Michael Banton, held that modern racism was born with the consolidation of race as a category in the biological sciences during the nineteenth century (Banton 1979). Even Banton and those who agreed with him, however, acknowledged important antecedents. Historian George Fredrickson, for example, found significant antecedents to modern racism in the growth of hereditarian religious antipathy toward Jews during the Middle Ages, as well as in Biblically grounded justifications for the African slave trade during the seventeenth and eighteenth century, though he agreed that the "full flower" of modern racism only became possible with the scientific paradigm of the nineteenth century (Fredrickson 2015).

Another influential position, taken among others by anthropologists Audrey and Brian Smedley, has contended that the invention of race predates scientific racism because it names an essentializing and hierarchical differentiation of humanity whose emergence one can already begin to discern through Europe's colonial encounter with new populations and civilizations in the Americas (Smedley and Smedley 2018). The Smedleys, as well as Peruvian social theorist Anibal Quijano, are prepared to go back at least to the sixteenth century, but no further, because, in Quijano's words, "the idea of race in its modern meaning, does not have a known history before the colonization of America" (Quijano 2000, 534).[1]

Over the last decade, however, the dating of race has been pushed ever further back. Geraldine Heng (2018) is one of several medievalist scholars who insist that the "invention of race" reaches back to the European Middle Ages (see also Bartlett 2001; Lampert 2004; Loomba 2009; and far more cautiously, Nirenberg 2007). Inspecting medieval representations of Jews, Muslims, Africans, and Asians, among others, Heng proposes that these populations were constituted as Europe's racial "others" already by the twelfth century, though not always in relation to what she calls a "body-centered phenomenon" (Heng 2018, 25). Anticipating the skepticism with which some might respond to calling such relations "racial" avant la lettre, Heng rhetorically enjoins their question, asking, "Why call something race, when many old terms—'ethnocentrism,' 'xenophobia,' 'premodern discriminations,' 'prejudice,' 'chauvinism' even 'fear of otherness and difference'—have been used comfortably for so long to characterize the genocides, brutalizations, executions, and mass expulsions of the medieval period?" (23). Heng answers that these other terms will not serve for several reasons. First, they are too general. Second, the refusal to describe medieval violence against difference as racism tends to reproduce a temporal divide between the modern and the premodern that cannot acknowledge the former as a "time of race." Finally, in her view, calling them something other than racial also "destigmatizes the impacts and consequences of certain laws, acts, practices and institutions in the medieval period, so that we cannot name them for what they are" (23).

Examined closely, Heng's argument appears circular. She asks us to call these medieval phenomena racial because, if we do not, we are denying their racialism and therefore denying that race existed in the Middle Ages. Heng's position also begs another question: If we were to embrace her theoretical assumption that race existed prior to any language of "race," why stop at the Middle Ages? Heng quickly finds herself one-upped by Benjamin Isaac (2013), who dares to leapfrog Heng by a full millennium. Isaac's survey of racism in classical antiquity focuses on the animus that was layered into Greco-Roman ideas about foreigners, which he presents as precursors to modern forms of racism. Isaac admits that the itinerary of his study "traces the history of discriminatory ideas rather than acts" (Isaac 2013, 2). Its focus, in other words, is on patterns of prejudice, bigotry, and cultural discrimination in the classical period, not on a project of power that would have been exercised materially or politically on its targets. Isaac can thus claim to discover the "invention of racism" in the classical world, but only because it is a racism that was invented without any related concept of "race" nor with any particular value for governing people and populations. Heng and Isaac both engage with rich archives for representing human difference in the ancient and medieval world. Their work also confirms the hostile views that ancient Greeks and Romans or medieval Europeans circulated regarding peoples they judged to be their moral inferiors. But neither really offers a racial account of medieval governance.

By contrast, Cedric Robinson's influential *Black Marxism* (2020) explicitly attempts a case for how medieval governance constituted a premodern regime of raciality. Robinson, who is primarily interested in showing how "racial capitalism" did not so much displace European feudalism as develop and extend the latter's mode of racial power, reaches all the way back to the ancient world described by Isaac. In Robinson's estimation, European feudalism was from the start a racializing mode of production that drew upon the ancient world's devaluation of the "barbarian's" cultural inferiority to establish an ethnoculturally rationalized division of labor that included medieval slavery and peonage. Robinson acknowledges that those divisions were different than those of today: they were often internal to European difference, serving to distinguish Genoese from Slav or Catalan from Greek. But in his view the divisions were already racialist.[2] Robinson further argues that the medieval "bourgeoisie" who emerged in the urban interstices of European feudalism, and who later became attached to the colonial expansions of the absolutist state, self-identified in ethno-racial terms that would prepare the way for later racial nationalisms such as Anglo-Saxonism or Teutonism (Robinson 2020, 27).

Although Robinson presents a political argument for how racial power was exercised in the Middle Ages, his argument (like Heng's and Isaac's) also suffers from a certain circularity: Robinson claims that we should recognize these feudal divisions of European labor as being "racial" because otherwise we would be disavowing their continuity with the capitalist racialisms of our own modern era. But why assume such a continuity if the various forms of othering, differentiating, devaluing, and inferiorizing that existed in the Middle Ages were not actually organized under the sign of race? As Heng and Isaac both acknowledge (though Robinson does not), neither the word "race," nor any of its etymological variants, existed in any premodern language of the eras they study. "Race" was neither a legal nor a political concept at that time. In fact, no attested appearance of the word can be found prior to about the fifteenth century.

How then might we think otherwise about the "invention of race?" The approach I will propose in this chapter rests on two basic principles. First, the invention of race cannot really be explained absent the invention of a discourse that names "race" as a political problem to be managed. And second, the political problem that "race" is invented to manage is fundamentally a problem of security. This does not mean that first (per Isaac or Heng) there was "prejudice" against Jews, Africans, or Saracens, then "race" was invented to codify it, and finally this discourse was enshrined as a project of security. Nor does it mean (in some variation of Robinson's analysis) that first there was a feudal division of labor, then that division became "racial" as a way of justifying it. What I will propose is a rather different story. Like Heng and Robinson, mine is a story that begins in the Middle Ages. But my starting point will concern instead the pastoral problem of the *indemnitas* of the church's souls. Only after explaining how this problem informed certain games of power associated with the governing of Christendom in relation to its spiritual threats will I turn (in the next chapter) to the event that could be called the "invention of race."

Pastoral Power as Regime of Security

Although no language of race per se existed in the Middle Ages, one can find there a language of security. Founded upon biblical passages that grounded the church's claim to spiritual responsibility for its parishioners, Christian security was organized around the idea of the *pignus spiritus*, or spiritual guarantee.

Found in the Latin of Jerome's Vulgate (the fourth-century CE translation of the Bible into Latin that became the official version used by the Roman Church), the phrase *pignus spiritus* occurs near the start of 2 Corinthians 1:21–22, when the apostle Paul greets the members of his Corinthian church with the words: "Qui autem confirmat nos vobiscum in Christo, et qui unxit nos Deus: qui et signavit nos, et dedit pignus Spiritus in cordibus nostris." The King James Bible translates this passage as follows: "Now he which establisheth us with you in Christ, and hath anointed us, is God; Who hath also sealed us, and given the earnest of the Spirit in our hearts."

The Latin *pignus* is translated in this passage by the English word "earnest," which, as in the current-day phrase "earnest money," means a means of securing or guaranteeing something. Paul is proposing that by bringing Christ to earth and unleashing the Holy Spirit, God has provided the "earnest" or security that will deliver the believer to Him.[3] This theme is echoed in the common Christian metaphor of Christ as the shepherd who protects the souls of his flock.[4] The medieval Roman Church, modeling itself on Paul's church in Corinth, promised always to act like Christ, delivering to its members the *pignus spiritus* by vigilantly steering their souls clear of the spiritual danger of damnation. The flock's security was also sometimes conveyed by the Latin word *indemnitas* (meaning "protection" or "security"), which appears for example in the 1215 canon laws of the Fourth Lateran Council, an important medieval legal corpus to which I will return at the end of this chapter. In those laws, the council decrees that no church under its jurisdiction should ever leave vacant a bishopric because of the threat this poses to the parishioners: "That the ravenous wolf may not invade the Lord's flock that is without a pastor, that a widowed church may not suffer grave loss in its properties, that danger to soul may be averted, and that provision may be made for the security [*indemnitas*] of the churches, we decree that a cathedral or regular church must not be without a bishop for more than three months."[5] *Indemnitas* designates the church's most basic aim: to lead in such a way as to avert "danger to the soul."

Though lacking the language of race, this project of pastoral security already involved what in the introduction I called a dialectic of body and soul. As we shall see, it also operated under the sign of war, looking to divide the population into camps of the threatened and those who threaten. Christian security sought to indemnify the population against forms of dangerous life found internal to the population but also interior to the self: snakes as well as tender hearts. To the extent that this chapter will contribute to the history of race, it will only do so indirectly as a preface, momentarily decentering the object itself (race) so as to explore the general mechanisms of power out of which race would eventually emerge, and whose features race would subsequently transform.

In *Security, Territory, Population*, Michel Foucault coined the phrase "pastoral power" to characterize this medieval regime (Foucault 2007, 115–226). His interest in the medieval pastorate was somewhat different than my own: he saw it as the chief precursor of modern governmentality, by which he meant a way of thinking and exercising power that differed from sovereign right or rule. By contrast to sovereignty's circular and self-serving logic (one rules in order to preserve one's rule), governmentality constituted strategies for "conducting the conduct" of a population toward a specific end.[6] It is in this respect that he saw governmentality as anticipated by the medieval pastorate, which did not after all concern itself centrally with the control of territory nor with the royal exercise of divine will. Rather, as I have already noted, pastoral power activated biblical references to God as a "shepherd" who cares for the spiritual well-being of his people, both as individuals and as members of a flock: all and one, *omnes et singulatim* (see Foucault 1986). Pastoral power undergirded the basic medieval ambiguity of the idea of the "church," which simultaneously named the totality of each and every one of its members (the flock), but also the hierarchical organization of clerics who safeguarded and led them (the principle of the shepherd). From this dual perspective, the church's charge was to watch, care, and *minister* to its population so as to ensure that they would remain faithful to God and be favored by him for their salvation. What Foucault thus stresses is that the pastorate was chiefly a "government of souls" focused on providing the *cura animarum* (care of souls) that would ensure the redemption of the flock. This was essentially a project of security, of *pignus spiritus*.

This attention to the salvation of "one and all" had what Foucault acknowledges to be a paradoxical quality. On the one hand, it involved a willingness to fight to protect the flock as a whole. A sheep whose "corruption is in danger of corrupting the entire flock, must be abandoned, possibly excluded, chased away and so forth" (Foucault 2007, 169). On the other hand, each sheep should be understood to be just as valuable as the entire flock. At times, one must place the entire flock at risk in order to seek to recover the stray lamb. Finally, there is the risk to the pastor himself. Alluding presumably to the passage from the Gospel of John that serves as an epigraph to this chapter, Foucault notes that the pastor "defends the sheep against wolves and wild beasts," but not only in the sense of giving his bodily life for them. He must also be prepared to wager his own soul. As he explains, "will not this person [the pastor] who is called upon to see, observe, and discover evil be exposed to temptation? Will not the evil of which he relieves the conscience of the person he directs, by the very act of relieving him, expose [him] to temptation? Will not learning of such horrible sins, seeing such beautiful sinners, precisely expose him to the risk of the death of his own soul at the moment he saves the soul of this sheep?" (171).

This pastoral model of conducting the population by no means exhausts the many mechanisms of power in the High Middle Ages. Viewing late medieval society from the perspective of the pastorate, for example, differs obviously from a broader focus on feudalism, which was at once a sociopolitical regime and a mode of production, concerned above all with the control of land and the attendant social relations of vassalage. Feudalism was indeed a system of power that focused on territory, production, and sovereign rule. But the era's more narrowly religious mode of pastoral power offered a different kind of political potential. Rather than centering on feudal right and its reciprocal obligations, it was grounded in a scrutiny and subjection of the truths of inner life, and their consistency with theological truth, since the care of the soul necessarily involved techniques for evaluating and correcting a people's conscience, faith, and loyalty to God. As such, in pastoral power the management of bodies and their behaviors proceeded by way of subjecting the truth of the soul to the truth of the church.

As I observed in the introduction, by the time he delivered the 1977–78 lectures collected in *Security, Territory, Population*, Foucault had taken a fateful step away from the seemingly different analytics of power-as-war that he had explored in his lecture series two years earlier (see Foucault 2003). This is unfortunate since the theme of security that is so central to the later lectures should have also concerned what the paradigm of war contributes to governmentality, which is no less concerned with the confronting and overcoming of risks faced by a population. Broadly understood, security always concerns itself with the defense of society. Contra Foucault, pastoral power was no peaceful regime for the regulation of conduct: it too was concerned with prevailing over threats. As Foucault tacitly acknowledged in some of the passages I have already cited, the salvation of the pastoral flock involves warding off wolves and wild beasts, rescuing the strayed lamb, and (for the pastor) endangering one's very soul in order to discern the spiritual condition of each and every member of the flock. These elements respectively suggest the pastoral motifs of external war (against the wolf), sabotage from within the flock (by the turned sheep or the wolf in sheep's clothing), and even civil war within one's own soul (against the danger of exposure to temptation). Each such skirmish was but a precursor to the final war described in Revelation between Satan's dragon and the Lamb of Christ. Pastoral power, hardly peace-like, was shot through with a bellicosity that moved decisively into the foreground during the High Middle Ages. And it is this theme, I intend to demonstrate, that eventually set in motion certain mechanisms of security through which the racism of inner life itself became possible.

Pastoral Warfare Within: The Biopolitics of Anti-heresy

A historical observation: in the early Middle Ages, Latin Christendom was politically and militarily weak, a sparsely populated and backward region of the world threatened by invading Vikings, Magyars, and Saracens from every direction. Yet sometime between 1000 and 1300 CE, the scholarship agrees, European power underwent a major expansion (see Bartlett 1994; Moore 2000). These developments can be observed across numerous domains (political, economic, territorial, intellectual) whose causal relationships to one another are complex and overdetermined. A certain paradox, however, seems clear: while this was an era of diminishing military threats to Western Europe, the discourse and practice of war gained substantially in importance. Rather than needing to defend itself against invaders, Latin Christendom now began conquering and absorbing new territories in Iberia, Scandinavia, Eastern Europe, the Balkans, and ultimately (with the Crusades) the Levant. But this heightened military prowess signaled other increases in scale and capacity. The so-called High Middle Ages saw an increasingly dense settlement of Western Europe, a rapid growth in population as well as in wealth (Bartlett 1994). As we shall see, it also saw certain concomitant changes in its political and religious technologies. What occurred in these centuries was, if you like, a certain take-off in power, an expansion in Latin Christendom's capacity to mobilize people and things.

The full extent of these changes lay well beyond the scope of this book, but what matters here is how this increased capacity was inextricable from a quantitative growth and a qualitative intensification of pastoral power. Growth is the simpler issue. In introducing his canonical study of Europe's take-off during the High Middle Ages, Robert Bartlett pointedly begins by counting the expanding number of bishoprics between 950 and 1300 CE, an approach he justifies because, in his words, "The theory of Latin Christendom was that of a cellular body, and the cells were the dioceses. Every part of Christendom was meant to be in a named and known see, and no part was meant to be in more than one see.... If small groups of countryfolk ever stated that 'We are not in any bishopric,' the immediate response was to condemn this as 'utterly wrong' and to assign them to one" (Bartlett 1994, 5). The growing number of pastoral cells making up the body of medieval Christendom derived in part from the conquest and conversion of new areas that had been peripheral to the Carolingian core of early medieval Europe, regions such as Scandinavia, Eastern Europe, Iberia, and so forth. But the expansion also concerned what Bartlett describes as a kind of internal colonization, a pressure toward cultural uniformity within the core regions that was at least partly accomplished by the work of the dioceses. Bartlett's observation of a medieval "political arithmetic" (the additive formula for bishoprics) thus points toward both a telescoping and microscoping of pastoral power—the placing of old as well as new populations under magnified clerical oversight in a kind of unitary cult that came to constitute the everyday meaning of the "making of Europe" (2–6). A larger flock with more shepherds, all under increasingly centralized church control and supreme papal authority: these new elements were critical to the governing of late feudal Europe's growing population, wealth, and power.

Yet it was not simply a quantitative change that took place. New tools became available to the shepherds as the church intensified pastoral power through a long series of reforms that multiplied its ability to regulate the population. What Bartlett calls the "new institutional and cultural uniformity in the Western Church" was propelled by fiercer insistence on both cultic and dogmatic orthodoxy in church practices, which also came to impute a quasi-racial, quasi-ethnic, and quasi-territorial delineation of membership in Christendom (Bartlett 1994, 197–268). A heightened use of the term *Christiana gens*, translated by Bartlett anachronistically as the "Christian race" but best apprehended more generically as a sense of Christian peoplehood, alludes to the sharpening delineation of those who dwelled within the flock of Christendom as opposed to what Bartlett calls "its mirror image: 'heathendom'" (250–53). The increased specification of the flock, in turn, was accompanied by a growing attention to its perceived endangerment.

Perhaps the most dramatic account of this medieval turn toward the proactive targeting of threat can be found in R. I. Moore's classic study *The Formation of a Persecuting Society* (2008). In his influential interpretation of the High Middle Ages, Moore tracks a spiraling relationship between fierce defense of theological orthodoxy and an equally vehement targeting of various subpopulations: suspected heretics, Jews, and lepers (these are Moore's focus), but also sodomites, witches, and others. The simultaneous stigmatization of these seemingly different groups was no accident, Moore argues, but an outgrowth of the church's Gregorian reforms.[7] On the surface, these top-down reforms, instituted by Pope Gregory VII and later likeminded popes, sought to purify the spiritual mission of the church. Looking to revive among the clergy the early church's "apostolic life" that many felt had become compromised by greed and worldly cares, these reforms abolished simony (the buying and selling of church positions) and mandated clerical celibacy.[8] On the one hand, reform was vital if the erstwhile shepherds of the church were to avoid degenerating into the untrustworthy "hired hands" that Jesus himself had warned about in the Gospel of John, clerics who lacked any sincere loyalty to their spiritual mission. But zeal to reform a corrupt church could easily tip into rejection of the church's authority tout court and thus into the exact opposite of the original intention. The impulse to denounce the church's impurity as a threat to the flock could itself drive the shepherd into becoming the most dangerous enemy of all: a heretical cleric who preaches against the church's authority from within the sheep pen. A priest advocating church reform like Peter of Bruys could quickly find him- or herself on the far side of the medieval church's dogma line, accused of having become the enemy of God's salvific plan (Moore 1996). Meanwhile, a reformer could point to the toleration of such a heretic as a sign that pastoral care was not sufficiently rigorous to protect the souls of the flock. "Why asleep, my bishops? Why are you the dogs that fail to bark?" admonished Philip the Chancellor, overseer of Notre Dame in Paris, preacher, and famed medieval lyric poet, in his anti-heresy poem *Dogmatum falsas species* (Trail 2006, 245).

Images of predatory wolves approaching the sheep pen were not at all unusual in medieval bestiaries. In an image from an Aberdeen manuscript, we see the analog of Philip's bishops—the sleeping shepherd who, failing to sound the alarm, leaves the flock exposed to the wolf's threat (see figure 1.1).[9] The wolf and the sleeping shepherd were closely linked figures, uniting to form a single crisis of the soul. As Bernard of Clairvaux put it in his denunciation of the evil work of the "heretical" reformer Henry of Le Mans, "A ravening wolf in sheep's clothing is abroad in your land, but as the Lord has shown, we know him by his fruits. The churches are without congregations, congregations are without priests, priests are without proper reverence, and, finally, Christians are without Christ" (Wakefield and Evans 1991, 122). A certain circular structure of power was at play in this game of medieval pastoral intensification. Reformist zeal against corruption could convert someone into a heretic, someone who in turn demonstrated to the orthodox that pastoral care was not taking sufficient care to protect the souls of the church, a situation requiring therefore even more forceful reform. The reformist project in this way conjured up the very figures it was designed to persecute. Or, put yet another way, the intensifying administration of pastoral conduct was the same spiraling force that, as it boomeranged, curved back into what Foucault has described as pastoral "counter-conduct" (Foucault 2007, 200–2), a countermove from within the pastorate against the direction it sought to lead the flock. The church's growing concern with the importance of proper conduct paradoxically energized those

FIGURE I.I. A wolf approaches sheep and their sleeping shepherd. Aberdeen Bestiary (English), ca. 1200. Aberdeen University Library, Univ. Lib. MS 24, fol. 16v–17v.

"wanting to be conducted differently, by other leaders (*conducteurs*) and other shepherds, toward other objectives and forms of salvation, and through other procedures and methods" (194).

These other paths of spiritual conduction were to have tremendous political implications. As Silvia Federici has argued, heretical movements and their theological claims opened space for peasants, artisans, and other social classes to resist a broad range of "social hierarchies and economic exploitation" by appealing to the idea that since Christ had no property those who claimed his authority should follow in his footsteps (Federici 2004, 34). In turn, she observes, the church would begin using the "charge of heresy to attack every form of social and political insubordination" (34). Heresy became the idiom of power's insecurity. From the perspective of the church, alternative shepherds were none other than disguised wolves in the sheep pen, or sometimes in the images of yet another Biblical metaphor, foxes in the Lord's vineyard whom the church needed to discover and expel.

As an issue for the church, heresy dates back to the earliest centuries of Christianity, but its importance had been marginal for many centuries since the defeat of such early sects as the Gnostics and Donatists. Now, for all these reasons, it moved swiftly into a renewed position of political theological prominence. As the church became increasingly preoccupied with quelling the burgeoning

Cathar and Waldensian movements, whose influence was suspected anywhere one saw signs of social or political resistance, its pastoral mission organized a new campaign of anti-heresy. The government of souls required new tactics and strategies with which to protect the population from Christ's enemies and ensure their salvation. To achieve these ends, the medieval church invented two new pastoral institutions, accompanied by a technological breakthrough for use by their shepherds.

The first development concerned the new "preaching" orders. Western Christianity possesses a long monastic tradition, but traditional orders like the Benedictines prayed for their own salvation through an ascetic practice they conducted behind cloistered walls. In the face of heretical threats, such "silent clergy" could be considered, in Innocent III's words, "dumb dogs who do not bark" and therefore left the sheep at the mercy of their predators (Ames 2009, 35). Around the twelfth and thirteenth centuries, therefore, new mendicant orders were formed with a notably different mission. The Dominican Order of "preaching friars," for example, was founded in 1216 to defend the "Catholicism" of church members by living among the people and sermonizing in vernacular tongues against the seductions of Catharism and other heterodoxies (Lea 2010, 243–302). As a new pastoral technique, preaching in common language became a way of using words as weapons to direct the population away from heretical appeals and back to Christ.

Preaching was a tactic for wooing back sheep tempted to stray. But what about those already abducted by heresy? The Inquisition was a second key pastoral innovation, closely linked to the first insofar as it was usually staffed by the same new mendicant orders who preached. Skill with words and discernment of another's thoughts were both prerequisites for these innovations. The church's juridical work had previously been characterized by accusatorial trial: someone accused someone else of a crime, and the church would frame the legal refereeing and resolution of the dispute. The Inquisition, by contrast, was based on a *persecutio* (prosecution) model of legal inquiry that was specifically aimed at the suppression of heresy: the inquisitor (often a Dominican or Franciscan friar) functioned simultaneously as judge and prosecutor of the alleged crime. Inquisitors first gathered evidence of possible heretical behavior from witnesses, before summoning a suspect, confronting them with the "truth" of what they had become, and urging them to confess and repent their heresy. As Talal Asad notes, although "judicial torture" was normally only permissible in cases where clear evidence existed of the commission of a crime, heresy was an exception to this rule because the crime was understood to be hidden, like the soul itself (Asad 1993, 95). The Inquisition was therefore, like later disciplinary apparatuses, designed to correct the soul by acting upon the body.[10] Because contrition was the ultimate objective, confessed heretics could be reconciled with the church if they performed the decreed acts of penance, but the ultimate punishment for unrepentant or recidivist heretics was a spectacular death (Lea 2010, 305–68).[11]

In addition to its new techniques for disciplining individual sheep, the Inquisition also advanced medieval power/knowledge about the nature of flocks. Paul Ormerod and Andrew Roach have observed a gradual shift that occurred between the twelfth and fourteenth centuries as inquisitional tribunals, which had begun by assuming that all heretics posed equally significant threats and required similar treatment, therefore often leading to mass killings and the destruction of the very flock that they had been charge with safeguarding, gradually became aware that certain individuals within heretical networks occupied the critical nodal points for heresy's ability to communicate and spread itself (Ormerod and Roach 2004). The Inquisition therefore became increasingly focused on how to identify and extract those special individuals. Ormerod and Roach suggest that the church had in effect grown aware that the flock of Christendom, and the circle of heretics within it, functioned according to the distributions that mathematicians now call "scale-free" networks. To defeat an army, of course, one seeks to kill the officers. To end a heresy, the equivalent move is to eliminate its "heresiarch," its propagator, along with the messengers whose sheer mobility or communicative literacy accelerates the population's infection by the heretical message. The population, in short, was not effectively administered as a uniform collectivity with a certain level of threat evenly distributed throughout. Rather, threats were concentrated at hubs usually associated with certain kinds of subpopulations, among the educated for instance, who could circulate appeals to scripture and use writing to communicate across geographical distance.

Preaching and Inquisition: these were the church's new spiritual weapons. If they did not suffice, however, then according to the medieval doctrine of the "two swords," the military needs of pastoral defense could make final recourse to the temporal sword of secular power. In addition to assigning secular authorities the task of executing discovered heretics, the church also claimed the right to summon princes as the military arm of the shepherd of Christ.[12] Seeking to defeat the Cathar heresy in southern France, for example, Pope Innocent III appealed to King Philip II of France in a letter of 1207, urgently requesting his military assistance on the grounds that "rapacious wolves in sheep's clothing, who seize and scatter the sheep, have entered into the kingdom itself. And since they do not fear ecclesiastical discipline, in so far as they are separated from the Church, to such an extent do they rage shamelessly against the sheep-pen of Christ. Yet they do so by so much the less in so far as they have finally found someone to resist them in the temporal world and to enforce God's cause upon them with the sword" (Léglu, Rist, and Taylor 2013, 36–37). The so-called Albigensian Crusade, a twenty-year-long war waged against fellow Christians, was the bloody outcome of this papal call to Christian arms. The expressed aim of *cura animarum* was to conduct a spiritual war on behalf of the eternal life of individual believers and thus Christendom itself. But since the protection of souls frequently required the marshaling of bodies, it could also lead to war on the battlefield.

Pastoral Warfare Without: Crusading against the Saracen

This militarized struggle against heresy was closely tied to the general medieval thematics of war we associate today with the Crusades. But the Crusades can also be viewed as the outward projection of the inward war against heresy. In a brilliant reading of the Crusades, Tomaž Mastnak (2001) has shown that these great wars against the "Saracens" of the Islamic world were inextricable from the era's pastoral themes. As Mastnak observes, the Crusades originated counterintuitively in a peace movement. Beginning in the eleventh century, local dioceses of the church began collaborating with common folk to eliminate the widespread violence of private wars regularly fought between Christian princes over wealth and territory. This movement, which called itself the "peace of God" and later the "truce of God," insisted that Christians must cease their incessant and sinful battles against one another, respecting their commonality under Christ (Mastnak 2001, 1–54). Yet Pope Gregory VII (of the Gregorian Reforms) would declare one necessary exception to this internal pacification of Christendom: war against other Christians was not only licit but moral if waged for love of Christ himself and for love of one's neighbors in an effort to protect their souls against heretical predation. In this respect, properly *holy* war, waged against the enemies of the church by the *milites Christi* (soldiers of Christ), shared the same underlying pastoral principle of *persecutio* as the Inquisition, namely that of "bringing the errant back into the Church" (32–33; see also 78–84).

This notable anti-heresy exception clause to the truce of God was joined by another form of licit war: the directing of Christendom's military capacities outward. War was an abomination when fought between Christians, but it offered a route to personal salvation when Christian soldiers fought together to grow the flock of Christendom itself. As Mastnak notes, Christendom never appeared anywhere on a map because it was in fact "mobile, moving space," not strictly territorial because it extended simply "wherever the Roman Church was obeyed" (Mastnak 2001, 123). A different way of spinning Mastnak's observation is to say that Christendom was primarily defined by the *Christiana gens* who followed Christ, and only secondarily by their elaborations of space: wherever the flock was, so was Christendom. And if, as Jesus himself explains in the Gospel of John, there are still other sheep not yet in the pen, then holy wars of conversion would serve his work, fulfilling the universalist promise of Christendom through conquests that would multiply his followers.

At first, the wars fought against Saracens in the Levant were not entirely different from wars of expansion into Scandinavia or Eastern Europe, or any other periphery of Christendom where pagan people dwelled.[13] What made them unique as "crusades" was less any special quality of the Saracens than the sheer fact that they ruled over the biblical "Holy Lands," site of Jesus's birth, death, and resurrection—hence a sacred homeland to be recovered through a military pilgrimage of the *Christiana gens*. The early crusades were caught up too in millennialist passions, which envisioned war with the Saracens as the first apocalyptic battles that might lead to the end of days and the Second Coming.[14] There was, therefore, a substantial theological weight to the Crusades, but not one, at least initially, that distinguished Saracens as a people from Vikings or Goths. They were yet another sect of idolatrous pagans who worshipped a false God—whether named Mahomet or even sometimes Saturn—to whom Crusaders might deliver the Gospel of Christ.

Over time, however, the Crusades were folded more overtly into the militant pastoral campaign against heresy through an alignment of the political theologies of the war within and the war without. To understand how this process occurred, it is necessary to consider the Crusades within the bigger picture of Christendom's expansion during these centuries. As Latin Christendom's frontiers moved eastward across Eastern Europe and the Mediterranean, northward toward Scandinavia, and southward through Iberia, the pastorate encountered Greek and Levantine (non-Roman) Christian sects, as well as pagan and Muslim communities, that now came under its rule. At issue was not only the question of how to govern these new populations, but predictably what dangerous effect they might have on Latin Christians. In addition to what I described earlier as the church reform movement's circular structure of power, another contributing factor to the anti-heresy efforts were the new contacts with Eastern Greek or Oriental Christians, who were widely feared to promote schismatic theological thinking. Meanwhile, on that western flank of Christendom's expansion known as the Iberian *Reconquista*, the issue of Islam stood openly in the foreground. Unlike many new subjects in the East, Muslims were not unorthodox Christian believers. Nevertheless, as Christian princes regained territory, and with it access to the rich literate culture of Moorish Spain,

Latin theologians encountered almost for the first time a firsthand written knowledge of Islam that challenged the reigning conception of the Saracens as pagans. It is primarily through the Spanish connection that Latin Christians came to reckon with Muslims, not as idolators but as monotheists who worshipped the biblical God according to their own revelation through the prophet Muhammad (Cruz and Hoeppner 1999, 63–66).

Crucial to this process was the publication in 1110 of the *Dialogi contra Iudaeos* (Dialogue against the Jews) by Petrus Alfonsi. Himself born a Jew in the town of Huesca under the rule of the Muslim kingdom of Saragossa, Alfonsi converted to Christianity in adulthood, approximately a decade after his home town was conquered in 1096 by the Christian kingdom of Aragon. Alfonsi's book is primarily a polemical dialogue between a Jew (Moses), who has theological faith in Rabbinic Judaism, and a newly converted Christian (Petrus), who overwhelms Moses with the indisputable truth of his Catholic faith. In the book's fifth *titulus*, however, Petrus briefly digresses by responding not to the flaws of Judaism but instead to those of Islam. Moses asks, is not the "religion of the Saracens" a viable alternative to Christianity for Jews like himself seeking a more persuasive faith? Petrus replies with a tale of Islam's fraudulent origins and theology: "It is not unknown to me [Petrus] who Mohammad was, how he falsely fashioned himself a prophet with a clever deception, and who his advisor was in contriving this" (Alfonsi 2006, 150). According to Petrus, Muhammad concocted Islam in a cabal with heterodox Jews and Nestorian and Jacobite Christian heretics, all of whom furnished deviant theological ingredients with which to mix the enticing brew. "Each one according to his own heresy" contributed attractive theological errors that might appeal to Jews and Christians (150). Given that Jews pray three times a day and Christians seven, for example, Muhammad settled on the number five, always making sure that "his law would be a little bit different from the law of Moses" (152). Petrus further explains that Muhammad exploited not only his follower's dogmatic predispositions but their sexual cravings as well, which he shared: "Mohammad loved women a great deal and was too much the voluptuary, and, just as he himself claimed, the power of the lust of forty men dwelled in him. And also, especially because the Arabs were very dissolute, he pandered to their desire, so that they would believe" (162). In short, Alfonsi presents Islam not merely as theologically fallacious, but as a kind of religious seduction, a treacherous law that elevates the "delights of the body [as] the highest good" in order to tempt humanity into disloyalty to Christ.[15]

Alfonsi's text innovatively positions Islam as a variant of Christian heresy, converting Mohammed into a heresiarch (the deceptive founder of a heresy) and further linking the belief's attraction to the pleasures of the flesh. This conflation of Islam with heresy (and Muhammed with heresiarchs), which dates to a far earlier era among Levantine Christians, made its way into the medieval West through this chaotic period in Iberian history (Tolan 2002).[16] Along with it, however, comes an account of the "dissolute" character of Arabs, which brings a new concept to the fore: the posited predisposition of Arabs as a population to carnal seduction, a quality that is not the *effect* of their conversion to Islam but rather part of its *cause*. "Dissolution," I suggest, represents a proto-racializing characterization, not because it generalizes an assumption about a population, or even because this generalization devalues or lowers this population's standing on some spectrum of humanity, but quite specifically because it names a dangerous tendency in the population's inward life, characteristic passions or desires that predispose it to embrace dangerous heresies. But it also suggests how the carnal, erotic, or sexual threat coproduces the predatory danger of heresy that will eventually be invested in race.

Alfonsi's widely circulated text promoted a new view of Saracens as people who had already received the Gospel, but, seduced by their heresiarch's duplicity, rejected God's truth in favor of dangerously errant beliefs. In this respect, the Saracens came to be modeled on heretics rather than pagans or heathens. The famous ninth abbot of the powerful monastery of Cluny, Peter the Venerable, who certainly read Alfonsi's polemic, championed Catholic orthodoxy by lifting his pen in battle against the followers of the heretical Peter of Bruys in his *Tractatus contra Petrubrussianos*. Shortly thereafter, Peter the Venerable would draw on Alfonsi (as well as on an early translation of the Qur'an) to write a refutation of Islam titled the *Summa totius heresis Saracenorum* (Summary of the entire heresy of Saracens). Calling it a "lethal plague," Peter characterizes it as the "dreg of all heresies, into which have flowed the remnants of all the diabolical sects that have arisen since the advent of the Savior" (Peter the Venerable 2016, 31).[17] Gradually, in response to the new convergence of heresy and Islam, a term emerged, that of "infidel," which identifies a group that is not quite Christian, worshipping the same God yet lacking any "fidelity" to the *fides catholica*—the catholic, or universal, faith.[18] Increasingly, the Crusades became understood as continuous with the internal war against heresy, as a struggle against infidelity's threat to Christendom's souls.

The Pastoral Reformulation of Anti-Judaism

In addition to his tracts against the Petrobrusian heretics and the Saracens, Peter the Venerable also wrote a third virulent polemic, *Against the Inveterate Obduracy of the Jews* (Peter the Venerable 2021). Peter's triad of theological enemies—the heretic, the Saracen, the Jew—were convergent figures in his vigilant war of letters against the threatening wolves of the High Middle Ages. As historian Dominique Iogna-Prat has shown, Peter's Cluniac polemics sought to order Christendom and define its limits through a peculiar kind of exclusion of Jews and Saracens: by comparing them with heretics, he implied a *need* for expulsion that actually presupposed a kind of belonging (Iogna-Prat 2003). To engage the Jews in such a pastoral war, however, required a substantive transformation in Latin Christendom's account of them.

For centuries prior to the Crusades, the Jews had possessed for Christendom a completely unique theological status and significance. Unlike the Saracens, Jews could never have been confused for pagans. Rather, they represented for the early church both its own ambivalent attitude toward the Hebrew Bible as well as the surviving descendants of the ancient New Testament Jews found in the Gospels and Pauline letters. As Jeremy Cohen has observed, early Christendom from at least the time of Augustine excoriated the Jews as the living remnant of that ancient "stiff-necked" people of the Bible who had rejected Christ's universal promise of redemption, clinging instead to the letter of the superseded Mosaic law (Cohen 1999). Jews were living fossils, a "historical anachronism" from an epoch before Christ's first coming, theologically vital to the church insofar as they provided a living reminder of the ancient truth of the story of Christ, as well as figuring the promise of the Second Coming (Funkenstein 1994, 177). Because on that future day the Jews would finally accept Christ's offer of redemption through the new covenant, although they deserved to be despised for their continued rejection of Christ, they also required toleration for the sake of his future return. Jews were permitted to dwell among Christians both as confirmation of the ancient story and as promise of the coming one. Neither pagan unbelievers nor part of Christendom, but truly sui generis, Jews, in the centuries preceding the Crusades and the war on heresy, lived a unique form of inclusive exclusion within Western medieval society based on their scriptural significance.

The pastorate's militant expansion, however, eroded this special theological standing of the Jews and refashioned their religious meaning, in part through an improved Christian understanding of Judaism as actually practiced. In addition to shedding light on Islam, Petrus Alfonsi's *Dialogue against the Jews* clarified features of postbiblical Judaism, including for instance the significance of the Talmud as a rabbinical reinterpretation of scriptural law that had transformed Jewish observance. Jews were apparently not a fossilized people still practicing the law of Moses as commanded in the Bible. On the contrary, the rabbinical oral tradition (and above all the Talmud) came to be seen as much like the Qur'an: a deceitful replacement scripture that had seduced Jews into betraying even their own law, and in this sense propagated a kind of heresy (Funkenstein 1994, 193–95). Judaism could now be viewed, in Amos Funkenstein's words, as "a secret, diabolical tradition," like other false doctrines encouraged by the Devil (320).

During the Crusades, anti-Jewish Christian discourse began yoking Jews and Saracens together for reasons that were sometimes politically straightforward: Jews were recognized as influential in the Islamic world of that era, and therefore viewable as the Saracens' allies in the Crusades (Cutler and Cutler 1986, 96; see also Anidjar 2003). With the new knowledge of Judaism and Islam, however, their conflation was also grounded in a positing of their heretical similarity: both people followed biblically corrupted dietary laws, performed circumcision, and subscribed to a dangerously false theology about the true God. Both had been misled by wicked rereadings of the Bible.

Cohen characterizes this ideological conflation of Jews and Muslims as a feature of high medieval theology that added them to the visages of the pastoral enemy: "As the crusades broadened the horizons of the Christian mentality, the world of the non-Christians assumed nuance and complexity; the Jews, who for centuries had functioned as the prime enemy in Christian religious polemic, began to share center-stage with Muslims (and heretics) such that the polemic against them developed in new directions and such that the insularity of their function—and, as a result their power—in the discourse of Christian theology were reduced" (Cohen 1997, 147–48). But if their theological uniqueness was diminished, the persecution of Jews was actually increased. Included now among the primary targets in the pastoral war against heresy, Jews became far more prone than before to violent pogroms (particularly ones tied to the Crusades) at the hands of Christians who viewed them as diabolical agents, more akin to witches than to Pharisees. No longer the unique "living letters of the law," Jews became an especially ancient breed of "wolf" with its own special threats to the flock (captured in the notorious "blood libel," for example).

Fourth Lateran Council: The Total Pastoral War against Errant Inner Life

In 1215, Pope Innocent III convened the massive Fourth Lateran Council (or Lateran IV), out of which emerged what is arguably the medieval Roman Church's most important body of canon law. All the aforementioned pastoral tactics and themes are gathered within its seventy-one canons into a consolidated agenda that sought to advance the pastorate's emerging strategies and tactics of security. I would like to review these canons so we can consider the overall strategy of power that pastoral security offered the Western church, but also discern the complex pastoral economy of body and soul that raised certain insolvable political problems for the pastoral exercise of power, problems that would come to feature centrally in the approaching racial turn.

In many ways, the Lateran IV gathering represented the apotheosis of high medieval pastoral power. Pope Innocent III, who summoned to his council church leaders from across Christendom, was arguably the most powerful pope in the history of the Latin Church. He not only inherited and expanded upon the Gregorian Reforms, but excelled in playing secular princes off against each other. He accelerated both the Crusades and the war on heresy, planning the Fourth Crusade himself and establishing a system of taxation to pay for it. He famously conducted the one Crusade that was waged against fellow Christians, the Albigensian Crusade of 1208, in which he summoned the king of France (in the letter cited above) to invade Languedoc. Finally, it was also Pope Innocent III who founded the Roman Inquisition, the church's pastoral institution par excellence for identifying heresy. In convening Lateran IV, through which he would launch the Fifth Crusade, Pope Innocent III consolidated all these various developments into a coherent political theological vision.

If there is an overriding agenda to Lateran IV, it could be neatly characterized by a passage in Canon 23 that invokes the Church's duty: "occurrere periculis animarum et ecclesiarium indemnitatibus providere" (to meet dangers to the soul and provide security to the Church).[19] Every major step in Lateran IV advances this logic of defending the flock against dangers, an aim equated with proactively protecting the church against its potential losses. How is this project of security to be accomplished? Lateran IV sequentially unfolds its animating pastoral logic. It begins with a careful spelling out of the *fides catholica*, the universal faith in a single God composed of three persons (Father, Son, Holy Spirit) but of only one essence. Contrary to the commonplace view that only under Protestantism did Christianity become centered on the importance of belief, Lateran IV attests to the critical significance of faithful belief as a linchpin of the post-Gregorian reformist medieval church. Lateran IV carefully specifies the *fides*, the creed or dogma, to which members of the church must cling if they are to avoid jeopardizing their souls. As Canon 1 stresses, "The devil and other demons were created by God naturally good, but they became evil by their own doing. Man, however, sinned at the prompting of the Devil."[20] Only those who cling to the *fides catholica* can be protected from those evil promptings. *Fides* delineates the sheep pen, which is itself a metaphor for the "Universal Church of the faithful, outside of which there is absolutely no salvation."[21] The pastoral work of the Church, then, is to protect the church's redemptive faith against those who seek to undo it. Even Greek Christians, with their equally ancient ritual traditions, must embrace the Latin Church because there can only be "one fold and one shepherd."[22]

In Lateran IV, the most important task for safeguarding the *fides catholica* was to denounce and forbid heresies. To that end, Canons 2 to 4 specified the various deviations from church dogma (by the mystic Joachim of Fiore and others) that must be rejected, arriving at the stern declaration that "we excommunicate and anathematize every heresy that raises against the holy, orthodox and Catholic faith which we have above explained; condemning all heretics under whatever names they may be known. They have different faces indeed but their tails are tied together inasmuch as they are alike in their pride."[23]

To safeguard against heresy, the Council's subsequent canons establish the new high standards of service to the church expected of the clergy at all levels, from the bishop down to the parish priest, forbidding worldly ambitions, decreeing celibacy, and above all insisting that Christians must never find themselves without a leading pastor who tends to their soul and ensures it is not sickened by sin, unrooted by foxes, or ravaged by wolves. Perhaps the best-known canon of Lateran IV was Canon 21, "Omnis utriusque sexus" (Everyone of either sex), the same decree that Foucault famously cites in the first volume of *The History of Sexuality* as an element in the intensification of confessional sexuality (Foucault 1990, 58–59). Lateran IV obviously did not invent the confession, but it systematized it and decreed that, at least once a year, every Christian must "confess all their sins" to their parish priest and perform the prescribed penance.[24] As Helen Birkett has noted in her study of Lateran IV's impact in medieval England, this law "necessitated a far reaching educational programme for the parish priests" to prepare them for this deepening of pastoral care (Birkett 2006, 201).

Earlier I presented the mendicant preaching tradition and the Inquisition as two exemplary new techniques of pastoral power in the High Middle Ages. Sacramental confession was a third such technique, and perhaps it was the most important of the three because it touched the entire flock. The confession offered a mechanism for inspecting the soul of each and every parishioner that, over time, would grow ever more intent upon producing the minutest truth of the self, down to the faintest hint of an illicit desire. In the context of Lateran IV, it is evident that the inner life illuminated by the confession concerns the sinfulness of both erotic urges and theological passions at the point of their interconnection. Heresy in the Middle Ages was widely associated with illicit sexual behavior. So too, as we have seen, were Saracens and Jews. And the wolf, of course, is a figure for the intertwining of heretical and sexual threat to the innocent lamb. It is a figure, above all, of seduction. When it comes to securing inner life, as we shall see throughout this book, race and sex are never that far apart because pastoral power is always concerned with the threat of the wrong passionate commitment, or what in erotico-religious terms we might call "infidelity." To whom or to what is one faithful? And at what point does the wrong faithfulness transform a sheep into an enemy against whom the other members of the flock must be protected? When does a tender heart allow entry to a snake that can ravage the flock?

The Problem of the Body in the Biopolitics of the Soul

The problem that desire poses to faith raises a fundamental question about the pastoral relationship of body and soul. We know that the pastorate was a government of souls. Its aim was to protect the eternal life that Christ had promised to all those who would have faith in him. In this sense, we could describe the pastorate as a premodern form of biopolitics. Admittedly, the pastorate did not much resemble the biopolitics that Foucault describes as emerging in the nineteenth century, the kind that dealt with populations as a "global mass that is affected by overall processes characteristic of birth, death, production, illness, and so on" (Foucault 2003, 242–3). That kind of biopolitics was statistical in its methods, and its targets were collections of aggregated bodies. But the pastorate nevertheless did seek to manage life at the collective as well as at the individual level, *omnes et singulatim*. It is just that we need to think about life in a different register.

Giorgio Agamben famously noted that there were two words for life in Greek, *zoe* and *bios*. The former refers to the bare, biological substrate of life that humans share with animals, while *bios* names the distinctly human, political life of the citizen (Agamben 1998, 2). But, in fact, there was also a third Greek word for life that is absent in Agamben's analysis: *psuchē* (ψυχή), which is alternately translated into English as "life" or "soul," and typically translated into Latin as *anima*.[25] *Psuchē* was also the Greek word used in the Septuagint to translate the Hebrew word *nefesh* (נֶפֶשׁ), which appears in the Vulgate as *anima* and also appears in English as "soul." Life has long been associated with the body in its movement, its warmth, its breath. But in Christianity especially, the soul was not just the locus of our spiritual being. It formed our participation in eternal life in Christ. The pastorate was therefore a biopolitics of *psuchē*. It represented an effort to manage the overall processes characteristic of spiritual redemption. And to achieves this it relied both upon early forms of discipline for individual sheep as well as biopolitical strategies directed at the flock as a whole. But if the biopolitics of the pastorate sought to improve the flock's prospects for eternal life as shaped in *this life*, then what conception of the relationship between soul and body did it depend upon?

Some answers to this question have presumably emerged in this chapter. The soul's redemption could not be protected without passing through the body. Preaching, for example, offered words that, passing through the ears, were conveyed by the body to the soul for its redemption. The inquisition inflicted torturous pain on the body to extract a confession that would lead the soul to contrition for its errors. And sacramental confession relied upon the soul's ability to inspect the body for feelings, passions, stirrings that might signal a potential risk to itself. Talal Asad has described this medieval testing of the body for the sake of protecting the soul as the emergence of a new way of detecting sinful *potentialities* (Asad 1993, 103). The body furnishes signs of risk, specifically the risk of an inclination to go astray. The same vigilance that must be directed outward toward others must therefore also be directed inward. Why? Because, explains Asad, one's body may also reveal the signs of the adversary: "Because it is a matter of flushing out from within the self the power of the Other, of the Enemy, who is hidden there under the appearance of oneself; because it is a matter of conducting an incessant fight against the Other whom one can't conquer without the help of the Almighty" (109).

The question, at heart, is whether and where within oneself the enemy is hiding. This is a possibility that exists both for the individual (the stir of the body that points toward the potential for sin) and at the corporate level (the members of the flock who may be led astray, or worse, who turn out to harbor wolves that have been mistaken for sheep). The enemy may even threaten from outside the flock, among the Jews or Saracens whose mere proximity might lead to infection by their perverse theology. The pastorate was therefore a multiscalar biopolitics that managed risk to the salvation of souls by governing the bodies of the church.

Epidermalizing the Soul?

It is in this context that I would like to consider a moment of play between soul and body in the canons of Lateran IV. In Canon 68 we find a law that is concerned with regulating the dress of both Jews and Saracens.[26] I will quote it in full:

> In some provinces a difference in dress distinguishes the Jews or Saracens from the Christians, but in certain others such a confusion has grown

up that they cannot be distinguished by any difference. Thus it happens at times that through error Christians have relations with the women of Jews or Saracens, and Jews and Saracens with Christian women. Therefore, that they may not, under pretext of error of this sort, excuse themselves in the future for the excesses of such prohibited intercourse, we decree that such Jews and Saracens of both sexes in every Christian province and at all times shall be marked off in the eyes of the public from other peoples through the character of their dress.[27]

This new rule apparently derived from a law developed for the Christian Kingdom of Jerusalem that had been decreed in 1120 by the so-called Council of Nablus in its twenty-five canons. Canon 16, the relevant one here, is very short and lacks any justificatory structure. It simply states that Saracen men and women may not dress in the Frankish style: "Si Sarracenus aut Sarracena francigeno more se induant, infiscentur" (Kedar 1999, 334).[28] The rule likely reflects the fact that Muslims constituted a majority in the Crusader kingdom and were, in any event, part of a local Levantine population whose Christians and Muslims could not be visibly distinguished by the European crusaders. The basis for this Lateran IV canon thus concerns from the start a specific Crusader-era problem concerning the inscrutability of interiority, what the canon calls a "confusion" caused when Jews and Saracens "cannot be distinguished by any visible difference" from Christians. So long as Jews and Saracens can be discerned by their dress, the flock can be properly regulated and the threat of infidelity contained. But the challenge arrives precisely when "Jew" or "Saracen" becomes a presence marked only on the inside.

The threat that this decree seeks to neutralize is borrowed directly from the discourse on heresy, which also sought to manage the dangerous gap that could exist between trustworthy outward appearance and inwardly hidden malice. Contrast Canon 68, for example, with an inquisitorial sermon about heretics of the same era that proposed that "Among Christians there are certain true Christians holding the true faith about Christ, and certain pseudochristians holding false faith, nevertheless they are both alike in Christianity, and the false ones are similar [to true Christians] in exterior appearance. For these false ones are those ministers of Satan about whom Paul speaks. . . . They are those false prophets who come to men in the clothing of sheep, but on the inside they are rapacious wolves" (Ames 2009, 41–42). This passage clarifies why it is so critical to inspect the entire flock. Just as one might hide within oneself (and even from oneself) a danger to one's eternal life, so the flock conceals within itself individual members who may threaten the corporate body. The principle of the shepherd is therefore the corporate correlative to the individual agency of self-inspection. And only by examining the body can one hope to discern the potential sin, the risks that the soul otherwise faces blindly.

Like the heretic in sheep's clothing, the Jews and Saracens of Canon 68 are infidels in disguise. Their unmarked status hazards a predatory seduction in which perverse "relations" might occur that are simultaneously erotic and religious. Jewish or Saracen infidelity could prove attractive to the wanton sheep even if those Jews or Saracens had not intended to damn their souls. God's enemy works in mysterious ways. It is in response to precisely such hidden threats that Cathars in the south of France were required by Saint Dominic (founder of the Dominican Order) to wear yellow crosses on their garments as ways of publicly identifying (and ridiculing) them before all as heretics (Weis 2002). This rule served as a form of enforcing penance through public humiliation, but it also sought to neutralize the corporate threat because all those who viewed the Cathar wearer of the yellow cross could recognize them as a heretic who put their soul's redemption in danger. So too, the cross reminded the heretic who wore it that if they were truly penitent, they must vigilantly watch for the inward return of their malign inclinations.

At nearly the same moment as the Cathar yellow cross, yellow badges were also developed and proscribed for Jews (Kisch 1942). These, and still other badges for other groups (Saracens, sorcerers, errant priests) embodying risk, emerged according to historian Joshua Trachtenberg (1943) alongside the Crusades and the war on heresy.[29] In the case of both Cathars and Jews, the yellow marking served to provide what in a future racial register we might call *giving these subjects a skin*: epidermalizing the wolf. They were meant to make visible on the bodily surface the enmity felt by this particular body toward the soul of the church. And yet, the badge alone could hardly overcome the threat that it was meant to mark. This is something we can see in a central epidermalizing paradox that it generated.

According to the terms of the pastoral metaphor, the unmarked heretic (or Jew or Saracen) is not actually undressed, for they are already, at least *in potentia*, a wolf in sheep's clothing. Inside their body, one can expect to find a soul bent on predation. But on its outside they wear the skin of a sheep. It is in order to overcome this disguise, which is already understood as a kind of masking outer skin, that now a further skin must be added. The wolf in sheep's clothing must be dressed a second time, now with the skin of a wolf overlaying that of the sheep so as to realign the truth of the inner self with this ultimate outer representation of the self. And the problem from the pastoral point of view, of course, lies in the fact that clothes may easily be shed. Or that one must know in advance who should be required to wear them. Even the Lateran IV canon could not avoid this paradox, presupposing as it does that the Jew and Saracen must be identified *before* they can be ordered to don the distinctive clothes that are meant to make them identifiable in the first place. No pastoral scrutiny, and no second skin, could ever guarantee the complete elimination of so circular a risk.

This problem finds an echo in the penultimate Canon 70, which was meant to address a problem that takes us to the very threshold of the invention of race. What, the canon asks, should be done about Jews who have converted to the church, yet continue to observe Jewish rituals, thus mixing the true faith with a false one? I again quote the canon's dictum in full:

> Since it is written, cursed is he who enters the land by two paths [Ecclesi-astes], and a garment that is woven from linen and wool together should not be put on [Deuteronomy], we therefore decree that such people shall be wholly prevented by the prelates of the churches from observing their old rite, so that those who freely offered themselves to the Christian religion may be kept to its observance by a salutary and necessary coercion [*salutiferae coactionis*]. For it is a lesser evil not to know the Lord's way than to go back on it after having known it.[30]

The final line confirms the classical theological position that the heretic and the infidel are far more wicked than the pagan since they have knowingly and there-fore willfully abandoned the Good Shepherd. In straying they may lead others astray, robbing them too of their eternal life. But it is here that the problem of the garment as second skin arises again, for if the sheep's wool is mixed invisibly with linen, if as a result the person with this Jewish admixture appears out-wardly as a Christian, do they not pose the greatest possible threat as someone whose Judaizing rites taint the sacred sacraments and the Catholic faith alike? It is important to note that the canon does not at all assume a malign intent by these converts. They are to be taken as people who have "freely offered them-selves to the Christian religion." Nevertheless, for the sake of their spiritual safety as well as all those around them, *omnes et singulatim*, one and all, it is critical that the church apply its *salutifera coactio*, its "salutary and necessary coercion."

This chapter has arrived at its terminus with this basic pastoral principle of "salutary and necessary coercion." In Lateran IV, the penultimate canons deal-ing with the Jews are followed by one long and final canon declaring a fifth Crusade to liberate the Holy Lands from the hands of the Saracen infidel. The holy war was yet another outward form of moral and positive force, the out-ward mirroring of the internal war against the threats to inner life. Consider the path of pastoral power as we have encountered it in this most canonical of medieval legal texts. Beginning with the problem of heresy and its seductions, establishing a pastoral response to that problem by such means as church-wide reform and universal sacramental confession, working through the twinned Jewish/Saracen threat, and ending with a call to launch a crusade, the Fourth Lateran Council brought into cohesive form the militarized pastoral strategy of power of the High Middle Ages.

The pastorate had developed a sophisticated means for conducting and protecting collective prospects for eternal life in a world of expanding wealth and population. These means were organized as tactics in a permanent war that would be waged against the soul's politico-theological enemies. But the pastorate did so by assuming that the enemy of eternal life, precisely because it too was lodged in the soul, required a regime of power that could examine, interrogate, and test the body for signs of its presence: the body of each individual Christian as well as the corporate body of all Christendom. While the operations of pastoral power did not yet identify this enemy within the population as racial, the problem of security that it established around the inscrutability of the internal enemy would provide the foundation upon which it could be established.

THE RACIAL TURN

Frayed Fabric and Dissimulating Danger

The converts [*conversos*] of Jewish lineage from your kingdoms are largely found to be unfaithful and heretics, who Judaize and keep the rites and ceremonies of Jews, apostatizing the chrismation and baptism they received, demonstrating through deeds and words that they received it on their skin and not in their hearts or in their will, such that their Christian color and name deceives Christians old in the catholic faith. —PERO SARMIENTO, "Letter of Supplication to the King of Castile"

By this time, I was in a high school that was predominantly Jewish. This meant that I was surrounded by people who were, by definition, beyond any hope of salvation, who laughed at the tracts and leaflets I brought to school. . . . The fact that I was dealing with Jews brought the whole question of color, which I had been desperately avoiding, into the terrified center of my mind. I realized that the Bible had been written by white men. I knew that, according to many Christians, I was a descendant of Ham, who had been cursed, and that I was therefore predestined to be a slave. This had nothing to do with anything I was, or contained, or could become; my fate had been sealed forever, from the beginning of time. —JAMES BALDWIN, *The Fire Next Time*

The Truth of Race

As we saw in chapter 1, the medieval European pastorate divided Christendom's population along multiple axes in its effort to extinguish the spiritual threats to its eternal life. To use its own pastoral metaphors, it took pains to distinguish the flock of believers from its predators, their shepherds from the sheep, the secure sheep from the vulnerable ones, and even the wolves concealed in sheep's clothing as opposed to the wolves exposed for who they truly are. Clergy and lay people, the faithful and the tempted, the orthodox and the heretical, Christians and infidels, these are merely some of the boundaries that the pastorate drew through the population to safeguard their souls. In routing these circuits of pastoral power, these distinctions also positioned people within various hierarchies. Populations were sorted and valued. Threats were identified. Friends were distinguished from enemies so that some might be defended and others attacked. Nevertheless, at no point did these pastoral demarcations introduce a language of race, even when they concerned the Jews or Saracens who would later be touched deeply by the practices of race. The pastoral game of truth employed other discourses: the languages of faith and infidelity, Catholicism, and heresy. Still, as James Baldwin acknowledges in the above epigraph, there is something in that pastoral Christian language for monitoring salvation and damnation—and perhaps especially in how Jews were targeted by that language—that quickly invokes the "whole question of color" and conjures up the status of racial Blackness as a fate "sealed forever" (Baldwin 1995, 45–46). This chapter hopes to explain why.

If medieval pastoral power seems relevant to the eventual contours of race, but was not yet itself explicitly a racial technology, then exactly when, how, and why did the language of race appear? To what uses was it first put? How did pastoral power shape the nascent game of race, and how did that game in turn come to reorganize the mechanisms of pastoral power? As posing my questions in this way might suggest, this chapter does not proceed by first postulating a definition of race whose truth it relies upon to determine how far back its existence goes or from whence it came. Instead, it begins with a deceptively simple genealogical question: Where do we first find the *language* of race? And what work did that language perform? It then raises the question of power: What changes in the pastoral regime of truth did this language of race begin to produce? In short, not what kind of difference *is* race, but what kind of difference did the advent of "race" *make*?

In order to answer these questions, I must acknowledge one respect in which I am in close agreement with Benjamin Isaac, Geraldine Heng, and others: it is important to decouple the assumed inseparability of race and modernity. For understandable reasons, scholars have long been predisposed to assume that the language, practice, and idea of race appeared only with and through the establishment of color-line racism as a facet of modern power. Even scholars such as Anibal Quijano and Agnes Smedley, who are prepared to go much further back than nineteenth-century scientific racism, date the origins of "race" to the modernity of plantocratic slavery and the "coloniality of power" in the New World. This chapter will eventually get to those same tremendous historical watersheds, but it does not begin there. It is a mistake to claim, like Anibal Quijano, that there is no known history of race prior to colonization. The earliest language of race began in late medieval Europe and in close relation to the themes of pastoral power from which it grew. This chapter will consider how the language of race emerged and wove its way through the complex and imbricated histories of forced religious conversions, expulsions, enslavements, conquests, and revolts that straddle the divide between the late medieval and early modern periods both in Spain and its colonies. The genealogy of the conceptions of race will be traced through a cluster of terms—*converso*, *morisco*, *cristiano viejo*, and *cristiano nuevo* (Old and New Christian)—that are no longer active, but whose consideration allows us to reevaluate the signification and power of other terms we thought we already knew: *race, color, passing.*

The Defective Fabric

The word "race," as several scholars have noted, has no history in classical Latin. It first entered European vocabulary through the Romance languages early in the fifteenth century, at the very moment when those languages were appearing as modern vernaculars distinct from Latin. In nascent French and Italian, the word was initially associated with the breeding of animals. Charles de Miramon observes an entry for *race* in one of the earliest French dictionaries, published in 1609, that starts with the following: "Race . . . means descent. Therefore, it is said that a man, a horse, a dog or another animal is from good or bad race" (de Miramon 2009, 200).[1] De Miramon suggests that the word was first applied to the animal world to describe the improvement of animals through breeding (a noble race of dogs), but subsequently was brought to bear on human nobility as a way to characterize the quality of aristocratic bloodlines. Race therefore began as a matter of zoological heredity and lineage before it took a political turn.[2]

Even earlier meanings in Spanish, however, suggest other trajectories. David Nirenberg has noted that "among [horse] breeders the word 'raza' quickly came to mean, in the first quarter of the fifteenth century, something like 'pedigree'" (Nirenberg 2009, 248), which is in keeping with the aforementioned usages in French and Italian. But Nirenberg also observes a different meaning: "At more or less the same time in Castilian poetry, 'raza' emerged as a way of describing a variety of defects linked to poetic speech, to sexuality, and especially to Judaism" (Nirenberg 2009, 249). In the Spanish language's first vernacular dictionary,

Elio Antonio de Nebrija's groundbreaking *Diccionario Latino-Español* of 1493, a related notion of race as defect is spelled out.[3] Nebrija's entry for *raça* (a medieval spelling of *raza*) includes two meanings, neither of which much resembles the French and Italian uses.

The first entry, associated with everyday language, is for *raça del sol*, meaning a "ray of sun." The second meaning, frequently used by the tailor's guild, according to historian Max Sebastian Hering Torres, is *raça del tela* or a "defect in the cloth." In his insightful reading of the dictionary entry, Torres suggests that these two meanings converged to describe a defect wherein an irregularity or fraying in the fabric allows the sun's rays to pass through it (Torres 2003, 9).[4] Sebastián de Covarrubias's *Tesoro de la lengua Castellana o Española* of 1611 offers a related but different meaning, noting the defect of *raza* as consisting in "the thread unlike the rest of the threads in the weft" (Lewis 2003, 193).[5] How would this sense of *raza* get mapped onto a breed or lineage? One answer is proposed in Joan Corominas's respected modern etymological *Diccionario crítico etimológico de la lengua Castellana*, which suggests that the Italian and French meanings of *raza*, drawn perhaps from the Latin *ratio* (in the sense of modality, species, or category), at some point came to be confused with an older and originary Hispanic meaning of *raça* as a thinness or defect in a cloth (Corominas 1954, 1019).[6]

It is not entirely obvious why a word describing an imperfection in fabric made the metaphorical leap of association in Spanish poetry to express the "defectiveness" of Jews, but we can nevertheless discern a certain swerve in the meaning of *raza* through which a concept of breed fused with that of defect to yield the politically consequential sense of a dangerously impaired lineage or genealogy. Perhaps this peculiar textile metaphor received motivation through rules like the Lateran Council canons of 1215 I discussed in chapter 1, which required Jews as well as Saracens to wear distinctive clothing so as to prevent unwanted interreligious sexual contact. Canon 70, you may recall, forbade all converted former Jews from reverting to Judaic rituals by way of a noticeably similar metaphor, quoting from Deuteronomy 22: "a garment that is woven together of woolen and linen ought not be put on."[7] The metaphorical redeployment of an imperfect textile to describe converts in fourteenth and fifteenth century Iberia might have made sense because the issue of a lineage tainted by a Jewish *raza* (stain, blemish, or defect) arose in a very specific context: growing social animosity toward a new and sizeable population of conversos, Iberian Jews who had been forcibly converted to Christianity but who were suspected of continuing to practice Jewish traditions, and suspected in a poetic sense of still wearing a "mixed" and thus defective garment.

Covarrubias's definition of the "thread that is different than the rest of the threads in the weft" is also metaphorically suggestive, since a lineage (*linaje* in Spanish), understood as a line, can metaphorically be described as a thread. A defective line, perhaps made of a different or inferior material, might weaken the entire (social) fabric it has been woven into, thinning it to the point of ripping the weft that binds together the warp's threads. Historian L. P. Harvey interprets the metaphorical action of *raça* as it came to apply to Jewish or Muslim lineages in much the same way: "a bolt of cloth, *sin raça* ('without any defect,' 'with no snags') was naturally worth more, and so by extension the ethnically pure were, for the purposes of the Inquisition, 'sin raza de judíos/moros': 'with no Jewish/Moorish blemish on their pedigree'" (Harvey 2006, 7n4).[8]

Perhaps the key observation regarding these metaphorical origins of the concept of race is that, in these early stages, the point of the word was not to ask, What race does one belong to? Because race named a defective condition, the question instead was, Who *has* race? Who damages the entire cloth when their line is woven into the whole? As Torres points out, *raza* in this sense of taint, stain, or defect usually appeared in a possessive form. So for example, to be pure of blood was to be someone who does not have *raza*, and to be an Old Christian was to be "without *raza*, stain, lineage and without evidence, reputation or rumour of these" (Torres 2012, 19).[9] At first, only those with Jewish ancestry "had race," but gradually others would be said to have race as well, certainly those with Moorish blood or heretical ancestry, but as we shall see, eventually Africans and Indians in the New World colonies.

A second theme of this metaphor of *raza* concerns a new kind of play between interiority and exteriority. I have already considered how in the Middle Ages the marking garment for the Jew, the Muslim, or the heretic served to epidermalize, to put on a second skin with which the body might signal visibly the threat that an otherwise invisible interiority might pose to the salvation of the flock. A garment often performed this epidermalizing task by means of its color. Jews and heretics, recall, were required to mark the infidelity of their souls by donning yellow cloth. To color someone was therefore incipiently a strategy of marking in the pastoral dialectic of body and soul. Read against this pastoral background, *raça* as a defective cloth or a mixed garment could potentially mean two different things. First, it might be a cloth that *signaled* a defect, like the yellow garments imposed on Cathar heretics in the Middle Ages. But it might also be a cloth that was itself defective by virtue of its own failure to signal properly. A flawed epidermis might be one that falls short of signifying (and thus exposing) the defect of the soul it garbs. This would be a skin that conceals what it should display if the flock's security is to be ensured; it fails to "color" as it should.

To pull all of this etymological speculation together, what if, instead of reading the earliest fifteenth century appearances of *raça* or *raza* as cognates for what we now mean by race, we read them primarily as signifying "taint" or "flaw," the thread that is not like the others? *Raza* provided a flexible and rich metaphor of defectiveness out of which complex operations of race eventually emerged. The challenge before us is to grasp what kind of defect this could be and why it posed above all a new problem of security that earlier forms of pastoral power had not anticipated.

From Jew to Converso

The earliest deployment of a logic of *raza* against the conversos of Spain occurred under unique circumstances. Compared with the rest of Western Europe, Spain possessed a much larger population of non-Christians stemming from its history of Moorish rule in the early Middle Ages. Although there is much debate as to whether Spain was ever quite the haven of religious coexistence and *convivencia* famously celebrated by María Rosa Menocal in her study *The Ornament of the World* (2009), medieval Spanish life certainly permitted a significant degree of cohabitation and cultural exchange among Christians, Muslims, and Jews that had no comparison elsewhere on the continent. This medieval multiculturalism began eroding on the Muslim side as early as the twelfth century with the Almoravid and Almohad invasions. Jews sometimes fled to Christian kingdoms in the north where multicultural *convivencia* persisted. Over the course of the thirteenth century, however, the wars of the *Reconquista* (the Christian "reconquest" of Spain's kingdoms that lay under Moorish rule), which relied heavily on crusading ideology against the Saracens, began to erode interreligious coexistence on the Christian side as well.[10] As in other regions of Europe, declaring war against the Muslim infidel could trigger pogroms against the Jews as a side effect. But there was another political element driving the anti-Jewish attacks in late medieval Spain that exceeds the pastoral logic of guarding the flock against infidelity. It is something that we can describe as an emergent urban-popular struggle against sovereignty. David Nirenberg writes that, as early as the twelfth century, "princely claims to powers of decision over Jews became a common feature of the medieval political landscape. In all of the emerging monarchies of western Europe, Jews began to be thought of as especially subject to royal power: 'serfs (or slaves) of the king's chamber' (*servi regie camerae*), according to a common legal formulation, or even the king's 'private thing'" (Nirenberg 2014, 77).

Since Jews were not part of the Christian flock, and thus formally speaking not subject to the church, they were, by the medieval logic of the two swords, subject only to secular authority. For this reason, there is a sense in which late medieval royal power found its purest expression in a king's special claim of ownership over Jews. However, the reverse also holds true: popular challenges to royal authority could be vividly articulated through confrontations with the king's Jews. To attack the Jews was to attack a "king's treasure" in a way that furnished a unique justificatory language. Since church canon law explicitly forbade secular rulers from granting Jews any authority over Christians, strong pastoral arguments could be mustered against kings in these terms. And in fact, prominent Jews were often appointed by kings as tax farmers (collectors), positioning them as lightning rods through which town dwellers especially could object to what they considered excessive taxation. Anytime a king's subjects felt they had been exploited or abused by him, they could complain that he was treating his fellow Christians as if they were Jews, as if in other words they were nothing more than his personal property. Worse, a king's authority could itself be described as Jewish—as exploitative and usurious. The condition of Jews as the pastoral enemy therefore began to converge during the late Middle Ages with their emergent status as intermediary targets in the new political struggles being fought over ascendant royal authority.

In 1391, one of the harshest waves of anti-Jewish violence in the history of medieval Europe swept across the towns of Spain. With strong encouragement from the anti-Jewish archdeacon of Écija, Ferrand Martínez, townspeople (first in Seville then in other cities) assaulted the Jews whom the recently coronated (thirteen-year-old) King Enrique III of Castile ostensibly owned and who would normally need to be protected by him. The rebels justified their actions according to the medieval logic of pastoral warfare, namely by insisting that the Christian flock was endangered by cohabitation with these Jewish enemies of the faith. But antimonarchical sentiments were tacitly at work. By forcing masses of Jews to convert, the rebels in effect deprived the king of his Jewish property in the name of expanding the church (Nirenberg 2014, 75–87).

Initially the mass conversion of the Jews after 1391 was celebrated as a miraculous victory. Over time, however, the consequences proved contentious. Once converted, and thus once Christians, these former Jews no longer faced traditional barriers to their social mobility. They could enter positions of administrative or economic power previously barred to Jews; they could enter all professions; they could even marry into Christian families. And perhaps above all, they could enforce the king's power to tax without doing so as Jews. Historically, Jews who converted had been legally entitled to full status as Christians. King Alfonso X's famous thirteenth-century juridical code, the *Siete partidas*, for example, had stipulated that "after any Jews have converted to Christianity, all persons in our kingdom shall honor them and no one shall dare to disparage them or their descendants concerning their Jewish past . . . And they shall have all the office and honors other Christians enjoy" (Carpenter 1986, 33).[11] The mass conversions of 1391, however, precipitated a historically unprecedented challenge to the royal statute's traditional principles. In the decades that followed that year's pogroms, many Spaniards not only refused to recognize the former Jews or their descendants—thereafter called *conversos* (converts), *cristianos nuevos* (New Christians), or *marranos* (a word with several possible meanings)—as full members of the flock, but instead maligned them as enemies.[12]

In his classic study of this phenomenon, Benzion Netanyahu claims that these events signified the earliest formation of modern racism out of what had formerly functioned as a variety of medieval religious hatred:

> Looking for a quality common to all Conversos, and at the same time so negative as to support the issuances of harsh, restrictive laws against them, the racial theorists believed that such a quality should not be sought in what the Marranos *did* or *believed*, but in what they *were* as human beings. This did not seem to be a difficult task. For what they were was determined by their ethnic origins—or rather, as they put it, by their race. Since race, they maintained, formed man's qualities and indeed his entire mental constitution, the Marranos, who were all offspring of Jews, retained the racial makeup of their forbears. (Netanyahu 1995, 982)[13]

The laws to which Netanyahu refers here are the so-called *limpieza de sangre* or blood purity statutes, anticonverso ordinances first instituted during this period to prohibit those with Jewish ancestry from assuming powerful public or private offices. Netanyahu reads this development as a turn away from demarcating Jews by faith (a religious distinction) and toward distinguishing them by ancestry, which for him launches the modern antisemitism that would lead straight to the Nuremburg laws and the full-blown genesis of modern racism. The process was more complex, however, as I will explain.

We have seen that the wolf in sheep's clothing was a classic figure of threat to the pastorate. Perhaps the gravest danger to the flock was posed by someone who looked like a faithful Christian but was actually a dissembler capable of seducing his or her neighbors into heresy. This is precisely why secular priestly inspection of the flock's inner life through the sacrament of confession and the investigative responsibilities of the Inquisition had been critical to the exercise of pastoral power. All the same, the traditional assumption concerning Jewish converts in the Middle Ages was that, even if one needed to guard against converts backsliding to their old Jewish rituals, still these converts would find redemption through their new faith in Christ. Eventually they and their descendants would fully join the sheep fold. The anticonverso polemicists of post-1391 Spain reversed this traditional assumption. While they admitted that individual converts could be sincere, they presumed that most *cristianos nuevos*, however much they appeared to be Christians, were predisposed to cling inwardly to their Jewishness. From one generation to the next, therefore, this line would have *raza*: they would threaten the social fabric.

This reversal drastically intensified the traditional pastoral problem of security, and in an unprecedented way. Netanyahu presumes that the "racial theorists" came up with an ideology justifying why New Christians should continue to be treated as Jews even after conversion. But this misses the most important feature of the new situation. The New Christians were not simply converts who continued to be treated as Jews. For those who feared them, they were in fact something new under the sun, and potentially more dangerous than the outward Jews they or their ancestors had once been. No longer directly subject to the king, and no longer excluded from the wider community, the conversos had gained entry into the Christian world. They had once been Jews; now they were nominally Christians. In actuality, however, they were now neither. They were a new hybrid subpopulation whose unique characteristics positioned them to smuggle both religious heresy and secular threat into the Christian community.

Baptizing the Skin but Not the Heart

We can observe the potency of this view of the converso in a well-known turning point in the history of antisemitism: the Toledan revolt of 1449. This was yet another antimonarchical uprising (against King Juan II), originally sparked by popular hostility toward a royal tax that the townspeople had refused to pay to Alonso Cota, a converso assistant to the king's constable. Among their demands, the rebels called on the king to bar conversos like Alonso Cota from all public positions where they could use their office to injure Toledo's *cristianos viejos*. In a letter of supplication to the king, the revolt's leader Pero Sarmiento complained:

It is notorious that the said don Álvaro de Luna, your constable, publicly defends and welcomes the *conversos* of Jewish lineage from your kingdoms, who are largely found to be unfaithful and heretics, who Judaize and keep the rites and ceremonies of Jews, apostatizing the chrismation [confirmation] and baptism they received, demonstrating through deeds and words that they received it on their skin and not in their hearts or in their will, such that their Christian color and name deceives Christians old in the catholic faith.[14]

This letter is nowhere near as well-known as a subsequent document by Sarmiento, written only after the king had failed to meet their requests: the *Sentencia-Estatuto* of Toledo, which scholars believe to contain Spain's first *limpieza de sangre* statutes. But the letter of supplication is interesting in its own right for its remarkable characterization of the converso problem. Let us review its rhetorical moves.

The issue that concerns Sarmiento is above all a probability: conversos are unfaithful "por la mayor parte," or for the most part. That a few may be faithful or trustworthy does not negate the threat of the majority's malice. On the contrary, a handful of faithful converts might distract Spaniards from the danger of the duplicitous majority. Regarding these unfaithful ones, writes Sarmiento, one can see by their words and deeds that they have only received the sacraments of conversion, "en el cuero e non en los coraçones ni en las voluntades," upon their skin (or hide) and not in their hearts nor in their wills. Sarmiento here draws a critical distinction between the converso's exterior presence, their skin as mere clothing or trappings of the body, and their interior life, the heart or the will that guides their intentions and faith. What does this distinction tell us about the converso defect or *raza*? It suggests that baptism has washed the body, but that its purifying waters have not reached the soul. Hence the converso is someone who now appears to be a Christian, whose skin indexes membership and provides entry into the flock, yet whose soul has been revealed (by words and deeds) not to be Christian at all. And this disjunction, this gap between the skin and soul is precisely what in Sarmiento's view allows "al fin que so color e nonbre de cristianos, prebaricando estroxesen las ánimas e cuerpos e faziendas de los cristianos viejos," allows that is, the conversos' Christian color and name to prevaricate or deceive, thereby destroying the souls, bodies, and estates of old Christians.

There is a curious play in this passage against the image of race as a defective thinness in the fabric, one perhaps allowing even the rays of the sun to penetrate through it. In Sarmiento's language, the skin of the converso might seem if anything too thick, for it blocks the purifying waters of baptismal conversion from penetrating into the soul. But viewed from another perspective, it could be said that the *cuero*, or skin, of the converso is a kind of thinned hybrid. It *looks* like the skin of a Christian, and indeed it shares its color. After all, the converso now dresses like a Christian, accepts the sacraments like a Christian, and thus looks like a Christian. Nevertheless, that exterior skin is flawed insofar as it instantiates the sin of deception, looking for all the world like the woven wool of a Christian sheep when it is really a blend with Jewish linen. The skin is thus thinned insofar as it exudes from the *inside* the toxicity of a Judaizing soul that taints its "words and deeds."

Perhaps the most interesting question to ask of Sarmiento's words is why he would speak of the "color" of Christians and what it might have meant in the 1440s. The European trade in African slaves is typically thought of as commencing only with the discovery and colonization of the Americas, but in fact it had begun earlier. Iberia's Moors had for centuries seized sub-Saharan Africans in war and brought them back as household slaves: Black Africans were therefore a visible presence in Iberia closely linked to Moorish history. Having ventured for several decades previous along the West African coast, the Portuguese were just beginning to trade in slaves from Africa at the time of the Toledan revolt. In the coming decades, they would sell their captives in the markets of Castile. But at the moment of Sarmiento's writing, the "color" of Christians probably referenced a lighter skin tone that contrasted with the sometimes tawnier hue of Moors and just perhaps the darker color of Africans enslaved by those Moors. The point is that Sarmiento's characterization of conversos as sharing the "color" of Old Christians was his way of suggesting that they now looked more like Old Christians than like the most proximate non-Christians. Skin color was emerging as one element among several outward signs (name, dress, skin) through which conversos were now disguised as ordinary members of the Christian flock.

If conversos now looked like Christians on the outside, their will or heart preserved the ancient animosity not only of Jews but also of their Moorish allies. Sarmiento confirms this association when he actually lists the "words and deeds" through which he claims the conversos have shown their true nature. In the *Sentencia-Estatuto*, Sarmiento accuses the conversos of having secretly waged "cruel war armed with blood and fire, inflicting slaughter, damage, and theft on us, as if they were Moors, enemies of the Christian faith" (Wolf 2008, 2). In this reactivation of the medieval linkage of the Jew and Saracen as twinned infidel enemies, the conversos become the descendants of Jews who once supported Moorish military assaults on the Christian-ruled city as well as the biblical Jews who betrayed Christ. But the new element, from the viewpoint of this anti-sovereign document, is the novel status of these conversos as *hidden* enemies: they cannot be readily recognized as were Jews of old, nor the Moors, with their distinctive "color and name." The converso therefore secretly breaches the security of Toledo's citizens, leaving them at the mercy of a negligent king. Like the pastorate's proverbial inattentive shepherd, the king is asleep in the pasture, endangering his own subjects by blindly trusting in the conversion of these half-sheep, half-wolf monsters.

The Moor's association with the converso's monstrous threat was central to one of the earliest and most widely read anticonverso tracts, the so-called *Tratado* or *Libro del Alboraique* (*Treatise* or *Book of the Alboraique*), which began circulating in Spain sometime between the 1460s and 1480s (just decades after the Toledan revolt).[15] The tract's title refers to al-Buraq, a magical steed found in the Islamic hadith tradition upon whose back Muhammad made the lightning-fast night journey from Mecca to Jerusalem, and then ascended from the Temple Mount to heaven and back.[16] Al-Buraq is said to be a hybrid creature freely mixing the features of different species. This legend was apparently familiar enough in post-Moorish Spain that the anonymous author of the *Tratado* used the Alboraique as a metaphorical figure with which to highlight the converso's unnatural qualities. Like Sarmiento, the anonymous author of the *Tratado* allowed that some conversos were now genuine Christians. It is in fact only those forcibly converted against their will, along with their descendants, whom the text characterizes as "Alboraiques." The book's author suggests that this is an appropriate name because these converts have "stubborn will and intention like Moors, and the Sabbath like Jews, and only the name of Christians, and are not Moors or Jews or Christians . . . though their will is to be Jews" (Gitlitz 1993, 123).

The *Tratado*'s frontispiece illustrates its opening claim that the hadithic Alboraique had twenty different features, including the mouth of a wolf, eyes of a human, body of an ox, and tail of a serpent (see figure 2.1). Not unlike Donald Trump's conjuring of a snake some five centuries later to figure multiple racial threats, the *Tratado* uses each animal that the Moors had allegedly attributed to Muhammad's steed to signify another of the converso's negative qualities.[17] The teeth, for example, which suggest a wolf's mouth, show that conversos are hypocrites who act under pretense. The human eyes, meanwhile, express the cruel converso's pretense of being a pious and decent person. In short, each body part augments the theme of the converso's dissembling nature. Even the Alboraique's gender proves treacherous. Although the frontispiece visibly shows the Alboraique with an erect penis, the *Tratado* explains that the creature is "not entirely male nor entirely female" (Gitlitz 1993, 124). I will return shortly to

FIGURE 2.1. Frontispiece of the *Tratado del Alboraique*, Biblioteca de Barcarrota edition, early 16th century. Biblioteca de Extremadura, Badajoz, Spain.

the significance of the Alboraique's ambiguous gender and sexual turpitude. For the moment, I wish to focus on an aspect of the Alboraique that is not actually visible in the illustration, since it concerns the question of its color. The Alboraique is described as possessing a skin, fur, or pelt of all possible colors, or "el pelaje de todas colores" (Lazar 1997, 216). Whatever evils are being done, the book observes, are "of the same color; for when they find themselves with Jews, they say: we are Jews; and when they find themselves among Christians, they say: we are Christians" (Gitlitz 1993, 137). Like a chameleon, the Alboraique disarms its neighbors by adjusting its outward hue to blend with its social surroundings. Precisely as in Sarmiento's letter, coloration appears in the *Tratado* not as a mark of inferiority but as a tactic in the game of concealment: the fact that certain bodies can signal the inward character of their soul simultaneously implies that other bodies can hide that character.

Although it depends on an anachronism, the converso panic in early modern Spain could be compared with much later anxieties in the United States about racial "passing." Like someone who passes, the converso raises for its regime of power all the possible dangers of dissimulatory boundary crossing. In other words, the very idea of a converso, like the person who passes, presupposes the possibility of transgressing a demarcating line that governs the population by bifurcating it. In the case of fifteenth-century Spain, of course, the border in question was not the North American color line but one drawn between Christians and their "others" (Jews, Moors). Like the passing subject, conversos triggered a need for security because they were "supposed" to look like people on the line's other side: by name, color, dress, behavior. It is not difficult to see that the very existence of that line as a problem of visibility is *constituted* by the converso, whose invention makes it the subject of disciplinary attention. The existence of the converso as a threat to the clarity and impermeability of the line therefore precipitates the need for new ways of disciplining the Christian population that proceed from the premise that some among them may not be "truly" Christian. *Limpieza de sangre* statutes will represent one important attempt to fortify the line as a militarized frontier, while new investigatory apparatuses will be developed to enforce it.

It is in these multiple senses that the converso constitutes a kind of proto-passing subject. But here the comparison reaches its limits. The situation of the converso differed from the case of racial passing in that the demarcating line presupposed here was still not yet a line of race. Jews and Moors, as the "others" of Iberian Christians, were *not* characterized by race. They were characterized by their infidelity, their lack of Christian faith. It is rather the converso *him or herself* who was first characterized as racial, not the population from which the converso "crossed over." To put this in the same anachronistic terms, it is as if the act of passing historically antedated and then itself retroactively constituted a color line. Yet even this characterization is not quite right, because at this early stage "color" was not yet the basis of the racial. Color was merely one factor, one instrument, part of the problem of someone's ability to feign Christianity. Conversos, for this reason, could just as easily be analogized to terrorists in a sleeper cell, or to underground communist spies. The figure of the converso represents a kind of forking path for the technologies of race that would lead to a wide range of future modes of racialization.

Of one thing we can be sure: the threat of the converso's suspected dissimulation depended on a historic resignification of the act of conversion. No problem of security could arise had conversion continued to mean what it had in the Middle Ages: an unambiguous act of spiritual amelioration, a washing of the soul and an embrace of Christ's salvation that literally turned a non-Christian into a Christian. But, as the first subject of race, the converso now raised the terrifying view of conversion as a malignant *feigning* of amelioration, an act of spiritual subterfuge that was at once a defect and a source of power. The *Tratado* shows us that the concept of genealogical purity, which entered the field of power in this era, precisely did not presuppose (as we often assume race to do) a straightforward sense of the superiority or higher quality (*calidad*) of the pure over the impure, or of one color over another, as for example one might find in the discourse of horse breeding. After all, within such a logic, the Alboraique would be but a pathetic mongrel, the purebred's inferior. Yet the Alboraique, precisely through the capacity for subterfuge granted by its impurity, became a hybrid monster to be especially feared (Gitlitz 1992).

Let us now return to the special problem of sexual turpitude. The *Tratado* explains at one point that it has described the Alboraique as "neither male nor female" because "Sodomy comes from the Jews," who "passed [it] to the Moors, and to the bad Christians, like Diego Arias, which was the beginning and the cause of the perdition that would come to Spain" (Gitlitz 1993, 137–38). Who was this Diego Arias? David Gitlitz explains that Arias was apparently a wealthy converso merchant and tax collector for King Enrique IV of Castile, who was nicknamed "Enrique el impotente," or Henry the Impotent (Gitlitz 1993, 131n47). His "impotence" concerned both his reputed shortcomings as a king and his failure to produce an heir, but also rumors that he engaged in sodomy with other men, allegedly including the converso Arias. Mobilizing those rumors, the *Tratado* paraphrases a satiric poem about the royal court in which Arias "flattens" the king's head to prove that, whenever Alboraiques "take a Christian into their power in debt or any other form of subjugation, [they] press him like grapes in a winepress and break him in many ways" (Gitlitz 1993, 131). Money, power, and sex all become confounded here as means of corruption. The converso wears away at the kingdom's strength by means of a sexual subjugation equated with debt, the crushing of its wealth or strength into impotence.

Yet this "flattening" would never have happened had Arias been a Jew rather than a converso. Precisely because its "many colors" means that it cannot be recognized on sight as a hybrid, the Alboraique's deceptive outer appearance (its camouflaging skin), which grants it entrance to Christian society, also admits it into the Christian royal court, and apparently even into the Christian king's body, introducing both a homosexual *and* a heterosexual threat into the realm. Converso sodomy precipitates the sexual corruption and weakening of even an Old Christian king. But converso heterosexuality produces the interracial threat of reproduction: its disguise allows it to breed and further mix monstrosity into the population through its progeny. The child of an Alboraique becomes another Alboraique, who, with each generation, further insinuates malicious intentions and further frays the fabric of the population. Predatory sexuality is therefore a critical dimension of the converso threat.

The Duality of Converso and Morisco Threat

The Toledan indictment of the conversos by comparing them with Moors, and indeed the making monstrous of conversos by way of a hadithic Muslim account, doubled back over the next few centuries to make converso-like targets of the Moorish inhabitants of the Spanish Christian kingdoms known as *mudejares* (from the Arabic for "those permitted to stay"). When Mudejares were forced to become Christian, their conversions would be subject to an analogous suspicion. As one Spanish writer of the sixteenth century succinctly wrote, "these descendants of the Mohammedan and Judaic races, cannot be distinguished by any visible extrinsic act, by any ocular external note or sign, from authentic Spaniards" (Martínez 2011, 63). But these linkages between the converso and Morisco populations were not simply a function of their similarity as dubious converts, nor even grounded in some imagined shared affinity with the Moorish past. Within the emergent logic of *raza*, or defect, what united them was a grander significance in the geopolitical present. This connection emerges in yet another polemical anticonverso text, the so-called *Carta de los Judíos de Constantinopla* (Letter of the Jews of Constantinople), a forgery that circulated widely across Spain in the late sixteenth century. By the time of the *Carta de los Judíos*, not only had *limpieza* statutes been widely implemented in many locales, but the monarchy of a united Spain had expelled all unconverted Jews from the realm, not because of any direct threat that Jews allegedly posed, but rather because of the indirect danger that the Jews might encourage malice among (and thereby increase the dangerousness of) the conversos. In other words, the proximity of Jews at the time was seen as increasing the risk of converso danger in the future. But the proximity of Muslims was also in play. The *Carta de los Judíos* illuminates this thinking in an interesting way.

Although scholars believe that the *Carta* was composed in the mid-sixteenth century, it poses as a much earlier exchange of letters between Spanish Jews, on the eve of their final expulsion from the kingdom in 1492, and their fellow Jews from the city of Constantinople. The forged document begins with a first letter in which Spain's Jews request advice regarding how to manage the impossible choice offered by the king between conversion to Christianity or expulsion from the realm. The second letter, in which the leading Jews of Constantinople reply, recommends the following course of action to Spain's Jews:

> Regarding what you state about the King of Spain compelling you to become Christians, let him do it for there is nothing that you can do to prevent it. Concerning what you write about the fact that they are seizing your goods, well turn your children into merchants so that, bit by bit, they may seize their goods. In connection with what you have said about their murdering you, well turn your sons into doctors and apothecaries, so that they may murder them. As regards what you say about their destroying your synagogues, turn your sons into clergymen and theologians, so that

they may destroy their churches. Finally, vis-à-vis what you have to say about the vexations that they make you suffer, strive so that your sons may become lawyers, attorneys, notaries and counsellors and that they should always know how public affairs work so that you may dominate them and win lands.... this way you will get your revenge. (Soyer 2014, 371–72)

This forgery proposes to expose the origins of a comprehensive conspiracy co-ordinated by a camouflaged internal enemy that has married into the popula-tion, spread across it, and now sits in wait to strike against all dimensions of Old Christian life. What deserves our attention, however, is why the city of Constantinople becomes the source of the conspiracy. In 1453, just four years after the Toledan rebels declared their *Estatutos*, Byzantine Constantinople fell to the Ottoman Turks. At the very moment that a unified Christian kingdom of Spain was consolidating its political power, a new Islamic power, the Otto-man Empire, was also launching a rapid westward conquest of the Mediterra-nean basin. This Ottoman presence would challenge Spanish power for several centuries.

At the moment of Constantinople's conquest, all that remained of Islamic Spain was the Moorish tributary state of Granada. Nevertheless, even before Granada's fall, the Moorish inhabitants of Christian kingdoms (or the Mude-jares) living in the southern reaches of Christian Spain were often feared to be potential fifth columnists whenever tension arose between Granada and its Christian neighbors. After Granada was conquered in 1492, the Mudejares launched a series of revolts, triggering the crown's decision in 1502 to require all Mudejares to either convert to Christianity or go into exile. It was this decree that resulted in a population known as the Moriscos who, as already noted, would come to be feared in a way that ran parallel to the conversos.[18]

If we return to the *Carta de los Judíos* forgery, we can see how the choice of Constantinople as the source of the conspiracy links the converso threat not only with the fear of Morisco revolt, but both of them with the geopoliti-cal challenge of an Ottoman empire that would presumably delight in rolling back the *Reconquista*. Conversos were conjoined with Moriscos as a potential fifth column preparing secret cooperation with the Turks. The defect or stain of Jewish or Moorish ancestry by this point in time had come to embody far more than a pastoral enemy of the flock, or even a poisoner of the social body; it indexed secret geopolitical collusions with enemies of an emergent Spanish imperial state. Panic about "passing," even at this early moment, already delin-eated the prototype of the secret agent or the political spy, a topic to which I will return in subsequent chapters.[19]

Technologies of Racial Security

From the viewpoint of racial power, it is important to consider the new technologies of security that would develop to regulate the problem of *raza*. As it consolidated power during the fifteenth and sixteenth centuries, the Spanish crown would assemble a game of security against the threat of race with tremendous disciplinary capacities. Certain elements, such as the establishment of the Spanish Inquisition, were largely variations on the technologies of pastoral power. Already in 1478, Isabella and Ferdinand had secured permission from the Vatican to establish this separate branch of the Inquisition whose special charge was to identify heretics and backsliders among the many converts from Judaism and, later, Islam.[20] Unlike its medieval predecessors, the Spanish Inquisition reported to the crown rather than to the pope, thereby acting from the start as a religious arm to the growing power of the Spanish absolutist state. By establishing an institution charged with rooting out the dissimulatory conversion associated with "Judaizing" and Morisco tendencies, the crown developed a governmental apparatus of surveilling power whose reach extended far deeper into daily life than the medieval inquisition ever had. Deborah Root characterizes the Spanish Inquisition of the late sixteenth century as a kind of crypto-Jewish/Muslim detection machine that sought to crack the private codes through which conversos or Moriscos concealed their inner lives (Root 1988). These clues were by no means restricted to the practice of Jewish or Muslim religious ritual. They came to include culinary, linguistic, and other cultural practices—or even feelings about such practices—that might expose the persistence of secret religious affiliation. As Root notes, these principles were then generalized into a system of examination across the population:

> The inquisitorial machine attempted to control Morisco heresies by extending policing to the entire community, both Old Christian and Morisco: a "true" Christian must and will enjoy pork. The surveillance of Moriscos was transformed into internal or self-policing by all Christians. Yet the problem of indeterminability was not solved; the Inquisition recognized that it was possible to dissimulate and to give only the appearance of pleasure when eating pork. The move into the private lives and into the kitchens of Moriscos and Old Christians alike only increased the unknowability of (internal) orthodoxy. (Root 1988, 129)

In these ways, the Spanish Inquisition trained its hermeneutic of suspicion on numerous domains of everyday behavior that had never before concerned its medieval predecessors. What it sought were outward cultural symptoms pointing toward the malignant hybridity of an otherwise hidden inner life.

As had been the case for heretics in earlier centuries, individuals discovered by the Spanish Inquisition to be practicing crypto-Jews or crypto-Muslims were mandated to display their shameful inner life in the public plaza. As part of a ritual of penance, the auto- da-fé (act of faith), the guilty would appear wearing a *sambenito*, a penitential garment made of yellow sackcloth that epidermalized their status as repentant betrayers of the faith (see figure 2.2). The *sambenito* essentially served to reverse the "Christian color" of the heretical converso or Morisco. Like the badges required of medieval Jews and heretics, it was typically yellow in color and accompanied by a pointed hat known as *la coraza*. The *sambenito* of a penitent person typically was covered with red crosses. But if the subject was considered impenitent, and sentenced to be burned at the stake, their *sambenito* resembled the one seen in figure 2.2: the dragons and demons adorning the garment's surface represented the evil soul of its wearer, along with an image of the public burning and future hellfires that awaited them.[21] The *sambenito* in this way exposed the defective inner life of its wearer, paradoxically stripping their capacity to "pass" as a good Christian by garbing them in their defect.[22] The notion of textile as a kind of outer skin evidently persisted at the time of the converso mutation even as the idea of the defective cloth itself became a guiding metaphor for the formation of race thinking. The hat of the *sambenito* would eventually make its way to French and Spanish Louisiana and become part of the festive reversals of Mardi Gras, paradoxically becoming the source of the conical hat of the Ku Klux Klan.[23]

In addition to inquisitorial pursuits of Judaizing and Morisco heresy, the blood purity statutes, although originally crafted by the Toledan insurrectionists as a means of challenging the monarchy, would within a matter of decades be coopted by the Spanish crown. And by contrast to the Spanish Inquisition's detection machine, these *limpieza* statutes, which entailed the Spanish Inquisition's entirely new duties of conducting genealogical research to ensure their enforcement, were emphatically *not* just modifications or intensifications of medieval inquisitorial techniques. If anything, they sought to bypass the entire medieval problem of identifying heretics within the population by developing an innovative technique of incipient racial knowledge/power embedded in temporal issues. This innovation extended heresy both backward and forward in time, or even more precisely, it traced the threat of race backward in order to look forward.

Limpieza statutes obviously could not be enforced unless one already possessed an apparatus capable of determining whether someone was *sin raza*,

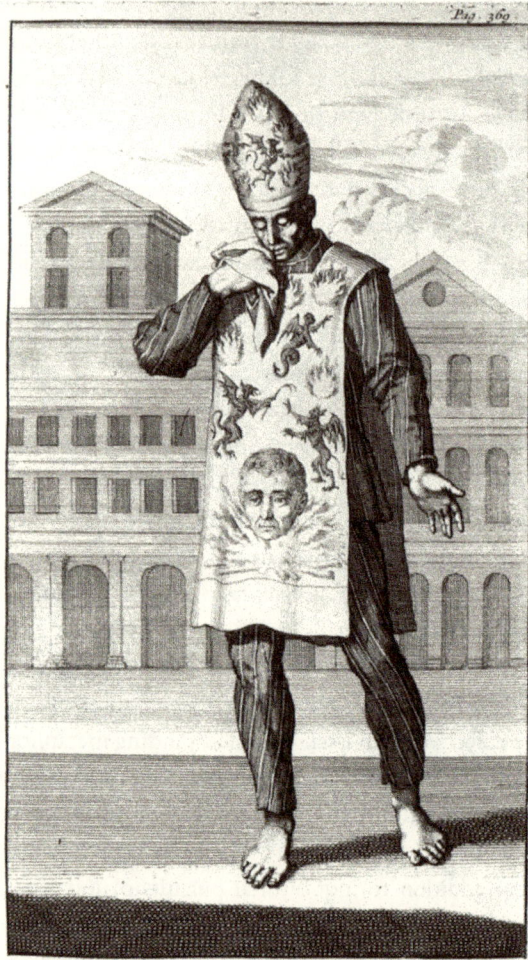

FIGURE 2.2. A figure
wearing a *sambenito*.
Phillipi a Limborch, *Historia inquisitionis* (History of the Inquisition)
(Amsterdam, 1692), 380.

*Vestitus relapsi vel impœnitentis comburendi
qui vocatur* Samarra.

without the stain or defect of Moorish or Jewish ancestry. The Inquisition was
therefore responsible for reconstructing the ancestry of candidates for proscribed
offices as well as suspects for a crime. But such genealogical investigations were
not necessarily meant to uncover an actual heresy. Rather, by ascertaining the
existence (or nonexistence) of an inward defect based on ancestry, they sought
to predict the likelihood of a future heresy. "Race" in this sense involved a technique of forecasting. *Limpieza* investigations sought to identify high-risk individuals within the population whose lineage predisposed them to become
dangerous dissimulators and who should therefore not be entrusted with

positions of power. Put another way, the converso or Morisco was not necessarily someone passing yesterday or even today, but rather a creature of the anterior future who might prove *to have been passing* at some unspecified future moment of otherwise unexpected vulnerability. Such hypothetical future risk was therefore to be mitigated preemptively through the security measure of *limpieza* rules that, contrary to the uncertainties of conversion, protected the longevity of well-being for faithful Old Christians, the crown and the church. The probabilistic logic of the *limpieza* statute here functioned rather like a modern security clearance.

Slavery, Colonization, and the Duality of *Casta* and *Raza*

Earlier I noted that the Ottoman Empire's takeoff layered a geopolitical dimension onto the converso and Morisco threat in Spain. But it also figures in the genealogy of race for a different reason: it pushed the early Iberian slave trade toward sub-Saharan Africa. Until the Ottoman victory at Constantinople, Iberia's Christian kingdoms had been distant parties to a Byzantine trade in Eastern European slaves. The very word "slave" in fact has an etymological connection to the Slavic population that was captured for this market.[24] But after the Ottoman victory, the Mediterranean slave trade in Slavs declined rapidly. It would come to be replaced with a new one led by the Portuguese, who conducted a growing slave trade down the western coast of Africa. Enslaved Africans had a long history in Iberia through the Moors, whose wealthier households had often used them for domestic labor. But as James Sweet puts it, "after the 1460s, the institution of slavery would be considered the preserve of black Africans"(Sweet 1997, 155).

Sweet has argued that a Moorish view of Black inferiority, which Iberian Christians inherited and expanded upon, was critical to the genesis of modern anti-Black racism in the West. The Portuguese without question drew upon a Moorish ideological inheritance to justify Black enslavement as early as the mid-fifteenth century. Nevertheless, at no point prior to the expansion of the Iberian slave trade into the Americas was the category of race—which at this time named the dangerous genealogical defect or stain of conversos or Moriscos—extended to Africans. Nor would it be for almost a hundred years after the conquest of the Americas. By the end of the sixteenth century, however, the new Iberian empires would begin integrating the language of race into their colonial administration. How exactly did the language of *raza* come to shape the regime of colonial power? In what remains of this chapter, my aim will be to analyze neither the greater story of the colonization of the Americas nor that of the transatlantic slave trade. Other scholars have addressed these topics far more knowledgably and eloquently than I could ever hope to do.[25] What I wish to account for here is something more specific: how the earliest practices of race-making originally directed at the conversos of Iberia came to be central to practices of colonial security in the Americas and, conversely, how the expanded project of colonial security propelled a reshaping of race itself as a technology of power.

From the start, the security of New World colonization relied upon the peninsular meaning of "race" as the stain or defect of a dangerous Jewish or Muslim lineage. Consider how quickly the Spanish crown moved to control the "race" of populations crossing the Atlantic. Cortez would not arrive in Mexico until 1519. Pizarro would only reach Peru in 1531. But already by 1508, the Spanish crown had decreed that "the descendants of Jews and Muslims burned or reconciled [by the Inquisition], up to the fourth generation" were forbidden from journeying to the New World (Soyer 2017, 406). In 1523, only two years after the final defeat of the Aztecs and the official founding of the colony of New Spain, as María Elena Martínez observes, the crown would publish another order forbidding all people who were "stained" from entering New Spain. And these were to be followed by "other decrees targeting Jews, Muslims, conversos, moriscos, Gypsies, heretics, and the descendants of those categories" (Martínez 2011, 128). It was therefore as a technology of border security that colonial power first made use of race.

Martínez suggests that these exclusionary *limpieza* decrees for the colonies arose from a utopian politico-theological impulse: "The tight relationship between the Spanish state and the church and the prevalence of Castilian providential notions of history at the time of the conquest produced a vision of the 'Indies' as a privileged space of purity, a region where Old Christians would make their faith flourish and the seeds of heresy would never sprout" (Martínez 2011, 128). Yet this vision of the colony as a theologically pure space appears to have been suffused with a fear of failure. These edicts would not have been deemed necessary nor applied so early had the colonies truly been deemed safe from the "seeds of heresy." On the contrary, this safety was predicated on a vigilant effort to keep those heretical seeds far from American shores, as if the soil were somehow dangerously fertile. Why might that be so?

As numerous historians have noted, the status distinctions developed (and legally enforced) among Spaniards, Indians, and Africans were not initially described through the language of *raza* at all. Instead, they were formalized through a different discourse, the so-called *sistema de las castas*, or caste system, of the Spanish colonies. *Casta* referred to ascending categories of prestige associated with bloodlines that soon became distinctions of color.[26] The caste system began as a triad, classifying individuals into one of the three populational categories: Spanish, Indian, and African. Over time, however, the caste system devised intermediary categories for every possible combination of the basic three: the *mulato* (half African, half Spanish), *mestizo* (half Indian, half Spanish), *zambo* (half Indian, half African), *castizo* (mostly European, some Indian), and so forth. *Casta*, like *raza*, therefore designated a genealogically acquired status. Yet the two were not the same thing. Offering a sixteenth-century example of how this difference between the terms actually functioned in the colonial situation, anthropologist Laura Lewis relates the telling story of "a Spanish woman suspected of witchcraft, who was asked by the Mexican inquisitors in the late sixteenth century whether her blood was 'clean' (*limpia*). She replied that she did not know if there was any 'evil (*mala*) raza' in her 'casta.'" Lewis then poses the crucial question: "What did she, in fact, mean?" (Lewis 2003, 23).

Casta here apparently referred to this woman's status as a "Spaniard" as opposed to being Indian, Black, or some other combination of these three categories. Since for us today race means precisely such things as being Black, Native, or white, her description of her *casta* reads to us a lot like race. And yet, as Lewis notes, when the word *raza* actually appears, it is doing different work. In asking whether she had any *mala raza* in her caste, the inquisitors were inquiring whether, above and beyond her caste position, this woman might also possess the stain or defect of Jewish, Moorish, or heretical origin. Critically, the question of race tended to emerge in the overarching security context of a risk analysis. Accused of witchcraft, this woman needed to be evaluated for the possibility of a stain or defect of race in her Spanish genealogy because this information would guide the inquisitors about the seriousness of the accusation and (if found guilty) the likelihood of her recidivism. I will touch on the special threat of witchcraft again in the next chapter, but as we can see, the "witch" was in this colonial context construed as something like a female Alboraique, a heretical danger availing herself of demoniac magical powers, whose special potency could be produced through the mixing of Jewish or Moorish blood with that of Christians.

Why the need to inquire about the stain of Jewish or Moorish race if, as I previously observed, such people had been excluded by royal decree from entering the Americas in the first place? The predictable answer is that, decrees notwithstanding, conversos had in fact arrived in the Spanish colonies. It was easy enough to purchase false documentation, to bribe, or (in later years) to enter via the ports of other colonial powers. As the pressures of the Inquisition intensified in metropolitan Spain during the sixteenth century, conversos sometimes sought to escape them by relocating to the colonies. By 1571, however, at least in large part because of increasing concern over this illicit migration, the crown responded by establishing three inquisitorial tribunals in the respective viceroyalties of New Spain (Mexico), Peru, and Cartagena de Indias (Colombia). As in the metropole, these tribunals would be tasked with conducting the blood purity investigations for important positions. They were also charged with investigating whether someone "had race" if they stood accused of heresy, witchcraft, or any kind of conspiratorial threat. Of particular concern was a population of "Portuguese" conversos descended from Spanish Jews who, during the expulsion of 1492, had fled across the border to Portugal. They had subsequently converted there when Portugal issued its own expulsion order in 1497, and some of their descendants had returned to Spain after 1580 when the Spanish and Portuguese crowns were united for a period of some sixty years. Portuguese merchants, who lived and worked in all of the colonies, were widely suspected of being conversos. By the late sixteenth century in fact, the words Portuguese, Jew, and converso had become virtual synonyms. The peninsular problem of *raza* therefore persisted in the colony, but through the very flexibility of the defect or stain as a political technique, it would now transfer itself to new populational targets for whom the political logic of *casta* would not suffice.

Anti-Indigeneity: The Threat of the Conquered

Perhaps the most obvious difference in the colonies when it came to *raza* was the multiplying risk of converted populations. By the sixteenth century, conversos and Moriscos were no longer Spain's only *neófitos*, or neophyte Christians. Indians and Africans were now part of the calculation. This fact illuminates the basic paradox in the Spanish attitude toward conversion. Despite the distrust of converts in the metropole, the Spanish imperial project presented the converting of Indigenous Americans as its highest spiritual objective. In the sixteenth century, Spain conceived itself as the church's temporal champion, fighting heretical Protestant powers on the European continent while winning over new converts in the Americas. But of necessity, sincere conversion needed to be a voluntary decision of the heart or will. A baptism only "skin deep" would not suffice. It was therefore difficult to reconcile the coercive force of military conquest, and the rapaciousness of the colonial settler class, with the vision of a freely chosen conversion (Lewis 2003, 16–18). After 1517, a largely symbolic attempt was made to reconcile these dueling logics by obliging Spain's conquistadors to present to Native peoples a *Requerimiento* (a demand or request) that offered them a "peaceful" option of accepting the monarch of Spain as their ruler and inviting the preaching of the gospel of Christ as savior. By accepting this option, they had committed to embracing Christ with their hearts. If they refused, however, Native peoples were lawfully subject to war and construable as pagans who had willfully refused the gift of redemption through the church.[27]

The *Requerimiento* was always a shaky solution to the ideological dilemma of a Christianizing conquest. Given that for conquered Native peoples, conversion (to Christianity) always entailed subjection (to the crown), this amounted to a coerced choice between the baptismal font or the sword, not unlike what the ancestors of the Iberian conversos had once faced. Native peoples often did not understand the reading aloud in Spanish of the *Requerimiento*, which thus made these performances into easy pretexts for military assault, colonization, and enslavement. In light of the indisputable violence in this history, how could colonial authorities really know whether a converted *Indio* (a Native of the Americas) was sincerely Christian? Was their professed faith genuine or was it instead the thinned cloth of another forced convert, shrouding an untrustworthy soul who sooner or later would conspire to expel from their ancestral lands the "Old Christians" of Spain? Tomaž Mastnak has observed that the famous 1550–51 debate between Bartolomé de las Casas and Juan Ginés de Sepúlveda put the status of America's Indigenous peoples on trial, primarily by weighing the aptness of a Muslim analogy: to what extent could Native peoples be judged, like the Turks or the Saracens, as enemies of Christendom against whom one could justly declare a permanent war (Mastnak 1994)?[28] For Sepúlveda, the Indian was a natural slave as Aristotle had defined it (someone born for subjugation), but because of his sinfulness, and because he had failed to respond appropriately to the *Requerimiento*, the Indian was also a new Turk; he could be treated as an infidel against whom one could justly wage war and subsequently enslave. For Las Casas, Native peoples were pagans with souls who had sufficiently demonstrated their receptivity to the word of God. One could not justly wage war against them, unless of course they had reneged on their conversion by somehow rebelling (openly or secretly) against God, church, and community, much as conversos stood accused of having done.

Over the course of the sixteenth century, the more pessimistic view gradually gained dominance. Colonial authorities increasingly came to suspect that *Indios* would revert to their pre-Hispanic idolatrous ways and, most alarmingly, employ the dark magic of Indian witchcraft and sorcery against their colonizers. Theories also emerged that the *Indios* were descendants of the lost ten tribes of Israel, and by implication shared the defect or flaw of Jews through their blood line. In 1555, just four years after the debate between Las Casas and Sepúlveda, Native peoples were banned from the priesthood on the grounds that Indigenous priests with their probable faulty or even malicious grasp of Christian theology might spread heresy and undermine colonial authority (Ricard 1974). *Limpieza* statutes began to sometimes apply to Native peoples. This growing pessimism about the conversion of Indians extended even to those of mixed blood (mestizos), who like the Iberian conversos could potentially use their "Christian color and name" to deceive the settler community. An example of this shift can be observed in a 1576 letter by Mexican inquisitors to the Suprema explaining that the "vile and despicable" population of mestizos and Indians were "not admitted into monasteries nor allowed to take the habit, but some were able to do both because of their white skin color, which allowed them to conceal their 'true descent,'" a descent that was not merely Indigenous but (according to the letter) ultimately traced back to Palestinian (Jewish) ancestry (Martínez 2011, 149). Mestizo and Indigenous converts, in short, were sometimes positioned as New World conversos, or as passing *Indios* who elicited a conspiratorial expectation similar to that expressed in the *Carta de los Judíos*. And this expectation was not entirely phantasmagoric: Indigenous rebellions occurred throughout the entire history of Spanish colonization, from the early 1519 "revolt of Enriquillo," a Taino leader on the island of Hispaniola born only eight years after the arrival of Christopher Columbus, right through the rebellion of the Incan Tupac Amaru II in 1780.[29]

Anti-Blackness: The Threat of the Enslaved

The expectation of threat ran deepest, however, when it came to the small but growing population of Africans in early New Spain. The Portuguese slave trade, as I noted earlier, dated back to the 1460s. But as the sixteenth century progressed, the traffic in African slaves was increasingly redirected across the Atlantic, first to the Caribbean colonies where the Native population had been eviscerated by the weapons and diseases of the colonizers, then to the American mainland, especially after the Spanish crown passed its "New Laws" prohibiting the enslavement of Native peoples. Although only a mere 3 percent of the total Atlantic slave trade would occur in the early decades between 1450 and 1600 as part of what P. C. Emmer calls the "First Atlantic System," characterized by Portuguese ships trading Africans in the Spanish colonies, it was here that anti-Blackness was first integrated into the game of racial power associated with chattel slavery (Emmer 1991, 75–78).[30]

As with Indigenous people, the uncertainty of conversion became of paramount concern to the maintenance of colonial power. Unlike Indigenous peoples, however, there could be no pretense that Africans enslaved by Portuguese traders had even a modicum of free will in their conversion. Because the crown mandated the ritual of baptism before arrival in the colonies, Africans were literally converted aboard slave ships, either during the middle passage itself or immediately after arriving in port (Lewis 2003, 20). Conversion for Africans was therefore if anything more compulsory than it had been for peninsular Jews and Mudejares. It was of a piece with the coerciveness of their worldly subjection as an enslaved population forcibly brought to replace the declining number of Indigenous laborers.

Among various justifications for the enslaving of Africans, one would become an important channel or circuit through which the language of race would begin to flow toward New World targets: the appeal to the biblical "Curse of Ham." This appeal referenced the ninth chapter of the book of Genesis in which, Ham, son of Noah, seeing the nakedness of his drunken father as he slept, summons his two brothers, Shem and Japeth, who respectfully respond by backing up into the room to cover their father. Upon awakening, Noah curses Ham through his son Canaan, declaring that he will be the "lowest of slaves" to Shem and Japeth. By identifying Black Africans as these cursed descendants of Ham, apologists turned this biblical story into a religious justification for the slave trade of their era.

The biblical Hamitic curse has sometimes been presented as evidence for a deep and archaic history of anti-Blackness in the West that predates the slave trade. In an influential essay, however, Benjamin Braude has argued persuasively against this view, arguing that it was only in the sixteenth century that highly polyphonic premodern understandings of the story were supplanted by slave-trade apologia (Braude 1997). In earlier centuries, Noahide genealogy was linked to the populations of a range of different and often overlapping geographical regions. For most of medieval history, for example, Ham was more strongly associated with what we consider Asian civilizations than with African ones. But it would be more accurate to say that the very conceptions of Africa and Asia were hazy in premodern Christian cultures, which did not recognize the continents to be distinctive land masses. For Braude, the narrowing of Ham's association to sub-Saharan Africans participated in a larger imaginative shift that included a cartographic breakthrough in envisioning the discreteness of the world's continents, a breakthrough tied not only to the "discovery of the Americas" by the Spanish, but equally to the "discovery of Africa" by Portuguese slaving journeys. During the first wave of European colonization, the emergent awareness of the world's variegated populations led to renewed interest in the genealogical passages in Genesis: the Noahide tale especially grew into a potential origin story for an increasingly urgent global genealogy of the peoples of the world. Only with the ramping up of the transatlantic slave trade during the late 1500s, therefore, did Europeans begin drawing on the "Curse of Ham" as a politico-theological rationale for the enslavement of Africans.

In the earliest of these late sixteenth- and seventeenth-century mobilizations of the Noahide story, an unmistakable theme of security initiates the fateful historical integration of anti-Blackness into the technology of race. This takes the form of what David Goldenberg has called a "dual curse," in which Spanish clerical colonialists began to claim that Noah's curse had not only condemned the descendants of Ham to be slaves, but simultaneously blackened them as a visible sign of the curse (Goldenberg 2017, 121–45). While there are certain precedents for the "dual curse" in premodern Islamic writings, the earliest known Christian use of the "dual curse" occurred in the Spanish viceroyalty of Peru, and in a striking political context. It was apparently the expressed claim of a Dominican friar who had adopted the pro-Indian tradition of Bartolemé de las Casas to a heretical extreme: Fray Francisco de la Cruz promoted an apocalyptic view that the church should be relocated to the religiously purer New World, that the Indigenous people should be liberated from colonial rule, and that, to facilitate this liberation, Africans should be enslaved in their place. For promoting this view, de la Cruz was tried by the colonial branch of the Spanish Inquisition. During his interrogation, de la Cruz explained to the Lima Inquisition in 1571 that his views had been divinely confirmed by an angelic revelation telling him that "the blacks are justly captives by just sentence of God for the sins of their fathers, and that in sign thereof God gave them that color ... and that moreover the conditions of the blacks is not convenient for liberty because they are untameable and bellicose and would disturb themselves and others if they were free" (Friede 1971, 417).

In de la Cruz's statement, the color black appears as the outward sign of an ineradicably sinful inward disposition, a concept that would continue to be elaborated.[31] In 1627, a Jesuit further elaborated this idea of black skin color's origin in sinful insubordination and rebellious bellicosity. Alonso de Sandoval, who had made it his life's mission to convert Africans at the docks of the Spanish Empire's main slave port in Cartagena, wrote in his book *De instauranda Aethiopum salute* (How to restore the salvation of the Ethiopians),

> The black skin of the Ethiopians not only comes from the curse Noah put on his son Ham ... but also is an innate or intrinsic part of how God

created them, so that in this extreme heat, the sons engendered were left this color, as a sign that they descend from a man who mocked his father, to punish his daring. Thus the Ethiopians descend from Ham, the first servant and slave that there ever was in the world, . . . whose punishment darkened the skin of his sons and descendants. . . . Thus blacks (negros) are also born as slaves, because God paints the sons of bad parents with a dark brush. (Goldenberg 2017, 123)[32]

Like the curse itself, Sandoval's reference to an "extreme heat" bears a dual meaning. It alludes to the hot tropical sun of Africa, which darkens the skin, but it also taps the common belief that the name "Ham" derived from the Hebrew word for hot, חַם (*cham*), suggesting the rebellious passion or fiery spirit of Ham's soul, and perhaps also the Hebrew word חום (*choom*), which means brown or dark.

In these early documents of anti-Blackness, color, conceived as divinely darkened skin, begins to participate for the first time in a racial dialectic of body and soul. It is converted along with the slave: Blackness becomes the literal epidermalization of an inward disposition to treachery. It produces the "anti-ness" of a hermeneutic of racial suspicion. Like the yellow garment of the penitent converso, black skin displays for all to see a person's genealogical descent as the "son of bad parents," in this case a progenitor (Ham) who in disrespectfully mocking his own father, subverted patriarchal authority. Color works, we could say, as a *naturalized* marker, or to invoke the pastoral language from which it draws, it functions like the *wolf naturally dressed in wolf's clothing*. If we contrast this to the figure of the converso, we might say that the Noahide story seems to present the curse as God's way of *preventing* dissimulation and *inhibiting* passing. The sons of Ham, with their sinful souls permanently marked on the body by their color, are denied the capacity to deceive. Color becomes a stabilizing force for populational demarcation, rendering transparent the difference between those who are blessed and those who are cursed.

This anti-Black perspective did not deter Sandoval from his commitment to conversion, however. As he pleads in the book's opening letter to the head of the Jesuit order, "although they are black, they can be washed clean by the purity and whiteness of Christ's blood. Pass your eyes over this book and you will see how many souls can be taken from the fires of hell to heaven" (Sandoval 2008, 7–8). Sandoval seems here to confidently trust conversion, as it had been in medieval times, as a salvific act. Yet his confident wording actually belies the same worry about converted Blacks that Sarmiento had expressed a hundred and fifty years earlier, namely he feels bound to assuage the reader's tacit doubt: what if the baptism of the convert might somehow *not* actually penetrate through the skin to the soul? What if they are not washed clean as one thinks? What if their souls remain in the fires of hell? If Blackness is an indelible mark, how would it ever be washed into "whiteness?" Perhaps, then, the problem of passing persists, though necessarily in a different form.

This would seem to be the subterranean nature of the justification of slavery since, like the *limpieza* statutes, it could represent a preemptive technology of security. Sandoval's account grounds the justice of African servitude not simply in an attribution of inferiority but rather in a view of the Noahide curse as a dual act, one that punishes the African's inner inclination to wickedness, while simultaneously protecting the flock against it. Although it promises the ameliorative purifying power of baptism's water, it also functions as a very early precursor to what Khalil Gibran Muhammad has called the "condemnation of blackness," in which skin color acts as a reified marker of one's predisposition toward criminality (Muhammad 2019).[33] Condemnation operates on two levels: as the disparaging signification of Blackness, but also as a consignment of Black populations to a subjugated status in the name of protecting all of those threatened by their inherent tendency toward sinful bellicosity, disrespect for authority, or (looking forward to the scientific racism studied by Muhammad and central to chapter 4 of this book) criminal violence.[34]

There is a certain paradox to the logic of the Noahide curse. The enslavement of Africans for labor was justified by an alleged curse stemming from a sinful insubordination inherited from their biblical ancestor. But Africans' threat of insubordination only actually existed for Spanish colonial authority because they had been forcibly seized and sold into slavery in the Americas. What we have had is the formation of New World slavery itself as a circular structure of power reminiscent of the circular structure of the threat of heresy in the Middle Ages, in which the security logic produces the threat it is supposed to defend against. As Colin Palmer points out in his excellent history of New Spain's Africans, the colonial regime worried continuously about its ability to control slaves and quell their anticipated resistance even as it permitted their numbers to swell (Palmer 2013, 119–20). A sincere conversion was critical to that process. According to Palmer, Africans were regularly called in by the Holy Inquisition of New Spain to face blasphemy charges anytime they stood accused of disrespecting the Christian God of the church (2013, 147–49). The suspicion at hand concerned a basic doubt as to whether conversion was actually leading Africans to the obedience of an ideal Christian servant. Reversion to pagan rituals and magic raised heightened concern, but the most extreme doubts about conversion's efficacy emerged around "Moorish" slaves, meaning

Africans suspected of formerly being Muslims. Even though Palmer's best guess is that only a few score ever lived in New Spain, by 1543 they would be explicitly banned by the Spanish crown from its colonies because they were considered to be especially "intractable and rebellious," and worse still, such slaves might act as "agents of Islam and, as such, would have a contaminating effect on the new Christians" (2013, 120).

African slaves posed two characteristic threats to colonial security (Palmer 2013, 119–44). The first was escape. Fugitive slaves would flee from the colonies to form maroon communities, where they could live freely and periodically raid Spanish colonial centers. Fugitivity, a key theme in Black studies today, was in some degree originally a conception of late pastoral power. The escaped slave's presumed relationship to the Christian flock was characterized by the term used to describe them: *los cimarrones*, which originally in Spanish referred to wild sheep or other escaped domesticated animals.[35] *Cimarrones* were thus former members of the flock who had passed as Christians only to flee the pen and escape back into the non-Christian wild. By demonstrating to enslaved Africans that a life outside of bondage within Christianity was possible, the very existence of the *cimarrones* subverted colonial security.

But colonial security always faced the more serious danger of a conspiracy by the enslaved to overthrow the colonial order altogether. The attempted slave insurrection appears as a recurring theme in the governance of New Spain. Colonial records mark the first attempted revolt as early as 1537, when an alleged conspirator "confessed" to a plot, thus allowing it to be thwarted. It is impossible to say whether this or later plots were real. What we can be sure about is that, in response to the expectation of such revolts, the language of colonial power began evolving toward a project of counterinsurgency. As early as 1553, we find documentation of the viceroy of New Spain employing a quantitative discourse of population that begins to calculate the ratio of likely friends to potential secret enemies of colonial power and combines Africans with other risky populations. The viceroy, for example, urged the emperor to reduce the licenses permitting the import of African slaves, writing, "This land is so full of negroes and mestizos that that they outnumber the Spanish greatly" (Palmer 2013, 135).

Of the various actual or alleged conspiracies attested to in the late sixteenth century, we can find the most details about a particular one that occurred in colonial Mexico City in 1612, thanks to the research of María Elena Martínez. On Easter week in that year, a group of Blacks and mulattos were arrested and accused of seeking to "decimate the Spanish population" and to "establish a black kingdom in New Spain" (Martínez 2004, 481). Their alleged objectives were to seize for themselves all major administrative positions and kill all the Spanish males, except for a few members of "religious orders" kept alive in order to train their children, while keeping the Spanish women for themselves. All we know for certain is that the accused were eventually found guilty, paraded through the streets of Mexico City, hung, decapitated after death, and their bodies left in the Zocalo as a public warning.

Martínez stresses that this story sits in a zone of factual uncertainty (Martínez 2004, 480–81). In this respect, it resembles others we have already encountered: the outbreak of heresies in the Middle Ages, the converso conspiracy attributed to the advice of Constantinople Jews, or Morisco fifth columns supporting Ottoman invasion. What is important in any of these cases ultimately is not which of these claims of conspiracy were true and which were false, but rather to grasp the *truth effect* associated with exposing a conspiracy attributed to these dangerous populations. In the case of the African slave conspiracy, one important truth effect of the investigation concerned its interplay with other political dangers to the Spanish Empire across the Atlantic. Martínez, for example, observes that the 1612 African conspiracy in New Spain occurred almost simultaneously with the expulsion of Spain's Moriscos between 1609 and 1614, which she describes as the years when

> anxieties over black conspiracies and rebellions in New Spain were at an all-time high, which suggests that dynamics in the metropole and colony were somehow influencing each other. At the very least, Spain's concerns about external enemies—in Europe mainly the Ottoman Empire and in Mexico British pirates—exacerbated anxieties on both sides of the Atlantic about perceived internal ones. Hence, just as Castile and Aragon were expelling their Moriscos and accusing them of being untrustworthy converts who were willing to act as a fifth column, New Spain's viceregal officials were describing the alleged conspirators of 1612, and all blacks and mulattoes in general, as "enemies of the republic," as an element that had to be excised from the body politic. (Martínez 2004, 506–7)

In the case of both Moriscos and Africans, religious heterodoxy amplified their ensoulment as the political enemy. Accused of using dark magic to kill Spaniards, the African conspirators of 1612 were cast simultaneously "as traitors to both the crown and the faith, as bad vassals and Christians" (Martínez 2004, 511). According to Martínez, the colonial correspondence about the case confirms that "rumors about their 'deviant' religious practices played a role in the handling of their case" (2004, 511). Finally, it was no coincidence that the arrests occurred during Holy Week, a period foregrounding the question of who belonged to the Christian community and, antithetically, who sympathized with the killing of Christ. As Martínez puts it, "Religious heterodoxy, conspiracies, poisonings, pacts with the Devil, and sexual excesses or depravities—these accusations were all common in Iberian (and, more broadly, European) anti-Semitic discourses and were frequently deployed before pogroms or other forms of religious, anti-Jewish, or anti-Muslim violence" (2004, 511–12). An African's faith was therefore intrinsically deserving of being treated suspiciously. If Africans had, per the Noahide curse, a genealogy of sinful ancestry, one that their color confirmed as a stain or defect threatening to the social fabric, then their appearance as a loyal servant could prove to be its own variation on passing, a means of waiting for the moment of revenge.

From Casta to Raza

Let us now return to the question of the relationship between *casta* (the caste system of the colonies) and *raza*. *Casta* assembled a hierarchical populational logic of the inferior and the superior, but as we have seen, *raza* invoked a warlike logic of the threat and the threatened. We have already seen a variety of threats achieved through populations "passing" as good Christians over the course of this chapter: converso conspiracies, Morisco fifth columns, Indigenous and African slave insurrectional plots. While the language of "race" at first fingered only the threats of conversos and Moriscos, the language of race came inexorably to apply to Indigenous and African populations. In at least one instance, these threats would in fact all be articulated into a single grand conspiracy against Spanish colonial power. I am referring here to the so-called great Jewish conspiracy of 1631 in the viceroyalty of Peru, sometimes known as the *gran complicidad*. This event symbolically crystalized race-making as a biopolitics of colonial population. Despite its description as a "Jewish conspiracy," Jewishness was only one dimension of the plot. To begin with, the event introduced geopolitical enemies into the allegations, much along the lines we saw at the earlier moment of the *Carta de los Judíos*. At this moment, the new external enemy was the Dutch, who had not only broken free from the Spanish Hapsburg monarchy to embrace Protestant heresy, but were now competing directly with the Iberian colonial powers. In addition to colonizing the eastern seaboard of North America, the Dutch had begun by the 1630s to seize sections of northeast Brazil away from the then unified Spanish-Portuguese crown. Finally, because the Dutch allowed Jews to worship freely, Spanish colonial authorities feared that Portuguese conversos hiding among their own merchant class might secretly support the Dutch cause.

According to Irene Silverblatt, the origins of the investigations into the *gran complicidad* began when Lima inquisitors gathered a growing body of testimony suggesting that some of the colony's most prominent citizens were secret conversos conspiring against the government. Significantly, they were believed to be seeking the support of Africans and Indigenous people. Alarmed at the alleged plan to hand Peru over to the Dutch, the colonial inquisitors abandoned the protocols set by the Madrid office. As Silverblatt characterizes it, "Inquisitors portrayed a Peru facing a serious threat: Portuguese-Judaizing-usurious-sabotaging spies lurked everywhere, ready to seduce Indians and Blacks to their cause. In light of this kind of menace, niceties of Inquisition law—including standards of evidence and the ratification of testimony—could be legitimately ignored" (Silverblatt 2004, 63).

Like the alleged Black revolt in Mexico City, it is difficult to know whether this plan had any basis in reality. More important is what the *gran complicidad* demonstrates about the consolidation of a colonial security apparatus. As in Iberia, the Peruvian Inquisition's various tactics (gathering testimony, conducting the inquisition of suspects, making use of torture to extort confessions) worked to unmask a class of Alboraiques (half Christian and half Jew, or now also half Spanish and half Portuguese) who were using their cover (their Christian color and name) in order to destroy colonial authority. We are dwelling in a conspiratorial universe parallel to the one dramatized by the *Carta de los Judíos*. But now conversos were aiming as well for "religious sabotage" that could stoke Africans and Indian revolt (Silverblatt 2004, 149). The *gran complicidad* crystallized fears that the colonial administration had been feeling for several decades. Already in 1610, for example, the *casa de contratación* (Peru's mercantile contracting house) had written ominously to the crown about a growing risk of collusion between the crypto-Jews and the Africans: "The Portuguese are so numerous that they outnumber the Castilians and the greater part of them is made up of *conversos* and impious people who hate Castile. Since they own a large number of slaves, they will seize the first opportunity to open the gates to the enemy and hand over the territory to them. Even without any outside assistance, they will outnumber the Castilians if they join forces with their slaves" (Soyer 2019, 215).

What the *casa* here offers the crown is a populational risk assessment, which foresees the additive threat of an emergent enemy-convert majority. What "equates" the various populations that are added together as enemy forces is the threat of "race," a sign that unites the entire set of untrustworthy conversions through whose conspiratorial efforts the colony might be unraveled.

The Birth of Whiteness

For perhaps a century and a half, *raza* had always meant a stain or blemish of Jewish or Muslim lineage discovered through genealogical investigations among Spaniards (or later in the colonies those who had at least part-Spanish blood). Gradually, claims that Native peoples were descended from the idolatrous Ten Tribes of Israel, or that Africans shared the cursed genealogy of Ham, began making their ancestry predictive of colonial betrayal as well. In 1602, Max Hering Torres tells us, the Bishop Prudencio Sandoval of Pamplona explicitly used the word *raza* to explain what was ineradicable about the danger of converso and African ancestry. Extolling the wisdom of Spain's "holy and wise" *limpieza* statutes, he noted that those rules ensured that "no one who has the race of convert may hold a benefice in it . . . because where there is someone of such a wicked race, even though there rarely are, these people are so malign that it only takes one to disturb many people" (Torres 2012, 23). While Sandoval agreed that Christian piety is meant to "embrace all," he nevertheless posed the rhetorical question, "Who can deny that the ill will of their ancient ingratitude and ignorance remains and persists in the descendant of Jews, as does the inseparable accident of their blackness in the Negroes?" (Torres 2012, 23).

No matter how many generations passed, conversos never lost their immorality. And this ineradicable depravity was something Sandoval wished to compare explicitly with the permanent Blackness of Africans: "Even when [the Blacks] mate with white women a thousand times, the children are [always] born with the dark color of their fathers. Thus, it is not sufficient for the Jew to be three-quarters hidalgo, or Old Christian, since only a single race infects and damages him, so that in their acts they are in any case Jews who are extremely dangerous in their communities" (Torres 2012, 24). I quote Sandoval at such length because in his words we can see how the indelible color of the African at last slides directly into the unalterable dangerousness of the converso's race, and indeed toward an imbricated condemnation of both populations.

We have already seen that the threat of the Alboraiques, the converso hybrids, stems from the fact that they can deceive with their "Christian color and name." In the colonial context, that color and name would explicitly become white. There the converso is someone who appears to be a genuine white Spaniard, who actually has a legitimate legal claim on the caste of white Spaniards. Nevertheless, that person has a stained lineage that inwardly preserves the evil inclinations—the *mala raza*—of a Jew. In Peru, conversos were sometimes known as *la mala casta blanca* (the bad white caste), meaning that they were the bad (racial) element within the superior caste of whites (Burns 2007, 189).

Whiteness could deceive by hiding race within it. By contrast to the converso, Sandoval presents the African as always wearing his race on his sleeve. There can be no deception because color is now presumed to reveal not only his caste but also his race.

In fact, Sandoval was wrong. The problem of passing had already come into existence as a constitutive technology of the early *sistema de las castas* in New Spain. It too featured a circular structure of power. In the classificatory logic of the *casta* system, between Africans and whites were "mulattos" (from the Portuguese for mule, an animal of mixed ancestry). Between mulattos and whites were "white mulattos." And between whites and "white mulattos" were "Moriscos," a one-eighth-African figure of the caste system who was "difficult at times to distinguish from the Spaniard" and who was named after precisely a population feared to be passing as Old Christian on the Iberian peninsula (Beltran 1945, 214). The color line (or more accurately the color zones) of early New Spain could only be constituted by a policing of the distinction between white and black that presupposed the possibility of an unmarked body still possessing race.

What made passing a problem of "race" and not just "caste," however, was the urgency of determining (in a way that one could not always from an in-spection of the body) whether someone (white or Black) was in fact a faithful Christian who did not have "race" and therefore was not predisposed to betray. Whether or not one presupposed in any given context the indelibility of color, the game of power anticipated dissimulation as the basis of racial threat. From the strict viewpoint of *casta*, perhaps, the blackness of the African marked an inferior legal status, one deserving the fewest rights and compatible with legal slavery. But from the perspective of *raza*, blackness indicated a probability of sinful desire to overturn rightful authority, a desire that needed to be coun-tered with security. The threat of Africans (and to a lesser degree Indians) *be-came racial* through this constitutive articulation with the danger of converted Jews and Moors.

Upon its arrival in the colonies in 1571, the Inquisition increasingly posed the question of how to classify Indians and Africans from the viewpoint of *raza*. Did Black or Indian blood indicate a genealogical defect of interiority comparable with that of conversos or Moriscos? Should those with Black or Indian lineage be similarly excluded from religious orders, political positions, or even roles in the Inquisition in the name of security? By the late sixteenth century the answer was a definitive yes. Consider the wording of a 1599 *pro-banza* (a document confirming one's pure-blooded ancestry) submitted by a candidate to the Franciscan order to show that he was descended from "a clean caste and generation, without the race or mixture of Moors, mulattoes, blacks, Jews and the newly converted to the Holy Catholic Faith and with no ties to persons punished by the Holy Office" (Martínez 2011, 164).

In this passage from the *probanza*, Black or mulatto no longer signifies just a caste. The *probanza* means to index a line of descent that is "without race or mixture" and hence "clean" of any possible contamination by an inward defect. Black ancestry generates a deficient hybridity analogous to that of converted Jews or Moors, and indeed all those whose newness to the faith or whose history of punishment by the Inquisition suggests an inner life that cannot be trusted within the Franciscan mendicant order. But just because skin color began, for the first time, to mark race, caste does not go away. Rather, we find a certain oscillation between the blackness of caste (inferior status) and the blackness of race (potential threat). Inferior status is after all a condition one might choose to accept. Were certain Africans actually good Christians and a loyal subjects, they would presumably understand and accede to their place within the caste system. But given the evident defect of race, special mechanisms of security become necessary because they cannot in fact be trusted to do so.

In the end, we might say that the invention of the color line became a compromise solution to the tension between *casta* and *raza*. Color, routed through the caste system, became an indicator of inferiority, not heresy or threat. But that inferiority of caste was linked with a distrust of the meaningfulness of their conversion, a distrust that began pulling back toward race. In lieu of a unitary body of Christendom, the new colonial model of power would elaborate a basic political distinction drawn between the Christian populations with ancestry from the core, clean blooded and *sin raza*, "without race," as opposed to those New Christians of the periphery, a distinction drawn by blood lines through which the caesurae and hierarchies of color were constituted. But Africans, Indians, and eventually all people of color would become the equivalent of the Turk or even the Jew *in potentia*, should they reveal by their actions that their conversion and docility as an inferior part of the flock has been feigned. By refusing their subjugation, they instantly revert to the status of the enemy in a permanent war that had both supplanted and broadened the medieval war on heresy.

In *Infrastructures of Race* (2017), his study of biopolitics in colonial Mexico, Daniel Nemser has shown how such politics of control translated themselves into the very geography of the colony. The Spanish empire, as a means of ensuring successful evangelism and extracting tribute, but also preventing the risk of riots, revolts, and threatening disorder (Nemser 2017, 101–4), established towns through which they could impose what they called a *concentración* of

Indians and Blacks, which could also be accompanied by its seeming opposite: *separación*, or segregation/compartmentalization. According to Nemser, these spatial infrastructures generally enacted forms of dispossession or primitive accumulation (2017, 165–71), but they were quite obviously also, politically speaking, means of controlling, surveilling, and disciplining populations that they subjected to racialization through a relentless hermeneutic of suspicion. "Concentration" in the Spanish colonies, he tells us, would finally become a technique of counterinsurgency that we can trace directly to the *campo de reconcentración* set up by the Spanish military in 1896 to incarcerate Black Cubans resisting their colonial rule (2017, 2). This camp was a historical prototype that would prepare the way for the British concentration camps used against the Boers in South Africa, the early concentration camps for Jews in Nazi Germany, and the internment camps housing Japanese Americans in the United States during World War II. *Raza* was more than a word. It was the retroactive explanation for a violent reorganization of human geography that it justified as a proactive use of force against imminent populational threat. It is in this deeper sense that *raza* completed the work of *casta*: it named the dangers that justified the bifurcations of ancestry and the divisions by color aimed at sorting the colony into respective populations of the threatened and the threatening, a segregation that it would physically impose through a politics of space. It is in these ways, and under these conditions, that the dialectic of body and soul began to produce race as a social effect: as the identificatory feature and as the practical stratification of a colonial society's perpetual need to defend its regime of power.

3

WESTPHALIAN REASON

The Political Theology of Sedition

There be two swords amongst Christians, the spiritual and temporal; and both have their due office and place in the maintenance of religion: but we may not take up the third sword, which is Mahomet's sword, or like unto it: that is, to propagate religion by wars, or by sanguinary persecutions to force consciences; except it be in cases of overt scandal, blasphemy, or intermixture of practice against the state; much less to nourish seditions; to authorize conspiracies and rebellions; to put the sword into the people's hands, and the like, tending to the subversion of all government, which is the ordinance of God. —SIR FRANCIS BACON, "Of Unity in Religion"

The fact is, of course, that our quarrel with the Catholics is not religious but political. The real indictment against the Roman Church is that it is, fundamentally and irredeemably, in its leadership, in politics, in thought, and largely in membership, actually and actively alien, un-American and usually anti-American. —HIRAM WESLEY EVANS, "The Klan's Fight for Americanism"

I must pass such sentence upon the principals in this diabolical conspiracy to destroy a God-fearing nation, which will demonstrate with finality that this nation's security must remain inviolate; that traffic in military secrets, whether promised by slavish devotion to a foreign ideology or by a desire for monetary gains must cease. —JUDGE IRVING KAUFMAN, Statement upon Sentencing Julius and Ethel Rosenberg

In 1594, a decade after the English defeated the Spanish Armada, courtiers in London exposed a secret plot to take the life of Queen Elizabeth of England. The aspiring regicide was Dr. Roderigo Lopez, her Majesty's personal physician, who had allegedly conspired with others to poison the queen (see Green 2003). Not coincidentally, Lopez was the son of a Portuguese Jewish physician who had converted to Catholicism back in 1497 (Green 2003, 13–29). And like his father before him, Lopez was assumed to practice Judaism in secret. Although some three hundred years had passed since the expulsion of England's Jews, Lopez's trial triggered a wave of public interest, especially in the English theater. Christopher Marlowe's *The Jew of Malta*, on stage in London during the trial, was renewed for a second run. Shakespeare is believed to have followed Lopez's trial closely. Four years later he would stage *The Merchant of Venice*, featuring Shylock, the mercenary Jew who scholars suspect was closely modeled on Lopez.

As the historian Peter Lake observes, Lopez's alleged identity as a converso who had "aped the outward forms of Christian religion" proffered a model for describing his duplicitous entry into the "service of queen Elizabeth intending to serve Philip of Spain" (Lake 2016, 453). Sir Francis Bacon, the famed writer and by then also an established figure in the highest circles of English government, wrote *A True Report of the Detestable Treason Intended by Doctor Roderigo Lopez* to indict the doctor's deceit, calling him this "*Lopez*, of Nation, a *Portugeze*, and suspected, to be in sect, secretly a *Jew*; (Though here he conformed Himself, to the Rites of *Christian Religion*;)" (Bacon 2012, 440). For Bacon, Lopez's religious chicanery modeled the double-dealing of his treason: he had outwardly conformed himself to her Majesty's loyal service even while inwardly plotting her murder.

In many ways, these accusations hurled against Dr. Lopez closely resemble Spanish allegations concerning converso *conspiridades*. They directly echo the *Carta* forgery, which had "revealed," among other things, how Constantinople's Jews had counseled Spain's Jews to "turn your sons into doctors and apothecaries" for the purpose of murdering Christians.[1] Not for nothing did Dr. Lopez's enemies accuse him of secret communications with the Constantinople Jewish community, whence he allegedly had planned to escape after the regicide (Lake 2016, 455).

Nevertheless, there are aspects to the Dr. Lopez story that cannot be contained by the model of the Iberian converso. To begin with, the plot was not at all understood as a scheme motivated by converso aims. Rather, it concerned a Catholic design to topple both the English state and its Protestant Church. Without an heir, Elizabeth's murder would have exposed the English throne to the predation of Spain's King Philip II, once the consort king of England by marriage to Elizabeth's Catholic sister, Queen Mary I. Lopez's plot was therefore understood as simultaneously political and religious in its designs, aiming to return the English throne to a foreign sovereign who might thereby restore England's church to Roman Catholicism.

In this respect, it was less significant that Roderigo Lopez was a Jew than that he was an immigrant from Portugal. Lopez belonged to a wider Portuguese émigré community then living in London. His fate had been sealed when several members of that community, ensnared in an intelligence dragnet, fingered him as a coconspirator. At the trial of these alleged coconspirators, prosecutor Sir Edward Coke advanced a case that amounted to guilt by ethnic belonging, indicting London's entire Portuguese community as a kind of papist fifth column (Philip II was then king of the combined Spanish and Portuguese kingdoms). "While 'poor protestants flighteth into this realm for religion,' Coke claimed, 'popish Portugals came only for treason'" (Lake 2016, 453). Lopez's treachery had less to do with his exceptional Jewishness per se than with his status as a dangerously placed dissimulating "Portugal," a papist conspirator working alongside a cohort of undercover Jesuit seminarians widely believed at that time to have slipped into England.

Portuguese-Spanish Catholicism trumped Jewishness. But there is another, final level to Lopez's treachery that was ultimately the most central to the case. As the trial unfolded, it was revealed that Dr. Lopez had worked in the service of a growing network of English state intelligence. An educated man who knew many languages and possessed wide contacts among the diverse Portuguese communities of Europe's port cities, Lopez had apparently been hired as an informant by Elizabeth's own government. Within official circles, therefore, he was already well known to be more than a mere doctor. What this conspiracy had actually unearthed, therefore, was not that Lopez had a secret political life, since the government already knew that, but rather that this secret life was itself a cover: Lopez was apparently operating as a double agent, pretending to advance English intelligence and state interests while covertly serving Spain. Neither could Lopez's threat to the state be reduced to endangerment of the queen. Elizabeth herself apparently never believed in the doctor's guilt. But this matter exceeded her Majesty's interests since the plot concerned the security of the English state, its one true faith, and its very capacity to govern, something that the queen merely figured in her status as "head of state." By 1593, a sizable state security apparatus had emerged that the queen no longer directly controlled. Dr. Lopez was charged with treason, prosecuted by key members of her Majesty's government, found guilty, and ultimately sentenced to death.

If we therefore step back to view the framing of Dr. Lopez's "plot," we can observe how its complex hermeneutic of suspicion posited dissimulations nested within deeper dissimulations, dangerous interiorities obscuring still deeper and more dangerous interiorities. Lopez was from a family that had concealed its Jewishness upon converting to Catholicism. In England, he had feigned conversion to Protestantism while staying secretly loyal to Catholicism. In London, he had "converted" to the cause of the English state, furnishing it with intelligence secretly gathered using the resources of his Catholic and Jewish background. But Lopez's "intelligencing" for the English state turned out to be yet another act of duplicity, just as his pretended Protestantism screened his papist political loyalties, while his Catholic background itself concealed an undertow of converso treachery (Campos 2002). The political threat of the converso's "race" had here become just one layer in the onion skin that wrapped itself around the soul of a more generalized and thus displaceable confessional sectarian danger to what this chapter calls Westphalian state security.

Dr. Lopez's threat to the English state indexes a mutation in the politics of ensoulment that, like the defective marking of "race" explored in the preceding chapter, is still with us today. It occupies the threshold at which the politics of identifying and exposing the inner life of race would be drawn into its long orbit around the Westphalian form of political power known as "reason of state." Lopez's trial can be seen as a prototype for future ones like the political prosecution of the Jewish couple Julius and Ethel Rosenberg some three centuries later for working on behalf of a foreign communist power to undermine American state security and (in Judge Irving Kaufman's apocalyptic words) "destroy a God-fearing nation" (Kaufman 2021).

Toward the Westphalian World of States

The proximate causes of this state-centered reconception of racial threat are complex. In chapter 2, I located the "birth of race" as part of a still quasi-medieval mutation in pastoral politics that occurred during the struggle to disempower conversos in mid-fifteenth-century Iberia. Emerging just before the "discovery" and conquest of the Americas, the new Iberian discourse of *raza* as a dangerously defective lineage with heretical tendencies proved a capacious strategy of power for governing the caste-differentiated population of the Spanish and Portuguese New World empires. Although, as Anibal Quijano and Immanuel Wallerstein have argued, the Iberian empires in the New World marked the origins of a geopolitical center-periphery relationship that would give birth to the capitalist world-system (Quijano and Wallerstein 1992), the empires' anchoring political vision (what Wallerstein would call their "geocul-ture") retained the medieval dream of Christian universalism.[2] The Spanish and Portuguese empires still pursued the Middle Age's eschatological hope to expand Christendom until all humanity had at last been brought under the dominion of the universal empire that anticipated the millennial promise of Christ's Second Coming. Invented in this context, race qualified yet abetted Christian universalism by introducing a political problem of security tied to expanding the flock, or converting new populations. The problem of secu-rity both justified the need for Catholic European rule over the Americas (to spread the gospel) and rationalized the imposition of caste hierarchies and the regulation of racial threat that might emerge from within the colonial popula-tion. Race named the threatening impediment to—and therefore the danger-ous enemy of—the universal dream of a millennial Christian empire, because certain people (those with "race") could not be trusted to take their conversion to Christianity to heart.

In those same centuries, however, the technologies of racial power would also begin a process of adaptation to a different set of political objectives. Even as Spain and Portugal expanded westward to build their universal empires, their political vision entered crisis in Europe when, beginning perhaps with Martin Luther's disputations in 1517, the Roman Catholic Church confronted the profound challenge eventually known as the Protestant Reformation. At first the Roman Church sought to meet this challenge through time-tested pas-toral strategies: condemning Luther and his followers as a new sect of heretics that should be defeated militarily with the help of the temporal sword. But although King Charles V, who ruled over both Spain and the Holy Roman Empire, warred for years against the princes supporting the new heresies, no final victory was achieved. What emerged instead was a Catholic-Protestant deadlock and a setting back of the grand ambitions of universal Catholic em-pire. The Peace of Augsburg signed in 1555 was a compromise that established the legitimacy of both Catholic and Lutheran "confessions" within the Holy Roman Empire on the general principle of *cuius regio, eius religio* (whose realm, his religion). The inhabitants of a realm would be expected either to follow the "religion" of their prince or depart from his realm if they would not. This new principle signals the genesis of an alternative geopolitical project that is often shorthanded as the Westphalian system of states, a world that dreamed, not of a single and unified empire, but instead of a perpetual peace among separate and independent states.

This Westphalian dream helped give rise to a normative Western narrative of liberal progress through state authority that still circulates today. According to that narrative, the Peace of Augsburg and (even more) its successor, the 1648 Treaty of Westphalia, should be viewed as successful way stations on the path toward religious freedom. They point toward the beneficent and enlightened decision to separate church and state that represents the philosophical and practical foundations of the secular West. How exactly does this narrative of secular historical progress work? For contemporary liberal philosophers such as John Rawls and Jeffrey Stout, that story goes something like this: Through the religious conflicts and hatreds that arose after the Reformation, the princes of Europe inflicted over a century's worth of bloodshed and destruction upon the continent. Yet only the unimaginable devastation of those wars made it possible for the princes at last to conclude that a better world was possible if they ceased killing in the name of faith and joined their former enemies in showing "toleration" for one another's religion. At first, in the Peace of Augsburg, they simply agreed to suffer the religion of their fellow princes. Almost a century later in the Treaty of Westphalia they further agreed to tolerate religious differences among their own subjects. Each treaty was therefore a stride toward a less bloody international order that would uphold the pluralistic commitments of secular values and prohibit religious violence.[3]

There are several serious problems with this narrative. First and foremost, in attributing the origins of (and the reason for) "religious tolerance" to the discovery of humanitarian and philosophically enlightened reason, it skillfully furnishes political legitimacy to the system of states that emerged at this exact historical juncture. Historians and international affairs scholars alike tell us that the Westphalian treaties ending the so-called Wars of Religion confirmed the absolute political authority of the mutually autonomous sovereign states that were its signatories. Whereas before, the jurisdictional claims of the church (and empire) had crosscut those of princes, now each prince was granted full authority over the temporal matters of people living within his territory, albeit with the expectation that he would respect the comparable authority that neighboring princes held over their people. The liberal narrative thus tacitly enshrines the secular state as the only proper guarantor of Western principles of political civility and religious tolerance.

In addition to serving as a legitimation narrative for the modern state (a political entity it assumes rather than explains), this normative liberal narrative also obscures a far more complex and interesting account of the Westphalian era. In this context, William Cavanaugh has asked what truths the philosophers have eclipsed with this waving of the bloody shirt of intolerant religiosity (Cavanaugh 1995). As Cavanaugh notes, the so-called Wars of Religion were far less motivated by "religion" than one might expect. The princes who fought these wars typically displayed far more interest in extending their own political power vis-à-vis opposing princes than they did in advancing any particular religious cause. Many of these principalities had been on the ascendancy well before the wars began, and they now used these wars as an opportunity to gain further advantage regardless of their implications for a Catholic or Protestant advantage. Perhaps the most glaring example was France, a Catholic kingdom whose monarchs nevertheless fought alongside Protestant powers during the Thirty Years' War because their primary competitor for a sphere of influence in Germany were the Hapsburg rulers of the Holy Roman Empire. Cavanaugh suggests therefore that these wars led not to the defeat of religious intolerance, but rather to a negotiated settlement that would cement the final triumph of the state as the sole form of political authority. The contemporary liberal narrative about Westphalia, in other words, has been adopted wholesale from the self-serving narrative of the victorious state's narrative about itself.

What Cavanaugh's critique does not explain, however, is the exact nature of this victorious entity called the state. Like the liberal philosophers he challenges, he assumes its existence rather than seeking to explain it. In the era leading up to Westphalia, many older political forms were in play among the principalities of Europe: kingdoms, dukedoms, free cities, and even republics (in Italy primarily). But the concept of the state *as such* was relatively new, an invention in fact of the sixteenth century that sought to encompass all of these different forms and structures of territorial government. The state was neither a particular kind of territory nor a particular kind of government. Rather, it was characterized by the objective of its new political rationality: the aim of *ratio status* (Latin), *ragione di stato* (Italian), *raison d'état* (French), or "reason of state" (English). The various Westphalian treaties of the sixteenth and seventeenth centuries gradually cemented reason of state as the overriding form of political prerogative in a Europe where religion would remain relevant to the exercise of politics, but only once it had been redefined as a secondary or supplemental entity lacking claim to such prerogative for itself.

What exactly was reason of state? In his intellectual history of the concept's early development in sixteenth-century Italy, Maurizio Viroli has condemned it as a form of political amorality that overtook an earlier (and superior) view of politics according to which princes were expected to rule over their subjects with wisdom and justice (Viroli 2005). Reason of state, he contends, replaced the principle of sagacious rule with a realpolitik focused on preserving the prince's power. While it captures something important about the role played by security in the emerging concept of the state, it is also misleading because, as Quentin Skinner has pointed out, the state's most critical feature was its differentiation from both the individual rulers (princes or magistrates) and the populace over whom they ruled (Skinner 1989).[4]

Reason of state can therefore be usefully understood as anti-Machiavellian in orientation, embodying an emergent principle of governmentality that would contrast sharply with Machiavelli's focus (at least as expressed in *The Prince*) on how a prince might best retain his principality. Compared with Machiavelli's circular logic (how does the prince stay a prince?), "reason of state" concerned itself with what Foucault's famous lecture on governmentality characterizes as the management of people and things toward some external end (Foucault 2007, 134).[5] What exactly was the state, then, if it was neither the prince nor the people? Even equating the state with the principality misses its level of abstraction. The "state" was neither just a kingdom (ruled by a king), nor a republic (governed by the citizenry), nor a commonwealth (a social body sharing a common good), but a realm of governability more abstractly conceived, something that could be any and all of these more particular domains, but only when viewed in a certain way.

When Foucault tried to unpack this peculiar new way of viewing a realm as a state, he turned to the revealing definitions offered by the Italian Renaissance thinker Giovanni Antonio Palazzo.[6] In Foucault's summary, Palazzo meant four related things with his concept of the state. First, the state was a domain, a place of rule. Second, it was a jurisdiction, a site of laws and customs. Third, the state was a "condition of life," a kind of status. And finally (and most crucially), the state was a "quality that means the thing remains what it is" (Foucault 2007, 338). The state therefore expresses a specified political formation with the capacity to preserve its own stability. It is quite literally a self-monitoring state of affairs that defends itself as domain, jurisdiction, and condition of life. Palazzo's more famous contemporary, Giovanni Botero, similarly defined reason of state as "knowledge of the means suitable to found, conserve and expand dominion," with the "greater work" consisting in the effort to "conserve the state" (Botero 2017, 4–7). The state may be grasped architectonically, as akin to an archway built of stone blocks that, because of the way that their mutual forces exert one upon the other along its curvature, maintains an overall stability without any external assistance. Reason of state therefore exists as a political rationality whose objective is the internal stability of the state, and on behalf of which it assembles an art of governance to preserve that stability, protecting against whatever misbalanced forces might put it at risk.

From whence might forces arrive that endanger the preservation of a state? One crucial source was expansion. For Botero, the state could not be characterized entirely by stability or self-preservation because the state was also something that sought to grow. Botero characterizes this as the use of "forces" to "expand the state," a problem that is secondary to that of "conservation" only in the sense that expansion functions as a kind of augmented conservation (Botero 2017, 121). The specific and unique problem faced by a state, in other words, was how to balance its forces so that its conservation would not be upended by its growth. Expansion must be kept proportional and run parallel to its earlier form so that the state remains as it was before, only more so: larger, wealthier, more powerful, but still the same state. To return to the architectonic metaphor, it acts as an archway perpetually enlarging itself, growing its stones, yet attempting to do so without unbalancing itself and sending itself tumbling down. The state, so viewed, is that realm, jurisdiction, and form of stability that must not be destabilized by disturbances associated with its own growth.

Like pastoral power, state power also concerned a problem of security. And it is here that one can grasp the indispensability of reason or *ratio* as an element in the definition of the state. Balancing the growth of the state's forces is something that requires ongoing calculation, a process of political reasoning. Although the "interests" have often been conceived as a concept tied to liberal political economy, it emerged first in the context of reason of state around the issue of calculating the "interest of state" (see Hirschman 2013).[7] The Latin word *interesse*, which entered English in the sixteenth century through French, originally referred to damage but also to compensation or *indemnity* for that damage.[8] "Interest of state" referred in part to calculations about how to mitigate potential damages to the state, or in other words, it concerned the reasoning process through which a state recalibrates its own forces in light of how those forces might damage it when they are grown. To this end, reason of state required an art of governance that calculates both the changing scale and direction (the vectors) of a state's expanding forces while also seeking ways to continually rebalance them so as to counter any unwanted destabilizing effect. It also names the interest of the state in intervening in those rebalancing efforts as it seeks (like interest in the pecuniary sense) to grow itself. Here were the essential problems and the overarching goals we can associate with reason of state.

Religion as a Technology of Reason of State

If we return now to Cavanaugh's powerful rereading of the Westphalian moment as signaling the state's triumph over the church, we can begin to make sense of the growing differentiation between the religious and the secular as a feature of reason of state. In regard to a concept of religion, we can view its early importance in the Augsburg notion of *cuius regio, eius religio*.[9] Here the word "religion" supplants an older idea of belonging to the church as a member of the flock. Religion now becomes a feature of the population associated with its faith, confession, devotion, or conscience, which must be politically managed because of its capacity to generate conflicts that destabilize the state.

This new statist concept of religion did not necessarily banish churches from post-Westphalian public life. In a close reading of the actual text of the Treaty of Westphalia, Jane O. Newman has shown how the word "religion" appears repeatedly in its articles as a term that actually requires people now associated with different churches to live peacefully "cheek by jowl" in the towns and principalities of the Holy Roman Empire (Newman 2012). The world was not so much made secular by the Westphalian treaties of the sixteenth and early seventeenth centuries, in other words, as it was made pluralistic through the invention of religion. Put another way, by the time of the 1648 Treaty of Westphalia, "religion" would name that abstractly defined element *shared* by Catholics and Protestants that henceforth they would be allowed to "profess and embrace," even when it differed from that of the "lord of the territory." According to the wording of the treaty, their "religion" should be "patiently suffer'd and tolerated, without any Hindrance or Impediment to attend their Devotions in their Houses and in private, with all Liberty of Conscience, and without any Inquisition or Trouble, and even to assist in their Neighbourhood, as often as they have a mind, at the publick Exercise of their Religion, or send their Children to foreign Schools of their Religion, or have them instructed in their Families by private Masters."[10] This tolerance, however, was always in the service of states' interests. Toleration was a strategy for ensuring the stability of the growing state, and it was therefore also always conditional upon uncompromising political loyalty to the lord who governed the state in which people resided. Sufferance would therefore only be granted, "provided the said Vassals and Subjects do their Duty in all other things, and hold themselves in due Obedience and Subjection, without giving occasion to any Disturbance or Commotion."[11]

"Disturbance or commotion" ("turbationibus" in the original) provides the crucial negative concept here. Religion needed to be a force for stability, and not its opposite. The critical importance of this provision had become clear to European princes as early as the German Peasants' War of 1525, arguably the opening chapter of the Wars of Religion, in which peasants had taken Luther's repudiation of church authority to justify uprisings against their own temporal rulers. Luther, who depended on just such princes for his own military protection, viciously indicted the peasantry for sacrilegiously misapplying the lesson of his own challenge to papal authority.[12] The Westphalian agreement can be seen as the formalization of a new political situation in which reason of state demoted both Catholicism and Protestantism to "religions" that would refrain from any commotion that might rock the state.[13]

Secularism as the Pastoralization of Reason of State

It was not only the new conception of religion that served the rise of reason of state, but equally that of the secular. This subtler point is easily obscured by our contemporary understanding of the secular as religion's antithesis. But in fact, what we conventionally call the rise of political secularism involved less a simple negation of the church than an absorption of pastoral themes and concerns into the structures of temporal government.[14] We see this in the word "secular" itself, which had once designated medieval Christendom's most pastoral features. "Secular" was originally used to distinguish parish priests—those "living 'in the world'"—from those clergy who lived "in 'religious' or 'regular' monastic seclusion."[15] "Secular" clergy carried out their ministry by caring for the souls of their parishioners and tending to their temporal (their practical or historical) needs or difficulties as they impinged on their hopes for redemption. In other words, it was the *secular* clergy who conducted the flock with the tools of pastoral power.[16]

Reason of state would become a secular enterprise in just this sense: it too attended to the worldly affairs of the souls under its jurisdiction. Secularism in the sixteenth and seventeenth centuries was only superficially about the subtraction of religion from the world of politics. Far more significant for the story of modern secularism was the process by which the shepherding of the body politic was transmuted into a central state objective. To be sure, the government of souls would be dramatically changed in that process. For the medieval pastorate, it had been the flock itself that required redemption as it approached the Kingdom of Heaven. In a world of reason of state, it was instead the state's salvation that required defense against the forces that might tear it apart. It was the state's future that was at stake, the state's soul that was at risk. This might seem like a dramatic turn away from concern with the many (the flock) to just the one (the state alone). But insofar as the state's singularity was routed through a pastoral conception of the body politic, it too turns out to have been (like the medieval church) paradoxically both plural and singular, *omnes et singulatim*. We can see how this paradox was preserved in the statist political theology of the "king's two bodies," a subject most famously associated with Ernst Kantorowicz's study of sixteenth- and early seventeenth-century Tudor and Stuart royal ideology (Kantorowicz 2016). As I will show in the remainder of this chapter, this paradoxical quality of a state that is simultaneously singular and plural is crucial to understanding how the Westphalian moment transformed the political technologies of race in enormously consequential ways.

For those whose familiarity with Kantorowicz runs through Carl Schmitt's and Giorgio Agamben's analyses of sovereign exception (Agamben 1998; Schmitt 2005), the doctrine of the king's two bodies explicates how royal sovereignty was invested with the Christological mystery of being simultaneously human and divine. Possessing both a material and a transcendent body, the king's mystical unity constituted the locus of his political theological authority. Kantorowicz, however, also showcases a different strain of Tudor political theology, adapted not from the sovereign rule of the divine father—the omnipotent God of the book of Genesis who willed the very world into existence—but instead from Christ the Son in the Gospel of John, a divine shepherd of men who leads the flock on the righteous path to their salvation (Kantorowicz 2016, 42–86). If the former yields a political theology of sovereignty, the latter reworks a pastoral political theology of government. Both tendencies are in play in Kantorowicz's work, but the latter frame, which has hardly been studied, was of equal importance in Westphalian reason.

In Tudor and Stuart jurisprudence, the political theology of government connected directly to the two-body doctrine. In addition to his natural body, of which his arms and legs (for example) were natural members, the king's corporate body politic was also composed of parts. According to the Law Report upon which Kantorowicz builds his argument, in this body politic, "the Members thereof are his Subjects and he and his Subjects together compose the Corporation . . . and he is incorporated with them, and they with him, and he is the Head and they are the Members, and he has sole Government of them" (Kantorowicz 2016, 13). What exactly is entailed by this notion of "sole government"? In this corporeal metaphor, the king becomes a "head" insofar as he acts as the body's unique organ of thought, judgment, and conduct. As its sovereign member, the head formulates the body's will but also its capacity for self-governance. As a self-executing synecdoche, the king is the body politic's unique governing member (its head), but the body politic thereby also becomes an extension of the king, his second body.

This doubled unity provided one common understanding of the stability of the state. It is an image that persists half a century later in the famously singular-yet-plural body found in the frontispiece to Thomas Hobbes's *Leviathan* (see figure 3.1). In Hobbes's image, the king is literally "head of state," wielding both the sword of sovereign power and the shepherd's staff whose secular power governs the flock. Through this dual exercise of sword and staff, the head must use

FIGURE 3.1. Frontispiece of Thomas Hobbes's *Leviathan* (London, 1651). Etching by Abraham Bosse.

its capacity for judgment to serve the weal of the commonwealth. A head interested only in its own sovereignty (like Machiavelli's prince) will soon begin to damage the body. A king's "sole government" is therefore nothing less than the full range of conduct through which he (as head) pursues his kingdom's flourishing by calculating and pursuing its state interest.

Toward the Enemy of State: From Treason to Sedition

Once the king-as-head is recognized as a political metaphor tied to the rise of reason of state, we can begin to analyze two attendant concepts that would serve to identify its enemies: treason and sedition. When sixteenth-century concepts of the body politic and the commonwealth drew on traditions of republican thought, they also borrowed from Cicero's classical figure of the traitor as the republic's hidden internal enemy (Cicero n.d.).[17] Conflating this Ciceronian traitor with the pastoral figure of the wolf, reason of state developed and deepened a discourse of treasonous crime that would permeate political life on the continent as well as in England. What exactly was treason? From the perspective of sovereignty, treason was a high crime that involved defying God's will by attacking the king. So conceived, treason was a kind of displaced heresy.[18] From a Ciceronian perspective, however, treason undermined the state through plots against its head.[19] Over the course of the sixteenth century, as Quentin Skinner observes, treason evolved from a crime against the king (as it had once been defined in England's 1350 statute on treason) to a crime committed against the state by virtue of its attack on the king in his capacity as head of state (Skinner 1989, 124). In traditional common law, treason was elevated above felonies and misdemeanors to become the third and gravest category of criminal law. In attacking the personage of the king or his deputies, the subject of treason assaulted the body politic's foundational capacity to govern itself.

In King James I of England's inaugural speech to Parliament in 1603, treason is metaphorically cast as a series of unholy threats to the sanctification of the monarch's two bodies. James proclaims that, "What God hath conjoineth then, let no man separate; I am the husband, and all the whole Island is my lawful wife; I am the head and it is my body; I am the shepherd and it is my flock" (quoted in Kantorowicz 2016, 223). With his opening metaphor of marriage, James sanctifies his rule over a unified British island through a theological appeal to Jesus's famous teachings against divorce.[20] But marriage is then followed with two further metaphors that, in the biblical tradition of poetic parallelism, propose themselves as variations on the original idea. Marital duties are first remapped onto the relation of head to body, an image that reworks the late medieval idea of the *corpus ecclesiae mysticum* (mystical body of the church)—the corporate body that the pope had used to declare his own governmental headship over church and Christendom.[21] Head and body then give way to the founding pastoral metaphor of the shepherd who guides the flock. The king is at once a husband, a head, and a pastor to his people.

What I wish to stress here is how each of James's three metaphors implicates an unholy enemy who jeopardizes the security of the state: some kind of treasonous person who dares to separate on three metaphorical levels "what God hath conjoineth." This monstrous person is successively the adulterous sodomite who seduces the wife, the traitor who "beheads" the state, or the heretical wolf who preys on the flock.

Alan Bray has observed how closely linked these various dangers were in the political imagination of Renaissance England. The sodomite in particular was someone whose inchoately sinful sexual proclivities (adultery, buggery, bestiality) undermined proper sexuality as defined in King James's vision of the marriage of the realm (Bray 1982, 18). The figure of the witch would also become a central preoccupation for "reason of state" in this period. Silvia Federici has famously analyzed the rise of witch-hunting as connected in both early modern Europe and the Americas to a "new concern, among European statists, and economists, with the question of reproduction and population size" (Federici

2004, 181). For Federici, the witch is a female figure of the transition to capitalism whose "rebel body" required expropriation due to her refusal of women's reproductive role. But we can find an even more explicit connection to the statist project of Westphalian body politics. King James himself, who thwarted several "treasonous plots" by witches during his kingship over Scotland (from the 1560s onward), presided over some of the bloodiest witch hunts in all of Europe (Young 2018, 155–62). James, who firmly believed in these threats, wrote a book in 1597 titled *Daemonologie* in which he explored the diabolical characteristics of witchcraft's necromancy, sexual debauchery, and summoning of evil spirits. James's book reiterates the divine antithesis between witchcraft and statecraft that the great French philosopher of sovereignty Jean Bodin had first articulated a few decades earlier.[22] Dr. Lopez's medicinal treason was consonant with witchcraft as the magical art of the enemy. And like Lopez, witches were often smeared by Jewish association, said to gather at night in councils known as "sabbats" to meet with the Devil.

All of these figures, then, could be used (much like the anticonverso trope of the Alboraique) to figure treason's diabolical threat to English reason of state. But high treason was merely the darkest umbra at the center of a greater shadow against which the state sought to act. Since treason was such a grave crime, its defendants were entitled to an elaborate trial. This body of law therefore offered no easy remedy for eliminating less severe threats to the state. Moreover, regimes of security seek to capture threat proactively, ahead of its actualization in the form of a foreseeable risk. Once someone had premeditated treason it was too late to prevent the birth of enmity and an acceleration of risk. What reason of state therefore needed to manage was not merely treason, but the crime of seeking to encourage it.

For Sir Francis Bacon, the great political thinker and statesman of the Tudor and Stuart era, the name for such a crime was "sedition." "Shepherds of people had need know the calendars of tempests in state," wrote Bacon in the opening to his famous essay on "Seditions and Troubles" (Bacon 1996, 366). Bacon's image of the calendar mediates between present risk and future threat since "shepherds of people" can mark upon it both the sign of risk that one has spotted today as well as the danger it foretells that might actualize tomorrow. As "heads of state," kings and their counselors seek a continuously felicitous state of affairs that can be figured as tranquil weather or good health. This calm vanishes with the advent of a tempest: a political rebellion, tumult, or act of treason. A tempest is whatever shatters the calm and shakes the state. Elsewhere in Bacon's oeuvre, instead of a ship at sea, the state sometimes appears (predictably) as a body. In place of the tempest, trouble appears as a disease or a physical deformation. The state's good health passes into a burning fever or an illness so serious as to yield a "distempered and unperfect body, continually subject to inflammations and convulsions" (Zeitlin 2018, 21).[23] Both the meteorological and the medical metaphors encourage a form of political reason that forecasts the fluctuations of risk through inspections of the body or physical world. Illnesses are portended by visible symptoms; likewise tempests are signaled by changes in the sky or water: clouds, changing light, wind, growing waves.

"Sedition" therefore heralded an approaching "tempest of state" yet was not itself that tempest. Like a worrisome blister on the face or a thunderhead on the horizon, sedition indicated danger ahead. Like treason, sedition constituted a crime against the state, but a lesser one that provided greater maneuvering room for the emergent apparatuses of state security. Sedition was a crime "defined and punished by the Court of Star Chamber," a subcommittee of the monarch's Privy Council of chief advisors tasked with prosecuting and judging all "crimes of state" (Manning 1980, 100). Francis Bacon, a member of the Privy Council under both Elizabeth and James, would eventually become clerk of the Court of Star Chamber in 1617 (Barnes 1962).

Sedition differed from treason in that the charge did not presume that the perpetrator intended to threaten the monarch directly. It supposed instead that the perpetrator's acts might rouse others to do so. Sedition's target was therefore not the king as such, but rather the preconditions of his stability as head of state. Derived from the Latin *seditio*, the word "sedition" had originally meant "violent party strife," forms of factionalism that lead toward civil war. But this now obsolete meaning was conjoined with a new one: "conduct or language inciting to rebellion against the constituted authority of a state."[24] Sedition was typically construed as a special form of libel (slander) directed against the state, which did not imply that the claims were false. On the contrary, true accusations could be judged even more likely to spark rebelliousness than false ones. According to an Elizabethan legal document apparently drafted for the aforementioned Court of Star Chamber, *sedition* was defined as "treasonable words" that "sought to divide and alienate 'the presente governors' from 'the sounde and well affected parte of the subiectes'" (Manning 1980, 100n3). The word "sedition" was sometimes spelled "seducioun" in Middle English, thereby acquiring a pseudo-etymological association with the Latin *seducere*, meaning to seduce.[25] Just as heresy involved the adulterous seduction of a Christian from their redemptive marriage to Christ, so sedition enticed subjects from their politico-theological marriage to the monarch. It was what Bacon called "licentious discourses against the state" (Bacon 1996, 366). Like an affair for a married couple, sedition had pride of place "amongst the signs of troubles"

of the approaching storm. It was a siren call to tempestuous infidelity that required security mechanisms for safeguarding the endangered marriage of king
and island, head and body, shepherd and flock.

The Invention of Population I: Seditions of the Belly

Why this new concern with the political potency of words in circulation? Bacon's discussion of sedition reveals that it was linked to the invention of a key
political concept: population. Foucauldian scholars (including Foucault himself)
often presume that populations grew into a "technical-political object of management and government" only in the late eighteenth century.[26] But population
had already emerged by the late sixteenth century as a quantifiable abstraction
necessary for assessing the risk of sedition and tumult. The word "population"
first appeared in English between the 1540s and 1570s, though initially as a term
for an "inhabited place" rather than its inhabitants.[27] There are two examples of
this obsolete usage, both in translated accounts of early Spanish voyages to the
Americas, where it replaces the Spanish words *lugares* and *poblaciónes* respectively. *Population* apparently entered English through such attention to places
where new inhabitants had been brought under imperial Spanish rule.

Bacon himself furnishes the *Oxford English Dictionary*'s first cited examples
of the now dominant second meaning of *population*, namely the "collective inhabitants" of a place.[28] But a closer inspection of Bacon's original texts shows
that he was using the word even more precisely than that. Especially as it appears in the essay on sedition (Bacon 1996), "population" designates the inhabitants of a place with common characteristics that can be used to calculate the
probabilities of a tempest. Because such calculations serve to manage the risk
in question, "population" in Baconian reason of state is above all a technology
of security. Bacon first introduces the word as he reflects on sedition's two principal causes. The first is "want and poverty in the estate," where sedition arises
from unmet material needs of the body politic's "belly" (Bacon 1996, 367). The
belly is that part of the body characteristically associated with hunger and sa-
tiation. Good governance requires discovering and meeting the belly's unmet
needs (standing in for the material things a population requires) before they turn
dangerous. To this end, Bacon proposes policy tools that would become central
to mercantilist political economy, such as "the opening and well-balancing of
trade; the cherishing of manufactures; the banishing of idleness; the repressing
of waste and excess by sumptuary laws; the improvement and husbanding of
the soil; the regulating of prices of things vendible; the moderating of taxes and
tributes; and the like" (Bacon 1996, 368).

Population becomes crucial at this point. One can neither calculate nor regulate the risk of sedition by attending solely to what he calls the realm's "store" or wealth. One must also solve for population—a second unknown in his equation—to determine whether the current store suffices. "Generally, it is to be foreseen that the population of a kingdom . . . do not exceed the stock of the kingdom which should maintain them. Neither is the population to be reckoned only by number; for a smaller number that spend more and earn less do wear out an estate sooner than a greater number that live lower and gather more" (Bacon 1996: 368). The population's overall characteristics as well as its internal differences (how much it spends, earns, gathers, or wears out) constitute what 150 years later would become known as "statistics," a word that (first in French, then English) originally designated knowledge of the forces of the state.[29] Bacon's early version of statistics, which calculated risks to the state's stability by deriving them from imbalances between store and population, offers a toolbox of policies for rebalancing them. For Bacon, both store and population are dependent variables. The former oscillates with every development in trade, harvest, or taxation, while the latter fluctuates as a result of shifting ratios of social class, new rates of consumption or productivity, wars, or epidemics. Each time either variable changes, its now unbalanced relation to the other jeopardizes the security of the state. To avoid tumults and factional violence, the state must therefore proactively recalibrate fluctuations in its ratio of stock and population. Foucault famously defined governmentality as the management of "people and things" toward a particular end. If "population" offers its conception of people and "stock" its version of things, then the end of Baconian governmentality is apparently the neutralization of sedition against the state through the balance of forces.

For seditions of the belly, Bacon foresaw danger in only one direction: the population could be too large. When a "surcharge of people" whose needs outstrip the store creates a prevailing state of poverty and want, seditious language will emerge that leads ineluctably toward a political tempest.[30] The grumblings of the belly should therefore count as an alarm bell, warning the state that it is time to right a growing imbalance of stock and population. But through what intervention? Bacon generally advocated two ways of managing a surplus population (Zeitlin 2018, 1–77). First, a monarch might wage war against the kingdom's enemies. In addition to whatever spoils this might deliver, war also solved the problem of surplus population through attrition on the battlefield.

Second, Bacon also strongly advocated settler colonial projects.[31] If war was the name of the first solution, that of the second was "plantation," a word conveying the aim of thinning surplus population at home by "replanting" it elsewhere on new soil, in Ireland and later North America. Originally, then, the word "plantation" was used to designate the colony itself (which grew settlers) rather than a commercial farm (which grew sugar or tobacco). Bacon celebrated plantations as "heroical works" because they reproduce the body politic: new plantations are the natural "children of former kingdoms" (Bacon 1996, 407). In a 1607 speech to the House of Commons, Bacon encouraged England to "issue and discharge the multitude" of its people to Ireland, a place where the bounty of nature "continually call unto us for our colonies and plantations" (Zeitlin 2018, 44n135). A fertile *terra nullius* and therefore a potential new store, Ireland was (like the Americas soon thereafter) a place for England to alleviate populational threats to the state through the transplantation of English subjects.[32] This Westphalian project of colonial planting illuminates how and why the English word "population" had been derived in the first place from Spanish writings about the "inhabited places" whose plantations had generated for that rival kingdom so much wealth and advantage.

Bacon's seditions of the belly undoubtedly indexed the turbulent birth of agrarian capitalism in sixteenth-century England.[33] The enclosures whose privatization of land had deprived many English inhabitants of their livelihood had given rise to "masterless men," "vagrants," "sturdy beggars," and other dangerous new categories of unemployed, unsubordinated lower classes. These were themselves populational forces unleashed by the growth of the early English state. Bacon's calculus of sedition therefore offered a means of battling what its shepherds viewed as a "many-headed hydra," a monstrous surplus population forever sprouting menacing new heads (Linebaugh and Rediker 2013, 2–4). Devised in an English context shaped by the destabilizing forces of incipient agrarian capitalism and settler colonial planning, Bacon's version of Westphalian reason of state was an early form of what Foucault called governmentality, assembling political economic tools for conducting "people and things" within the context of an emergent capitalist world-system. As that system gradually relocated its core from Iberia to the North Atlantic, it took shape as a series of maritime commercial empires characterized by Westphalian states in its metropolitan core and settler colonies along its periphery.

The Invention of Population II: Papist and Puritan Seditions of the Head

Bacon's second major explanation for sedition, however, is only more circuitously about the birth of capitalism and transatlantic colonialism. This was not a kind necessarily caused by material need or physical hunger, but instead by what he calls "discontentment" (Bacon 1996, 367). The threatening image of the many-headed hydra was even more apt here. If physical need and economic coercion incite seditions of the belly, then discontentment instigates what could perhaps be described as seditions of the head insofar as they concern ideological as opposed to material causes of unhappiness. "Discontentments," Bacon explains, "are in the politic body like to humors in the natural, which are apt to gather a preternatural heat and to inflame" (Bacon 1996, 367–68).[34] That is, like humors, they express states of mind or spirit that affect the overall disposition of the body politic. To call them seditions of the head might seem paradoxical since the head was supposed to refer to those who govern (the king, the Privy Council). But insofar as they encouraged usurpations of the king's status, they reflected Bacon's warning that "shepherds of state" must beware any "likely or fit head whereunto discontented persons may resort, and under whom they may join" (Bacon 1996, 370).

Like want, seditions of discontentment could be calculated only by reference to the population. But here a different political arithmetic was needed: the statistics of public opinion. The political economy of public opinion, like that of wealth, offered an art of government for conducting the relationship between people and things. With public opinion, however, the concern was not with material objects needed for corporeal life, but instead with the inner things of the public's conscience. The art of public opinion dealt less with a population divided among social classes that produced or consumed the realm's treasure at different rates. It treated instead a population divided by its underlying regard for the body politic.[35] And these regards, as one would expect during the long sixteenth-century of the Westphalian transition, were frequently assessed along religious lines.

As a political philosopher, Bacon wrote abstractly about the nature of the threat that discontentment signaled for "shepherds of state." But as a statesman and advisor to two monarchs, the particular seditious threat that concerned Bacon most was "papist" discontentment. In part, Bacon's concern derived from the religious wars and factional conflicts that he had personally witnessed while studying as a young man in France during the reign of Henry III, a French king killed by a Catholic assassin (Zeitlin 2018, 28–29). But Bacon's attention to "popery" also reflected England's distinctive status as a Protestant state where civil and religious authority had been fused. Ever since King Henry VIII's schism with Rome in the 1530s, the English monarch's "sole government" over the body politic included both temporal and ecclesiastical authority. Yet this tenuously fused power had already once been reversed in the 1550s when Henry's Catholic daughter Mary Tudor returned the Church of England to Rome. After Mary's death, although her successor Elizabeth restored the Church of England to Protestantism and induced Parliament to declare her the church's "supreme governor," the realm's significant number of Catholics early in her reign remained a potentially seditious faction.

In his 1584 "letter of advice" to the queen, the young Francis Bacon had characterized the situation since the so-called Elizabethan Religious Settlement in this way:

> the happiness of your [Majesty's] present Estate can no way be encumbered, but by your strong factious Subjects, and your foreign enemies: Your strong factious Subjects be the Papistes: strong I account them, because both in number they are (at the least) able to make a great Army, and, by their mutual Confidence and Intelligence, may soon bring to pass an uniting: factious I call them, because they are discontented, of whom in all reason of State your Majesty must determine, if you suffer them to be strong, to make them better Content, or if you will discontent them, to make them weaker. (Bacon 2012, 22)

Many shared Bacon's view that Britain's Catholics represented a potent fifth column for the pope and Catholic Spain.[36] In 1569 the queen had faced down two Catholic-led revolts in northern England and Ireland. But worse yet was Pope Pius V's bull of 1570 that excommunicated Elizabeth for heresy, declaring her illegitimate, absolving her subjects from expectation of allegiance, and threatening further excommunication against all who persisted in obeying the queen.[37] Moreover, the pope endorsed a mission sending Jesuit priests to England in order to rescue Catholicism, a mission construed by Elizabeth's government as an effort to subvert the kingdom through sedition.

State defenses against papist threat became a kind of permanent condition. Here, for instance, is how the 1585 Act against the Jesuits and Seminarists characterized the danger:

> Daily do [the Jesuits, seminarists, and other priests] come and are sent, into this realm of England and other of the queen's majesty's dominions, of purpose (as has appeared, as well by sundry of their own examinations and confessions, as by divers other manifest means and proofs) not only to withdraw her highness's subjects from their due obedience to her majesty, but also to stir up and move sedition, rebellion, and open hostility within the same her highness's realms and dominions, to the great endangering of the safety of her most royal person, and to the utter ruin, desolation, and overthrow of the whole realm.[38]

By the early seventeenth century, the Papist had become the dominant figure for the "enemy of state," reaching its apotheosis in Guy Fawkes's so-called Gunpowder Plot against James I.

The figuring of the papist threat in relation to English reason of state is compellingly illustrated in a 1643 broadsheet image titled "The Kingdomes monster vncloaked from Heaven: the Popish conspirators, malignant plotters, and cruell Irish, in one body to destroy kingdome, religion and lawes: but under colour to defend them, etc." (see figure 3.2). Although published nine years before the frontispiece of Hobbes's *Leviathan*, this image appears almost as its exact inversion. Whereas Hobbes's stately figure is crowned by a large single head (the king's) governing from atop a multitudinous body politic, here the "Kingdomes monster" owns but a single body sprouting three necks that each lead to a myriad of monstrous heads, including papist conspirators, malignant plotters, and cruel Irish. The plantation of Ireland, it would seem, had already folded immigrants into the fear of popery.

Although this sketch from the start of the English Civil War comes not from the king's viewpoint, but instead as a parliamentarian attack on the monstrous combination of Papists and Cavaliers, it maintains a Westphalian vision of "reason of state" endangered. The proliferating heads sitting atop the monstrous body have fragmented the unified sovereign will of the body politic into an exponentiated multiplicity of threat. Wickedly seeking the destruction of stately government, they control four hands reaching out with sword, torch, rope, and dagger to aggress against the various aspects of the English state: kingdom, church, parliament, and city. To the monster's left stands a small demoniac homunculus, connecting popery to the treasonous magic of witchcraft and sorcery. This secondary demon sports both a penile barbed tail and a small erection, while the monster itself displays an ambiguous appendage that might be either. Popish sodomy, as Alan Bray notes, was envisioned as a powerfully hybrid monstrosity, combining the threats of religious, sexual, and political difference (Bray 1982, 17–20). Like the *Tratado del Alboraique* before it, this polemical sketch purports to expose a malevolently lascivious creature whose truth consists in its lust for treachery. Exposure is critical because this truth remains concealed from the eye of state power by a vast cloak that exactly inverts the *sambenito* or the yellow cross of the medieval Jew: it acts as a deceptive outer skin (a sheep's clothing) to hide predatory intentions. If, as the verbiage accompanying the image indicates, only Heaven itself has uncloaked this monstrous "sedition of the head," then, absent such a miracle, how might ordinary state intelligence successfully alert the shepherds of state?

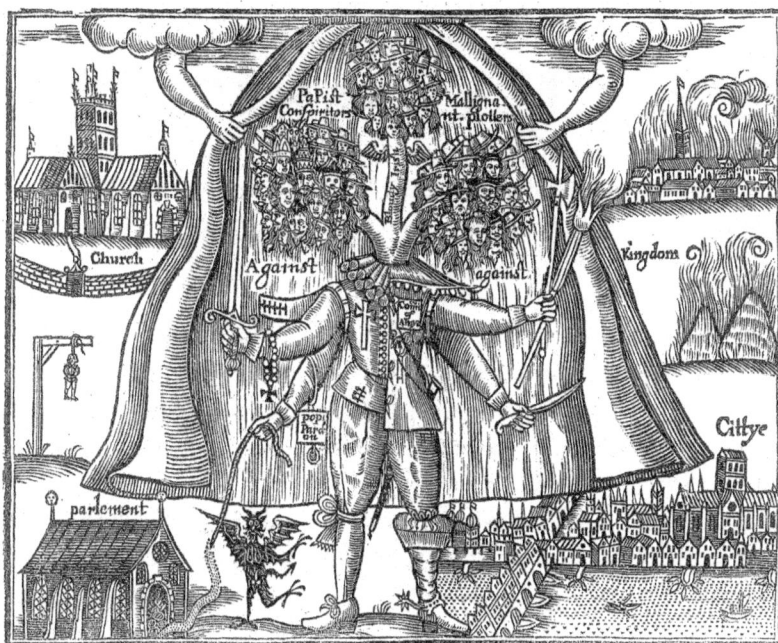

FIGURE 3.2. The Popish conspiratorial threat as sketched in an anonymous broadsheet (London, 1643).

One answer was to listen for the seditious words that emanated from behind the cloak, for the Westphalian moment was characterized by the growing significance of the printing press as a tool of public opinion. In England, as many contemporaries recognized, a massive increase in pamphleteering beginning in the 1570s and 1580s had produced a powerful new medium for the rapid yet anonymous circulation of seditious claims, rumors, and slanders (see Raymond 2006). Catholic missions could set up secret print shops to disseminate their "libels," a word originally meaning any small book but that now became tinged with the intention of seditious slander and smear.[39] These libels could in turn undermine the allegiance of a people still not far removed from Catholicism. The multiheaded papist threat could therefore be conceived by the Elizabethan and Jacobean state as the outcome of a successful conspiracy to sway a seditious faction (including for example the Portuguese merchant community of London) into conspiracy with the queen's foreign enemies.

As if the papist threat were not enough, the state was also detecting early signs of yet another seditious faction among those "hotter" Protestants who, believing that the Church of England had not left popery far enough behind, felt that it should cleanse itself of idolatrous Roman rituals and clerical despotism. Although in the late sixteenth century these "zealous" and critical Protestants mostly remained as members of the Church of England, their challenges to episcopal authority could lead logically to skepticism regarding the monarch's spiritual authority as the church's "supreme governor." There was reason, therefore, to view these "puritan" arguments as potentially seditious.

It was these radical Protestants (more than the Papists) who actually made the fiercest use of pamphleteering to influence public opinion. Most famous were the anonymous and ferociously anti-episcopal "Marprelate" pamphlets published throughout 1588 and 1589. Using scathing sacrilegious humor to attack clerical pretentiousness, their author condemned the Church of England's self-important clergy as nothing less than "petty Antichrists, petty popes, proud prelates, intolerable withstanders of reformation, enemies of the gospel and most covetous wretched priests" (Anonymous, n.d.). Such statements exploited antipapist sentiment in ways that threatened English reason of state from the other side. In a 1589 letter on the queen's religious policy, Bacon complained that some of these "godly" people, crossing the line from mere religious fervor to political menace, had begun to "vaunt of their strength and number of their partizans and followers, and to vse Communications that their Cause would preuaile though with vproare and violence; Then it appeared to bee noe more Zeal, noe more Conscience, but mere faction and division" (Bacon 2012, 228).

As some Puritans began withdrawing from the church, the crown decreed a legal Act against Puritans designed to halt the "wicked and dangerous practices of [these] seditious sectaries and disloyal persons" by imprisoning anyone who refused to attend church services or who used print or speeches to "deny, withstand, and impugn her majesty's power and authority in causes ecclesiastical, united, and annexed to the imperial crown."[40]

State Security and the Covert Technologies of Intelligence

It was in relation to these new political objectives regarding the population that an incipient security state began to coalesce around a growing ensemble of techniques for waging war against seditious enemies of the state. Although part of this war simply involved criminalizing "seditious libel" through the Crown's aforementioned acts, these laws were also allied with important new political technologies of surveillance, propaganda, and militarism used to identify and neutralize seditious Papists or Puritans (Breight 1996). Certain medieval inquisitorial techniques such as interrogation and confession were predictably adapted to new ends by the state (Bacon was an official interrogator for

Her Majesty's government). Now, however, these venerable modes of prosecutorial examination would be integrated into an innovative apparatus of governmental investigation becoming known as "intelligence." Formerly a word designating one's capacities for understanding or referring to items of information, "intelligence" in the late sixteenth century acquired a secondary meaning as espionage: the comprehending of politically valuable information through secret tactics and covert institutions of the state.[41] These covert tactics and institutions were developed by Queen Elizabeth's principal secretary, Sir Francis Walsingham, who founded an office of "intelligencers" famous for its new techniques of countersubversion, including the use of a standing network of informants and double agents, the interception of correspondence, and even the use of cryptographic techniques for breaking codes (see Hutchinson 2007; Cooper 2011).

"Intelligence" can be compared with "statistics" in that it too sought to produce knowledge about the forces of the state. But intelligence was distinguished in two ways. First, it was knowledge secretly discovered by the state through its covert operations and kept secret until the moment when its revelation served reason of state: the timing of disclosure was part of its intelligence. Second, intelligence was knowledge regarding a threat. Unlike statistics, in other words, it concerned not so much the forces of the state itself as the relationship of those forces to hostile ones potentially arrayed against it. Intelligence involved secret knowledge about the machinations of foreign powers or their domestic agents, including the growing international spy networks of Westphalian states. But on the domestic front it also involved secret knowledge about the gravest of treasonous plots or the most mundane of seditious activities. It was through intelligence that plots against the life of the queen, such as the 1571 Ridolfi Plot, the 1586 Babington Plot, and the Lopez Plot of 1594, were discovered and foiled. Intelligence also worked to employ propaganda for counteracting seditious libels. It included the secret commissioning of pamphlets to insinuate counter-rumors or to slander seditious authors.[42] As historian Peter Lake puts it, "fire was to be met with fire as the regime and its agents used the full range of contemporary media—cheap print, performance . . . , and planted rumour—to convince a popular audience," but most especially when it came to the righteousness of its "anti-popish cause" (Lake 2016, 44). And finally, words would not only be met with words. Intelligence also exposed the identity of anonymous pamphleteers who could then be legally charged with sedition and severely punished. The guilty had their right hands cut off in public spectacles intended as a forceful warning to potential libelers.[43]

What made uses of intelligence to rebalance public opinion and neutralize "seditions of the head" so emphatically Westphalian was their positioning of religion as a key political threat to the state. Consider, to cite one example, the opening sentences sworn in the Oath of Supremacy required of anyone taking office (civil or ecclesiastical) in Elizabethan England:

> I, A. B., do utterly testify and declare in my conscience that the Queen's Highness is the only supreme governor of this realm, and of all other her Highness's dominions and countries, as well in all spiritual or ecclesiastical things or causes, as temporal, and that no foreign prince, person, prelate, state or potentate hath or ought to have any jurisdiction, power, superiority, pre-eminence or authority ecclesiastical or spiritual within this realm; and therefore I do utterly renounce and forsake all foreign jurisdictions, powers, superiorities and authorities.[44]

Any Catholic taking this oath was also swearing that the queen, not the pope, was supreme governor of matters "spiritual or ecclesiastical." Since Catholics could not vow loyalty to the state without betraying their religion, nor preserve their religious faith without perjuring themselves through a false assertion of state loyalty, by definition they could not swear this oath honestly. To speak it at all was to lie. Although intended to ensure loyalty, this oath therefore could easily produce "discontentment" through the same circular structure of power that I have discussed throughout this book.

Urging a strategic use of toleration, Bacon encouraged Elizabeth to strike from the Oath of Supremacy those sentences asserting the spiritual supremacy of the queen, leaving only the promise to show faithfulness to her against foreign princes. Even had the crown accepted this advice, however (and it did not), the key outcome of such an oath is that, even when the state tolerated or suffered Catholic conscience, it would always need to leaven that tolerance with suspicion. A Catholic who believed in the pope's spiritual authority was always politically speaking a potential Papist and therefore a riskier subject. A similar suspicion would become part of the necessary calculation regarding those "godly" people whose rejection of Anglican clerical hierarchy verged on disavowing the English monarch's authority. Just as Catholics became Papists during the late sixteenth century, so "godly people" would increasingly be called Puritans, people whose purism had thus run "from one extreame to another," as Bacon expressed it in a telling turn of phrase (Bacon 2012, 232).[45]

Race and Reason of State

To what extent should this governmental war against threats of papist and puritan treason be construed as reconstituting Catholics and "godly" nonconforming Protestants as racial others to an emergent national body politic? There are certainly obvious reasons to answer in the negative. First, Papists and Puritans were never characterized as "races," but instead (as we have seen) as "factions" or "sectories." Perhaps the best way to grasp this distinction is to remember that, until Henry VIII declared the Church of England independent of Rome, nearly the entire English population was Catholic. Under his rule they became Protestant, under his daughter Mary they became Catholic again, then under Elizabeth they again became Protestant. In short, English Catholics of the sixteenth century could hardly be characterized as a fixed minority. It cannot even be said that Catholics are those who remained with the Roman Church when the population of England crossed a religious boundary from Catholicism to Protestantism. Rather (to borrow a formulation used by the Tejanos of Texas), the border crossed them, and more than once. In Elizabethan England, people who openly objected to the top-down separation from Catholicism or who refused to attend a Protestant Church of England became known as the "recusants" who so often stood in the crosshairs of antipapist political action. Because many recusants were found among the nobility, such as the Catholic earls who waged the 1569 Rising of the North against Queen Elizabeth, or even the Catholic Mary Queen of Scots, long feared (and eventually executed) by the Tudor state as a claimant to the throne, aristocratic Catholics were legitimately feared as a rival "head" that endangered the state.

But while elite recusants formed an identifiable Catholic contingent within the population, the risk of a papist faction extended beyond it. The sixteenth-century "conversion" of England's entire population from Catholicism to Anglican Protestantism produced a certain universalized variation of what I described in the preceding chapter as the epistemological uncertainty of the converso character. How could the state really know who among those now claiming membership of the Church of England might surreptitiously continue to practice Catholicism? Who among the "conformists" in outward practice secretly maintained a loyalty to Rome? Such people did in fact exist.[46] English historians have sometimes called them crypto-Catholics, analogous to the converso crypto-Jews of Spain. In the Westphalian era, the counterfeit worshipper posed a generalized problem. In Europe's Catholic states, it was recognized that some people concealed their Protestantism by attending Catholic Mass, while in

Protestant states, others concealed their Catholicism by worshipping in Protestant churches. Such religious dissemblers were known as Nicodemites, a term for those who masked their inner "conscience" out of political expediency.[47] In England's version of this problem, therefore, the papist threat extended beyond known recusants into an indefinite populational fraction that might either still secretly be Catholic or at least secretly still feel attracted to Catholicism.[48] Like medieval heresy before it, the papist threat was a seductive and unbounded possibility, requiring permanent vigilance against the seditious libel that enticed its readers back to popery.

The puritan threat took similar form at the other end of the religious spectrum. Although "recusancy" had originally been used to name Catholic dissenters, antirecusancy laws were also applied to Protestant nonconformists who refused to attend church. Exactly as with Catholicism, the prospect of religious dissimulation expanded the Puritan problem into the same zone of epistemological uncertainty: any member of the Church of England could hypothetically still be attending its services even while covertly sympathizing with Puritans who considered the church insufficiently reformed. The Puritan threat of treason was therefore an equally indefinite one whose seditious reaches into the population could not be decisively measured through the mere consideration of people's outward "conformity" to the church.

It is here that we arrive at the technique of power described in this book's introduction as the *universalizing* pincer of racial ensoulment, a technique whose political effect might easily be mistaken for a "racism without race" (Balibar 1991a, 21). The figure of the seditious Papist, while it embodied the Catholic threat of a "sectory" within the population, could not definitively be used to demarcate that threat's limit. Likewise, while the figure of the Puritan demarcated a faction of nonconformists, it too could not be used to draw a reliable line through the population. The game of power posed this question: What must reason of state do if it can never distinguish with absolute certainty the faithful members of the Church of England from the crypto-Catholics or "nonconforming conformists" dwelling among them? These populations, which could always be enlarged by successful acts of sedition, had no reliable markers by which they might be recognized. Counteracting their spread would therefore require a permanent monitoring apparatus of state intelligence.

The dual Catholic/Puritan danger marks a political innovation in the mapping of racial threat, no longer as a linear spectrum from good to evil, but instead a bell curve, with racial danger exponentiating at either end. Defined against two indeterminate Papist and Puritan extremes, good membership in the English body politic would come to be situated in what the Anglican tradition has sometimes called the *via media* (middle way).[49] The hypothesis of the *via media* graphed a populational majority whose religious moderation suggested a "marriage" to the state that enjoyed a high degree of trust. The faithfulness of this proper Anglican body politic remained metaphorically bound to proper sexuality, wedlock, chastity, and goodness. To either side, however, one descended into a presumed—though imprecisely bounded—minority "faction" of the population whose extremity of conscience signaled a high propensity for falling into disloyalty, an inclination toward wicked seduction, treasonous "sodometrie," or even the diabolics of witchcraft or sorcery. If one were to plot this *via media* demarcation of state loyalty on a graph, the bell curve would reflect the very distribution of probability that would later become standard to biopolitical analyses of population.

While English "reason of state" had its unique features, there was nothing exclusive in its placement of maximal state loyalty at the apex of a curve distributing population on either side of two religiously seditious extremes. In France, monarchic loyalty was also defended on a middle ground that required protection from the Huguenot Protestant fanaticism, on one end, and the Holy League's overly zealous Catholicism at the other. French *raison d'état* asserted the primacy of state interest against any subordination to—or subversion by— either wing of conscience. *Raison d'état* rationalized the St. Bartholomew's Day massacre of Huguenot leaders in 1572. A few decades later, it justified the French king's alliance with Sweden, the Netherlands, and Protestant German princes in order to rebalance power against the Hapsburg rulers of Spain and the Holy Roman Empire (Church 2015). As in England, good government in France required an ensemble of techniques for mitigating the risk of sedition whenever either Protestant or Catholic religiosity exceeded its proper bounds. In the name of managing the population's discontent, Westphalian political rationality gradually birthed the security state. Whether through the judicious use of intelligence, the rhetorical power of the pulpit, mandated loyalty oaths, special policing laws, or ideological force applied through pamphleteering or religious schooling, its search for the objects of Westphalian suspicion involved the continuous assessment and preemptive confrontation with potentially seditious elements on either side of an ideological middle ground.[50]

Antipopery and the Color Line

What relationship do these new religious targets of Westphalian state security bear to the genealogy of racial power explored in this book? What connection does the figure of the treasonous Papist bear to that of the dissimulating converso or the conspiring African slave? Let me turn to a few brief historical snapshots that suggest how the field of racial power was modified as it integrated reason of state's permanent war against confessional treason. Consider, for instance, the English colony of New York, 15 percent of whose population in 1741 were enslaved Africans working in the homes of merchants. In that year, three African slaves apparently stole goods from a local store and disposed of them at a local tavern whose white owners had agreed to resell them. Shortly after the slaves were apprehended, a wave of fires broke out. Were these fires somehow connected to the theft? Was the crime they had planned something greater than petty larceny? New York Supreme Court Justice David Horsmanden, convinced that it was, began a search for witnesses. Once an indentured servant girl of the tavern owner agreed to testify, the purported scope of the conspiracy rapidly expanded. The purported alliance of poor whites and African slaves behind the fires pointed increasingly toward revolutionary intrigue. The crucial turn occurred, however, when indictments grew to include half a dozen "Spanish slaves," Black sailors formerly from Spanish Caribbean colonies. Not only were these Black sailors believed to be fiercer than local Africans, but they were presumably faithful to Catholicism. At this stage, the trial blossomed into high-stakes allegations of an elaborately conceived papist effort to entice slaves to destroy the colony on behalf of French and Spanish foreign interests. It climaxed with the apprehension of Jon Ury, an itinerant Latin teacher accused of hiding his identity as the "popish priest" who had secretly masterminded the entire conspiracy. Ury's priestly status was indispensable to the prosecution's account. Not only was he accused of plotting the entire scheme, but worse, of attracting accomplices by offering priestly absolution to all the conspirators, including African slaves whom he had recruited to kill their masters.

In the prosecutorial account, Catholicism merely pretended to be a religion when in fact it was (to use Bacon's term from a century and a half earlier) all *faction*. A seditious politics masquerading as mere confession, Catholicism was a recruiting dogma, tempting Africans into treasonous violence against their racial subordination. Catholicism's evil was therefore lodged, not as heresy against a true Protestant faith, but rather in its own faithless political treason against the racial state. In Judge Horsmanden's words, Ury and other popish priests (as yet undiscovered) were "infernal agents" who had sought the "horrible, detestable purpose, as the devastation of this city, and the massacre of its inhabitants, to be perpetrated by the hands of our own slaves," and they had done so by "debauching their slaves, and acquainting themselves of such white people as might be most likely seduced to their detestable purposes" (Zabin 2004, 153–54). Yet this Catholic principle of seduction into treason, precisely by eliciting the evil of a cross-racial conspiracy, also conspired to undo the racial security of the color line. Horsmanden's journal notes a divine sign apparently offered of this truth: after two of the chief conspirators, one white and one Black, were hung in the city square, the onlookers observed "wondrous phenomenons" in which the white man had changed hues to a "deep shining black, rather blacker than the negro placed by him," while the African, in turn had become "somewhat bleached or turned whitish, insomuch as it occasioned a remark, that Hughson [the white] and he had changed colors" (Zabin 2004, 130). This wondrous trading of the two conspirator's skin pigmentation, I would suggest, marked the imagined underlying truth of the papist threat: what had been at first conceived as a slave revolt against New York's white masters had now, with the addition of popery, become an ideologically inspired act of treason against the color line of the colonial-racial state.

Almost two centuries after the 1741 New York conspiracy, the American Ku Klux Klan still denounced Catholicism as a seditious enemy of the racial state. Rarely is attention paid to how or why the second Klan's anti-Blackness was folded into a comprehensive defense of the white Anglo-Saxon Protestant (Nordic) character of the racial state against what it claimed were a multitude of coordinated political threats that also included Jews, Catholics, and immigrants (Gordon 2017, 1–11). Just as Catholicism had been targeted as a religious threat to the Elizabethan and Jacobean state, so here again the Klan sought to prevent its corrupt ecclesiastical hierarchy from taking control of Protestant republics like the United States.

Let me sum up. Antipopery was but an early though persistent variant of the larger innovation that reason of state introduced into the field of racial power. In this innovation's most general terms, the state's security apparatuses would need to govern a permanent if fluctuating risk that some populational factions (typically its extremes) would grow attracted to rival authorities and subversive religiosities. In relation to the particularizing force of a color line, for example, the Ku Klux Klan urged the racial state to battle the threat that its multiracial body could be seduced away from its "marriage" to the sole governance of its white head, perhaps by Catholicism, but later, for instance, by communism. The crucial insight into Westphalian racism therefore is not that it constituted Catholics or other religious populations as a racial group (although it sometimes could), but rather that it constituted Catholicism as a generalized racial threat through its ability to incite populational enemies, including ones that transgressed (or at least sought the transgression of) the color line. What is important, in other words, is the form rather than the content of antipopery. Its "anti-ness" in relation to the wrong sort of religious affiliation would prove highly flexible as a technology of racial power. In Bacon's own time, Islam was widely conceived as a religion that did not respect the authority of the state, as I will discuss further below. Jews would represent yet another religious group whose theology (loyalty to their own law) threatened because it precluded loyalty to the state. In the late eighteenth and early nineteenth century, as we will see in the next chapter, Jacobinism would become an "atheistic" antireligion of revolutionary sedition. And from the mid-nineteenth century onward, anticommunism would operate in ways strikingly analogous to antipopery. When the FBI opened a file on Martin Luther King Jr. on his presumed communist loyalties, the purpose was to expose him as seeking not racial justice as he claimed but instead the treasonous demise of the America's racial state on behalf of a foreign ideology (communism) and a foreign power (the Soviet Union).

Islamophobia: Westphalian Reason on the International Scale

I end this discussion of Westphalian racial reason by unpacking its paradigmatic positioning of the Muslim as a ground for the figure of the Papist. Consider, for example, that although it was Catholics and Puritans that (as we have seen) Francis Bacon feared might wage a religious war against the Stuart state, he warned against this danger in the following way:

> There be two swords amongst Christians, the spiritual and temporal; and both have their due office and place in the maintenance of religion: but we may not take up the third sword, which is Mahomet's sword, or like unto it: that is, to propagate religion by wars, or by sanguinary persecutions to force consciences; except it be in cases of overt scandal, blasphemy, or intermixture of practice against the state; much less to nourish seditions; to authorize conspiracies and rebellions; to put the sword into the people's hands, and the like, tending to the subversion of all government, which is the ordinance of God. (Bacon 1996, 346)

Similarly in the next century, when John Locke pointedly excluded Catholics from his plea for religious toleration, he explained its grounds by analogy to Muslims:

> It is ridiculous for any one to profess himself to be a *Mahumetan* only in his religion, but in everything else a faithful subject to a Christian magistrate, whilst at the same time he acknowledges himself bound to yield blind obedience to the *Mufti* of *Constantinople*, who himself is entirely obedient to the *Ottoman* Emperor and frames the feigned oracles of that religion according to his pleasure. But this Mahometan living amongst

Christians would yet more apparently renounce their government if he acknowledged the same person to be head of his Church who is the supreme magistrate in the state. (Locke 2016, 50)

Why would sedition be generally characterized by Bacon as the work of "Mahomet's sword?" And why would the comparatively distant religion of Islam furnish Locke with his clinching argument against the Catholic confounding of church and state, religious and political authority, private belief and public loyalty?

One answer may be found in Locke's implication that the Ottoman emperor was *dangerous* as the magistrate of a nearby power who did not honor the authority of his neighboring states. The era's Westphalian order of states was premised on "reason of state," not only as a matter of internal stability, but also as an external stability that rested upon two principles: the mutual respect of states for one another's sovereignty, and a balance of power among them that maintained an overarching state of peace. Foucault calls the technologies developed in support of this project the "military-diplomatic apparatus" of reason of state (Foucault 2007: 296–306). This was an outward looking machinery for relationships among states that together produced, in place of the old dream of Christendom, the new idea of Europe.

For Foucault it was this balance of power that produced the new idea of European unity only out of a competition of states and the play of forces. But if the goal was at least *symbolically* to rationalize the interstate system's "just wars" that established colonies for European states, then we can say that the diplomatic-military system also operationalized "Europe" as a geopolitical coalition constitutive of the new capitalist world-system's core. Here the idea of "Europe" grounded a geopolitical order in which capitalism was spread militarily (via primitive accumulation). Europe, understood as a system of sovereign states, was deemed uniquely fit to conquer and rule over the nonsovereign periphery: this was the inception of the colonial "nomos of the earth" that Carl Schmitt appropriately termed the *ius publicum Europaeum* (European public law) (Schmitt 2003). This imperial unity of a *ius publicum Europaeum* collectively dominated the expanding colonial periphery of the world-system while also policing its borders against forces in that part of the globe that still lay outside it. It was precisely this unity that emerged through the "victory of states" in the so-called Wars of Religion. By asserting the primacy of European states' collective interests as a *state system* against all religions that exceeded their proper bounds, the Westphalian peace forged an international order that made possible the colonial world.

This makes it clearer, however, why the threat of religion with a political interest found its ultimate representation in the Ottoman Empire. The Ottoman Empire and the Islamic world that it represented was, of course, immediately adjacent to the emergent space of Europe, so that the expansion of the interstate system (on its way to becoming a genuinely global world-system) was pitted symbolically against exactly that part of the world that geographically represented its limit or border. In a short essay that extends his brilliant study of the medieval crusades, Tomaž Mastnak has argued that the idea of Europe was born out of a vison of "chasing the Turk out of Europe" (Mastnak 2003, 208). Although in practice many European powers established alliances with the Ottomans, the political conception of a European order of states was envisioned through its war against what was *represented* by the Ottoman Empire, a non-Christian realm at Europe's edge that lacked the European qualities deemed necessary to becoming a genuinely European state. The border between Europe and the Ottomans was deployed as what I have elsewhere called a racial dogma line (Medovoi 2012a). On the near side of that line, one finds states willing to respect one another's sovereignty, and thus prepared to join in a place of perpetual peace called Europe. On the far side, one finds the racial otherness of a rogue state that sees its civil authority as extending on a religious basis to all Muslims, and that therefore refuses to recognize the sovereignty of other states.

For medieval Christendom, the Muslim had been the ultimate infidel, the agent of the Antichrist. For the secular state system of Westphalian Europe, this notion of infidelity was now reconceived as a pernicious disloyalty to the political form of the state itself in its fundamental difference from a church. What the Muslim domain of the Ottoman Empire represented as Europe's immediate outside was an unwillingness to guarantee religion's harmlessness to the state. Protestants and Catholics alike, when attacking one another for their failures to separate religion from political authority, labeled the other a "Mahometan" or a Turk (see Heath 1988).[51] It was in this era that the Orientalist trope of the *Turkish despot* emerged as a unifying political motif, and that a genuinely Saidian discourse of Orientalism emerged in dialogue with Westphalian "reason of state." Knowledge of the East became a kind of foreign intelligence about the ideological forces arrayed against the entire state system of Europe. In this sense, the era of reason of state was racially predicated upon what, to rephrase Étienne Balibar, we might call a generalized anti-Islamism, one in which any religion that interfered in the authorities of princes was the equivalent of Islam, and in which any state that did not respect the sovereignty of its peers (including the encouragement of seditious or treasonous behavior by minority populations) was the equivalent of the Turks.[52] Reason of state did not merely set in motion the individual interests of individual states. It also set in motion the overarching interest of a European order of states that would be defined against the Turk as a prototype for later notions of the totalitarian or rogue state, a state that, whether communist (the Soviet Union), Third Worldist (Chávez's Venezuela), or Islamist (postrevolutionary Iran), threatened world order through its embrace of a dogma viewed as a politico-theological threat to the interstate system itself. Westphalian reason reorganized the game of racial power around a geopolitical problem of seditious threat to state security that, on the international scale, is still with us today.

4

———

RACIAL LIBERALISM, RACIAL CAPITALISM
Ensouling Property's Adversaries

Abstractedly speaking, government, as well as liberty, is good; yet could I, in common sense, ten years ago, have felicitated France on her enjoyment of a government (for she then had a government) without inquiry what the nature of that government was, or how it was administered? Can I now congratulate the same nation upon its freedom? Is it because liberty in the abstract may be classed amongst the blessings of mankind, that I am seriously to felicitate a madman who has escaped from the protecting restraint and wholesome darkness of his cell on his restoration to the enjoyment of light and liberty? Am I to congratulate a highwayman and murderer who has broke prison upon the recovery of his natural rights? —EDMUND BURKE, *Reflections on the Revolution in France*

Should a rattlesnake, or a mad dog, be tried before killing? Should a murderer, incendiary, or highwayman, caught in the act, be allowed to complete it and to appeal to all the delays and chances of law? If you, or your people, or your property, be feloniously attacked, will you await the laws, or will you act at once in self-defense? If a mad man be on the streets, marauding and slaying all he meets, must we take out a warrant for him, arrest and try him, before we disable him and stop his wild career? The negro who has just been lynched at Charlottesville was far worse than any rattlesnake or mad dog, far worse than any mad man or criminal and by his nature and course had outlawed himself utterly. —Editorial, *Wilmington Messenger* (North Carolina), 1898

A spectre is haunting Europe, the spectre of Communism. —KARL MARX AND FRIEDRICH ENGELS, *Manifesto of the Communist Party*

Rethinking Racial Capitalism

In this chapter I will pivot at last to the transition through which racial power became one of capitalism's enduring features. As explained in the introduction, this book considers race as part of what Dipesh Chakrabarty has called capitalism's "History One": it does not treat the history of race as something with which capitalism merely found a way to coexist. Rather, it proposes this history to represent one of capitalism's key political preconditions. In this sense I am thinking with and through the scholarly paradigm that studies "racial capitalism." I am doing so, however, in a rather unconventional way. My focus in this chapter will not center on a race/class problematic that addresses race-making as primarily a technique for the naturalization of inequality, exploitation, or expropriation. My focus instead will concern a race/value/security problematic that reproduces capitalism on a political level.

"Racial capitalism" can be a useful conceptual framework insofar as it allows us to move simultaneously in two critical directions. On the one hand, it lends focus to the argument that racial power cannot be adequately critiqued or challenged outside the determining conditions of capital accumulation. At the same time, the racial capitalist frame challenges the presumption found among certain more orthodox Marxisms that racism is a residual or "merely ideological" political issue that is secondary to capitalism's inexorable bifurcation of the population into two antagonistic social classes: capitalists and proletarians. If capitalism is a universalizing social force, then to call it racial capitalism, as Arun Kundani understands it (Kundani 2020), and as Ingrid Diran has usefully elaborated (Diran 2021), is apparently to recognize how and why capitalism operationalizes its own failure "to universalize itself."

The American academy's understanding of "racial capitalism" has typically been derived from Cedric Robinson's *Black Marxism* (2020), which argues (as noted in chapter 1) that capitalism grew out of preexisting racial divisions of labor found in European feudalism, including an active slave trade in the Mediterranean.[1] Capitalism, according to Robinson, emerged out of feudal conditions that were already fully racialized, and whose populational divisions were used to organize its colonial expansion and to prepare the groundwork for its earliest regime of labor—plantocratic chattel slavery.

Although this book has proposed a precapitalist genealogy of race dramatically different than Robinson's, one that hearkens back not to feudal divisions of labor but instead to the feudal era's reliance on pastoral power and the government of souls, I agree with him that race not only predates capitalism but was essential to its development. For Robinson, race's operations as a discourse for explaining and justifying the division of labor mean that, even today it should be theorized above all in relation to what Sarika Chandra and Christopher Chen call a "race/class problematic" (Chandra and Chen 2022). Race so grasped becomes, in Stuart Hall's famous words, "the modality by which class is lived" (Hall 1996, 55), the way that we are made to live our position within a capitalist division of labor.[2]

This analysis is indispensable, yet I will argue that racial capitalism needs further theorization. Consider, for example, an approach that would emphasize the expropriative logic of settler colonial violence. Here racial differentiation centrally concerns not the segmenting of labor but instead the distinguishing of settlers from Native peoples in ways that authorize the expropriation of land and resources. This approach to racial capitalism also has roots in Marxist traditions, primarily through the analysis of Western imperialism developed by Rosa Luxemburg (2015) and V. I. Lenin (1920). It was further elaborated during the twentieth century by Third World Marxists, and has more recently been adopted by such Indigenous scholars as Jodi Byrd (2011) and Glen Coulthard (2014).

These distinctive emphases on labor and land can be synthesized, as we see in the work of such scholars as Onur Ulas Ince and Robert Nichols, who have potently reworked the concept of "primitive accumulation" (Ince 2014; Nichols 2021). In contrast to Marx, for whom primitive accumulation was a transitional phase of coercively expropriative violence that prepared the way for conventional accumulation by separating traditional producers from their means of production, Ince and Nichols have argued that primitive accumulation is a recurring phenomenon. They draw here on Luxemburg's revisionary insight that expropriative forms of accumulation reemerge under capitalism whenever it reaches a limit to its growth that necessitates a new absorption (expropriation) of noncapitalist life worlds. Nichols, as well as Byrd, Jodi Melamed, Alyosha Goldstein, and Chandan Reddy, have argued that such expropriative accumulation always shadows the extraction of surplus value by waged capitalist production (Byrd et al. 2018).

When settler colonialism is theorized alongside the color-lining of labor, racialization can be grasped as a general idiom for explicating capitalist processes of differentiated expropriation: "race" becomes a discourse through which capitalism has historically answered the question of which populations will become juridical subjects submitted to routine exploitation by the formal equality of the wage form and which ones will become second-class or nonjuridical subjects who face naked forms of violent dispossession. In his synthesis of this combined approach, Michael Dawson writes that "the associated binary that expropriation under capitalism divides the world into distinguishes racialized superior and inferior humans. Sometimes and in some places this binary is framed as 'human/subhuman'; in others, as 'full citizens/second-class citizens' or 'civilized/uncivilized.' In each case the division marked a racialized group whose labor, property, and bodies could be subject to expropriation, exploitation, and violation without recourse to (particularly civic/political) resources available to those classified as fully human" (Dawson 2016, 149). In her endorsement of Dawson, Nancy Fraser likewise argues that capitalism has always utilized "race" to sort its populations in relation to two distinct, yet highly imbricated accumulation logics: that of exploitation (the extraction of surplus value) and that of expropriation (the seizure of wealth) (Fraser 2016). In this sense, the valorization process itself has historically relied on technologies of racial differentiation.

This synthesis represents a major step forward in the critical analysis of racial capitalism, yet even here I would contend that something important is missing. Arguments that construe racialization as the direct effect of capitalist exploitation and expropriation are powerful but also limiting. They are powerful because they provide an analysis of racial capitalism that addresses the conditions of possibility for its expanded reproduction—that is, the conditions of possibility for capital accumulation. They are limiting, however, because they narrow the intelligibility of those reproductive conditions to a narrowly economic register of the political—that is, to the violence that occurs through the appropriation of land, resources, and labor. Yet violence may also be necessary to enable certain political conditions that only indirectly enable the expanded reproduction of capitalism.

This problem is usefully raised in Barnaby Raine's thoughtful response to Fraser's reading of "race" as a sorting task for capitalism's exploitation/expropriation distinction. Raine, while acknowledging the value of Fraser's account, nevertheless asks what would happen to our view of racial capitalism "if we started instead from Islamophobia or anti-Semitism? Those seem today to interact with capitalism at a level that is less foundational (immediately enabling commodity production) and more political: Islamophobia sustains imperialism and anti-Semitism is a fetishistic discourse of ostensible anti-elitism. Both of those readings should hint at how Islamophobia and anti-Semitism are connected to capitalism, but in slightly different ways than a focus on settler colonialism and primitive accumulation as the generative moments for (all) racism might suggest" (Raine 2019, n.p.).[3] If, for example, we take up Moishe Postone's analysis of antisemitism as a right-wing fetishization of the Jew used to figure finance capital's abstract power (Postone 1980), what kind of approach to "racial capitalism" would we need to successfully integrate such a racialization process alongside the others? The same question could be asked of Iyko Day's incisive reading of anti-Asian racism as a settler colonial variant on the Postonian fetishization of "alien capital" (Day 2016). Do such analyses posit the raciality of racial capitalism in a way that can be successfully integrated with theories focused on the hyperexploitation of a labor force or the seizure of land? And what about Islamophobic racism that is directed at the "terror" of an immigrant's religious difference, as Junaid Rana (2011) among others has considered it? If we place our analyses of these diverse racisms alongside one another, can we discern any overarching account of racial capitalism that might plausibly explain their mutual relationships?

Perhaps the place to begin is to consider how racial capitalism as such would need to be retheorized if we treated it as something more than an economic system, even a violent or expropriative one. As a mode of production that constitutes a social totality (and not just a growing quantity of capital), capitalism must generate power as well as value to reproduce itself. And power is not always directly in the service of creating value even when its dynamics act as value's precondition. Here I find useful a distinction drawn by the neo-Marxist French regulation school.[4] The regulationists have argued, contrary to mainstream liberal "equilibrium theories of the market," that capitalist production is incapable of regulating itself. Instead, its tendency toward multiple forms of crisis forces a reliance upon political technologies that, even while not themselves elements in the accumulation process, still play a critical role in stabilizing the conditions required for accumulation to proceed (Boyer 1990). The regulationists therefore heuristically distinguish a "regime of accumulation," which names the material processes associated with the actual production of surplus value, from something they call a "mode of regulation," by which they mean the various legal, political, and cultural technologies through which a "regime of accumulation" is sustained (Boyer 1990, 36–53).[5] As regimes of accumulation enter moments of crisis that transform them, their political requirements also change. Meanwhile, as political technologies evolve, the kinds of accumulation they can support may presumably shift as well. Capitalism's history, viewed from this regulationist perspective, follows a dialectical path of ever-shifting points of convergence and contradiction between accumulation and regulation, value and power.

There is another way to pose the relationship between accumulation and regulation that the regulation school does not consider, perhaps because the point appears overly philosophical for a group of economists (however heterodox they might be). While the accumulation of capital is a process that depends on the abstraction of the value form, regulation can be said to depend on a different abstraction, the political one that in this book I have been calling "security." In a critical tradition that begins with Marx, runs through the Frankfurt school, and culminates in Moishe Postone, the abstractness of the value form is understood as not merely conceptual. It is a real abstraction that, once materially instantiated, begins to operate as an independent historical force capable of dominating human life.[6] One underlying argument of this chapter is that, under capitalism, security too becomes a real abstraction, though one that differentiates even as it universalizes. As a biopolitical project, the liberal regime of security that capitalism has adopted seeks to measure and thereby commensurate all people or things as forces that might either enhance or endanger the well-being and smooth operation of a "free society." Like value, security is material force that quantifies and calculates. To that end, security enumerates and distinguishes those in the population who ensoul (as we shall see) the freedom of a liberal society from those who ensoul a threat to that freedom. The so-called abstractness of modern citizenship, viewed from this perspective, is just one side of the real abstraction of security. It is always paired with the abstractness of threat: the measuring of the various dangerous counterparts of the citizen from whom the citizen must be defended. Security's biopolitical analysis and measurement of the population for the threat it contains then boomerang back to subject and dominate that population's life. People are disciplined and regulated not only by *how* they are sorted, but as well by the brute fact that they *will* be sorted. This is where racism in its broadest sense becomes critical to capitalist development: not simply as a structuring element of racial capitalism's regimes of accumulation, nor just as an alibi for class, but also and at the same time as constitutive of its historic modes of regulation and its techniques of governance.

Before proceeding further, I should provide a caveat. The story of racial capitalism does not really begin in this chapter of my book. While the rise of a language of *raza* arguably occurred at the Iberian dusk of medieval power, its relocation to the New World played a key part in the expropriation of Native lands and the importation of slave labor from Africa by the early Iberian colonial empires. Chapter 2 therefore was already engaged with what Marx once called the "rosy dawn of the era of capitalist production." Meanwhile, chapter 3, in addressing the rise of the Westphalian state and its mode of political reason, considered the management of "seditions of the belly" among the metropolitan peasantry in an era of accelerating land enclosures and incipient agrarian capitalism. Moreover, the uses of antipopery by the early modern English state's security regime were instrumental for the Elizabethan "plantation" of Ireland, which in turn prepared the way for massive English settler colonial expansion during the next century. So, racial capitalism has already made an appearance in this book. Nevertheless, this chapter, which presupposes the "birth of race" and the "rise of the state" as treated in chapters 2 and 3, respectively, will now consider in a more explicit way how liberal technologies of ensoulment put the racial into racial capitalism.

Racial Liberalism, Police, and the Mode of Regulation

My guiding hypothesis here will be that racial capitalism, a four-hundred-year-old mode of production whose history includes several successive regimes of capital accumulation (plantocratic, industrial monopoly, Fordist and post-Fordist regimes), has always relied upon multipronged and continuously evolving modes of regulation that constitute so many distinct episodes in the political history of *racial liberalism*.[7] Liberalism, with its possessive individuals, its civil society of fungible exchange, and its discourse of liberty, has long provided capitalism with both a veneer to mask its acts of extraction and a mode of regulating the populations that are subjected to those processes. In this way, liberalism offers capitalism both ideological legitimation *and* a political strategy of governance. In a famous scene in the first volume of *Capital*, Marx described liberal market society as one whose governing power sits above—and thereby screens from view—the "hidden abode of production" (Marx 1977, 279). As he put it, "There alone [in the "noisy" sphere of exchange] rule Freedom, Equality, Property and Bentham" (Marx 2004, 280). But if capitalism is always a racial capitalism, then in what sense have liberalism and its abstractions always operated as a *racial* liberalism? What do freedom, equality, property, and Bentham have to do with race?

In his 1977–78 lectures, collected as *Security, Territory, Population*, Foucault approaches liberalism as a new governmental logic that emerged during the eighteenth century through a decisive break with reason of state and its economic analogs, cameralism and mercantilism (Foucault 2007). Reason of state had exercised a project of governance that it called "police," by which was meant the state's use of its accumulated knowledge/power regarding people and things to maximize the wealth produced by the economy/population couplet. Bacon's policies for balancing the state's store and its population exemplified this kind of police.[8] In sharp contrast, liberalism sought to limit rather than expand governmental action over the market: in this sense it called for the dismantling of cameralist police. Liberalism's reasoning for the dismantling of police was that state intervention could only impede the market's operation as a self-ordering homeostatic machinery for economic veridiction (truth telling). Markets possessed their own natural laws, which when left uninterfered with, could solve economic problems (shortages, gluts, imbalances). The best way to increase social wealth was therefore to permit the market to use its own exchange process to discover and implement the truth about prices, distributions, and efficiencies. Policing only interfered with this natural ability.

While Foucault's account captures one important aspect of liberalism's strategy of governance, it misses entirely another side of its operations. Even as liberalism withdrew police from direct regulation of the market, in the name of security it would expand and intensify police power in relationship to the population's potential threats to the "freedom" of the market. Mark Neocleous calls this redefinition of police a turn toward the "fabrication of social order" through the safeguarding of private property (Neocleous 2021). In a strikingly parallel analysis, Bernard Harcourt has shown how liberalism, from its inception, consistently advanced two seemingly opposed yet ultimately congruent regulatory projects: on one side, a withdrawal of government or a maximization of laissez-faire when it comes to market regulation, but on the other, a government of "unlimited penality" when it comes to policing and incarcerating populations whose disordered passions might imperil the smooth functioning of that same market (Harcourt 2011, 38–41).[9]

As we shall see, this reconception of police power would become the cornerstone of racial liberalism. It expresses the form that liberal power would take to ensure that those who cannot be governed safely by means of freedom are governed in a different way. According to Markus Dirk Dubber, police power began as a legal concept derived from the right of the head of the Greco-Roman household (the *pater familias*) to discipline and punish all members of his household, even unto death, in the name of its well-being. For this reason, the origins of police power are tied to *oikonomos*, the law of the household (Dubber 2005). This explains why police was originally connected to economic policy, but also why it could easily be redirected toward the social ordering of populations by means of force. The common assumption that police primarily concerns law enforcement is a mistake. Unlike ordinary juridical power, police power is both anticipatory and absolute without being strictly speaking a legal power itself. Police forces provide security for the good order of the public household. They can therefore intervene to regulate disorder even in circumstances where the law has been obeyed; conversely, they can choose to tolerate "good order" even if it involves behavior that is technically violating the law. Police power is therefore distinct from legal power, nor is it clear which power is supreme. Laws may be legislated to delimit police power, but these limits must always be defined negatively and on an ad hoc basis given that the future-oriented objective of policing—protecting good order against unforeseeable dangers—requires discretionary license.

Neither Neocleous's nor Dubber's analysis of police power directly considers how or why racial distinctions have been so central to its exercise, but we find some clues in Domenico Losurdo's compelling counterhistory of liberalism. Losurdo, who carefully traces the "unique twin birth" of liberalism and chattel slavery (in fact a triplet birth when one adds settler colonial conquest of Native land in the Americas), explains that liberalism, even at the abstract level of its principles, has never really concerned itself with individual freedom per se. Rather, what liberalism celebrates above all is the sacred space of freedom that it calls "society," which properly belongs to a propertied class whose self-government is protected therein. This sacred space, Losurdo suggests, is defined through borders that demarcate it from a profane, illiberal exterior where freedom is absent (Losurdo 2011, 297–322). Losurdo characterizes this dividing line between liberalism's sacred and profane spaces in racial capitalist terms that reflect "the self-consciousness of a class of owners of slaves and servants that was being formed as the capitalist system began to emerge and establish itself, thanks in part to those ruthless practices of expropriation and oppression implemented in the metropolis, and especially the colonies, which Marx described as 'original capitalist accumulation'" (Losurdo 2011, 309).

Losurdo's frame, while illuminating, might wrongly be taken to imply that liberalism's profane space is a byproduct of its hypocritical relationship to its abstract principles, a double standard that insincerely refuses to some the freedom it allegedly promises to all. Yet if liberalism were simply an ideology of universal freedom that had failed to deliver, and if racial capitalism were merely a capitalism that had failed to universalize itself, one would expect its racial discourse to simply devalue or inferiorize racialized populations. Some would be deserving of freedom, others not. But this is precisely what we do not find: the analysis of liberalism and capitalism as failed universalisms is not in itself sufficient to explain the *anti* quality that drives such bellicose projects as anti-Blackness, anti-Indigeneity, anti-immigration, or antisemitism. Those to whom liberalism would deny human freedom are not merely governed as an infrahumanity; they are policed as the probable *enemies* of humanity's sacred freedom, as the potential ensoulment of evil.

The particularizing bellicosity of this racial structure can be observed in the allegorical identification expressed by many early liberals with the "chosen people" of the Old Testament, and above all with their conquest of the promised land from the Canaanites (Losurdo 2011, 309–10). The Canaanites are the enemy of the Israelites, not simply because they lack "chosenness" but because their wicked worship of other gods tempts the Israelites to abandon the sacred circle of their camp. It is this danger that necessitates the Israelites' preemptive war and occupation of Canaan. The "land of milk and honey" is also a holy land because it is cleansed of dangerous Canaanite abominations. This liberal metaphor suggests why Losurdo's account of the *enclosure* of liberalism's sacred realm of freedom should be retheorized as a spatialization of martial power, the drawing of a militarized frontier of security, and the *battlefront* for a certain kind of race war that is always presented as a defensive action.[10] Freedom's boundaries, as we shall see, define liberal space as a first step toward protecting it on the principle that a clear border is a secure one. Let us consider how liberalism came to conceive itself as the project of freedom's security.

Securing Society: The Antecedent of John Locke

Liberal security, as I will show, is grounded in the defense of private property, a concept whose earliest and most influential formulation belongs to John Locke. Locke stands out as a political philosopher who argued that the right to property actually *preexists* the social contract. It is already there in the state of nature whenever someone "mixes" their labor with the world to make something that thereby becomes their own. With this hypothesis, Locke articulated what would become known as the "labor theory of property" that became central both to the liberal tradition of political economy and Marxist critiques of it. Locke was also famously a colonial administrator involved in the design of British settlement in North America, and more than a few scholars have explored the relationship between his theory of property and the principles of racial domination.[11] In his *Second Treatise on Government*, for example, Locke provided a clear and influential philosophical justification for the seizure of Native land in the Americas. Locke explains property right by describing the "Law of Reason" that "makes the deer that *Indian's* who hath killed it" (Locke 2016, 16). But he also observes, the "*chief matter of property*" is not "the Fruits of the Earth and the Beasts that subsist on it, but the Earth it self" (Locke 2016, 17). The Indians may keep the deer they kill, but if they do not know how to productively cultivate the land in the way that God commanded in his biblical injunction for man to "master the earth," then it is entirely within the right of settlers to "inclose" the land. For God did not mean for the earth to "remain common and uncultivated. He gave it to the use of the Industrious and the Rational (and Labour was to be *his Title* to it); not to the Fancy and the Covetousness of the Quarrelsom and Contentious" (Locke 2016, 18).

Once money comes into existence (which, like property, Locke also considers a presocial phenomenon), it becomes possible to cultivate far more land than someone can actually use as an individual. Money can be used to sell the fruits of one's land to other people for their own use. Money can also be used, of course, to hire wage laborers or indeed to purchase slaves to perform this labor. Although Locke professed philosophical abhorrence of slavery, his *Second Treatise* also acknowledges its existence and permits it insofar as the slave is normatively defined as the loser of a just war whose life has been forfeited "by some Act that deserves Death" (Locke 2016, 14).[12]

We could say, then, that Locke's philosophy of civil government repeatedly sought to resolve contradictions between freedom and unfreedom, ownership and expropriation, in ways that ultimately legitimated both the plantocratic regime of capital accumulation then emerging in North America and the Caribbean, as well as the early agrarian capitalism unfolding in Britain around the same time.[13] Read in relation to these passages, race becomes the effect of Locke's laws of property and slavery. It names and characterizes those who find themselves outside his sacred society because of their lack of "industry" and "rationality," or their loss of freedom due to defeat in war.

Nevertheless, these are not the passages in Locke's treatise that are most central to my account of racial capitalism, for although they do connect racial difference to the imperative to accumulate value (mastering the earth via the power of money), they do not yet connect it to a second and closely related imperative: ensuring the *security* of that accumulation process. In what way does the sanctified realm of Lockean freedom lead to the racialization of threats from those who stand outside it? How does racial liberalism generate a need to posit its enemies?[14] And how does it develop, through that process, a modern conception of police power? For these questions we must turn to different passages from Locke's *Second Treatise*.

In Locke's political philosophy, security stands as the primary objective of government. But unlike earlier thinkers tied to reason of state, Locke saw security as something that the state provided not in order to protect itself, but instead to preserve a "society" that natural individuals form when they join together in a social contract. Government is merely a supplementary creation, charged by society with providing security. Why does Locke believe society requires security in the first place? The answer can be discerned in how he defines civil society as the antithesis of civil war: "civil society," he explains, is a "state of peace, amongst those who are of it" (Locke 2016, 105). But this state of peace is something that must be actively created in response to the harrowing potential for its opposite. Locke devotes the entire third chapter of his *Second Treatise* to the "State of War," which can come about because there always exist certain individuals who pose a violent threat to the peaceable arrangement of the social contract: "he that in the State of Society would take away the *Freedom* belonging to those of that Society or Common-wealth must be supposed to design to take away from them every thing else, and so be looked on as in a *State of War*" (Locke 2016, 11).

For Locke as well as for his contemporary, Thomas Hobbes, this state of war had already existed in the state of nature. For Hobbes it existed among everyone in the famous "war of all against all." For Locke, as well shall see, this state of war obtained only with some individuals, the "quarellsom and contentious" ones who disobey God's natural laws respecting property. The transition from the state of nature to the state of society is motivated precisely by the opportunity it offers to establish a civil government that will wield the magistrate's temporal sword against these enemies of the propertied person. With the social contract, the warfare among individuals that occurs in the state of nature is now folded into society's interior. It takes the shape of a permanent war that liberalism will call "policing." As Marx famously put it, "Security is the highest social concept of civil [i.e., bourgeois] society, the concept of *police*, expressing the fact that the whole of society exists only in order to guarantee to each of its members the preservation of his person, his rights, and his property" (Marx and Engels 2018, 46). But if liberalism's underlying assumption is that society must always be defended, who exactly ensouls the illiberal threat to property that must be guarded against?

I would like to consider the trajectories of two distinct but related targets of liberal policing. The first suspect, refracted through the racial prism of colonial capitalism as well as early metropolitan capitalism in Europe, maps loosely onto microthreats to the regime of capital accumulation. This figure includes among its avatars the poor, the indigent, the pauper, the vagrant, the slave, and above all the criminal. Beyond these, meanwhile, lurks a second threat to liberal society. This suspect, who emerges out of the religious hostilities of the English Civil War, and who ensouls the permanent threat of revolution, is the principal concern of what will become known as "political police." Here we confront a catalog of ideological enemies: the fanatic, the revolutionary, the abolitionist, even the communist. As we shall see, these dual enemies of propertied society amount to a liberal redescription of reason of state's two modes of sedition: those of the "belly" and the "head." The criminal and political clusters of suspects—and the issues they each raise—are distinctive, yet regularly cross paths and are inevitably dialectically related under liberalism. Slaves, after all, can always become insurrectional abolitionists, and the poor can always become revolutionaries.

In the end, these two figures reach the zenith of their capacity to threaten when they overlap and coincide. It is not difficult to see how these figures organize the basis for a mode of regulation that tacitly defends capitalism by openly defending liberal society: the policing of criminal suspects stabilizes the regime of property while the policing of political ones protects against social upheaval. Let us examine each of them more closely.

Enemy One: The Criminal Threat of the Unpropertied

The words "property" and "propriety" today have diverged in their principal meanings. Property today indicates a thing or quality one possesses, while propriety suggests a proper or correct standing. In their earliest senses, however, the two words were largely interchangeable. Locke in fact used the word "propriety" in several places in the first edition of the *Second Treatise* before later amending them to "property" (see Locke 2016, 20, 172n36). The words continue to be closely related even today: a "proprietor" is an owner and "proprietary" is to have a special possession of something. Propriety, of course, involves possessing good qualities, or having good properties. Liberalism, borrowing from earlier aristocratic conceptions of the propertied, braided these connotations together at the foundational level of its political philosophy. The freedom of the sacred realm belonged to the propertied, or those whose properties were appropriate because they had properly appropriated (properly made their own) the world around them. This in turn meant they possessed the unique quality (propriety) that makes for a proper individual in a liberal society. In liberal discourse the principle of freedom melts imperceptibly into a concept of proprietary ownership. For Locke, "property" is a word that subsumes life and liberty as well as possessions. All of these are "property" since life and liberty are the foundation of our individual property, the first things which we must first possess if we are to appropriate anything further in the world.

This primacy of property reflects what C. B. Macpherson famously termed liberalism's concept of "possessive individualism" (Macpherson 1962). In his own readings of Locke and Hobbes, Macpherson showed that the liberal tradition, from its earliest stages, defined freedom as an exclusive ownership over oneself, or as Locke famously puts it, that "every Man has a Property in his own Person" (Locke 2016, 15). One might notice here how Locke's concept of the free individual represents an exceptional case tacitly defined in relation to slavery. Slavery is a situation in which a man has property in *another* person. But the liberal individual is a man who has property in his *own* person, whose slave, in other words, coincides with his own body. The philosophical background here appears to be a Cartesian one in which the soul is the master of the body. To be a good liberal subject is to control one's own body in the sense of using it *properly*, for proper purposes that do not violate the principle of property itself. Tacit are the following two assumptions: if one does not use one's body properly, it might be better for another soul to have property in it who *will* use it properly; and conversely, if a person improperly tries to seize control of a proper possessive individual, they act as an enemy of property. Such a transgressor who threatens someone's life or freedom (a murderer, a kidnapper) thereby threatens both the individual's most basic property in themselves, as well as their society, understood here as a transactional arena for proper propertied exchange. This is the case because the liberal tradition, by defining the free individual in Macpherson's words as a "proprietor of his own person or capacities, owing nothing to society for them," thereby envisions society as a transactional arena composed of "a lot of free individuals related to each other as proprietors of their own capacities and of what they have acquired by their exercise. Society consists of relations of exchange between proprietors. Political society [the state] becomes a calculated device for the protection of this property and for the maintenance of an orderly relation of exchange" (Macpherson 1962, 3). But what then of those people who are *not* deemed possessive individuals? Some might be children, women, the mad, the infirm. But beyond the sacred realm of liberal transactional society there were also many versions of Locke's "Common Enemy," those whom we might call the antipossessive adversary of proper commerce.

Let us therefore begin with the most literal figure for so abstract an enemy, namely the criminal or thief, someone who, instead of properly acquiring property, by mixing with nature their own labor (or more likely mixing it with the labor of those in their employ), instead robs another individual, improperly depriving them of their property. This figure represents a double threat to liberal society. Through theft they steal the reward owed to possessive individuals for the industry of their efforts. But in addition, they also show the indigent how to successfully avoid the call to labor, thereby encouraging idleness and further criminality. What kind of person does liberalism actually suspect of thievery or robbery? Hobbes pessimistically argued that, absent a social contract, any of us might seize whatever we can from others. We are therefore all at heart potential enemies of propertied liberal society, and the Hobbesian Leviathan serves no other purpose than to "overawe" and dissuade us one and all (*omnes et singulatim*) from such impropriety. In this tradition, which runs from Hobbes through Cesare Beccaria and Jeremy Bentham, police and penality are technologies of power pitted against the general human tendency to violate one another's freedom whenever it serves our interests.[15] Criminal threat to society is therefore universally distributed across the population.

There is another tradition, however, which begins with Locke's view that justice precedes society. As I pointed out earlier, even in a state of nature, Locke expected people to obey God's natural laws forbidding theft, murder, and criminality. Most of humankind understands that it is an unnatural offense to seize another's property. Nevertheless, some people appear to violate this God-given norm. As Locke puts it, "In transgressing the Law of Nature, the Offender declares himself to live by another Rule, than that of reason and common Equity, which is that measure God has set to the actions of Men, for their mutual security: and so he becomes dangerous to Mankind" (Locke 2016, 6). Because such people are prepared to "trespass against the whole Species, and the Peace and Safety of it," and therefore represent an imminent danger to their fellow humans, a permanent state of war obtains with them (Locke 2016, 6). Locke's notable use of the word "trespass" suggests both a transgression of a law and an encroachment on what belongs properly to another. For Locke, such people are "unnatural" in the sense that they constitute a subpopulation of humanity lacking the moral compass offered by natural law. Between Locke's criminal particularism (only some) and Hobbes's universalism (we are all inclined), we can find a proto-sociological zone of probabilities (all of us might, but with different probabilities).

The preemptive managing and targeting of these probabilities for criminal disorder is the work of police power. It is a war for security that rests on a logic of risk. Police cannot be everywhere, so how should it assess the probability of crime across the various sectors of the populace, and how should it concentrate the powers of its vigilance?

The Hobbesian position, which presumes that we are all capable of joining this criminal faction when it serves our interests, represents the universalizing pincer of liberal security, explaining why the policing of society must be enacted as broadly as possible with the fewest possible exceptions. Police stories featuring the respectable man who is later discovered, in Rousseau's words, to be a "public enemy" who has "broken the social contract," clarify that we can never be sure where the border of society is actually located (Rousseau 1983, 32).

In the Lockean view, by contrast, it is relatively clear where one should patrol. This distinctive liberal tradition traces from Locke's own "Offender" through the French physiocrat François Quesnay, who, a century later, would name such unnatural criminals *hommes pervers*. Policing should be concentrated on certain known populations of people who habitually defy the market's natural laws, short-circuiting the exchange of property through their theft. The market's smooth functioning, therefore, will depend on a properly aimed and entirely vigilant regime of policing and incarceration.[16] Another century later the *homme pervers* would be updated again in Cesare Lombroso's sociology of "criminal man," one who was born ready to violate the law and whose physiognomy alerts us to this inward tendency (Lombroso 2006).[17] The target of policing in this tradition is the vagabond, the beggar, the masterless man, the Black, the Indian.

Although liberalism provided a regulatory framework for capital accumulation, its conception of property was not reducible to economic wealth. Rather, a broad conception of property/propriety provided the indication of a fully possessive individual—someone sovereign in their economic self-sufficiency, in their capacity for political self-government, and even in their sexual self-possession. It was this combination of "properties" that provided the broad foundation upon which a liberal society could charge police power with safeguarding the reproduction of capital accumulation. Foucault's famous analysis of the bourgeoisie's "possession" of their sexuality (Foucault 1990) should be read in relation to this expectation for propertied and proprietary membership in the liberal society. The bourgeois family was both an institution for the ownership and transmission of private wealth, and a kind of "container" within which the possession and control of sexuality could demonstrate one's liberal belonging. Women too could therefore ensoul the threat of the unpropertied criminal through sexual impropriety. Lombroso argued in his symmetrical investigation of "la donna delinquent," or the "criminal woman," that the prostitute was to the bourgeois wife what the male criminal was to her husband: a physiologically specifiable abnormal whose disordered passions threatened liberal stability (Lombroso and Ferrero 2004). Police power was therefore directed at the prostitute alongside Foucault's assortment of other nineteenth-century figures who jeopardized sexual propriety—the pervert, the masturbating child, the hysterical woman. These figures condensed power's various "lines of attack" to render sexuality a precious yet vulnerable thing that needed to be controlled or possessed (Foucault 1990, 146–49).

The Hobbesian and Lockean conceptions of criminality, though seemingly opposites, worked in tandem to produce liberal police power. The former authorized the universal license of police to protect the "law and order" of property even against those whom one would not normally distrust (figures resembling the unsuspected converso who destroys society from the inside), while the latter established permanent suspect populations whose entirely predictable delinquent proclivity could be specially policed. Adapting the older Iberian concept of race-as-defect, liberalism would signify with the concept of the "unpropertied" not simply the *inferior populations* lacking in property or propriety, but also the *dangerous classes* who menace and degrade it.

Possessive Individualism and Plantocratic Colonial Racism

It was in the slavery-based Caribbean and North American settler colonies that the liberal war on property's enemies were first mapped systematically onto a racial capitalist color line. The colonial planation system was no holdover from premodern feudal agrarianism, but in fact one of capitalism's originary regimes of accumulation.[18] Their spiraling circuits of sugar and tobacco production unambiguously enacted what Marx calls the general formula for capital (M-C-M'): money was converted into commodities and labor to produce something that got sold for more money. Capitalism's industrial "factory" in fact finds its etymology in the plantocracy's "factoryes:" the word was first used to name trading posts that served as human warehouses for enslaved Africans before they were shipped to the sugar plantations in the West Indies.[19] The plantations would also come to be called factories, here in their more modern sense as sites for a production process. Even if that process was preindustrial, still, as Sidney Mintz points out, it utilized a vast pool of laborers subjected to a regime of continuous disciplinary intensification that aimed, no less than the later industrial factory, to maximize the surplus portion of the value produced (Mintz 1986).[20] For nearly a century, as Peter Linebaugh and Marcus Rediker demonstrate, this body of coerced labor was obtained, not only from Africa, but also from British "vagabonds," Irish and others captured or "barbadoesed" in imperial wars, and enslaved peoples. Although early commercial planters across the Atlantic required this "mongrel" population, they also feared them as a "many-headed hydra" (Linebaugh and Rediker 2013, 1–7). By the late seventeenth century, however, in response to dangerous alliances forged among the unpropertied during such colonial labor revolts as Bacon's Rebellion in the Virginia colony, the planter class began adapting the Iberian logic of color-as-race to the distinctly liberal political and juridical needs of the North Atlantic European colonies.[21]

At this threshold, possessive individualism first became a means of mapping the sacred boundary of liberal society onto the color line. What Cheryl Harris calls the legal phenomenon of "whiteness as property" (Harris 1993), and what George Lipsitz has relatedly called the "possessive investment in whiteness" (Lipsitz 2006), represents a complex encoding of "color" as a racial matrix through which the early liberal principle of self-ownership could be marked in relation to its antithesis.[22] Whiteness came to signify for North American settlers the ontological ground of property-in-oneself, paradigmatically understood as a state of owning one's own whiteness. Yet that possession bore a circular logic since whiteness itself served as the master signifier and marker of the *very capacity* for self-ownership. According to this tautology of possessive racial liberalism, one bears the social capacities of the possessive individual because one is white, yet one can own one's whiteness only because one is a possessive individual. Whiteness thereby becomes the "common property" of the propertied, that which is *proprietary* to them. Through a reworking of the Iberian concept of race-as-defect, meanwhile, "color" came to signal the no less circular binary opposite of whiteness-as-property. Color marked a defect in possessive capacity that framed and rationalized the conditions of enslavement and social death. Through this liberalization of the Iberian discourse of *raza*, the forcible expropriation of enslaved African labor and violent dispossession of Indigenous people's land could be articulated to a plantocratic color line that demarcated the liberal colonial society in need of protection from those whose expropriation was no crime. The color line distinguished the colonial society of possessive individuals from a population ontologized as the *absence* or voiding of property-in-oneself.

It is a mistake, however, to think that racial liberalism produces Blackness as pure absence. Saidiya Hartman, in a painfully careful reading of *State of Missouri v. Celia, a Slave*—an 1855 legal case in which a slave woman was repeatedly raped by her owner until she at last defended herself by killing him—observes the apparent paradox that Celia "could neither give nor refuse (sexual) consent, nor offer reasonable resistance," yet when it came to killing her owner, her personal will suddenly became worthy of acknowledging: Celia became a legal person just long enough to be subject to criminal prosecution as a murderer (Hartman 1997, 82). Hartman explains this paradox through the legal presumption of what she calls "positing the black as a criminal," a strategy of power that acknowledged their personhood only at the "site on which the 'crimes' of the dominant class and of the state were externalized in the form of a threat" (82). The slave was thus always a special combination of two things: both a piece of property and a potentially dangerous criminal. Stephen Best has characterized this situation as the legal condition of "the slave's two bodies" (Best 2004, 5–9). Like the slave in the Spanish colony who had both caste (inferior standing) and race (a characteristic of threat), so was the slave of British colonial America politically doubled. On the one hand, they constituted a body that, when docile, was legally reduced to chattel and disallowed any expression of will other than the master's. But when resistive—when construable as expressing a will hostile to the masters—the enslaved person reverted to a negative form of legal personhood as the lawless enemy who endangers the possessive individual. It is worth noting here that the question of will, intention, and desire at the crux of this legal moment of criminality, which Best would associate with the "second body" of the slave, could more vividly be characterized as the positing of a *criminal soul* inhabiting the body that belongs properly to someone else (the master). This felonious spiritual double of the slave was a prime enemy of plantocratic liberal society: the figure who most emphatically assaulted its founding principle of property through the paradigmatic act of criminal self-theft or demonic self-possession.

I will come back to this trope of demonic possession later in this chapter as I explore racial liberalism's relation to political threat. But for now, I simply want to stress that liberal anti-Blackness was anchored in this legal standing of the enslaved African as a paradoxical combination of chattel property with a fundamental moral threat to property. It is at this site of suspicion that we need to locate the slave as the target of the earliest iterations of modern police power: the colonial slave patrol, whose policing power shored up a color line designed to fabricate the well-ordered plantocratic liberal society, protect its citizens, and subject its slaves. This history provides the origins of what Nikhil Singh has called the "whiteness of police" (Singh 2014), while also illuminating its historical persistence through the postbellum era, when the plantocratic positing of the slave's criminal soul was succeeded by a correlative metropolitan logic that Khalil Gibran Muhammad has called the sociological "condemnation of blackness." Policing would remain "white" after the US Civil War in relation to this transfiguration of Blackness into a sign of statistically probable criminality (Muhammad 2019).[23]

In the plantation colonies, using police to constitute the liberal border between freedom and chattel slavery *as a color line* diminished the risk of a grand coalition of the unpropertied (a fear correlative to Spain's *gran complicidad*). In colonies such as Virginia and Carolina it offered poor Europeans a limited partnership in whiteness as property/propriety with threshold social standing.[24] Whiteness, as Cheryl Harris puts it, became "a shield against slavery and the color line, for poor whites" (Harris 1993, 1720–21). This granting of whiteness to the minimally propertied, however, also inflicted a certain precarity because their proximity to the color line as barely-white left their dubious propertied status highly vulnerable to revocation. They too became objects of racial suspicion since preserving the frontier of whiteness required surveillance for signs of sympathy, fraternization, or even alliance with those on its far side.[25] In effect, the color line projected a racial borderland throughout which heightened vigilance and suspicion was required. Nevertheless, the very fact that both the liberalization of the Iberian category of race and the revised liberal police function applied to it were reactive processes—defensive maneuvers of power designed to anticipate not just crime but equally the political threat of colonial and slave rebellion—already points toward a second enemy of liberal society that featured its own complex genealogy.

Enemy Two: The Extremist Threat of the Improper

Liberal police power also addressed threat from a second direction, not just from the unpropertied but from the fanatically improper: the principled and politicized enemies of property. As noted in the preceding chapter, sixteenth-century Westphalian reason had already established intelligence agencies to target the seditious ideas and opinions that endangered the state. Some two centuries later, liberalism similarly sought to police ideas, opinions, and beliefs, but by asking a slightly different question: not whose opinions threaten the state, but rather whose ideas endanger the civil society, liberal freedom, and private property that the state had been designed to protect in the first place?

In Locke's oeuvre, the earliest origins of this politicized enemy appear not in the *Second Treatise*, but instead in his *Letter Concerning Toleration*, where he argues that differences in religious opinions or beliefs do not constitute a sufficient reason to exclude someone from civil life. Locke's letter is widely celebrated as a step forward toward the tolerant society promised by liberalism, but it too produced sacred boundaries beyond which, in his view, toleration would only lead to its opposite. The concept of society in the *Letter* actually bears a double meaning since Locke is adjudicating the proper (normative) relationship between two kinds of society: the civil and the religious.[26] Civil society, as we saw in the *Second Treatise*, emerges when our bodily needs, which we satisfy with the property we create through labor, find protection through a social contract leading to civil government. In the *Letter*, Locke stresses that such civil interests involve "Life, Liberty, Health," as well the "Possession of outward things" (Locke 2016, 128). The anticipated enemy of civil society is therefore the one we have already considered: the person who fails to ensoul a possessive individual.

The *Letter*, however, is primarily interested in something else: what we might call the possession of *inward things*. Foremost among all one's inward possessions is one's soul or eternal life. Accompanying it are the spiritual things that the soul possesses, namely its dispensations toward salvation or the contents of its conscience. This could be called Locke's *inward*, as opposed to his *outward*, account of the possessive individual. In step with this inwardly possessive individual, Locke also proposes an inward sort of society. For Locke, a religious society (as opposed to a civil one) is called a "church." A church is a society because (like civil society) it represents a voluntary association of possessive individuals "membering" together the like-minded persons gathered for worship according to their shared beliefs about how to save their souls. Churches are therefore based upon what Locke repeatedly calls common "opinions" or "beliefs" about what makes for *spiritual security*.

Locke is often presented as the philosopher who made religion into a private matter, but he argues for toleration not because civil affairs are public and religious ones private. Rather, the governance of civil and religious affairs should be separated so they can remain mutually independent. The magistrate who administers civil society should not meddle with people's religious decisions or practices just as people's religious views and lives should never undermine the magistrate's authority over civil matters. Since both domains involve societies (voluntary associations of individuals), they can both be considered public spaces.[27] Locke argues that because one finds such "variety and contradiction in the opinions in religion" (Locke 2016, 130) and therefore such disagreement about the path to salvation, freedom is even more crucial for inward than for civil life: people must not be forced into worship in hiding, nor in professing what they do not believe, because

> Neither the profession of any articles of faith, nor the conformity to any outward form of worship (as has been already said), can be available to the salvation of souls, unless the truth of the one and the acceptableness of the other unto God be thoroughly believed by those that so profess and practise. But penalties are no way capable to produce such belief. It is only light and evidence that can work a change in men's opinions; which light can in no way proceed from corporal sufferings or other penalties. (Locke 2016, 129–30)

Locke establishes here a parallel norm for inwardly possessive individuals, a principle of *free exchange* of religious professions that is analogous to the exchange of outward property in civil society. We might call this the commerce of (religious) ideas. Religions must be publicly confessed in order to produce what in liberal theory will eventually become known as the "marketplace of ideas."[28] Liberal society enforces not only a free exchange of goods whose truth-speaking about value will increase the common wealth, but also a free exchange of "opinions" that will yield another veridiction, here about the religious beliefs whose demonstrated spiritual value will ultimately save more souls.[29]

One critical asymmetry exists, however, between Locke's visions of commerce in outward property and in religious opinions (inward properties): certain religious views must not be tolerated because they intrinsically challenge the independence of inward and outward commerce. These are opinions or beliefs that, in Locke's view, "break the publick Peace of Societies," disrupting outward commerce by reviving a threat of civil war (Locke 2016, 150). It is this anomaly, as we shall see, that leads the regulation of opinion—and the boundary setting for toleration—to emerge as such a vital political objective for racial capitalism's liberal mode of regulation.

What ideas count as such a breaking of the public peace? Locke offers a list and, not surprisingly, the principle that "society must be defended" organizes its rationale. First, he explains, "No Opinions contrary to human Society, or to those moral Rules which are necessary to the preservation of Civil Society." All "Doctrines of Religion" that "manifestly undermine the Foundations of Society" must not be tolerated (Locke 2016, 157). Presumably ideas that promote violence, insurrection, or seizure of property in any sense would fall into such a category. Locke then turns to a "more secret Evil, but more dangerous to the Commonwealth," namely dissembling variations of the same sorts of opinions. These situations occur where members of a sect arrogate to themselves "some peculiar Prerogative, covered over with a specious shew of deceitful words, but in effect opposite to the Civil Right of the Community" (Locke 2016, 157). Locke's tacit examples here are, in keeping with the prime enemy of "reason of state," English Catholics who assert that "*Faith is not be kept with Hereticks*" or that "Kings excommunicated forfeit their Crowns and Kingdoms" (Locke 2016, 157–58). Both assertions promise to betray one's fellow members of society, as well the government that was established to protect their property. It is not just the content of the ideas themselves that can prove antisocial, but also the way they are held: antisociality increases if one conceals these dangerous beliefs under a mask of ostensible sociability. Locke's third category consists in churches that expect their members to "*ipso facto* deliver themselves up to the Protection and Service of another Prince," since this expects a magistrate to "suffer his own People to be listed, as it were, for Souldiers against his own Government" (Locke 2016, 158). As I observed in the preceding chapter, Locke offers up the "Mahometan" as the paradigmatic religious believer who makes inappropriate political claims. Locke also offers another forbidden opinion ensouled in the atheist, someone who cannot be trusted at all since "Promises, Covenants, and Oaths, which are the Bonds of Humane Society, can have no hold upon an Atheist" (Locke 2016, 159).

What is noteworthy about Locke's list of insufferables is that, even though it includes paradigmatic examples of those whose antisocial opinions make them intolerable (Catholics, Muslims, and atheists), ultimately the limits of toleration must be defined abstractly as the set of all inward opinions or doctrines that make improper religious claims to authority over civil society. In theory a Catholic willing to "keep faith" with heretics, or a Muslim who repudiates loyalty to the Turkish sultan, could be tolerated. What ultimately matters is whether their opinions "tend to establish Domination over others, or Civil Impunity to the Church in which they are taught" (Locke 2016, 159).

Zealotry and Fanaticism: From Religious to Political Extremism

Locke has a special name for this abstractly defined set of all people (of any religion or irreligion) who hold such uncivil opinions: they are "zealots," people who "condemn all things that are not of their mode" to the point of inflicting injury on civil society (Locke 2016, 140). A zealot is more than someone with excessive "zeal" or enthusiasm for their own opinions. The word derives from the Greek word *zelotes*, which Jerome's Vulgate Bible applies in its Latin form as an epithet to the apostle Simon the Zealot, a follower of Jesus whose Jewish sect advocated violent resistance to Roman rule.[30] A zealot is therefore someone who, because of their religious opinions, incites rebellion against the civil government. Locke considers zealotry to be insincere since it attacks the civil life of the very people whose spiritual life it claims to love (Locke 2016, 140).

If we keep in mind Locke's account of government as a product of the social contract, zealots are enemies of society as well as the state. Their actions endanger other people's property, whether their civil property (because zealots threaten the state that exists to protect that property) or their inward property (since zealots will threaten one's soul in the name of saving it). Zealots reject the civil marketplace of formalized competition among religious ideas in favor of an unrestrained civil war of religious ideas that spills into violence. In a liberal frame, therefore, the zealot is a politicized *homme pervers*. Like the unpropertied who are inclined to criminality, so are Catholics, Mahometans, and even atheists predisposed toward zealotry: they too harbor disordered passions that encourage violation of the liberal rules of sociality. That they might also be dissimulators who merely feign propriety further heightens the challenge of securing against their threat. The abstraction of the zealot must never be *reduced* to the concrete of the Catholic or the atheist. To do so is to enact the very intolerance that liberalism rejects. But one should certainly *suspect* Catholics, Muslims, or atheists given the probability that they are zealots.

Zealotry was Locke's personally preferred term, but more widely used in the following centuries was *fanaticism*. The derogatory concept of the "fanatic," as Arturo Toscano has noted, emerged alongside the Protestant Reformation to describe those who challenged the state's confessional authority over religion (Toscano 2017). In the preliberal era, the fanatic therefore already ensouled a seditious enemy of Westphalian reason of state. The English word "fanatic" entered usage in the seventeenth century as a term for "excessive and mistaken enthusiasm, esp. in religious matters," but in the second half of the century, during the English Civil War, it became increasingly "applied to nonconformists [outside the Church of England] as a hostile epithet," much like the word "Puritan" had before it.[31] This philological detail reveals something important about how the problem of dangerous *religious* ideas would be reshaped between the late sixteenth and late seventeenth centuries into a problem of dangerous *political* ideas.

In chapter 3 I described how "reason of state" sorted the realm's population along a curve that placed the loyal and trustworthy (Anglican) middle between two religious extremes: the Catholic and the Puritan factions, both predisposed to seditious views. We might call this Puritan-Anglican-Catholic sequence, with increasingly probable traitors at both ends, the Westphalian English state's *political spectrum of religion*. Beginning with Locke's *Letter Concerning Toleration*, this spectrum would undergo a process of gradual secularization through a series of liberal substitutions. Over the course of the late seventeenth and eighteenth centuries, the Westphalian political spectrum of religions would become the template for the *ideological spectrum of modern politics*. Locke's letter itself takes the first step by substituting liberal society itself (the civil society of toleration) at its center in lieu of the Anglican church and state. Although his catalog of the zealous groups who must be excluded from the sphere of toleration includes only churches, and although he encourages toleration only for religious associations, Locke's criteria for distinguishing the tolerable from the intolerable could as easily be applied to associations sharing political opinions. His questions need only be slightly reframed: Are their *political* opinions so zealous as to threaten the authority of the magistrate and thereby the "publick peace"?

In his study of the modern concept of fanaticism, Zachary Goldsmith characterizes this period between the late seventeenth century and the French Revolution as a critical *Sattelzeit*, or transition time, during which the secular political meaning of the fanatic was consolidated. It is in this period, he explains, that "the concept of fanaticism undergoes a disinvestment of much of its religious meaning and is reinvested with political meaning and understood in a new political fashion" (Goldsmith 2019, 83). The fanatic, in short, became a figure of liberal political theology. Following Locke's substitution at the spectrum's center, new ones would now occur at its two extremes. At the "right" end of the new scale, the Papist/Mahometan would be superseded by the abstracted figure of the "reactionary," a conservative extremist zealously seeking to undo liberalism's progress toward freedom. The word "reactionary" appeared in the English language in 1799, borrowed from a French cognate (*réactionnaire*) used to describe the French Revolution's illiberal enemies who sought "a reversion to a former state of affairs."[32] The reactionary classifies and ensouls the illiberal who values freedom not at all. Though Catholics and other religious groups were often still so positioned, they now were so in an overtly political idiom. The Catholic who blindly obeys the pope or a foreign Catholic king, the Jew who clings to a theocratic religion, the Muslim who obeys the sultan of the Ottomans—these are people whose *political* opinions (albeit guided by their religion) seek historical reversion to a past that, by its very nature, rejects the regulatory ideal of a liberal exchange of political ideas.[33] The reactionary however, need not be religious. Such a person could, for example, believe in absolutist monarchy and reject civil society as the embodiment of popular sovereignty.

On the "left," meanwhile, the excessively reformist Puritan would be reformulated as the radical or extreme universalist, a fanatic who believes in freedom too much and too abstractly. Unlike the reactionary who rejects liberty, the fanatic threatens civil society through an excessive and improper commitment to freedom so over-universalizing that it short-circuits the liberal rules of engagement. Such "radicals," in digging for the root of the problem, threaten to uproot civil society altogether, often by pursuing freedom for precisely those unpropertied subjects who lack a proper capacity.[34] In addition to pursuing such extreme ends, the fanatic might also advocate the use of extreme means, abandoning the marketplace of rationally competing ideas to wage an unlimited war of propaganda and civil violence.[35]

From Church to Party

As a political theological figure for the enemy of possessive individualism, the propagandizing fanatic evoked illiberal threats of invisible parties and secret societies. I noted earlier how Locke used the word "church" to describe voluntary associations formed around shared religious belief. About a century later, the word "party" would come to signify its secular analog: a voluntary association based upon shared political beliefs. In the process, the word "party" began shedding negative associations that had once made it synonymous with "faction" and "sect," Westphalian words for dangerous fractions of the population.[36] Edmund Burke, the reputed conservative writer, thinker, and politician, was among the first to formulate this positive sense of "party," which he defined as "a body of men united, for promoting by their joint endeavors the national interest, upon some particular principle in which they are all agreed" (Burke 1999b, 146). Himself a Whig Member of Parliament, Burke defended political parties as positive institutions so long as their goals were transparent and their methods to achieve them just. In Burke's view, a multiplicity of parties could offset the threat of any one faction improperly seizing power.[37] As this view spread, "parties" became for liberalism what the "balance of power" was to the Westphalian "system of states": a key tool for organizing potentially clashing forces into a stable arrangement.[38] This is the political technology we have come to know as liberal democracy, whereby parties, competing in a constitutionally mandated electoral process, permit possessive individuals to exercise their political opinions (Parekh 1992).[39] What the party system of liberal democracy encourages above all is not an imperative to think from the universal viewpoint of society as such (parties may remain sectional in their interests), but rather an imperative to pacify the antagonisms that result from differences of opinion. A party system sublimates antagonisms by routing them through a temporally delimited rivalry during an electoral campaign for control of government.[40] The electoral campaign in fact becomes the pacified liberal democratic alternative to the military campaign. Liberal democracy is also liberal insofar as it subjects political conduct to the promise of *market veridiction in the realm of political ideas* by means of "fair competition" among political platforms and nominated magistrates. Like the market in goods, party-based electoral democracy is driven by a logic of interests, with the best outcome in governance assured through the "invisible hand" of the electoral process.[41]

Liberal democracy, however, sometimes retained the negative connotation of *party* or *faction* to indict fanatical organizations that opposed society's common interests by organizing secretly and using illiberal means to achieve their ends. Burke's attacks on the Jacobin "party" in his 1790 polemic *Reflections on the Revolution in France* was critical to this political turn. Notwithstanding his fame as the father of modern conservatism, Burke was a self-understood liberal, a Whig, whose antipathy toward even the earliest phases of the French Revolution derived not from its espousal of liberty per se, but rather from what he decried as liberty's "fanatical" universalization. To us, the 1789 Declaration of the Rights of Man and Citizen may appear a benign declaration of core liberal principles, describing the "goal of any political association" to be the "conservation of the nature and imprescriptible rights of man. These rights are liberty, property, security, and resistance to oppression."[42] Yet the Declaration's failure to specify limits on which men were entitled to this guarantee of liberty signaled for Burke its fanaticism. As he famously asks near the opening of the

Reflections, "Is it because liberty in the abstract may be classed amongst the blessings of mankind, that I am seriously to felicitate a madman who has escaped from the protecting restraint and wholesome darkness of his cell on his restoration to the enjoyment of light and liberty? Am I to congratulate a highwayman and murderer who has broke prison upon the recovery of his natural rights?" (Burke 2014, 8). Burke here figures the dangerous, abnormal man in order to advance the argument that liberal society's borders must be policed in liberty's defense. Nothing more grievously threatens liberty than granting it to such a dangerous class of men: the mad, the criminal, the murderous. Any fanatic who would celebrate their freedom proves himself to be equally mad or criminal, recklessly willing to dissolve the sacred realm of liberal society back into its profane opposite.

Burke's rhetorical question transfers the necessary application of police power from ordinary criminals and madmen to political revolutionaries. His analogy suggests that those who extend freedom beyond its proper limits ensoul a criminal ideological zealotry that terrorizes civil society no less than the highwayman. For Burke, at his historical moment, France's riotous Jacobin revolutionaries were actively menacing Great Britain's carefully circumscribed liberal democratic order, its constitutionally framed society of possessive individuals, attentive to the proper limits of freedom and committed to the electoral pacification of conflicts. By 1796, in the wake of the Jacobin Reign of Terror, Burke would pronounce his prophecies in *Reflections* to have shown their veracity. The French revolutionary government had predictably devolved into a violently radical pseudo-republic capable of murdering the king while enfranchising the sansculottes, the "breechless" commoners or workers of Paris.[43] The Jacobins had roused the unpropertied masses not only to defeat France's traditional ruling classes, but also, through a *levée en masse* (universal conscription of young males), to crush all the professional armies of Europe. In his "Letters on a Regicide Peace," which fiercely opposed the British government's peace overtures toward the French Jacobins, Burke transformed ordinary Lockean security (the perpetual war against civil society's criminal enemies) into a multicontinental holy war against the universal Jacobin threat to proper and propertied liberalism. Jacobins were a party, but not in the good sense. They met in Masonic "secret societies." They formed "cabals" (a word drawn from the Jewish tradition of kabbalah, indicating secret knowledge). They pretended to be liberal, but their multipronged conspiracy against the society, church, and state of the ancien régime had recklessly shattered any hope for proper French freedom. These Jacobins had become for Burke what Arturo Toscano characterizes as "the very archetype of the modern fanatic: a reckless innovator 'possessed with a spirit of proselytism in the most fanatical degree'; zealously attacking religion 'in the spirit of a monk'; laying waste to custom, property and manners" (Toscano 2017, xiii). Jacobins were like Locke's Catholics in that their aims were "covered over with a specious shew of deceitful words" (Locke 2016, 157), but also like his atheists insofar as they were a godless party whose words could not be trusted. Neither transparently aiming for the common good nor playing by the rules of the marketplace of ideas, Jacobins for Burke epitomized the worst sense of "party," a secret faction bent on driving the "swinish multitude" toward revolution (Burke 2014, 81).

For at least two centuries after 1789, revolution would constitute a permanent image of the political threat to liberal democracy. Although in the proverbial last instance, this menace would attach to concrete political upheavals— the French Revolution, the Haitian Revolution, the revolutions of 1848, the Russian and Chinese Revolutions—to focus too narrowly on such specific uprisings is to miss, in Geoff Mann's apt words, how the "anxious memory" and the threat of revolution as a "popular rejection of the existing order" would matter politically, "even when the streets are quiet and all is calm" (Mann 2017, 84). Liberal police power would follow Burke's lead, extending its domain from managing ordinary criminality to countering this enduring political peril of radical upheaval. When it came to this danger, liberalism suddenly stopped worrying about whether one was governing too much (laissez-faire), always asking instead if one was governing too little (proving soft on revolutionary parties). This kind of police power would sometimes become known in the nineteenth century as the "political police."[44]

French Jacobins, Black Jacobins: The Possessive Power of Revolutionary Slaves

The political police differed from its ordinary counterpart in that it addressed a collective and arguably more powerful kind of threat. Consider Burke's fears about what made revolutionary France so immensely powerful on the European battlefield: neither that nation's large size nor its great population or vast resources. These were conventional and familiar forces of the state that Westphalian reason had already learned to balance out through myriad techniques of international alliance and policy. Rather, what made revolutionary France formidable was Jacobin ideology's uncanny ability to possess the entire social bodies of nations and infuse them with a demonic strength on every battlefield. In Burke's hyperbolic prose, Jacobinism represented a spectral criminality, devouring and destroying a nation's liberal spirit, which it then replaced with its own fanatical energies. This is the inner possessive individual's dark counterpart:

> It is the [Jacobin] faction that makes them truly dreadful. The faction is the evil spirit that possesses the body of France; that informs it as a soul; that stamps upon it's ambition, and upon all it's pursuits, a characteristic mark, which strongly distinguishes them from the same general passions, and the same general views, in other men and in other communities. It is that spirit which inspires into them a new, a pernicious, and desolating activity. Constituted as France was ten years ago, it was not in that France to shake, to shatter, and to overwhelm Europe in the manner that we behold. (Burke 1999a, 154–55)

The military campaign Burke now considered necessary was in effect an *exorcism*, an always-already belated war waged against the demonic possession of a society of possessive individuals. Better to have anticipated and thwarted this (dis)possession before such a war became necessary. Better to have policed before the crime was committed. Such was the rhetorical aim of Burke's *Reflections*, to alert his readers to the dangers posed by certain English political societies before their foolish sympathy for the Jacobin regime could seduce Britain into becoming similarly possessed (Burke 2014, 4–5).

The "characteristic mark" that is "stamped" upon Jacobin France's ambitions, as a sign of its dangerousness, would seem akin to a racial marking except for the fact that it is stamped on the soul rather than the body. But ensoulment, as I have argued throughout this book, always proceeds through a suspicious inspection of the body. How might the "body" of a European nation like France look different when possessed by Jacobinism? One answer to this question found expression in a caricature of the Jacobin terror etched by the political cartoonist Richard Newton (see figure 4.1). Is this an image of revolutionary France? Yes and no. In a brief analysis, Raphael Hörmann has argued that the "s" missing from the French word *sans* (without) in the cartoon's title, "A Real San-Culotte," overtly connected it to the wealthy French slave colony of Saint-Domingue, already one year along its path to becoming the independent nation of Haiti. In Hörmann's reading, this gothic image participated in the rise of the "Black Jacobin" as a "specter of the revolutionary Black Atlantic" that would haunt Western liberalism at the turn of the nineteenth century (Hörmann 2017, 29–30). It visualizes the same animating "evil spirit" of the Jacobin faction that Burke was urging his readers to exorcise from the body politic. What historical context accounts for this strange split image, half French, half Haitian?

FIGURE 4.1. "A Real San-Culotte!!," London, 1792. Hand-colored etching by Richard Newton. British Museum, 1948.0214.350.

Although Haiti would not achieve independence for another twelve years, by 1792 (the year of the sketch), the former slave and future governor of a free Saint-Domingue, Toussaint L'Ouverture, had already encouraged revolt among those enslaved, seizing an opportunity opened by the colony's conflicting factional responses to the revolution: royalist planters versus republicans, another faction of white planters seeking independence from France along US lines, free *gens de couleur* (mulattos) seeking revolutionary French citizenship, as well as Spanish and British rival powers exploiting the vulnerabilities of French internal divisions. As the colony degenerated into factional and international warfare, the embattled Jacobin governor of Saint-Domingue, Léger-Félicité Sonthonax, desperately moved to unilaterally emancipate all slaves willing to support his military defense of French revolutionary rule. This emancipation proclamation of 1793 (seventy years earlier than Lincoln's) persuaded L'Ouverture and his army of the formerly enslaved to join forces with Sonthonax, quickly shifting the tide against the royalist planters and toward a Black-Jacobin entente.

This led to an admittedly brief ideological and military alliance that would horrify moderate liberals like Burke, not to mention the plantocratic liberal elites in other European colonies.[45] Seeking official approval in France for his proclamation, Sonthonax sent three pro-emancipationist delegates to represent Saint-Domingue in the French revolutionary assembly. They arrived in Paris in 1794, at the revolutionary apex of the most radical wing of the Jacobins. According to C. L. R. James's classic account, when the three delegates arrived—one Black, one mulatto, and one white—Simon Camboulet, a Jacobin member of the assembly and nephew of the famous anticolonial historian Guillaume Reynal, rose and spoke: "Since *1789* the aristocracy of birth and the aristocracy of religion have been destroyed; but the aristocracy of the skin still remains. That too is now at its last gasp, and equality has been consecrated. A black man, a yellow man, are about to join this Convention in the name of the free citizens of San Domingo" (James 1989, 139–40).

Bellay, the Black delegate from Saint-Domingue, reportedly delivered a fiery speech the next day pledging support for the revolution and calling for the abolition of slavery. Another delegate rose to motion that abolition be approved without debate: "When drawing up the constitution of the French people we paid not attention to the unhappy Negroes. Posterity will bear us a great reproach for that. Let us repair that wrong—let us proclaim the Liberty of the Negroes. Mr. President, do not suffer the Convention to dishonor itself by a discussion" (James 1989, 139–40). This earliest of all European acts to abolish slavery apparently passed by acclamation and with great applause.

When word reached Haiti, it kindled a general uprising that ended slavery in the colony once and for all. It is this historical conjuncture that sits at the heart of James's argument about the world historical importance of the "Black Jacobins." Though the window of solidarity lasted only a few years before the French Revolution took its Thermidorian reactionary turn, Haiti's revolutionaries liberated themselves in alliance with radical Jacobins whom they in turn had radicalized by appealing for an act of revolutionary abolition that exceeded all expectations of the Declaration of Rights of Man and Citizen.

Let us return then to Newton's caricature of the "Real San-Culotte," which is simultaneously an image of the French and the Haitian Revolutions, combining them in order to express a racial panic regarding this emergent Black Jacobin conjuncture. What exactly does it reveal about the work of racial ensoulment in the racial liberal age of revolutionary threat? Hörmann offers one answer through his observation that, in the rhetoric of split figures like this caricature, "one half usually reveals the true essence of the other" (Hörmann 2017, 31). The *real* sansculotte is therefore exposed as a marauding slave. His French workingman's liberty cap is shown to be devil horns. The tools on his belt, already with a dripping knife, transform into the fierce weaponry of the African spear. The boot that stands upon the blood-red earth of France becomes a cloven hoof that strides upon America (Saint-Domingue). The smile gives way to the snaked tongue and noxious fumes that emanate from the dark mouth. In all these ways, the sansculotte is revealed to be what Hörmann calls a "menacing black figure, half devil, half African rebel" (Hörmann 2017, 31). In this reading, the white skin of the sansculotte fraudulently disguises a soul that the cartoonist rhetorically uncloaks. Peeling away the white skin, the cartoon shows us the underlying Blackness that would have properly marked what is invisibly layered below. So exposed, the caricature ensouls the sansculotte in such a way as to produce the combined "anti-ness" of both anti-Blackness and counterrevolution. In Newton's cartoon, Blackness constitutes not an inferior body type but an exteriorizing metaphor for a diabolical spirit of revolution. In pastoral terms, it characterizes the wolfishness of the predator who has disguised himself in sheep's clothing.

Hörmann's interpretation of the sketch, however, could be complemented by another that foregrounds not just the two half-images, but also the line that cleaves them. When so read, this caricature appears to figure the color line itself, the racial border that produces the binary of white and black. So read, the image finds a precedent in the trope of the unnaturally hybrid steed Alboraique, whose combined animal and human features indexed the converso threat in early modern Spain. In the image, what I am calling the color line appears as a vertical stripe that, standing directly over England, extends farther down by a descending phallic devil-tail that is broken by the surface of the ocean. This broken tail, which visually fissures the stripe, nonetheless threatens to pierce the isle of England, much like the sansculotte's dripping dagger. The phallic tail is decisively dark in tone, yet it is also noticeably displaced toward the white side of the image. It signifies the color line's confounding and fracturing, illustrative of an ominous trespass by Blackness onto the white side of the image.

From the viewpoint of this fissured color line, the sansculotte threatens not because he is really a Black devil in disguise, but because through his revolutionary action he is shattering the line that *distinguishes* him from his Black counterpart. The Black devil, meanwhile, through his diabolical revolt, also challenges racial distinction by claiming a liberty that should be reserved for the white form. The two half figures, in other words, imperil the color line through a joint revolutionary attack on the frontier it instantiates. On one side, a white personage proximate enough to the color line to lack all but the barest property and propriety, behaving as if he were Black; on the other a Black who arrogates to himself, not just the liberty, but also the police power that properly belongs to a white.

The powerful political charge of this split figure personifies the double-edged quality of what Susan Buck-Morss once called the "root metaphor of Western political philosophy," namely the image of the slave as an expression for "everything that was evil about power relations" (Buck-Morss 2000, 821). In her masterful reading of Hegel's political philosophy against the unacknowledged context of the Haitian revolution, she suggests that the slave figured as the "conceptual antithesis" of the Enlightenment's "highest and universal political value," the "freedom of man" (Buck-Morss 2000, 821). Indexing such classic statements as Jean-Jacques Rousseau's assertion in *The Social Contract* that "Man is born free and is everywhere in chains" (Rousseau 1983, 8), Buck-Morss suggests that Hegel was influenced by the symbolic use of the irons binding African slaves in the West Indies to express the "tyranny" of metropolitan France's ancien régime. The enlightenment allegory of enslavement also carried enormous implications flowing in the opposite political direction: if one condemns monarchy *because* it is slavery, then how can one disavow the political evil of actual chattel slavery without falling into blatant hypocrisy? Given this fundamental allegory, does not a revolt against slavery necessarily become the archetypical revolutionary act of a people's self-liberation?

For Burke and his fellow racial liberals, this revolutionary claim on "freedom" expressed the reckless love of liberty in the abstract, precisely what he so feared in the Jacobin spirit: political passion for the self-liberation of the enslaved was nothing less than extolling the criminal freedom of the high-wayman or the murderer. This was no metaphor for Burke, but something he meant quite literally. French Jacobinism, which Burke describes elsewhere as a "revolt of the enterprising talents of a country against its property" and a movement that "does not make confiscations for crimes, but makes crimes for confiscations," had finally encouraged the African "property" of the planters to kill their owners (Burke 2014, 309). In places like France and Haiti, society had abandoned security to become "more like a den of outlaws upon a doubtful frontier; a lewd tavern for the revels and debauches of banditti, assassins, bravos, smugglers, and their more desperate paramours . . . This system of manners in it-self is at war with all orderly and moral society, and is in its neighborhood unsafe" (Burke 2014, 315). Burke's "doubtful frontier" echoes the vertical line that sepa-rates the French sansculotte from the Black "San Culotte" in the caricature, while the "den of outlaws" or "tavern" echoes as a spatial metaphor the image of France's body as an interior space corrupted by an evil Jacobin spirit. Both images, for what it is worth, are to be found in his 1796 "Letters on a Regicide Peace."

By that year, not only had Toussaint L'Ouverture's army overthrown slavery in Saint-Domingue, but it had also soundly bloodied and defeated a British force sent to invade the French colony. Arguing against a proposed peace ne-gotiation with the revolutionary French government, Burke sketches a com-pletely imaginary scene whose crowning horror becomes the perversion of justice at the hands of violent Black Jacobins. How would his reader feel, he asks, had *their* British monarch (and not the French) been murdered by revo-lutionaries, had *they* (and not French royalists) been driven into exile, and had neighboring nations approved their extradition to face certain execution at the hands of the revolutionaries? Even as he paints this picture, Burke perceptibly shifts the scene of the fantasized extradition from an imaginary revolution-ary England to bloody Saint-Domingue, substituting for the French Jacobins their Haitian counterparts: "How must we feel, if the pride and flower of the English Nobility and Gentry, who might escape the pestilential clime, and the devouring sword, should, if taken prisoners, be delivered over as rebel subjects, to be condemned as rebels, as traitors, as the vilest of all criminals, by tribunals formed of Maroon negro slaves, covered over with the blood of their masters, who were made free and organized into judges, for their robberies and mur-ders?" (Burke 1868, 222).

The answer Burke expects to his question—How must we feel?—is evi-dently a sense of racial panic produced through a synthesis of gothic horror with political terror. Horror, that gothic feeling emerging culturally at around this time, concerns the uncanniness of entering the darks spaces that invert

Enlightenment values, in this case the topsy-turvy discharge of juridical reason at the dark hands of bloody Maroon slaves. Meanwhile, terror, another emergent political concept in the eighteenth century, entwined several different associations, as Ronald Schechter has shown, that began with the sublime power of kings to overawe their political enemies, a power now in the filthy possession of the swinish multitude in France and, worse yet, among ex-slaves in the colony (Schechter 2018).[46] In this last tropological turn, we can view the birth of liberal racial panic through this fusing of gothic horror and revolutionary terror; it is the invention of a new political danger that would invest anti-Blackness with a statist project of counterrevolutionary security.

America's Black Jacobins

In the United States, home-grown versions of this trope of the Black Jacobin menace would circulate after each of the nineteenth century's major slave revolts. Cast as a revolutionary spirit bent on overthrowing not just slavery but the color line that produces racial difference, the Black Jacobin appeared as the figure that is born whenever the dangerous soul of the revolutionary takes possession of the slave's body. The earliest case of Black Jacobin panic in the United States was nearly simultaneous with Haitian emancipation: in 1798, at a moment of rising anxiety among the Federalist faction about pro-French conspiracies in America, a prominent Northern minister claimed to have discovered a letter from an Illuminati "mother agency in France with local agencies in Virginia, St. Domingo, and New York City," which (as he explained in his public sermon) revealed "preparations for a French invasion of America with armies of blacks from St. Domingo" (Tise 1990, 200). It was Northern ministers like these who initially emphasized the Jacobin element. Their Burkean indictment of the French Revolution as the American Revolution's fanatical and atheistic double, and as the source of ongoing insurrection, disorder, and threat to the stability of American liberal society, became, according to Larry E. Tise (1990), the place where coherent proslavery political arguments would first find expression in the United States. Federalist ministers would develop a Burkean-style counterrevolutionary ideology aimed at the dangers of Jacobinism that, over time, would be adopted by Southern planters and politically fused with more conventional fears of "servile revolt" into the expectation of a Black Jacobin revolutionary threat. After all, the inspiration of Haiti was felt everywhere in the Americas. As Laurent Dubois observes: "Within one month after the 1791 uprising, slaves in Jamaica were singing songs about it," and within a few years masters "from Virginia to Louisiana to Cub and Brazil were complaining of a new 'insolence' on the part of their slaves, which they often attributed to aware-ness of the successful black revolution" (Dubois 2005, 304).

One early southern articulation of Jacobinism with slave revolt occurred in 1800 when Gabriel Prosser, an enslaved man who, inspired both by the emancipation of Saint-Domingue and by the French National Council's of-ficial abolition of slavery (six years earlier), plotted a revolt of the enslaved in Richmond, Virginia. Prosser had hoped that his insurrection would be joined by Virginia's Jacobin-inspired artisan clubs to form a united cross-racial up-rising of unpropertied workers ready to advance a revolutionary democracy (Egerton 2000, 8). The clubs did not join, and Gabriel Prosser's plan to abduct the governor of Virginia failed, yet the event added credibility to the idea that revolutionary ideology and revolts of the enslaved went hand in hand.

Nineteen years later, the language of Black Jacobin threat reappeared on an even larger scale in the revolt attempted by Denmark Vesey, an ex-slave living as a free man in Charleston, South Carolina. Vesey, who had briefly worked in his youth in Saint-Domingue and spoke French, approached not only Charles-ton's slaves but also "French slaves" in the countryside who had arrived with their fleeing masters from Saint-Domingue. Suggesting that the Haitian presi-dent might lend support if they initiated the struggle to liberate themselves, Vesey allegedly persuaded over nine thousand slaves to join his plan to con-verge on Charleston, seize its arsenal, and escape by sea to Haiti or Africa. The revolt, scheduled for July 14, 1822, Bastille Day, was exposed to the authorities several weeks before that date, and Vesey was executed along with seventy-five alleged coconspirators.[47]

By the 1830s, as abolitionism gained political momentum, proslavery ide-ology sharpened around a counterrevolutionary defense against the depreda-tions of a Black Jacobin abolitionist uprising. Just as the early Federalists had feared the power of Jacobin propaganda in the 1790s, so now would proslav-ery state governments in the South organize around neutralizing the threat of abolitionist propaganda. A key event here was the political response to David Walker's *Appeal to the Coloured Citizens of the World, but in Particular and Expressly to Those of the United States of America*, originally published in 1829. Walker, another black Charlestonian who had lived in the city at the same time as Vesey and attended the same African Methodist Episcopal church, wrote and published his appeal after he had moved to Boston. The appeal represented a unique challenge to slavery, not only for the polemical words it contained, but more importantly because Walker did not write to a white public, nor even to his fellow free blacks, but instead to the enslaved. Celebrating Haiti as "the glory of the blacks and terror of tyrants," Walker's appeal urges his "afflicted brethren" to shed their servile spirit, predicting that sooner or later the world would witness a great revolutionary uprising against black enslavement: "The whites want slaves, and want us for their slaves, but some of them will curse the day they ever saw us. As true as the sun ever shone in its meridian splendor, my colour will root some of them out of the very face of the earth" (Walker 1830, 23).

In Boston, Walker provided copies to sailors who would distribute them in Southern ports to individuals who could then disseminate them widely. Although Walker's appeal never refers to Jacobinism, in the third edition of his pamphlet he slyly introduces the American Revolution, asking why Americans are "so very terrified respecting my book?" Why, he asks, "do they search vessels, &c. when entering the harbours of tyrannical States, to see if any of my Books can be found, for fear that my brethren will get them to read?" (Walker 1830, 82).

Walker offers this answer: "Perhaps the Americans do their very best to keep my Brethren from receiving and reading my 'Appeal' for fear they will find in it an extract which I made from their Declaration of Independence, which says, 'we hold these truths to be self-evident, that all men are created equal'" (Walker 1830, 82). And in an explicit appeal to revolution: "Hear your language further! 'But when a long train of abuses and usurpation, pursuing invariably the same object, evinces a design to reduce them under absolute despotism, it is their *right*, it is their *duty*, to throw off such government, and to provide new guards for their future security'" (85).

Walker's militant deployment of the "root metaphor of Western political philosophy" provoked a powerful political reaction. Walker's biographer Peter Hincks has observed that, across the South, "authorities were aware that they were up against a strategy the likes of which they had never seen before. Despite claims that Gabriel Prosser had ties with the French, and that Denmark Vesey had ties with the Haitians, all previous conspiracies had been overwhelmingly local, with a few spreading over a handful of counties. Now authorities were confronted with a plan that not only hoped to embrace the entire South but was actually being orchestrated from a distant Northern city" (Hincks 2006, 239).

Virginia and Georgia held special secret legislative meetings to extend state police power so that the secret networks of the pamphlet's dissemination might be discovered. It was largely at this time that Southern lawmakers prohibited the teaching of literacy even to free Blacks. And although slave patrols in states such as South Carolina and Virginia date much further back, they were greatly expanded and their names changed to the contemporary term "police" after the circulation of Walker's pamphlet.[48] Yet for all these efforts, two years later, the Nat Turner revolt suggested that the threat of bloody insurrection had not been eliminated. Vesey's and Prosser's revolts and Walker's pamphleteering can be rightly celebrated as courageous attempts to overthrow the slavery of plantocratic capitalism under impossibly difficult and dangerous conditions. But they should also be recognized as moments when the scope and focus of police action designed to counter the threat of a Black Jacobin slave revolt would be expanded into an ever more powerful system of populational control and patrol that would prepare the way for twentieth-century policing.

We can learn much about the logic of racial ensoulment following these events from a polemical proslavery tract that appeared shortly after Vesey's attempted revolt. Written by a white Charlestonian named Edwin C. Holland, the tract presents itself as *A Refutation of the Calumnies Circulated against the Southern and Western States Respecting the Institution and Existence of Slavery among Them*, but to this ideological rebuttal it also adds a concluding analysis in part of its title, concerning the *Actual State and Condition of Their Negro Population*. While the refutation is directed at Northern abolitionists, the populational analysis concerns the development of a racial threat to white South Carolina's liberal society. Every actual, aborted, or even fantasized conspiracy or revolt by the enslaved of the South is chronicled as evidence of the enslaved African's innate aggression and propensity for violence. Holland hyperbolically concludes, "our Negros are truly the Jacobins of the country; that they are the *anarchists* and the *domestic enemy*; the *common enemy of civilized society*, and the barbarians who would, IF THEY COULD, become the DESTROYERS *of our race*" (Holland 1822, 86). This polemic conflates the American South's enslaved Africans with both the French and Haitian Jacobins, and even with Locke's "common enemy."

But there is more to notice about Holland's language. While the abolitionist would suggest that slavery is what produces the enmity of the enslaved, Holland steadfastly insists on the reverse: slavery has become a necessary tool for checking an enemy population. Below the appearance of the plantation system, Holland sees among the enslaved a smoldering longing for race war that will ignite whenever a revolutionary spark might encourage among them "wild and visionary ideas of freedom" (Holland 1822, 70). Abolitionists therefore must take full responsibility for catalyzing the enslaved's "disposition to insurrection and plunder" into such a state that it has now "ripened into open rebellion"(62).

But Holland also explicitly racializes the "color" of political deceit at the moment when his description of this "common enemy" conflates the chromatic designation of skin (blackness) with the demonic threat of inscrutability (darkness), and thus with evil's gothic power of self-concealment, a power that will nonetheless ultimately be exposed and defeated: "Their treachery, though it walks only in the gloom and shadow of midnight and shows its 'dark and dangerous brow' at that dead hour, so suited for its evil machinations, still will always be detected; nor can the most elaborate ingenuity hide it from prevention. There is no secrecy so profound enough to conceal such a Heaven offending sin" (Holland 1822, 78). Holland's language reflects how and why, for the liberal plantocracy, Blackness never simply signified inferiority. It signified as well a horrible enmity that allowed the plantation system to combine its disciplining of slave labor with violent anticipations of sinister revolt (Rosenthal 2019, 9–48). For the slaveholder, the color of the enslaved African was always also racial in the earlier Iberian sense: a Hamitic sign of the "gloom and shadow" or the "dark and dangerous brow" of "evil machinations" that the regime of the color line was designed to police and defend against in the Lockean name of that "first and great law of nature—SELF-PRESERVATION" (Holland 1822, 62).

From the Abolition of Slavery to the Persistence of the Color Line

I opened this chapter by juxtaposing two epigraphs. One originally appeared in a newspaper in Wilmington, North Carolina, in 1898, but I discovered it while reading Bryan Wagner's fascinating study of Black vernacular traditions and the law (Wagner 2009). The newspaper editorial, which histrionically justifies the public lynching of a Black man by describing him as a "rattlesnake" who must be crushed *before* he bites, is cited by Wagner as a text that illustrates the political reasoning of postbellum Southern "police power." Wagner shows us two things about that power. Firstly, it shows us how racial lynching operated within the logic of a police action that deputized all white people as its potential agents. Secondly, it shows how racialized police action assumes a kind of temporal emergency where, as Wagner explains, "the time is always right for action whether the offense is happening in the past, present, or future. Delay in every case is fatal. The stakes remain the same whether the offender completes his action (as purportedly is the case with the negro in Charlottesville), is caught red-handed (the case with the incendiary or highwayman), or merely implies the threat by his nature (like the rattlesnake or mad dog)" (Wagner 2009, 19).

Wagner proposes that in this way American police power has rendered Blackness as a state of "statelessness," akin presumably to Hannah Arendt's definition of the stateless as those who are exposed to violence because, without a state to defend them, they have been denied "the right to have rights" (Arendt 1973, 296–97). I would argue slightly differently that the condition of Blackness in Wagner's example does not truly exemplify "statelessness" insofar as the state in question obsessively targets its Black population. Far from state-less, Blacks in the Jim Crow South endured a permanent condition of being treated as the probable "enemy of state." The state's very legitimacy was in fact derived from its claim to defend society against the threat of Blackness, and from its need for police power to do so. The condition of Blackness, therefore, is better understood as a racial liberal variation of what Giorgio Agamben has called "inclusive exclusion," a special case of belonging to the population that is premised on a nonbelonging to the society, thus to the status of the exception rather than the exclusion (Agamben 1998, 21–22).

Consider now the Wilmington editorial's uncanny repetition of Edmund Burke's indictment of the French Revolution, which he had accused of reck-lessly extending liberty "in the abstract" to the "highwayman," the "murderer," or the "madman." In both cases, extending liberty to the criminal is itself a political crime. The Wilmington editorial probably did not knowingly repli-cate Burke's verbiage, but it certainly reworked its liberal technology of pro-ducing freedom's enemy: to be sure, instead of the Jacobin, that enemy is now the postbellum Black man, always already to be anticipated as a "highwayman," "murderer," or "madman." And because the extension of legal rights to such a man is understood as posing so basic a social threat, opposition to the lynching of Black men demonstrates the same flagrant disregard for the well-being of civil society as the Jacobin project of emancipation. Blacks and those who sympa-thize with them (like Trump's snake and the woman who takes him in) converge into a single dangerous class clustered along the color line's borderlands. The editorial articulates a two-faced racial enemy whose threat resembles the split image of the "Real San-Culotte."

A line of descent can be traced from the figure that Locke called the "Of-fender" who is "Dangerous to Mankind," through Burke's "highwayman" or "murderer," on to Holland's "*domestic enemy*. . . . who would, IF THEY COULD, become the DESTROYERS *of our race*," and arriving at the "rattlesnake" of the Wilmington paper. This line of descent zig-zags between the criminal and the political enemy for a reason: the political enemy was a special kind of criminal, while the criminal could also be viewed as an emergent political enemy. The mad dog or rattlesnake of Wilmingtonian Jim Crow racism would find later counterparts in the "violent" Scottsboro Boys of the 1930s, the dangerous "crim-inals" incarcerated in the prison-industrial complex of the 1980s and 1990s, and the Trumpian figure of the snake evoked by right-wing populism today. Twentieth- and twenty-first-century anti-Blackness would rely on both faces of this doubled enemy of liberal society—the criminal and revolutionary—

and would therefore also mobilize features of the Burkean fanatic. These continuities show us not that anti-Blackness is a constant and unchanging feature of American political culture, but rather that the history of racial power has involved a series of strategic rearticulations of Blackness that have always occurred as elements in what David Harvey has called the "spatial fixes" of capitalism (Harvey 2001). This is so because Harvey's spatial fixes have always relied as well on *racial* fixes that involve the drawing and redrawing of a populational frontier.[49] North American anti-Blackness as the security logic of chattel slavery grew out of a certain racial fix for the political instability that the early plantation rebellions of "mongrel labor" posed to plantocratic colonial capitalism. After slavery's abolition, the radical possibilities of American Reconstruction were quelled through the racial liberal enactment of a "Jim Crow fix," a hierarchical segregation of the population across a reconstituted color line that shored up postbellum agrarian capitalism by resecuring the propertied status of whiteness and (with it) the continued segmentation of rural labor.[50] Finally, with the defeat of Jim Crow in the second half of the twentieth century, and the challenge posed to the color line by a complex interaction of Black freedom struggles with official liberal antiracism, we encounter what Ruth Wilson Gilmore has called the "Prison Fix," the establishment of an expanded carceral-policing regime that simultaneously found a means of utilizing surplus land, capital, and population through the growth of prisons, but also promised a renewed security against what Nixon, Reagan, and others viewed as the new domestic political enemy associated with militant antiracist movements (Gilmore 2007, 87–127).[51]

The post-Fordist carceral regime has generated its own accumulation processes (the prison-industrial complex as an industrial sector) while simultaneously neutralizing a new round of political challenges to racial capitalism (antiracist and Black Power movements). We might say that what links nineteenth-century slavery abolitionism with the mid-twentieth-century Black civil rights movement's Jim Crow abolitionism, and with movements today for prison and police abolition, are not simply the fact that they share abolition as a political strategy, but also *what* they have each tried to abolish: the institutional forms of the North American color line that liberal police power has established and patrolled in their respective eras. This was true for Du Bois's radical post-Reconstruction concept of "abolition democracy," and it is true today in relation to police and prison abolition. In each case, when taken to its fullest conclusion, abolition attempts to dismantle racial liberalism's series of cordons sanitaires between a sacred realm of white liberty protected by police power and a profane world "stained" with politico-racial criminality whose populations are subjected to that police power in the name of the threat they are alleged to represent.[52]

From Jacobin to Communist: Evolutions of the Revolutionary Enemy

In 1840, just seven years after slavery had been abolished in the British Empire, Pierre-Joseph Proudhon opened his treatise *What Is Property?* with these words:

> If I were asked to answer the following question: *What is slavery?* and I should answer in one word, *It is murder*, my meaning would be understood at once. No extended argument would be required to show that the power to take from a man his thought, his will, his personality, is a power of life and death; and that to enslave a man is to kill him. Why, then, to this other question: *What is property?* may I not likewise answer, *It is robbery*, without the certainty of being misunderstood; the second proposition being no other than a transformation of the first? (Proudhon 1993, 13)

For Proudhon, a truly free society would require the abolition of both slavery and private property as manifestations of one and the same liberal regime of social domination. The two forms of abolition are intertwined since one can only have slavery by means of a social death that "murders" people in treating them as private property, and one can only have private property by murdering the lifeworld of people who must be kept separated from possession so they can become "unpropertied." But notice as well that Proudhon's formulation "property is theft" offers a brilliantly inverted mirror image of the liberal credo: whereas for Locke and his successors, it was the propertied classes who face the threat of theft from the unpropertied, Proudhon insists that it is the propertied who have robbed the poor and the destitute. It is the propertied, he insists, who are the real highwaymen, the real robbers, and the true murderers. And it is therefore the poor who must be defended against the wealthy, not the reverse.

While abolitionists challenged plantocratic capitalism's founding antinomy of slavery and mastery, the contemporaneous radicalism championed by Proudhon and his successors confronted the related yet distinct conditions of metropolitan capitalism. By the early nineteenth century, a globally integrated plantocratic-metropolitan regime of capital accumulation was expanding rapidly by means of the cotton commodity chain. Explosive growth in cotton plantations during the 1820s and 1830s in the American South, as Sven Beckert has detailed, was part and parcel of the equally rapid rise of industrial manufacturing as the cotton was shipped to Manchester, England, and other major processing centers where it was spun and woven into textiles for the world market (Beckert 2015). It was during the 1820s in the industrial zone of this massive new scale of accumulation that European leftist movements, variously called radical, socialist, agrarian, populist, or communist, first began advocating that private property be "socialized." By the 1840s, "socialism" and "communism" would emerge as the two predominant names for metropolitan revolutionary programs to abolish private property and thereby create a genuinely free and equal society.

The two names, socialism and communism, differed primarily in their relationship to militancy. "Socialism" was generally a term claimed by utopian followers of Charles Fourier and others who sought a social revolution led by example not force (see Johnstone 1967, 123). By contrast, the word "communism," when it emerged around 1840, was closely associated with several Parisian secret societies advocating political revolution.[53] The term first achieved notoriety when a secret society member attempted to assassinate King Louis-Phillipe of France. During the trial, Bertel Nygaard observes, the word "communism" evolved from an unfamiliar name for an obscure wing of radical French politics into a universal scourge of capitalist modernity. It would thereafter be associated with "anarchy, social disintegration, murder, pillage, plunder" and characterized as a "chaos of every lustful drive and every moral anomaly" that one finds in "the veritable dunghill of the big cities" (Nygaard 2016, 14). With this characterization, we find the earliest racial liberal articulation of a new game of power, a long-lasting and flexible counterrevolutionary policing strategy that we have come to know as "anticommunism." Like the abolitionist, the communist offered another founding ideological enemy of liberal society descended from the Jacobin fanatic.[54] Anticommunism would, of course, be used against actual communist movements. But its real power was found in a wider application of police tactics to any perceived development within the population that might destabilize property's claim to social order.

Marx and Engels's *Manifesto of the Communist Party* was in meaningful ways not really the platform of an actual political party, but instead a polemical rhetorical response to the rapid expansion of this anticommunist strategy of power. Consider a very early anticommunist cartoon, published (like "A Real San-Culotte!!" before it) in Britain's *Punch* magazine (see figure 4.2). It appeared in a December 1848 issue focused on that year's wave of political revolutions across the European continent. Although these were mostly bourgeois revolutions seeking to establish liberal democracies with which to enfranchise

THE REPUBLICAN MEDAL,   AND   ITS REVERSE.

FIGURE 4.2. Cartoon comparing republicanism and communism, *Punch*, December 2, 1848.

the propertied, the upheavals also involved radical and working-class elements seeking much more. The third French Revolution in February 1848, which replaced Louis-Phillipe's July Monarchy with a moderate republican government, was notably followed four months later by *les journées de Juin* (the June Days), a popular uprising of Paris's working poor supported by radical republicans and socialists. It would be violently crushed by the new republic.[55] This is the context in which the *Punch* cartoon featured a pair of panels showing first the face of a French republican medal, then "its reverse."[56] There is a deceptive complexity to these images. The face of the "republican medal" replicates the features found on the front of the *grand sceau de la République française*, the Great Seal of the French Republic still used today, which had in fact been designed just a few months prior to the *Punch* cartoon. It features "Marianne," the French figure of Liberty, who also stands in New York harbor (Agulhon 1981, 12–21; see also Hunt 1984, 91–93). The revolutionary creed "Liberté, Egalité, Fraternité," which encircles the top of the medal, however, is normally found on the *rear* side of the seal. Here it is relocated to the front to facilitate a critical contrast.

The cartoon's counterrevolutionary message emerges in part through the double meaning of its title "The Republican Medal, and Its Reverse." It could refer to two distinct medals, one republican and another its opposite, in which case the second image appears as the conceptual (antirepublican) antithesis of the first. If the "reverse," however, refers literally to the rear side of a single medal, then the two images turn out to express the *same* republican values. Of course, these meanings may also be combined: the rear may seem to be the antithesis of the front only to prove to be its deeper truth. So read, this cartoon functions much like "A Real San-Culotte!!," exposing the malignant communist soul that has disguised itself in the bodily form of Marianne. She who purports to stand for liberty, equality, and fraternity turns out to endorse (wittingly or unwittingly, we cannot say) the violent aims of socialism, communism, and atheism.

Since the Jacobin was already associated with fanaticism, the medal's front image facilitates the refiguring of the fanatic as communist. At "face value," however, the medal begins by suggesting that the republican looks like a proper liberal subject. One must flip over this republican medal in order to surface the latent communist meaning of French revolutionary values. These allegations emerge out of the precise substitutions offered in the second image for each element appearing in the first. The original encircling revolutionary slogan "Liberté, Egalité, Fraternité" is now replaced by the new slogans, "Socialism, Communism, Atheism," whose violent fanaticism is verified by what we see in the new illustrations. First, Marianne's divine image is supplanted by a menacing bearded man. With a broad face and wide nose, long hair, two pistols in his belt, and a bayonet and torch in his hands, he looks outward with his feet firmly planted atop "property" and "religion," two sacred values that he grinds into the earth. This feature replaces Marianne's foot, which stands on the yoke symbolizing human subjection. If Marianne symbolizes the sacred struggle for liberation, the "reverse" figure's revolutionary aims appear to be only murder and destruction of the propertied.

It is especially difficult to interpret the exact racial implications of the communist's features. Is he a swarthy working-class militant of Britain's own Chartist movement engaged in an ideologized "sedition of the belly?" Is he a barbaric or militant French or German foreigner who threatens Britain like the Irish Catholic once did Stuart England? Might he even be a bearded Jew?[57] Though there is no definitive answer, the figure seems to evoke some unspecified menace. This is a man whose countenance racially marks him as an ideologically motivated enemy of proper freedom. And the gender contrast with Marianne also evokes in the faintest of ways a sexualization of the violent threat to liberty.

The *Punch* sketch's theme of the fanatical destroyer masking themselves in French revolutionary values traces back to the emergence of modern conspiracy theory in the 1790s, for example in the writings of the reactionary Jesuit priest, Augustin Barruel, a contemporary of Burke's, who wrote a three-volume account of the Jacobins as a secret conspiratorial group that had worked for decades as undercover enemies of society, religion, and the monarchy, hatching plots within existing secret societies such as the Masonic lodges (Barruel 1799). The line from Jacobin to communist conspiracy could also be drawn through the memory of François-Noël Babeuf's so-called Conjuration des Égaux, or Conspiracy of the Equals, in 1796, an attempted coup that sought to reverse the Thermidorian reaction of that moment in the French Revolution, and was supported by radical Jacobins who were arguably the first modern advocates of the abolition of private property.[58]

But the anticommunist targeting of secret revolutionary threats was by no means phantasmagoric. As Eric Hobsbawm observes, although the French Revolution had been a cataclysmic but unintended event, for the next generation of revolutionaries it offered a model of social change they could seek to replicate. The upheavals of 1848 were (like slave insurrections) usually planned by activists working underground (Hobsbawm 1996, 123–27). Anticommunist political policing thus participated in a spiraling game of power as conservative regimes sought to infiltrate and break revolutionary plots that in response became increasingly secretive. This game encouraged the institutional form of what Hobsbawm calls the "secret insurrectional brotherhood," the building of conspirator organizations such as the Carbonari in Italy or Louis Blanqui's Société des Saisons in France. These brotherhoods actualized what had once been Augustin Barruel's fantasy, revolutionary groups modeled on the Freemasons, all the way down to the adoption of Masonic rituals and initiations into secret knowledge (Hobsbawm 1996, 112–17).[59] It was in fact just such a Parisian revolutionary secret society, initially named the League of Outlaws, then renamed the League of the Just after moving to London, that became Marx's and Engels's early political home.[60]

New international and cross-border "political police" and sometimes "secret police" organizations and federations would expand through this confrontational game between the mid-nineteenth-century counterrevolutionary state and the threat of the revolutionary "secret society."[61] The Police Union of German States in 1851, for example, was set up for the purpose of exchanging useful political information about religious organizations, Freemason societies, labor unions, student groups, or any other institution suspected of presenting a revolutionary danger to public order (Deflem 1996). Sometimes called "information without noise," such interstate intelligence networks assisted national political police in monitoring or even infiltrating suspicious organizations so as to determine which ones were merely reformist, and which were secretly interested in the violent overthrow of property. Because the risk logic of political police presumed that one can never predict in advance the threats that might exist to good order, political police, with their growing mechanisms of surveillance, constituted a technology of power whose asymptotic target concerned the entire population.

A Specter Haunting Europe

When Marx and Engels were charged with writing a manifesto on behalf of their political organization in London, by then known as the League of Communists, they already belonged to precisely the kind of "party" that the *Punch* sketch would decry: a revolutionary communist "society" passing itself off as a French-influenced advocate of liberty and equality. Over the course of the 1840s, communism had become the subject of expanding allegations of violent political criminality, but also spectrality. Peter Osborne notes a book about French communism, written as early as 1842 by the liberal economist Lorenz von Stein, that had already sounded an alarm concerning this dangerous *Gespenst* (a specter, spook, ghost, nightmare, or even hobgoblin). This word makes another appearance in a keyword essay on communism, penned by German socialist Wilhelm Schulz in 1846 (and definitively read by Marx and Engels), where communism is acknowledged as having "become a threatening spectre [*drohenden Gespenst*] for those who fear and with which others seek to create fear" (Osborne 2000, 73). Schulz's reference to such political uses of the communist "specter" hearkens back to Burke's Jacobin "evil spirit," which terrorizes through its supernatural power to possess or haunt European nations. Marx evidently seized upon Schulz's observation for his opening gambit in the *Manifesto of the Communist Party*.

Marx and Engels's titling of their document a "manifesto" instead of the more traditional socialist genre, the catechistic *Glaubenbekenntnis* (confession of faith), indicates their awareness that polemical humor might be effective as a means of waging war against the anticommunist ensoulment of their movement as an evil spirit. A manifesto seeks to make something manifest; it proclaims political aims that have previously been obscured or misunderstood due to the mobilization of a panic. In the modern era, a manifesto is frequently presented as a response to the spectralization or demonization of a radical social or artistic movement. It declares itself to be not only a list of the movement's goals but also a public antidote for the false accusations mounted against it.

Marx and Engels declared the radical objectives of their Communist Party, which had in fact once been a de facto secret society, in order to combat the phantasmatic figure of the "communist," the same demonizing figure that appears on the reverse of the aforementioned Republican medal. If the "spectre of communism" was now "haunting Europe," and had become a convenient way to decry and dismiss all parties out of power, then actual communists would now "openly, in the face of the whole world, publish their views, their aims, their tendencies, and meet this nursery tale of the Spectre of Communism with a manifesto of the party itself" (Marx and Engels 2018, 473). The *Manifesto* presents both a detailed plan and a playful response to the norms of liberal democracy, a *party platform* with which to replace the communist's status as a floating political signifier for threat. The platform contains even a sexual agenda, responding to allegations that communism erotically threatens liberal society by seeking to "socialize" the crime of prostitution through the creation of a "community of women."[62] Like David Walker's *Appeal*, the *Manifesto* attempted to boomerang the power that racial liberalism itself had invested in the threat to property into a different kind of force that could be weaponized against liberal police and its bourgeois society. In American studies especially, anticommunism is usually studied as a phenomenon of mid-twentieth-century Cold War political culture, with occasional consideration of the Palmer Raids and Red Scare that push a bit further back to the aftermath of World War I and the Russian Revolution. But as we can see, it emerged far earlier. By the middle of the nineteenth century anticommunism had already become a constitutive technology of liberal security.[63]

In what ways can anticommunism be understood specifically as a technology of *racial power*? I would suggest in answer that, like the abolitionist Black Jacobin, the communist became someone whose attempted abolition of private property signaled a threat that required the fractionalized policing of the population. During the decades when it became clear that the racism of the color line would survive slavery's demise, the communist abolition of private property became a highly influential political framework for envisioning its overthrow, since what was the color line if not a boundary to establish a racially defined right to private property? The Black radical tradition can be said to be descended from this recognition that the end of slavery was merely the first step toward advancing a wider, deeper, and more radical politics of abolition that could only succeed by imagining the total abolition of racial capitalism along with its liberal juridico-political infrastructure.

Black radicals who articulated such politics, including W. E. B. Du Bois, C. L. R. James, and Richard Wright, sometimes called themselves communists. But the police powers of the liberal state did not wait for them to so self-identify. As Charisse Burden-Stelly has shown, twentieth-century American racial capitalism came to depend politically on a tight interweaving of anti-Blackness and anticommunism (Burden-Stelly 2020). American political police would apply a hermeneutic of suspicion to the Black call for liberty, equality, and fraternity, which like the Republican medal, they could flip over into anticipations of violence and destruction of white property, propriety, and religion. This pattern can be observed with special clarity in the FBI's Counterintelligence Program

(COINTELPRO) campaign against Martin Luther King Jr., a nonrevolutionary liberal activist who, by demanding the abolition of Jim Crow, apparently signaled a threat to white property/propriety that quickly brought a communist threat into political focus (Garrow 1981). Communism's association with racial threat also carried over into the sexual domain. The nineteenth-century fear that communism sought a "community of women" would under Jim Crow become reenvisioned as the sly communist promotion of miscegenation and racial "agglomeration": the color line could be abolished just as effectively through a sexual attack. "Race Mixing is Communism" was not an uncommon political placard at postwar white supremacist rallies.

But anticommunism's relationship to anti-Blackness is only one aspect of its centrality to twentieth-century racial liberalism. A similar trajectory can be traced in communism's relationship to anticolonial politics, and in imperial reactions to the development of Third World communism. Insofar as the abolition of private property became a way of envisioning the abolition of European territorial claims over the African, Asian, and Caribbean colonies of the British, French, and other European empires, and insofar as communism offered a critical frame for analyzing and indicting multiple colonial histories of resource extraction, expropriation of land, destruction of traditional ways of life, and enforcement of market dependency, it proposed a project of colonial liberation that went far deeper than the liberal promise of nominal independence. As communism's influence in anticolonial struggles grew, anticommunism expanded first into the application of political police power in the colonies, and later into the internationalization of anticommunist counterinsurgency, a police project that Kristin Williams argues was first developed by US domestic policing, but would expand rapidly in the twentieth century as the US security state supplanted the global reach of the former European imperial powers (Williams 2011). America's informal control over a globalized conception of liberal society (the "free world") would be enforced both by the international projection of its military force and by a covert counterinsurgency regime that trained Third World client states in the tactics of political police.

I would like to close these reflections on what we might term "racial anticommunism" by returning to the enigmatic image of the communist revolutionary in the December 1848 *Punch* cartoon. He is, after all, neither an enslaved African nor a colonial subject, yet this dangerous bearded communist still bears the burden of racial signification. I would propose that we read him as an early political representation of the "alien immigrant." Beginning as early as the 1790s, the British Parliament passed the Aliens Act, the first of successive laws that mandated the policing of foreigners entering Britain in order to exclude propagandists for the French revolution. The United States followed suit in 1798 with its own Alien and Sedition Acts, which were similarly aimed at expelling foreign agitators. Like all police, the new "border police" that emerged out of such laws were meant to anticipate problems, not just remediate them after the fact. Their goal, in other words, was not to apprehend someone who had spread propaganda or committed sedition, but rather to develop techniques for barring the entry of all foreigners who might even hypothetically threaten to do so. Ideological profiling was therefore essential to the task of border control from its inception. Although Britain's original Alien Acts concerned the Jacobin threat, in 1848 another round of acts was passed to prohibit the entry of communists. The figure on the reverse side of the *Punch* magazine cartoon appears to be just such a communist "alien," akin to one that appears in a different *Punch* cartoon of the same year (see figure 4.3).

In this sketch, John Bull, icon of British nationalism, proclaims, "I'll 'propaganda' you, you meddling French Scoundrel," booting him off the White Cliffs of Dover and scattering in the process his broadsheets, in which historically older terms for Westphalian state threat ("sedition," "disaffection," "treason") are now accompanied by the new threat of "communism."[64] The French scoundrel, albeit a European, is again ominously racial, bearded yet vaguely effeminate, and with an almost monkey-like appearance. The communist apparently ensouled a perpetually floating but ideally perceptible foreign threat—now French, now German, now Russian, now Jewish—that demanded vigilant inspection of the population for propagandistic spreaders of the spectral communist contagion. If we recall the ambiguous nature of Trump's "snake," that inchoately and unspecified someone/something who is permitted entry into the home from the outside, then the *spectrally* racial quality of communism—its central role in mobilizing a racism of the soul that demands a political policing of the population—materializes before our eyes.

In the late nineteenth century, following both the bloody crushing of the Paris Commune in France and the Haymarket affair in the United States, border policing became increasingly integral to the modern nation-state's governance of the population. Increasingly centralized, it also began to involve the collection of biometric data that could be processed by new technologies of the surveillance state for the purposes of sorting the flow of populations across borders. New identification practices were developed for this purpose such as the issuing of passports and visas designed to control immigration and, especially, to apprehend foreign radicals and anarchists suspected of revolutionary aims (Shirk 2019). The biopolitics of modern populations develops in part from this problem of how to conduct populational flows in ways that can detect the rare

FIGURE 4.3. "John Bull's Alien Act," *Punch*, April 29, 1848.

but important revolutionary threats they carry, right through the contemporary terror suspect. These are the developments through which political policing would develop at last into what Timothy Melley has called the liberal state's "covert sphere" of operations (Melley 2012), a domain that runs alongside the transparent public sphere of liberal society yet claims a unique right to maintain its secrecy in the name of the security it provides for its transparent counterpart.

From the Jacobin to the Threat of Abstract Capital

We have seen how nineteenth-century racial liberalism targeted both abolitionism and communism as conspiratorial threats associated with an overly abstract and universalizing fanaticism for freedom. But there is another sense of abstraction taken too far that also connects to the policing of conspiracies. Here too a line of descent can be drawn from Edmund Burke's earliest diatribes against the French Revolution. In this case, however, the relevant peril highlighted by Burke concerns neither revolutionary principles nor slave revolts, but instead pecuniary ambitions. It focuses on the speculators and the "new moneyed interests" as an ascending calculative power of certain classes who, by doing whatever money wanted, precipitated the revolutionary destruction that began in 1789. These betrayers are (to use Burke's words) the "directors in assignats, and trustees for the sale of Church lands, attorneys, agents, money-jobbers, speculators, and adventurers, composing an ignoble oligarchy, founded on the destruction of the crown, the Church, the nobility, and the people" (Burke 2014, 199).

Although this threat of moneyed abstraction could be traced earlier, for example to the "Portuguese" merchant conversos of seventeenth-century Spanish Peru's *gran complicidad*, its power would accelerate and gain a specifically revolutionary spin alongside the industrial capitalism of the nineteenth century and capital's growing ability to dominate social life by impersonal means. Marx's conception of capital, as Moishe Postone has pointed out, is double sided (Postone 1980). It can take the concrete or congealed forms of machinery, factories, raw materials, and other material instruments of production. But at the same time, capital possesses an abstract side insofar as it embodies the value form that is associated with the abstract labor time it congeals. Insofar as capital's pursuit of greater relative surplus value drives a search for ever greater productivity, and because money—capital in its "liquid" financial form—is always seeking these most productive outlets, it is a feature of capitalism to trigger powerful social upheavals.

In Postone's powerful analysis, the political reactions to such upheavals may take a racially fetishized form. As I noted early in this chapter, Moishe Postone reads modern antisemitism as a key element in the right-wing expression of anticapitalist sentiment, one that converts the Jew into a target of what he calls a "one-sided attack on the abstract" (Postone 1980, 112). Although capital is always constituted through a dialectic of the concrete and the abstract, in Postone's analysis, antisemitism singles out the abstract side of capital as its pernicious aspect, as pure speculation and amorality, while celebrating its concrete manifestations as the productive embodiment of a society's wealth and national interests.

Why would Jews be so singled out as the racial representatives of abstract capital? Postone offers several reasons. He notes the long association of Jews with money, something this book has touched upon, for example, in the anti-converso attacks that were motivated by the Jewishness of tax collectors. He also observes that the take-off of industrial capitalism roughly coincided with the "political and civil emancipation" of the Jews. Finally, he observes that, because Jews were never considered members of the nation in which they lived, their civil claims as citizens of their respective nation-states were always a matter of "pure abstraction." In this way, Jews could be identified with the "rootless-ness" and the "internationalism" of abstract capital. I would only add to these points the observation that the figure of liberalism's "enemy" is no less abstract than the citizen who constitutes its society. Both figures are political effects of a prior act of abstraction that proceeds from the biopolitical bifurcation of the population into the threatened and the threatening.

Indicting amoral internationalism or cosmopolitanism was therefore an inverted way of finding Jews to be disloyal to the nation in whose state they resided, of describing them as enemies who appeared as citizens by means of the camouflaging qualities of abstract belonging that actually derived from their human embodiment of money itself. The longer genealogy this book has tracked clarifies why this might be so, and in so doing complicates Postone's no-tion that modern antisemitism was distinctively different from the religious anti-Jewishness that dates back to late medieval times. We have seen that Jews were tied from the Middle Ages onward to a notion of "infidelity," a stiff-necked unwillingness to keep proper faith with God, with Christ, or for that matter even with their own biblical religion (Talmudic Judaism, as I noted in chapter 1, was already seen as a kind of infidelity to their biblical role as believers in the Law of Moses). Such infidelity amounts to a standing in which Jews were inside the European population, but also outside in the sense of acting as principal enemies of the flock. The modern association of Jews with the abstract domination of finance capital can be seen as the insertion of this political logic of the cam-ouflaged Jewish threat into a representation of capital itself, and as itself an abstraction of the earlier charge that the Jew ensouled a diabolical threat.

The form of political reason at stake in a war against Jews as the embodi-ment of the abstract side of capital comes into stronger focus if we consider Noam Yuran's observation that there is a sense in which capital brings to life a certain abstraction of desire that he calls "what money wants" (Yuran 2014). Once money becomes capital (i.e., once it begins serving the purpose of accu-mulation and enters into an M-C-M' cycle), by definition it comes to objectify the characteristics of desire that we usually associate with human subjectivity, a Jew's perhaps. What money always "wants" is to breed more of itself, to in-crease itself quantitatively. But the power unleashed by capital in this respect will periodically take the form of what Joseph Schumpeter many years later would famously call the "gale of creative destruction" (Schumpeter 2004, 84) that might seem to have been what somebody "wanted." As in the scene of primitive accumulation or violent expropriation, and indeed whenever capital's inability to regulate itself reaches a point of crisis and disruption, capital can pivot suddenly to destroy or eradicate a way of life in order to build upon the ruins an opportunity for fresh accumulation, a chance to make more money. This ghostlike subjectivity of financial power has been described by Joseph Vogl, riffing on Marx and Engels, as "das Gespenst des Kapital" (the specter of capital) (Vogl 2014). In this respect, "what money wants" stands as a second-order abstraction from the Lockean society of possessive individuals who seek to increase the wealth and prosperity of their society through favorable exchanges. It is a specter that enters into the exchange process seemingly in order to destroy the society that grounds it. When this happens, money is experienced as placing a liberal society in the same position as the violently expropriated. It can appear in fetishized form as a kind of reverse colonialism in which the Jew or some similarly racialized figure ensouls finance capital as a force that, having no national or social allegiance, does not hesitate to liquidate the property of liberal society in order to do something more lucrative with it. This is the logic that Burke was already formulating in the 1790s when he accused financiers of acting to unravel the very fabric of French society on the eve of the Revolution, unleashing unprecedented destruction on a grand European power for the sake of monetary gain. Germany, in the aftermath of World War I, would be susceptible to similar Nazi accusations that Jewish bankers had collaborated with the allies in a racial plot to destroy their society (Klotz 2005). And today, in the United States, well along its twenty-first-century decline as a capitalist hegemon, we see the rise of a similar discourse of racialized financial enemies, a subject to which I will return in my conclusion. Such threats represent a peculiar variation on Toscano's "fanaticism" (Toscano 2017) that he would probably not recognize as such since it essentially concerns the fanatical amorality of money, something to which (as to Locke's atheist) promises or oaths mean nothing, and which will employ any means necessary to achieve its own ends (i.e., breeding more of itself). In such moments, money also becomes conceived as a force of "infidelity," sexualized alternately as a pimp or a prostitute with no genuine loyalty to society. Sex and money become equated as amoral forms of "commerce" seeking to unravel the fabric of liberal society.

The antisemitic narrative of Jewish conspiracy was closely associated with all these themes, but it now becomes clearer why Jews could be associated with finance capital and communism simultaneously since liberalism treated them as twin forms of fanatical disloyalty to the possessive individuals of their society. If the Jew was a foreigner inside the homeland, this foreigner could equally be the communist propagandist who had crossed the border to spread the contagion of revolution, or a financier who circulates capital across the border for self-enrichment through some profitable disruption of liberal society. Either or both versions of enmity would, of course, be presumed to hide themselves behind a plausible deniability, waiting like an early modern converso for the right time to strike.

Such racialized politics converged with the emergent forms of modern conspiracy theory. Over the course of the nineteenth century, Barruel's allegation of a Freemason revolutionary plot to destroy France would be synthesized with that of a secret pan-European Jewish cabal to yield the modern vision of a Judeo-Masonic conspiracy whose apotheosis is found in that master forgery, *The Protocols of the Meetings of the Learned Elders of Zion*. Although scholarship on the *Protocols* is vast, with many competing theories of its textual history, most scholars believe that it was assembled by Russian secret police agents working in France in the 1890s around the time of the Dreyfus Affair as a propagandistic tool to quell revolutionary turbulence in late Tsarist Russia (Webman 2011). It was a political narrative, in other words, of police power.

The *Protocols* purportedly transcribe the sayings of a Jewish Masonic organization bent on world domination that, in the third protocol, characterizes its own global threat through an array of images: the "symbolic snake" of Judaism that will lock "all the states of Europe . . . in its coil as in a powerful vice," the infliction of "economic slavery," the arms of Jewish "social masonry," the destruction of the "Goyim," and the uses of hunger to enforce the "right of capital" (Nilus 1965, 17–20). The significance of the symbolic snake, which appeared on the cover of many early editions of the *Protocols*, also maintains this studied ambiguity of many illicit forces (see figure 4.4).[65]

Did the Jewish Masonic snake, an early prototype for the Trumpian serpent, symbolize the global circulation of capital constricting the world? Did it convey the political encirclement of communist revolution? Was it a fanatical appropriation of the world's liberal democracies by a malevolent cabal? Apparently, it was all these things. Even today, when antisemitic white supremacists chant "Jews will not replace us" (Rosenberg 2017), they are expressing fear of a secret plan to demolish their (white Anglo-Saxon) society so it can be supplanted with a more profitable one that sates what the *Protocols* call the "hunger and rights of capital." The populational "replacement" theory in question typically concerns foreigners whose cheaper labor will financially benefit an amoral Jewish form of property at the expense of the legitimate possessive individuals who truly deserve capital's blessing. This conspiracy theory sees no contradiction, therefore, if the foreigners promoted by the bankers are also being seduced by the Jews' communist propaganda into mounting a revolutionary threat. This is merely a way for the Jews to attack them from both directions at once. What the regressively anticapitalist form of antisemitism fears, paradoxically, is its own social death at the hands of capital's pursuit of "creative destruction."

FIGURE 4.4. Cover of *The Protocols of the Meetings of the Learned Elders of Zion* (London: Britons Publishing Society, 1978), depicting Jews collectively as a snake.

THE PROTOCOLS
OF THE MEETINGS OF THE
LEARNED ELDERS OF ZION
TRANSLATED BY VICTOR E. MARSDEN

Although Postone was specifically concerned with understanding the exterminationist logic of Nazi antisemitism, it is important to see that Jews are by no means its unique targets. Racisms grounded in the politics of what Iyko Day calls "romantic anticapitalism" have taken many forms. Anti-Asian racism, as she shows, has also been tied to the threat of abstract capital, and particularly in the context of settler colonies such as the United States, where the alien, rootless, international secret aims of "what money wants" have been anchored in the figure of the Asian immigrant (Day 2016). Amy Chua has analyzed racisms directed at what she calls "market-privileged minorities" in the late twentieth-century era of economic globalization that targeted a wide range of populations (Chua 2004). Such racisms paradoxically draw on anticapitalist feeling to call for the reinvigoration of a racial liberal society that, by cleansing itself of a threatening financialized minority, promises to realign that society with the regime of private property that has at least apparently (and sometimes in actuality) begun to threaten it. This romantic anticapitalist mode of liberal racism becomes most virulent in moments of transition between regimes of capital accumulation, when the forces of social disruption are politically ensouled in the bodies of a scapegoated population.

Coda

Throughout this long chapter, what I have tried to suggest above all is that the accumulation strategies of racial capitalism have always required the politically stabilizing force of a racial liberalism that proclaims the security of a sacred free society as its highest priority, and to that end directs an ever expanding anticipatory and preemptive set of police powers against a range of announced enemies: criminals, ideological fanatics, and finally even financial adversaries who ensoul the amorality of capital. These multiple genealogical tracks demonstrate that racial capitalism is in fact a politically complex phenomenon that cannot be easily reduced to a singular structure of racism. The forms of ensoulment that accompany its history are diverse and historically contingent. Although we can make the general point that racial liberalism has always involved a dual war that pits police power against the respective threats of criminality and fanaticism, this war has been both conceptually and practically reformulated many times in relation to different targets that respond to changing historical contingencies, political indeterminacies, and especially the processes of abstraction that are required to characterize its threats. With each phase of capital accumulation we find new racial targets for liberal police power. These include among them the endangerment of property associated with the predation of the poor, or with liberal and enlightenment projects of emancipation being taken too far, threats to dismantle possessive whiteness, to abolish private property, and even to destroy liberal society on behalf of capital accumulation itself. Racial capitalism, it turns out, can deploy even anticapitalist sentiments to produce its racial enemies, as it did in the case of Nazi antisemitism and as it does in anti-Asian racism today.

One important conclusion we can draw, however, is that we must be careful when we say that racial capitalism is a capitalism that fails to universalize itself. It would perhaps be more helpful to say that it is a capitalism that optimizes its universal goal of accumulation by differentiating its populations along axes of enmity. What is also universalized in the process is the reach of security as a real abstraction whose technologies of policing defend capital accumulation, while what get particularized are the populations whose threats to property require those police powers to continually reestablish and reinforce the biopolitical boundaries that serve to produce race. The capitalist division of labor is protected by racial power on multiple levels: as a policing action against the poor, as a shoring of the logic of property through a defense of the color line, and as a counterrevolutionary covert sphere that undermines radical social movements. The couplet we need to think most about here is not race and class (at least not in isolation). It is race and security. Accumulation has only survived as capitalism's unique objective because racial security has always acted as liberalism's highest value.

CONCLUSION

The Many-Headed Hydra

Although we still live in a world of racial capitalism, the liberal regime of security that governs it today has obviously changed considerably from that of the nineteenth century. In this brief conclusion, I will make no real attempt to do justice to the complex history of racism as a politics of security in the late nineteenth and twentieth centuries. A chapter or even a book could be devoted to each of its major moments: the globalization of the color line that accompanied the capitalist imperialism of Western powers, the trajectory from modern antisemitism to fascism and the Holocaust of European Jewry, the emergence of an official liberal antiracism after World War II, the Cold War's complex reconfiguration of racialization in the face of both decolonization and Third World communism, the racial politics of neoliberal globalization that followed the "golden age" of Fordist capitalism, and finally the reshaping of racial power through the crisis of that neoliberal order in the twenty-first century. What I offer here as a modest alternative is a very short usable history of the current racial conjuncture that I considered in this book's introduction via Donald Trump's uses of Oscar Brown's "The Snake" as a late fascist fable of racial threat.

The right-wing populism that has exploded into prominence both in the United States and across the globe today has a distinctive political quality that we could call its capacity for *racial proliferation*. Reversing the hegemony of what Jodi Melamed has called "official antiracism" of the post–World War II period (Melamed 2011), the new populist Right has revivified longstanding targets of racial threat. Trump's language of "American carnage" calls for a muscular security state unafraid of confrontation with Black criminality (Black Lives Matter as a plot against police order) and fanatical political violence (antifa "radicals" running loose in the streets). At the same time, it kneads into these ingredients a number of figures that have grown especially conspicuous since the turn of this century: the "radical Muslim terrorist" bent on mass destruction, the Latin American migrant who murders or rapes, even the globalist Jew who financially exploits and dispossesses ordinary Americans. Less a single snake, perhaps the most appropriate name for this assemblage would be what Peter Linebaugh and Marcus Rediker once called the "many-headed hydra" (Linebaugh and Rediker 2013), a multiplicitous racial menace from which Trumpism promises to protect the American people. I would therefore like to end this book with a brief consideration of two questions. First, how did we get here, or what kind of genealogical itinerary might take us from the liberal project of nineteenth century racial capitalism to our post-neoliberal moment's tightly braided deployments of color-line racism, nativist xenophobia, antisemitism, and Islamophobia? And secondly, what is to be done? If the current conjuncture represents a potent revival of racism as a militarized politics of security, then what are the implications for how we should conduct the antiracist struggle?

A Quick Journey from Early Racial Capitalism to the Present Moment

In the preceding chapter, I discussed how racial liberalism came to govern and regulate capitalism in relation to the threats associated with several of these populational types: the African slave, the fanatical revolutionary, the migrant foreigner, the financialized Jew. Each of these constitutes a pattern of racialization that liberalism would persist in targeting over the centuries, albeit in ways that continued to evolve alongside the development of capitalism itself. The color line, for example, which had been used to bifurcate the New World plantocratic population according to a logic of property, became central as well to the racial power of nineteenth-century industrial imperialism in Asia and Africa. This "global color line," to use W. E. B. Du Bois's pioneering term (Du Bois 2007, 32), imposed a biopolitical distinction between metropolitan and colonized populations that would frame the hyperexploitation of colonial labor, land, and natural resources on behalf of the world market.[1]

The alien migrant who threatens the national border also developed out of the security logic of nineteenth-century racial liberalism. Though at first indexing the need for new police technologies of national security and border control to contain seditious threats in the wake of the French Revolution, it was not long before the alien migrant would come to figure the pauperized "reserve army of labor" whose urban poverty was associated with criminality and social unrest. The politics of the "border" followed the migrant even after entering the territory of the industrial nation-state because the native/foreign boundary was reproduced in multitudinous ways within its political geography. This political process, which Sandro Mezzadra and Brett Neilson have called "border as method" (Mezzadra and Neilson 2013), was born through the new immigration controls laws of the late nineteenth and early twentieth centuries, which along with various formal and informal codes of employment and residence, permitted police power to begin regulating the size and distribution of the surplus population in accordance with the cycles of capital accumulation.[2] Labor forces would be multiplied and divided, proliferated and segmented, by means of a border logic. But it was primarily in the name of national security rather than economic exigency that this form of control was exercised. As a foreigner who lacked the presumption of national loyalty and propriety granted the "native" citizen, the migrant's entry was conceived as a social risk that concretized the threat of abstract labor to liberal society. It was the *sheer need* for such a large quantity of labor that produced the concern for a multiplication of the size and intensity of the "dangerous classes," with migrants distilling for police power an especially powerful alien concentration of the criminal and disordered passions that menace property.[3]

This conception of the heightened risk associated with the migrant was itself a mode of racialization, one organized in relation to the national border rather than the color line, but which interacted with the latter in complex ways. In nineteenth-century Britain, it had been the Irish above all who ensouled the dangerous immigrant class, a perception of compounded both by the older racial tradition of antipopery as well as the newer colonial-racial threat of "Fenian" political violence as symbolized by public attention to the "skirmishing" campaigns and such mass-mediated hyperevents as the Jubilee Plot.[4] In the United States, as a rich historical scholarship has shown, nativism has invoked a long succession of dangerous immigrants: here too the papist disloyalties of the Irishman were invoked early on, but the ensuing decades would see nativist appeals to the demographic "yellow peril" posed by Asian "coolies" that would precipitate the first immigrational control laws—the Chinese Exclusion Act of 1882—as well as the criminality of Italians in the early twentieth century, Mexicans throughout the twentieth century, and in today's most recent revival, the menacing "caravans" of Central Americans.[5] As this list reminds us, the alien migrant from the other side of the "border" was sometimes but not always deemed a person of color. Scholars of these immigrant populations are sometimes tempted to say that the Irish, Italians, and Jews were either "not white" or possessed a "whiteness of a different color" even though, from a strictly legal point of view, they did in fact always count as white.[6] I propose that we should acknowledge a distinctive threat of *alien raciality* that could work intersectionally with the color line without necessarily being reduced to it. Once this kind of intersectionality is grasped, a framing context emerges for what Mae M. Ngai has called the impossible yet ubiquitous figure of the "illegal alien," the subject who stands at precisely the legal point where the alien and the person of color converge (Ngai 2014).[7]

In addition to such nativist racial security, Jews were also subjected to other modes of racialization that require some specification. The hereticalization of medieval Jews discussed in chapter 1, as well as the Iberian racialization of "converted" Jews addressed in chapter 2, would both find afterlives in the era of racial capitalism: modern racial power would sometimes attribute to the Jew a counterfeit whiteness that concealed beneath it criminal or communist malice.[8] Finally, not reducible to any of these modes of antisemitism is the Postonian analysis discussed in the preceding chapter, when the Jew comes to represent financial capital's threat to annihilate the society within which it circulates (see Postone 1980). If the migrant represented the abstract threat of the laboring population, then here we find its inverse in a fetishization of capital. Jews-as-finance still ensouled a foreign will, but they did so by figuring what capital "wants" through the image of rootless international bankers, the globality of financial interests, or even the "cosmopolitanism" of a secret conspiratorial cabal.[9] In the long aftermath of World War I, it was this version of antisemitism that, in advancing the right-wing narrative that a Jewish and socialist "stab in the back" was responsible for Germany's defeat, enabled the Nazi seizure of power. The question I will take forward from here is why it is that we find a similar pattern of antisemitism ascendant today alongside a reinvigorated anti-migrant xenophobia and a renewal of color-line racism.

The Question of the Religious Enemy

Unlike the modes of racialization I have been discussing, the menace of the "radical Islamic terrorist" does *not* trace back in any obvious way to the nineteenth-century forms and figures of metropolitan or settler colonial racial liberalism discussed in the last chapter. Did the powerful spectacle of the 9/11 attacks really produce the threat of the Muslim terrorist ex nihilo? Or is there a racial genealogy we can specify for this twenty-first-century object of security? It is true that, over the course of this book, we have encountered several antecedents for the modern terrorist's dangerous religiosity in the wolflike predations of the pastorate's heretics, the conspiratorial intentions of Iberian conversos and Moriscos, and perhaps especially the seditious and treasonous religious fanaticism of "papists" in Westphalian Tudor Britain. In chapter three, I also noted that the "Mahometan" became an archetypical figure for religious threat to the state within the logic of Westphalian reason. Like these earlier figures, the Muslim terrorist has become a populational type associated with a theological animus that authorizes apparatuses of state security capable of discovering and rooting them out from the surrounding population. This form of racial power does therefore have some precedent.

What does require an explanation, however, is the return of such a religious enemy so long after the concept of fanatical threat had apparently been secularized in the liberal era. The course of the eighteenth and early nineteenth century was one in which, as we saw, the Westphalian management of religious fanaticism on the European continent and its American colonies was transubstantiated into a system of liberal police power pitted against the kinds of radical political fanaticisms that catalyzed slave insurrections, Jacobin upheavals, communist overthrows, or even (perversely) the financial destruction of proper liberal societies. Why would antifanaticism revert to the management of a religious threat at the end of this long era?[10]

This question is best answered by qualifying one of its premises: the concept of religious fanaticism did not in fact disappear entirely in the eighteenth and nineteenth centuries, but persisted on the margins alongside political fanaticism. We can see this in numerous places, for example in the ongoing demonization of Mormonism as a fanatical religion marked by an unchristian heretical theology, a lack of national loyalty, and an immoral (polygamous) responsibility for secretly conducting a sexual slave trade to obtain white women. The case of anti-Mormonism reminds us as well that anti-Catholicism did not vanish after the nineteenth century, nor did anti-Judaism vanish as a basis for antisemitism. Below and sometimes running as a counterpoint to liberal threats of criminality and political fanaticism were persistently religious racial undercurrents.

If instead of looking only at the European and American continents, we also glance eastward at the expansion of European imperialism in the nineteenth century, we find explicitly racialized religious threat operating alongside the globalized color line as a major theme in colonial governance.[11] As Edward Said famously showed, the power/knowledge regime of Orientalism, which conceived the East as a civilizational unity of passive despotism, emphasized the necessity of accumulating linguistic, cultural, and historical knowledge about the Orient in order to discern the best way to govern Eastern peoples deemed incapable of governing themselves (Said 1979). Standing beyond this more generic mode of Orientalism, moreover, was a specifically *religionized* form of Orientalist racism—what we now call Islamophobia—that occupies a unique place in the larger Orientalist framework because it explained where, when, and under what conditions Oriental populations could become *unruly* and dangerous to colonial power. This modality of racism drew on the older Westphalian archetype of Mahometan disrespect for the authority of the state, but now put it into governmental practice as a vehicle for managing anticolonial animus toward the imperial power.[12]

To the best of my knowledge, this Islamophobic politics of counteracting Orientalist racial threat first surfaced in relation to British rule in India when, after 1857, the British East India Company, which had utilized a complex system of client states to govern South Asia, confronted an unexpected series of military revolts that are collectively known as the Indian Mutiny or the Sepoy Rebellion. In India it is sometimes also called the First War of Independence. These powerful uprisings, which nearly swept the British charter company out of South Asia, led the British home government to drastically alter its governmental approach to South Asian colonialism: the East India Company was stripped of its authority as the United Kingdom imposed for the first time the imperial form of direct sovereign rule known as the Raj.[13]

Established to guarantee colonial security, the Raj formulated a militarized regime of intelligence gathering to preempt further revolts. The India Police Act of 1861 instituted a regime of colonial police, modeled on the Royal Irish Constabulary, designed to "ensure no repetition of the 'mutiny' by their subjects" (Das and Verma 1998, 361). The accumulation of Orientalist knowledge was critical to this endeavor, but especially a certain blend of political, theological, and statistical analysis of Muslims predicated on their standing as a hostile faction within the South Asian population. South Asian Orientalism attributed the special enmity Muslims allegedly felt for the Raj to a potent combination of two matters: political resentment, given their lost status as the former (Moghul) conquerors of South Asia, but also an anti-Westphalian characterization of their religion. Lord Mayo, the fourth viceroy of India, in his attempt to understand the causes of the 1857 Sepoy Rebellion, posed the Raj's overriding political question this way: Are Indian Muslims bound by conscience to rebel against the queen?[14] "Conscience" reinvoked the confessional divide of Westphalian politics in a new colonial context: Was there something in the theological nature of Islam itself that rendered rebelliousness an endemic feature of colonial rule in India and therefore a permanent political problem for the Raj?

Mayo received his most detailed answer from W. W. Hunter, a leading figure in the Indian Civil Service whom he had commissioned to carry out a statistical survey of the population and its attributes. In a remarkable book of Orientalist expert knowledge about the demographic and theological sources of the Sepoy Rebellion, Hunter concluded that while Islam did not *necessarily* promote rebellion, nevertheless, its theological principle of "jihad," could always be interpreted by the more fanatical elements as requiring revolt against non-Muslim rulers. At a minimum, therefore, the Muslim population of India would always be *assessing* an obligation to rebel. While not all Muslims were fanatics, they nevertheless comprised a sizeable population within the larger complex of "Asiatic races" that Hunter concluded to be comparatively and statistically "predisposed to violence and rebellion, with the potential to agitate otherwise-docile Hindus into anti-imperial action" (Morgenstein Fuerst 2017, 35). Anticipating Narendra Modi by over a century, Hunter suggested that the "Indian Musalmans" constituted a "Standing Rebel Camp on our Frontier"(Hunter 1876, 9) and ensured a "Chronic Conspiracy within our Territory" (44). The pacification of this threat would require ongoing educational, legislative, and cultural tactics to keep jihadism in check, with a military readiness waiting in the background if those softer tactics failed.

Muslim threat became a critical element in the militarized language that Ranajit Guha has famously called the "prose of counterinsurgency," a complex system of codes through which the Raj interpreted and responded to peasant revolts (Guha 1994). British India developed a regime of colonial counterinsurgency that, like pastoral antiheresy, Westphalian antipopery, liberal anticommunism, and other modes of securitizing racial power, would employ militarized tactics of detection, infiltration, and neutralization to defeat insurrectionists who had apparently been possessed by what at least one British special commissioner called a "*fanatical spirit of religious superstition*" (Guha 1994, 79).[15]

The British Raj's permanent war against Muslim fanaticism, in some respects, repeated the struggle against the French Jacobin spirit that had infected European nations half a century earlier. It also paralleled the roughly contemporaneous international political police actions to contain the "specter of communism" on the European continent. We can see in each of these cases a political technology aimed at preventing spiritual "possession" by the enemy, or what would much later become known in the secular language of American Vietnam War policy as the "hearts and minds" strategy of anti–anticolonial warfare. But there was one important difference. Unlike Jacobins and communists, rebellious peasants in nineteenth-century India were not, according to the Raj's prose of counterinsurgency, trying to create a new world too liberal for its own good. Their objective was, more like the French reactionary, to roll back "colonial progress" and reverse civilizational momentum to a time before the European arrival. The colonial account of Muslim fanaticism involved what Johannes Fabian has famously called the "denial of coevalness" (Fabian 2014). Its religiosity expressed the Orient's desire for a precolonial past, not a revolutionary future.

Toward the end of the nineteenth century, religious fanaticism faded as the central problem of enmity in Europe's Asian and African colonies. In response to such leftist anticolonial projects as early twentieth-century Pan-Africanism, and accelerating in the wake of the successful Russian Revolution, colonial counterinsurgency as a strategy of racial power would shift its attention instead to a globalized anticipation of the communist threat that had already long been the focus of counterrevolutionary security in Europe.[16] Anticommunist counterinsurgency reached its zenith during the Cold War when the victories of communist movements in the Third World were taken to indicate not a political will to overthrow Western imperialism, but instead a seduction by the Soviet communist specter. Like revolutionary France before it, the Soviet Union appeared as the contagious source of a highly potent revolutionary spirit against which the "Free World" needed to hold the line. And this political line was tacitly mapped onto Du Bois's global color line since twentieth-century communism was widely conceived by Cold War counterinsurgency campaigns as a nonwhite neo-Jacobinism being spread across Asia, Africa, and the Americas by charismatic revolutionary leaders of color such as Mao Zedong, Ho Chi Minh, Fidel Castro, Kwame Nkrumah, Che Guevara, and many others.[17] For this reason, the Cold War (as I have argued elsewhere) was fought by the United States and its (considerably diminished) European allies as a displaced race war that treated revolutionary socialism as its own inward racial marker of fanatical populations (Medovoi 2007). The color line and political radicalism produced mutually constitutive markers for the imperial security state in which the African or Asian body indexed the communist anticolonial soul, and that soul evinced itself in the Asian or African body. To the American security state, the communist was always a racial enemy even if only by virtue of their ambition to abolish the colonial color line, while the person of color presented an ideological risk if only because of their special vulnerability to communist seduction.

In such a Cold War world, the Raj's older form of Islamophobic counterinsurgency faded into near invisibility. By the last third of the twentieth century, however, it would slowly creep back into view. As the Black radical tradition weakened in the United States under the anticommunist assault, Malcolm X and the Nation of Islam gained prominence as new antiracist and anticolonial champions. This formation, which Sohail Daulatzai has called the "Muslim International" (Daulatzai 2012), in part because of the linkages developed between African Americans and national liberation movements in Africa and the Middle East, itself became a growing concern for domestic US counterinsurgency. The FBI's Counterintelligence Program (COINTELPRO) built extensive files not only on Malcolm X but also on numerous radical Black Islamist figures and organizations in the United States.[18] The following decade saw several new inflection points for the reemerging suspicion of political Islamism, including the Palestine Liberation Organization's attack on Israeli athletes at the Munich Olympics in 1972, followed the next year by an oil embargo that triggered the so-called international energy crisis.

The key trigger for a fuller reactivation of Islamophobia, however, arguably occurred with the Iranian Revolution of 1979. Not only did Iran present for the first time an Islamist, as opposed to a communist, path for Third World revolution, but through the ensuing hostage crisis and its instigators' rhetorical attacks on the United States as the "Great Satan," it demonstrated that an Islamic revolution could be just as hostile toward American geopolitical power as a communist one. A new political language for the dangers of Islamic enmity developed with a redefinition of the word "fundamentalism," which inherited, but also substantially revised, the threat of "fanaticism." Prior to 1979, "fundamentalist" was a pejorative name for a scriptural literalist in the United States, whose doctrinal commitments to the "divine word" of the Bible expressed a rearguard, possibly hapless, opposition to the liberalism, progress, and freedom accepted by more moderate members of their church.[19] With the Iranian Revolution, the words "fundamentalist" and "fundamentalism" underwent a shift, evolving to describe the political aspirations of Shi'a leaders in Iran.[20]

"Fundamentalism" was at first used by progressive liberals who disliked the conservative scriptural literalists at home. Theologians like Martin Marty, one of the word's most important popularizers, argued that communists, American evangelicals, and the Iranian ayatollahs were equally "fundamentalist" in their rigid and fanatical commitment to their dogmas, which they militantly forced on other people as political realities.[21] But within short order, the term would be picked up by Ronald Reagan, whose election to the presidency came in no small part through his tough talk directed at the ayatollahs as well as the communists. As America's first neoliberal president, Reagan touted the nation's return to market solutions for its economic problems. At the same time, however, he was also America's first neoconservative president, calling for a militarily strong state whose global mission aligned with God's own fundamental values. As he put it in his famous 1983 "evil empire" speech to the National Association of Evangelicals, "freedom prospers only where the blessings of God are avidly sought and humbly accepted" (Reagan 1983). Meanwhile, Reagan preserved the older hostile view of fundamentalism only for the foreign dogmas he opposed abroad, whether Muslim or communist. If one wonders how communism, an overtly atheist revolutionary movement, could possibly be reframed as fundamentalist (as opposed to a Jacobinesque fanaticism), consider Reagan's citation in this same speech of Whittaker Chambers, the one-time communist turned US spy, to describe Marxism-Leninism as "actually the second-oldest faith, first proclaimed in the Garden of Eden with the words of temptation, 'Ye shall be as gods'" (Reagan 1983).

Globalization's Enemies

When the Cold War came to a close, and with it nearly a century and a half of anticommunist counterrevolutionary politics stretching from 1848 to 1991, some Cold Warriors like Francis Fukuyama proclaimed the end of ideological contestation and thus the end of history (Fukuyama 1989). But in fact, if one looks closely, this era in which liberal freedom celebrated the defeat of its communist archenemy was really one in which the technologies of security steadily reconstituted themselves in relation to new threats, nominated first by a *racial neoliberalism* committed to the geopolitical project of globalization, and more recently, in our own turbulent period of global retrenchment and revivified nationalisms, by an intensifying politics of late fascist *crisis populism* whose proliferation of racial enemies, like that of 1930s fascism, has drawn generously from across the long history of security explored in this book (Medovoi 2007).

I would define racial neoliberalism analogously to the racial liberalism that I described in chapter 4: it has offered a revised mode of political regulation for racial capitalism in the decades since the high globalization of the 1990s.[22] As Quinn Slobodian has shown, the globalist variant of neoliberalism can trace its intellectual ancestry all the way to the end of World War II in the writings and agendas of the so-called Geneva school of neoliberal thinkers (Slobodian 2018). According to Slobodian, the Geneva school envisioned—and was ultimately successful in bringing to fruition—a global governance regime built out of top-down international institutions—first the International Monetary Fund (IMF) and the General Agreement on Tariffs and Trade (GATT), later the World Trade Organization (WTO)—endowed with the power to prevent individual states from intervening in the global marketplace on behalf of their citizens. Slobodian's thesis might seem compatible with that of Wendy Brown, who has characterized neoliberalism as above all a depoliticizing project that degrades the public sphere and dismantles democracy in the name of a market logic (Brown 2015). By contrast, Slobodian understands the global governance regime that neoliberals built as a political project in its own right. I would argue that, like its nineteenth-century liberal predecessor, neoliberalism was always *simultaneously* a depoliticizing and a politicizing project. It buffered capitalism from democratic political intervention by reallocating many social relations to market processes and administrative agencies located on a global scale, as Slobodian shows, but it also mobilized state and interstate police powers to defend the charmed circle of neoliberal market society from populations and parties hostile to its marketization projects. Austerity campaigns were not just ways to enforce market relations, after all, but also a means to punishing states and nations that had sought alternatives to them (Medovoi 2002). "Rogue states" like Iran who refused to cooperate with the global governance regime could face broad international sanctions while, by the time of the Balkans crisis of the 1990s, international military intervention could be presented as a police action. Neoliberalism shared with classic liberalism a project of security against the *homme pervers* of the global era, a figure that was widely associated with a fundamentalist reaction against modernity.

This is the form of political reason that informed Samuel Huntington's highly influential "clash of civilizations" thesis, for example, where he suggested that "la revanche de Dieu," the revenge of God, was the new animating force behind civilizational opposition to global economic integration. "The fundamentalist movements can have significant political impact," wrote Huntington. "They are, however, only the surface waves of a much broader and more fundamental religious tide that is giving a different cast to human life at the end of the twentieth-century" (Huntington 1996, 96). While Huntington considered Christian religious revival to be loosely consistent with the secular universalist claims of Western civilization, Islam's resurgence threatened this because of its "resemblance to Marxism, with scriptural texts, a vision of the perfect society, commitment to fundamental change, [and a] rejection of the powers that be and the nation state" (Huntington 1996, 111).[23]

In a similar vein, Benjamin Barber's 1994 book *Jihad vs. McWorld: Terrorism's Challenge to Democracy* revived "jihad" as a metaphor for all tradition or tribal-based forms of resistance to the global expansion of capitalism, and like Huntington he did not hesitate to make Islamic religiosity into the archetype for globalization's chief terrorizing enemy.[24] Here Barber followed in the very long footsteps of John Locke's presentation of the "Mahometan" as the paradigmatic *exemplar* of uncivil religiosity. Barber foresaw a coming struggle between the interstate system itself (globalization) and stateless enemies who refused incorporation. In this revised version of racial (neo)liberalism, the new enemies of civil society were still to be found *within* society, but since civil society was now global in scale, this simply meant that the world population itself harbored enemies of its own global future.

Barber was no huge fan of neoliberalism: his concern was with saving national democracy, not global capital markets. Nevertheless, on September 11, 2001, the consequences of invoking "jihad" as the generic term for non-state-based resistance to globalization became painfully clear. The declaration of a "global war on terror" reconstituted the futurity of globalization as a choice between *two* future roads: progress toward the asymptote of a fully integrated neoliberal globe, or a grim alternative to it pursued by Islamic terrorists who were, in George W. Bush's words to Congress, the "heirs of all the murderous ideologies of the twentieth-century," enemies of freedom who were "willing to sacrifice human life to their radical visions" (Bush 2001). When Bush declared a "war on terror," he emphasized that this was not just "America's fight. And what is at stake is not just America's freedom. This is the world's fight. This is civilization's fight. This is the fight of all who believe in progress and pluralism, tolerance and freedom" (Bush 2001). And indeed, the "global" securitizing premise of what Bush himself called a "global war on terror" has since offered many opportunities for nations to present themselves as the world's soldiers fighting in new racial battlefields on behalf of a global neoliberal society, often against Muslims: from Israel's occupation of Palestine, and Modi's aggression toward India's "jihadist" Muslim minority, to China's internment and reeducation programs waged against its Uighur population. In effect, the "war on terror" helped to revivify a wartime conception of state-based security for the post-Cold War era.

But in addition to the top-down security state's mode of post-9/11 Islamophobic governance, a form of racial power from below was also emerging at the same time, in this instance one that concerned *national* peoples defending themselves against internal racial enemies that they associated with global forces. Consider the stories that populate Amy Chua's *World on Fire* (2004), a book in which she discussed the growing forms of hatred directed in the nineties and aughts at those she called "market dominant" minorities in different parts of the world—diasporic Chinese in the Asian Pacific, Jews in post-Soviet Russia, South Asians in Africa. These populations had become targets of racial violence because, to the surrounding impoverished populations, they had come to embody the alien financial pressures imposed by a conspiratorial world market. Arjun Appadurai, in his similar and roughly contemporaneous cautionary book about the cultural politics of globalization, *The Fear of Small Numbers* (2006), also observed a growing "geography of anger" and violence attached to the political responses to globalization. As Appadurai noted, this anger had a demographic dimension associated with national minorities who stood in for the threat of populations situated outside the national border. Although neither Chua nor Appadurai named it as such, what had begun to emerge here was a new antiglobalist breed of romantic anticapitalism whose racial animus, which would coalesce into a crisis populism, sometimes aimed at the job-stealing threat of dangerous migrant laboring classes, and at other times was directed at the parasitism of affluent monied minorities on the Postonian model of modern antisemitism.

Crisis Populism: The Assemblage of the Hydra

The political world we inhabit today has been shaped by both of the afore-mentioned racial dynamics. One of the many heads of Trump's hydra is what he insistently called the "radical Muslim terrorist," and one of the key policies that he enacted upon election—the so-called Muslim travel ban—reflects his war against that enemy. In this sense, the new far-right populism we see today is an inheritor of the strategy of top-down governance through Islamophobic security. It speaks as a state that promises to keep liberal society safe against its fanatically religious global enemy. At the same time, however, the new populism has managed to incorporate the bottom-up popular anti-immigrant and antisemitic enmity into its politics. Unlike neoliberal globalization, it presents itself as antiglobalist and anti-elitist, combining in an unprecedented way the counterterrorist 9/11 security state with a militant promise to defend its national people against the amoral forces of cheapened labor (immigrants) and hostile capital (Jews and Asians). Its proliferation of threat draws on the flexible racism of classical fascism , which had itself targeted a diverse range of populations: Jews, Roma, communists, trade unionists, Slavs, gays, and lesbians. Yet, as Alberto Toscano has suggested, right-wing populism today also draws on tropes of color-line and colonial racism that date back to earlier phases of racial capitalism (Toscano 2023).

This late-fascist populist synthesis is one that began to coalesce during the Great Recession that followed the financial crisis of 2008. It would be hard to overestimate the global political implications of the tremendous discrepancy between how international governance resolved the financial crisis itself—by bailing out the banks—and the shock austerity model that it enforced on the global population. Globally, some thirty million jobs were lost, world trade declined by some 15 percent, and ordinary people experienced a catastrophic loss in real wealth (Kalleberg and von Wachter 2017). It was the fallout from 2008 that pushed right-wing populist movements into electoral viability as they leveraged a growing hatred of an international order, with its compliant domestic governments, that had rescued banks and financial institutions while leaving national populations to face their economic pain on their own. The US Tea Party began its slow but inexorable takeover of the Republican Party, the pro-Brexit UK Independence Party (UKIP) was founded in Britain and Alternative für Deutschland (AfD) established in Germany (Judis 2016, 39–108). It was also after 2008 that Modi's Bharatiya Janata Party (BJP) took power in India.[25] All of these movements or political parties would present themselves as eager to wage war against a "corrupt political establishment" that betrays the people so it can profit either from capital flight to other parts of the world or, insofar as jobs remain domestic, purchasing the cheap labor of ethnic minorities and foreigners whose immigration they encourage.

I should at least note too how the slow-motion unraveling of the Arab Spring between 2010 and 2012, which culminated in the largest refugee crisis since World War II, amplified in Europe *both* the antiterror logic launched in 2001 *and* the right-wing populism born of 2008. It is no surprise that, in the wake of the heightened unemployment produced by the Great Recession, the massive influx of immigrants provided ready scapegoats for the experience of economic distress. Latin American migration to the United States in this era functioned in much the same way.

Certain theorists of populism, including Ernesto Laclau and Chantal Mouffe, acknowledge that populism depends not merely on collective identification around "the people," but also on a political narrative that presumes antagonism (see Laclau 2005; Mouffe 2005). Yet they view this antagonism as a positive feature because it ensures that the very things that neoliberalism once sought to depoliticize are once again being repoliticized and reintroduced into the field of democracy. Antagonism produces the "demands" on the state that restores a "people" as the articulating subject of politics. In the specific case of right-wing populisms, however, the process of repoliticization that we are witnessing is premised on a demand that the state defend the people against its populational enemies. Drawing together the Islamophobia of the "war on terror," the post-2008 "betrayals" of enemy capital and corrupt elites, and the threat of "criminal migrants" during the last decade, the new right-wing populism has produced a highly flexible politics of late fascist racial enmity that has seized control of the security state in more than a few parts of the world. It is this conjuncture that has brought the Trumpian snake into its contemporary racial alignment.

Partha Chatterjee has brilliantly posited the question of whether this new kind of populism might in fact represent a "revolt of the people against being turned into populations as things" (Chatterjee 2019, 68). The people/population couplet is in fact critical to its political logic. Populism defines the population as those who dwell among the people but who are not of them, neither deserving their rights nor sharing their interests. Unlike the leftist antiglobalization movements of the nineties, whose binary narrative challenged the institutional regimes of global finance recognizable in the forms of Wall Street, NAFTA, the WTO, the European Union, and even the United Nations in the name of the diverse populations of the globe, right-wing populism triangulates a narrative with three singular characters: the national people, the corrupt elites, and then a shifting third populational figure who is at best an unfair competitor and at worst a nefarious foe. In fact, neither the corrupt elites nor the shifting third figure truly belong to the people: they function as complementary populational enemies, living among but not belonging.

Through this triangulated threat, populist anger is neatly deflected away from the elites qua elites, since the problem is not their excessive wealth and power per se but only their *corruption*. Right-wing populism promises to usher in a loyal elite in racialized national terms, not one dominated (for example) by Jewish bankers who privilege minorities, or Muslims, or Mexicans, or Chinese business partners over the "people." Right-wing populism promises to install a leadership committed to a racial conception of who belongs to the people, which is to say, in the terms of this book, a conception of the people that defines them in opposition to the full range of potential enemies ensouled among them.

Racial Enemies and the Concept of the Political

If neoliberalism's ruination has unleashed a new late fascist variety of racial populist politics that proliferates political enemies in the name of national peoplehood, what then does this suggest about the direction antiracism should take today? Let me tackle this question in two steps. First, I will revisit some general principles that emerge from the approach to racism that this book offers—the logic of security—so we can consider in a generalizable way what it means to challenge the production of enmity. After that, I will turn to the conditions of the contemporary conjuncture, a conjuncture in which the undoing of a global neoliberal order has triggered a capitalist retrenchment that unleashes profound political fragility.

At first glance, the overarching analysis of race I have offered throughout this book might seem consistent with Carl Schmitt's influential but contentious claim that "politics" always concerns itself with a friend/enemy distinction (Schmitt 2008). If, as I have argued, race is what is produced when regimes of security fractionalize the population along an axis of anticipated enmity, Schmitt's "political" and my version of the "racial" would seem to be kindred terms that name intimately related operations. To offer a pithy formulation for the era of racial capitalism, we could say that capitalist production produces class, but that the *politics* of capitalism produces race. The division of labor that constitutes the relations of production for a particular regime of capital accumulation is governed by institutions whose technologies of race-making target the potential rebelliousness of labor as a threat to liberal society, as we have seen, but also establish a range of other populational threats that will require policing.[26]

In formulating it as a product of the "political," I do not mean to suggest that race is necessarily produced by the state. This book has shown how churches, parties, and societies can act as the subject that articulates friend/enemy distinctions just as readily as states. "Race," it would be more accurate to say, is what results from a *politicization of the population* regardless of whether that population constitutes the flock of the church, the body politic of the state, the political unity of the party, or the common property of bourgeois civil society. And what politicization of a population (at least in this sense) always involves is the discovery of an enmity *internal to it*, an existential threat that produces an expectation of war. Here Schmitt is again useful insofar as he posits war as the limit concept of politics. To act politically is not necessarily to engage in war, but it is at least to prepare for the possibility because, as he puts it, "to the enemy concept belongs the ever present possibility of combat" (Schmitt 2008, 32). Insofar as an enemy is one whose very soul longs for your destruction, to act politically is to prepare for the moment when the "existential negation of the enemy" (33) becomes the only possible solution.

If we view racial power as political in this sense, we can begin to see how and why security as a form of political reason works to reproduce relations of inequality, domination, or exclusion, but also why it can also lead to the politics of assimilation, expulsion, or genocide. War is not always instantiated by combat. It may also involve occupation, annexation, or even truce. It produces collateral damage. It deploys spies and intelligence, it incarcerates its prisoners of war. Seen across such a broad terrain of bellicosity, inequality and domination can become racialized conditions precisely because they are rationalized as strategies of security: they become the means of reducing an inimical population's social power and its capacity to threaten. Nor should this threat of race be taken to be entirely in the domain of the fictional or putative, a cognitive error produced by the circulation of a stereotype. Insofar as the production of race actualizes a practice of war, the enforcement of inequality and domination often doubles back to *realize* the enmity it is meant to control. Racialization tends to yield what throughout this book I have called a circular structure of power, a feedback loop of the political that continually reinforces and reanimates the friend/enemy character of the racial distinction. Assimilation, insofar as it is a disciplinary process meant to supplant inimical loyalties among the target population with an instilled allegiance to the relevant church, party, state or society, appears as yet another strategy to reduce racial threat. And finally, modern genocide represents what the Nazi's infamously called a "final solution" to the problem of the enemy: eliminating it altogether by exercising the right to kill in the name of what A. Dirk Moses has called "permanent security" (Moses 2021).[27]

But it at this point that the Schmittian concept of the political begins to fail as a resource for the analysis of racial power. From whence, for example, comes such an extreme notion of existential threat that Schmitt associated with "the political?" In *The Concept of the Political* (2008)at least, Schmitt insisted that it would be a mistake to associate the political with any other domain (the moral, the aesthetic, the economic) because of its unique criteria. Rather than distinguishing good from evil, beautiful from ugly, profitable from unprofitable, the political responds with its own unique antithesis—friend and enemy—that Schmitt insists "cannot be directly reduced to the others" (Schmitt 2008, 26). This position, however, flies in the face even of his own insights. Ten years prior to this work, Schmitt had suggested that the significant political concepts of his time were always "secularized theological concepts" (Schmitt 2005, 36). His special focus in the earlier study was sovereignty, which he argued was modeled on a God who both establishes the law and can suspend it. But the theology of the divine sovereign God figures more than omnipotence: it expresses as well the righteousness of absolute good. Indeed, as Adam Kotsko has pointed out in his analysis of political theology and the problem of evil, Western theology has long linked omnipotence and goodness as part of sovereignty's founding conundrum (Kotsko 2016, 5–8): if God is all powerful and all good, how can he allow evil to exist? The classic move of theodicy, in Western Christianity at least, was a certain splitting of divine power so as to produce a distinctive agent of evil—the demonic. Satan, as Kotsko explains, emerges as an antithetical source of (im)moral action that allows for a human decision, a freedom of will to act either as God's enemy or remain loyal to him.[28] If we put Schmitt's two works together, no doubt in a way that he would not appreciate, then the friend/enemy political distinction appears as a secularization of the moral-religious antithesis of good and evil. The concept of race, running (as this book has shown) along a genealogical track of ever-changing figures of enmity connected to ever-changing historical circumstances—the wolf-like heretic, the malicious converso, the wicked Papist, the rebellious slave, the nihilistic revolutionary, and the destructive terrorist—bear the politico-theological mark of the political enemy constituted as a variant on God's adversary. To condense the point I am making, "race" is a strategy of power grounded in the deployment of a "secularized theological concept"—the opponent of God—that generates a political enemy always already imbued with the metaphysics of evil. "Race" presupposes the inclination of a population of souls toward the destruction of the good, an inclination that augurs a final war. When Schmitt says that to the political concept of the enemy "belongs the ever present possibility of combat," he has himself secularized the eschaton as the theological horizon of the political.

Schmitt wrote *The Concept of the Political* in 1932, just as the National Socialist Party that he had endorsed was about to take power in Germany. Once it did, Nazism would in fact move Germany increasingly onto a war footing, not only with other European powers (what Schmitt would later refer to as "conventional enemies"), but also with a host of internal enemies that the Nazis identified as threats to the Aryan race that constituted that portion of the German population in need of being defended. These enemies—socialists, communists, Jews, Roma, gays—represented the multiheaded hydra of fascism in the Nazi era. Schmitt's "concept of the political," in other words, was a historical collaborator in the logic of racial power that this book has sought to map, not its impartial analyst. For Schmitt, one cannot produce a polity without a willingness to identify and prepare for battle with its existential enemies.[29] This theologization of enmity may at least in part explain why Schmitt fails to consider the *statistical* production of *probable* enemies. Schmitt is always seeking an absolute and sovereign decision about the enemy that produces both an existential unity and an unambiguous domain of the good. But in fact, what makes enemy-making so effective as a strategy of power when it comes to populations is its regulatory capacity for gradation, fractionality, probability, statistical calculation, and, in the final instance, an uncertainty that requires policing. Although Schmitt's writings can therefore illuminate for us the logic that makes racial enmity so central to modern political life, they ultimately offer us no way of imagining alternatives to the theologized perpetuation of racial enemies nor to the permanent preparation for a race war that always appears at the end of time.

We need to take several additional steps in order to ground an analysis of racial security that offers a genuine tool kit for antiracism. First, we need to see that Schmitt makes a subtle but enormously consequential error when he claimed that the "concept of the political" concerns the *decision* about who is the friend and who is the enemy. The political is best understood as the means by which a friend/enemy relation is retroactively produced through a process of *policing*. The political, in other words, is that which *produces* enemies and friends. It does not simply identify them. Secondly, we need to see how this production of the friend/enemy distinction is part of a larger process that governs the entire population, and not only those who are deemed its racial enemies. To grasp this, we must break with Schmitt's tendency to only discuss the side of the enemy when it comes to his friend/enemy antinomy. What happens when we reflect on the political role played by the "friend" as well? My aim here is not to stand Schmitt on his head by promoting the friend or the decision about friendship as the basis of the political. It is rather to help us observe how the joint deployment of *both sides* of the friend/enemy antinomy constitutes what I have called the *game* of racial power. Racial regimes work to discipline and govern the behavior of both "friends" and "enemies" precisely by subjecting everyone to the sorting process. The "friend," after all, is not at all identical with the political order that *polices* the friend/enemy distinction, but acts as a position internal to the rules of the game and their mapping of a battle line (a color line, a national border, but really any populational fractionalization in the name of enmity).[30] To return briefly to the terrain of political theology, the "friend" names the portion of the population that a certain politics aligns with the good and that it therefore deems supportive of the race-making through which populational threat is policed. But those deemed "friends" do not thereby escape subjection to the exercise of racial power, though they will obviously experience it in very different ways. Whites who assist escaped slaves, citizens who offer aid to migrants at the border, liberals who are "fellow-travelers" with the Communist Party, all of these people, when exposed as giving aid and comfort to the enemy of a permanent war constituted by racial power, can be subjected to a police scrutiny that seeks out the enemy-adjacent, the enemy-sympathizing, or even the enemy-camouflaged. A disciplinary process is therefore tightly connected to the position of the friend, and a series of political technologies are at work to impose it. For this reason, the friend/enemy distinction of racial power cannot simply be described as a means by which one group of people dominate another. It is more fully comprehended as a technology of permanent policing by means of which the entire population is differentially subjected to a racial determination that disciplines and regiments their political behavior.

In a certain way, this argument runs parallel to the *Wertkritik* challenge to so-called traditional Marxism for adopting the "standpoint of labor" and assuming that capitalist domination will be overcome when workers achieve a final victory in their class struggle with the capitalists.[31] Precisely because racial power represents the domination of the population by means of a real abstraction, it cannot be dissolved through a warlike defeat of white supremacists, nativists, Islamophobes, or antisemites. What must in fact be abolished is not *only* white supremacy, or Islamophobia, or nativism, or antisemitism, but the very security technologies that *produce them* by exercising a permanent suspicion about our souls, measuring us as a populational datum of racial threat, and ultimately sorting us into degrees of the threatening and the threatened.

What Is to Be Done?

This point seems more important than ever given the historical conjuncture at which we have arrived. The proliferation of racial enemies spawned by right-wing crisis populisms over the last decade—migrants and Muslims, people of color, liberals as well as radicals, corrupt establishments and fake news, treasonous parties, foreign bankers and Chinese viruses—seems inextricable from a broad intensification of abstract violence, rooted in the era of neoliberal austerity, which first accompanied the global economic order of the late twentieth century, and then only intensified in the aftermath of the Great Recession. A post–Cold War world once marked politically by technocratic "third way" governments, economically by free trade agreements and organizations, and subjectively by "responsibilized" (market-embedded moral) selves, has disintegrated. As the corrosive effects of capital accumulation and its attendant crises swamp the neoliberal political arrangements that once served as its mode of regulation, we face a populist proliferation of enemies who are held accountable for the "creative destruction" of capital, the migratory dislocations of populations, and the contemporary resurgence of geopolitical bellicosities. But this is not all. Climate change and the zoonomic spread of viral pandemics may also be counted as the perpetration of indirect and unintended violence by the sheer force of the unintended consequences of "what money wants." It is these very real forms of violence that populist movements ensoul as threat—threats from traveling caravans, competitors for diminishing water and food supplies, perpetrators of "Chinese flus," or even the executors of vaccination conspiracies. These enemies take other forms as well that echo various moments in the long history I have explored in this book. Crisis populisms can declare a fascistic race war against treasonous political parties and factions—democrats, liberals, labor parties, but also alleged "uniparties" (covert and conspiratorial unities of superficially different political parties) and fictious conspiracies of elites engaged in an updated blood libel (think QAnon)—as well as against sexual conceptions of threat against the proper body, for example against the peril of "trans" people who ensoul for populism the seductive sexual-political-racial danger to the proper gendering and racial loyalty of children. If, as Jasbir Puar and Amit Rai have shown, the murderous violence of the "war on terror" in the early 2000s drew justification from the queer monstrosity invested in the terrorist, so now the mobilization of trans panic generates an analogous racial threat (Puar and Rai 2002). The lashing out at public schools for teaching "critical race theory" on the one hand, and using "pronouns" on the other, should not be analyzed as two separate attacks but seen as parallel moves in the deployment of a racism of inner life that seeks to police the inculcation of improper desires by a multiheaded racial enemy with recycled features of the heretic, Alboraique, the sodomite, and seditionist. With this openly martial invitation to meet on a racial battlefield, we therefore live in a time when, perhaps more than ever, we need to take great care that antiracist efforts are not just *redirecting* the distribution of racial enmity (declaring populists to be the true enemy, for example, and marching off to battle) but focused instead on what would be required to reduce and hopefully *dismantle* it altogether. What then should be done? What kind of language and activism do we need? Perhaps most pressingly, what shall we do with the insight that the language of political struggle risks inflaming the problem of enmity rather than addressing it?

I must confess that I find myself deeply uncertain how to answer these difficult questions. No doubt there will be ways to employ this book's analysis of racism that I do not foresee. My principal hope is simply that I will have provided some usable theoretical and historical lessons that can be drawn upon by people with sharper political acumen than I possess. At the moment, however, I find myself wavering between two rather different responses, each with its promises and pitfalls. I would therefore like to take a parting glance at the two strategic directions that have been on my mind over the course of writing this book. The first direction brings together the vital antiracist traditions of abolitionism and nonviolent action. Abolitionism is arguably the most careful and insightful tradition we have when it comes to theorizing the materiality and the material consequences of the technologies through which racial power has been constituted. The economic and political institutions undergirding plantocratic slavery were abolitionism's first focus, of course, but beginning in his book *Black Reconstruction*, W. E. B. Du Bois famously extended the purview of abolitionism by arguing that the elimination of slavery was only an inadequate first step toward producing genuine democracy (Du Bois 2021). The abolition of slavery in and of itself left untouched so many other racial technologies (private property, criminal law, social apartheid, the police, the prison) that would continue to enforce the color line, while leaving entirely unanswered the question of what new technologies of power might organize a form of democratic governance that did *not* rely upon racial power. So broadened, what Angela Davis calls "abolition democracy" has ever since sought to dismantle the technologies of racial security—regimes of policing, incarceration, legal discrimination—so that they may be replaced by new political technologies associated not with security but instead with logics of empowerment or capacity building (Davis 2005).

The challenge facing the abolitionist project is that, as we have seen, it is not in and of itself immune to capture by the logic of permanent war that produces racial power. Abolitionism and communism in the nineteenth century, we saw, were easily made into specters of threat that could be channeled right back into a wide variety of racial security projects: the criminality of people of color, the danger and perversion of foreigners, the Bolshevik disloyalty of Jews. And the project of abolition, precisely because it seems from the viewpoint of security, to express a call to disarmament and therefore precarity, can be pulled back into the alarmist politics of enemy-making.[32] This seems all the more true when abolitionist projects are willing to call for the use of violence.

What might become possible, then, if we bring together the ends of abolitionism with the tradition of nonviolent strategy as a means of evading the logic of permanent war? Nonviolent or direct action, which was widely developed in anticolonial, civil rights, and antiauthoritarian campaigns, has always focused on the question of how the forms of power that produce a regime of governance are most effectively undone. In the writings of Mahatma Gandhi, Martin Luther King Jr., and Gene Sharp, war is alleged to be an ineffective strategy for social change because it tends to reinforce the political authority of existing regimes and rulers by bolstering their appeal to security. Nonviolent action rejects the model of war when it eschews the use of violence against any part of the population. If it does attack, it aims solely at the machinery of power rather than the people, at the "force of evil rather than against persons who are caught in these forces," as Martin Luther King Jr. once put it (King 1957). It thereby becomes compatible with philosophical pacifism.

We should not forget, meanwhile, that nonviolent direct action also exists in the socialist (and in the anarchist) tradition. The strike, after all, can also be viewed as an attack on the machinery of power rather than on its owners. And while the strike might seem to have a modest aim—better terms of work for a certain group of workers—that narrow view is misleading. Strikes often have much wider aims than the immediate interests of the workers who take action. This grows clearest when we turn to the concept of the general strike, which is fundamentally solidaristic in its intent and often used to bring down political regimes. We catch a glimpse of the possible breadth of this tradition in Du Bois's famous description of the flight of enslaved Africans northward during the Civil War as a kind of general strike against the plantocracy (Du Bois 2021, 55-83). What makes nonviolence *strategically* important is the challenge it creates for an existing regime to activate a counterpolitics of security. Instead of accelerating a logic of war, one possible hope regarding nonviolent action is that it will encourage sympathizers to withdraw their active or even tacit support for the regime in question, denying its institutions and technologies of power the various forms of participation upon which it relies.

Even when so supplemented with nonviolent strategy, however, abolitionist projects will surely still stand accused of engaging in a political struggle, of treating proponents and leaders of a racial regime as the enemy, of employing "strategies and tactics," and therefore of being engaged in an antagonism that still looks like war. Even Gene Sharp, the famous theorist of nonviolent action, sometimes proposed nonviolence as a smarter or better way to conduct revolutionary struggle (Sharp 1973). The ongoing challenge for abolitionist/nonviolent approaches to antiracism, therefore, will be that they have not been entirely withdrawn from the politics of the friend/enemy distinction, nor the project of combat, and therefore remain at risk of being drawn into the game of racial power. Gandhi did become a political enemy of the British Empire, King became a "danger" to national security. Strikes are regularly met with violence. And perhaps this problem is a strategically unavoidable feature of antiracist action.

There is a second approach to antiracism that would pull even further away from the logic of war that undergirds the politics of security. I mean here a reparative approach that attempts to do entirely away with racial power's hermeneutics of suspicion. In this approach, the observation is that the paradigm of struggle always produces the enmity of camps and the distrust of those who might support the other side. Abolishing racial power is here understood as refusing that logic fundamentally, avoiding any knowledge/power formation that appears to bifurcate populations in favor of ones that seek to unify them or heal differences. These are the approaches associated with projects of restorative justice, political reconciliation, and the activist production of mutual trust as a prelude to envisioning futures of mutual aid that undermine the production of populational divides. In other words, these are approaches that attempt not so much to defeat the hermeneutic of suspicion on the terrain of struggle as to enact, wherever and whenever possible, activities generative of a hermeneutic of trust that might someday supplant it by offering populations an alternative to the politics of security. Indigenous conceptions of justice are often premised on this kind of restorative work, which treats actually existing enmity as a kind of wound in need of healing if a better future is to be had. Olúfhemi O. Táíwò has similarly proposed that reparations for plantocratic slavery and colonialism should also be thought of in this way, not simply as a way for individuals to make amends for the past, but as a spiraling path toward a post–climate crisis future where shared world-making could at last replace race-making (Táíwò 2022).

Such reparative antiracism seems daring at this political moment. It turns away from direct struggle against the contemporary proliferation of enemies in favor of asking how to ameliorate enmity by means of nonpolitical actions and projects that are not based on the friend/enemy antinomy. Another name for this kind of work might be disarmament. Under current conditions, disarmament is a project that would only become possible when people begin to conclude that the permanent preparation for war is ultimately more dangerous and damaging than de-escalation. It requires also a utopian capacity to imagine that discarding the weapons of suspicion and the machineries of war could produce a better world than the one that a logic of security has asked us to envision and trust. But is unilateral disarmament of this sort a foolhardy strategy, particularly in a world where this logic of war already undergirds massive inequalities? If forms of impersonal abstraction domination form the basis of racial power, does withdrawal from the battlefield mean an acceding to the technologies of power? For all its good intentions, it might well prove, as Patricia Stuelke has argued, to be little more than a means of turning oneself into an unwitting ally of "neoliberal empire's 'anti-politics machine'" (Stuelke 2021, 217). A more generous way of posing Stuelke's criticism might be to ask whether it makes any sense to attempt an amelioration of actually existing racial enmity before we have first attempted to quell the forces that continue to generate it in the first place?

This counterargument would echo Marx's famous critique of the utopian socialists in the *Manifesto* of the *Communist Party* as people who "wish to attain their ends by peaceful means, and endeavor, by small experiments, necessarily doomed to failure, and by the force of example, to pave the way for the new social Gospel" (Marx and Engels 2018, 498). To withdraw from politics in favor of repair seems both visionary and impossibly dangerous. And to accept Marx's criticism is to conclude that one must throw oneself back into the political struggle associated with the antagonisms of our social conjuncture. Is the idea of "disarmament" preposterous, for example, when it comes to class conflict and social inequality? Does such a project just ensure that there will be no resistance at all to a world saturated with exploitation and expropriation of the many?

I understand these concerns, but I also want to suggest that if we take seriously the idea that capitalism's racialized regime of political regulation is necessary for accumulation to proceed, then it might actually make sense to see racism as capitalism's weakest link, and to imagine that if we can significantly reduce the politics of enmity this book describes, it will actually make it far more difficult for capitalism to proceed as normal. A political regime that is organized through the crystalized fear of crime, revolution, and terror, immigrant hordes, people of color, or Jews—all this ensures the imperative of policing. Such forces make anything other than a romantic and racialized anticapitalism very difficult to achieve. The reduction of racial power and the diminished policing of threats would therefore perhaps make possible new ways of acting politically to transform the mode of production—new ways of emancipating ourselves from racial capitalism—that are not available now.

Perhaps the distinctions I have drawn between abolition and repair are ultimately also too quick. Even Stuelke acknowledges that her criticism of the "reparative turn" is not meant to express a criticism of material reparations. If, as Ruth Wilson Gilmore argues, abolition always requires more than acts of undoing or dismantling so as to replace the technologies of racial power with new infrastructures that literally create a new place (the place of "Reconstruction"), then abolition and reparation may yet prove to be the same project (Gilmore 2022, 483). What we need to build through reparation will prove to be the anticipatory successor of what we need to abolish.

In dividing this conclusion into its two sections—the historical and the theoretical—I have perhaps only shown that these strategic explorations of abolitionist nonviolence and reparative disarmament come at the worst possible moment. The global proliferation of right-wing populisms has heightened the political demand for security and threatened accelerated violence against those targeted as the racial enemies of an ethno-nationally defined people. It is hard to avoid feeling a call to arms rather than a call to drop them. It is hard not to confront racism on the battlefield by declaring the new crypto-fascist features of crisis populism to be the political enemy of our time. This might therefore be among the most difficult of moments to discern how we can advance antiracism by abolishing security. But I want to suggest, nevertheless, that grasping the inner life of race, understanding its investment in the processes of ensoulment that lead to a logic of war, will be useful regardless of which strategy of antiracism we ultimately adopt.

The one thing about which abolitionism will surely prove correct is in its insistence that technologies of control and institutions of policing are the means by which power circulates through the population. It is ultimately this ensemble of apparatuses—acting as racial capitalism's political infrastructure—and not some segment of the population, that is the real enemy of human liberation from both racism per se and from its accompanying processes of exploitation and expropriation. Finding a way to abolish these technologies, and thereby to interrupt the bifurcation of the population into friends and enemies, may be no easier or more likely to succeed than the revolution against private property that Marx once foretold. But the destination, if not the pathway to it, at least makes sense.

Notes

INTRODUCTION. ENSOULMENT: A STRATEGY OF RACIAL POWER

Epigraph: "The Snake," a song written by Oscar Brown Jr., first appeared on his album *Tell It Like It Is!* (1963). A cover version recorded in 1968 became a hit for the soul singer Al Wilson.

1. Although W. E. B. Du Bois coined the term "color line" in *The Philadelphia Negro* (1995, 116), he popularized it in *The Souls of Black Folk* through his famous pronouncement, "The problem of the Twentieth Century is the problem of the color-line" (2007, 32).

2. For an account of the Charlottesville white supremacist rally, see Rosenberg 2017.

3. It would be impossible to provide a bibliography that does justice to the history of this investigation in a single footnote, especially since this entire book will be engaging with this corpus of questions. I should mention, however, a handful of very different kinds of studies to suggest the range of scholarly interventions that have been attempted. In a classic study, *Racism: A Brief History* (2015), George Fredrickson explores the long-term historical linkages and comparative relations between modern antisemitism and color line racism; J. Kameron Carter's *Race: A Theological Account* (2008) locates the basis of all forms of racism in the specification of the Jews as obstacles to the universal-izing aims of Christian theology; Junaid Rana's *Terrifying Muslims: Race and Labor in the South Asian Diaspora* (2011) considers the historical intertwining of race and religion as an informing context to anti-immigrant racisms in the present moment; and Sohail Daulatzai's *Black Star, Crescent Moon* (2012) considers twentieth-century Black Islam as an anti-imperial political formation that relied on the imaginative interplay of the Muslim Third World and Black freedom struggles. These and many other studies have sought to show how Islamophobia, antisemitism, and anti-Blackness share common his-tories that must be thought together if the political work of race-making is to be grasped comprehensively.

4. For more on Oscar Brown Jr., see the "Biographical/Historical Note" in the guide to his papers, collected at Howard University (DCAAP 2016, 4).

5. Evelyn Alsultany's thoughtful analysis of post-9/11 media representations of Arabs and Muslims supports the view that Trump's probabilistic mode of racialization is nothing

new. As she notes, media images of Arab or Muslims as terrorists were always balanced with positive counterimages meant to immunize programs from accusations that they "stereotyped" Arabs or Muslims as haters (Alsultany 2012). A statistical racism could thereby present itself as postracial. Asultany echoes Mahmood Mamdani's analysis of the "good Muslim/bad Muslim" binary (Mamdani 2005), which allegorically reduces a biopolitical statistical racism to the two Cold War figures that forecast the dueling possibilities for Muslim inner life.

6. I am alluding here to David Theo Goldberg's pithy book title, *The Threat of Race* (2009).

7. For a masterful history of the religious tradition that turned sex into sin and the snake into a figure of evil, see Pagels 1989.

8. By "police" I here mean not only what we mean more narrowly by police today, but more broadly the management of a population through the use of "intelligence" (information about the population) and "policy" (techniques of acting on that information). "Policy" and "police" share the same etymology, and in fact, the first meaning of "police" was as a synonym for policy. I will discuss this genealogy in chapter 4.

9. On counterinsurgency, see Guha 1994. See also Manu Karuka's account of US imperial expansion as always taking the form of a reactive and fragile countersovereignty (2019).

10. The original formulation appears in Carl von Clausewitz's *On War* (1989, 87).

11. This said, note that the original French phrase this translates is "Tiens, un nègre" (Fanon 1952, 90), which is perhaps better translated as "Here, a n—gger." The original captures a sense of observation, coupled with racial fear and loathing, without locking it into the visual register.

12. Jennifer Lynn Stover (2016), however, astutely shows how the color line also concerns a regime of *audibility*.

13. Special thanks to Zahid Chaudhary for drawing my attention to the importance of stressing this reversibility of racial power.

14. Two key novels in the tradition that interest Gayle Wald are James Weldon Johnson's *Autobiography of an Ex-Colored Man* ([1912] 1990) and Nella Larsen's *Passing* ([1929] 1986), both of which concern surreptitiously crossing the line in order to thwart it.

15. "Antisurveillance" could be defined as the neutralization of a regime's tactics of surveillance. See Monahan 2015.

16. The threat of passing was intensified during the early twentieth century with the legal institution of the "one-drop rule" as the legal definition of Blackness.

17. I thank Anoop Mirpuri for his crucial feedback and intervention in my account of passing. The language I use in this paragraph is indebted to his comments. For his own account of how passing operates as a technology of racism in the context of professional sports, see Mirpuri 2010.

18. It is in exactly this context that Du Bois famously activates a militarized terminology of the twoness of the Black soul: "two souls, two thoughts, two unreconciled strivings; two warring ideals in one dark body" (2007, 8).

19. I thank a helpful anonymous reader's report for suggesting this incisive formulation.

20. This reflects the classic formulation for fetishistic disavowal in *The Sublime Object of Ideology* (Žižek 2019, 28–30).

21. Junaid Rana's rich exploration of the "race-ing of religion" over the *longue durée* (2007) has been immensely illuminating and useful to my work.

22. At the time I wrote "Dogma-Line Racism" (2012a), I conceived color and dogma as two different axes through which race gets mapped. Though I would still argue that this is a useful approach, I now prefer to think of race as a game of power that alternates between a particularizing and a universalizing mode of population management. I will elaborate on this conception in the coming pages.

23. Thanks to Judith Butler for calling my attention to this distinction: the racism of "interiority" that Jasbir Puar (2011) explores should not be mistaken for a "racism without race."

24. In the essay "Algeria Unveiled," Frantz Fanon demonstrates this logic perfectly. The veil becomes an indicator of a potential resister, but the absence of the veil, denoting the apparently "modern" or "secular" Algerian woman, may represent an even deeper form of deception perpetrated by the revolutionary woman (2004, 53–55).

25. Étienne Balibar's discussion of racism as relying on both a universalizing and a particularizing logic bears an oblique relationship to the dual heremeneutics of suspicion I describe here. For Balibar, the focus is on racism's scale—that is, how it operates both above and below the level of the nation. While that distinction matters for my analysis, my focus is on whether the threat of race should be secured in relation to part or all of the population. The question, in other words, is whether the boundary conditions for racial threat tend to bifurcate the population, run coterminous with the boundary of the population, or striate both its inside and its outside. See Balibar 1991b.

26. The TV series *Homeland* ran for eight seasons from 2011 to 2020.

27. I have explored this argument in my essay "Swords and Regulation" (Medovoi 2012b). A briefer but similar discussion appears in chapter 4 of this book.

28. Albeit in tremendously different and frequently incompatible ways, I would include here the work of Cedric Robinson, Barbara Jeane Fields, Robin Kelley, Ruth Wilson Gilmore, Walter Johnson, Iyko Day, Moishe Postone, Hylton White, and Jodi Melamed.

1. RACE BEFORE RACE: THE FLOCK AND THE WOLF

Epigraphs: The Gospel of John is quoted from the New Revised Standard Version found in the *HarperCollins Study Bible* (Attridge 1989, 1834–1835). The full text of Philip the Chancellor's poem, written some time before 1250, is reproduced in Traill 2006 (245). For the *Protocols of the Meetings of the Learned Elders of Zion*, see Nilus 1965. This forged work was first published in Russia in about 1903.

1. Elsewhere, Aníbal Quijano writes, "Con la formación de América se establece une categoría mental nueva, la idea de 'raza.' Desde el inicio de la conquista, los vencedores inician una discusión históricamente fundamental para las posteriores relaciones entre las gentes de este mundo" (With the formation of the Americas, a new mental category was established, the idea of "race." From the start of the conquest, the victors initiated a discussion historically fundamental for subsequent relations between the peoples of the world) (Quijano 1995, 5), translation mine. The Smedleys similarly write, "*Race* as a mode of describing and categorizing human beings appeared in the languages of the Spanish, Portuguese, Italians, French, Germans, Dutch, and English as these groups established

colonial empires in the New World and Asia and set about dealing with their heteroge-neous populations" (Smedley and Smedley 2018, 14).

2. C. J. Robinson observes that even modest Catalan and Italian families had domestic slaves who might be "Tartar, Greek, Armenian, Russian, Bulgarian, Turkish, Circassian, Slavonic, Cretan, Arab, African (Mori), and occasionally Chinese (Cathay)" (Robinson 2020, 16). This, for him, illustrates the "racial" differences of the division of labor in the Middle Ages that would prepare the way for racial capitalism. William Robinson, Salvador Rangel, and Hilbourne A. Watson (2022) have attacked this argument, pointing out that slavery was ubiquitous elsewhere in the world in those centuries, and in no way especially central to Europe's division of labor.

3. The original Koine Greek word translated in the Vulgate by the Latin *pignus* is ἀρραβῶν, or *arrabōn*, which likewise can mean the deposit, earnest, or security on a loan.

4. The New Testament metaphor derives from the Hebrew Bible, in references to King David as a shepherd, for example, or in the famous "The Lord is my shepherd" (Psalm 23:1). But the pastoral metaphor took on an outsized importance in medieval Christian-ity that it never played in Judaism.

5. "Fourth Lateran Council—1215," in Tanner 1990, 246.

6. In Foucault's account, the logic of sovereign power is circular: its end is to maintain itself (2007, 98). Governmentality, by contrast, seeks ends external to itself, such as the well-being of the population or the accumulation of capital. For the pastorate, that end was the redemption of souls.

7. R. I. Moore reads these persecutions in a quasi-psychoanalytic vein. He represents these attacks as acts of repression perpetrated by elites who sought to protect and purify medieval culture of its feared "others." My approach is to read Moore against Moore by focusing on the way that the pastorate was a productive form of power, managing the population by creating the very transgressions that it then policed. This rereading of Moore reflects the criticism of later scholars that Moore produced a kind of teleological reading of European intolerance; see Nirenberg 1996, 1–17; Nederman 2010, 13–24; and Peters 2006, 14–15. The productively circular (as opposed to merely repressive) structure of pastoral power clarifies why it could spiral in numerous directions in different regions and over time. One such historically momentous spiral, as I will suggest in the next chap-ter, led to the production of race.

8. In the process of purifying the church, Gregory VII and others also sought to elevate the pope's authority over all other bishops as well as temporal rulers. Gregory proved victorious over the Holy Roman emperor during the so-called investiture conflicts. These reforms therefore also represented an insistence on the priority of pastoral over sovereign authority. The church's responsibility for the salvation of the Christian flock meant that the church not only should not be expected to yield to the decrees of secular rulers, but more importantly that the pope reserved the right to summon Europe's princes to exer-cise the temporal sword against Christ's enemies.

9. For more on wolves in medieval bestiaries, and the image in figure 1.1, see "Wolf," Medieval Bestiary, 2023, https://bestiary.ca/beasts/beast180.htm.

10. For an excellent analysis of the medieval disciplinary process, see Given 1997, 218–20.

11. There was no single, unified Inquisition formed at one moment. Rather, a range of inquisitorial tribunals emerged under various authorities, some papal, some secular, some under the mendicant orders themselves. See Given 1997, 16.

12. See Robinson 2008 for a useful intellectual history of the doctrine of the "two swords."

13. Popular works like *La Chanson de Roland* not only depicted Saracens as pagans, but regularly confused them with Slavs. See Cruz and Hoeppner 1999.

14. The apocalyptic imagination of the Crusades is discussed by Jessalyn Lea Bird (2004, 24). Joachim of Fiore, whose heterodox views on the Trinity were indicted in Lateran IV's canons, was famous for a mystical account of end times that possibly influenced Pope Innocent III's commitment to the Crusades.

15. The comparatively accurate knowledge about Islam found in Petrus Alfonsi's text is not spoken by the Christian character Petrus, but instead by the Jewish Moses, who describes Islam in great detail as a prelude to asking Petrus why he did not convert to Islam instead of Christianity. When viewed as a dramatic reenactment of Alfonsi's own decision to convert, Moses's section of the dialogue seems less an account of Islamic law waiting to be rationally critiqued by Petrus than the eyeing of a diabolical alternative path that his former self might have taken. It is in this sense that the religion of the Saracens turns out to be a heretical threat in the world of Alfonsi's dialogue—a faith that could potentially seduce Jews away from the *right* conversion.

16. Tolan (2002) shows that Alfonsi's account of Muhammad is taken quite directly from an eighth-century eastern Christian polemic against Islam known as the *Risalat al-Kindi*.

17. Peter the Venerable makes this comment in a letter to the famed preacher Bernard of Clairvaux, which is included in the translated edition of the *Summa* (Peter the Venerable 2016).

18. The earliest use of the word "infidel" indicated in the *Oxford English Dictionary* is an appearance in Thomas Malory's *Le Morte d'Arthur* (1485), where Malory speaks of "Two honderd sarasyns or Infydeles." The OED defines this usage as referring, from a "Christian point of view," to "an adherent of a religion opposed to Christianity esp. a Muslim, a Saracen (the earliest sense in English); also (more rarely), applied to a Jew, or a pagan." "Infidel, N., Sense 1.a.," *Oxford English Dictionary*, Oxford UP, https://doi.org/10.1093/OED/1670975593, accessed December 16, 2023. The English word derives etymologically from the Old French *infidéle*, also of the fifteenth to sixteenth century, which in turn comes from the Latin *infidelis* (unfaithful; by extension, unbelieving). The Latin word is certainly ancient, appearing in the Vulgate, for example, as in the line from 2 Corinthians: 6:15: "quae autem conventio Christi ad Belial aut quae pars fideli cum infidele?" (And what concord hath Christ with Belial? Or what part have the faithful with the unbeliever?). But only in the late Middle Ages did the term *infidelis* begin to single out Saracens as well as Jews in this indicative way that is inflected by heretical thought.

19. "Fourth Lateran Council—1215," in Tanner 1990, 246. All translations from this source are my own.

20. "Fourth Lateran Council—1215," in Tanner 1990, 230.

21. "Fourth Lateran Council—1215," in Tanner 1990, 230.

22. This pastoral formula is taken directly from John 10:16.

23. "Fourth Lateran Council—1215," in Tanner 1990, 243.

24. "Fourth Lateran Council—1215," in Tanner 1990, 245.

25. Aristotle's uses of the term, which appears in the title of his important book *On the Soul* (*Peri psuchēs*), are discussed in Ackrill 1972.

26. Canons 67 through 69 concern the Jews. Canon 67 requires Jews to tithe the church on the grounds that they have already stolen much of their wealth from Christians who would have previously tithed. Canon 69 reiterates that Jews should never be given public office since "under cover of them they are very hostile to Christians" ("Fourth Lateran Council—1215," in Tanner 1990, 266).

27. "Fourth Lateran Council—1215," in Tanner 1990, 266.

28. David N. Friedenreich observes that laws had long existed forbidding marriage or sexual intercourse between Jews and Christians, but that this Crusader law was the first to add a requirement concerning Jewish and Saracen dress (2011, 56–57). The text of Canon 16 may be translated, "If a Saracen man or woman dresses in Frankish manner, they will be infiscated" (special thanks to Livia Tenzer for this translation); the penalty refers to the seizing of a person's property on behalf of the "fisc" or public purse.

29. In his classic *The Devil and the Jews*, Joshua Trachtenberg (1943, 180) writes:

> The introduction of the Jew badge coincided with the start of the Inquisition and the war against heresy. This chronological correspondence was not accidental by any means. It became the policy of the Church to expose all its enemies to public notice and execration by means of distinctive signs—Jews, Saracens, sorcerers, priests convicted of irregular practices, heretics. These signs were intended to differ for each group, but they varied from place to place and were often so nearly alike and so clumsily designed (consisting usually of pieces of colored felt sewn to the outer garments) that they could be distinguished from one another only with difficulty, and often not at all.

30. "Fourth Lateran Council—1215," in Tanner 1990, 267.

2. THE RACIAL TURN: FRAYED FABRIC AND DISSIMULATING DANGER

Epigraphs: Pero Sarmiento's letter, dated 1449, is quoted from Salgado 2018. For the quote from *The Fire Next Time*, first published in 1963, see Baldwin 1995, 34.

1. The definition is taken from Jean Nicot's *Thrésor de la langue françoise* (1609). The dictionary obviously catalogs words that were already in use.

2. See also Cooley (2022), who explores how this discourse of the breeding of animals came to shape race. I will be following another pathway associated with a different etymology of the word.

3. Nebrija's work was not a pure vernacular dictionary, but a Latin-Spanish dictionary. Still, it was apparently the first dictionary to define Spanish words.

4. An exhibit at the Casa de Sefarad in Córdoba, Spain, claims that Nebrija was repeatedly investigated by the Spanish Inquisition and that the famous critic Americo Castro believed he was a converso. If true, it is ironic that Nebrija's *Diccionario* is the first place we find the Spanish word *raça* written and defined.

5. Covarrubias's text on race is translated by Laura A. Lewis (2003, 193n53). The original wording may be found in the entry on "raza" in Covarrubias 1611; https://www.google.com/books/edition/Tesoro_de_la_lengua_castellana_o_espa%C3%B1o/qKm8nzelynUC?hl=en&gbpv=1&printsec=frontcover.

6. Corominas writes that *raza* "vino a confundirse con el viejo y castizo *raça* 'realeza o defecto en el paño'" (came to be confused with the older Castilian *raça*, meaning a defect in the cloth) (Corominas 1954, 1019), translation mine.

7. "Fourth Lateran Council—1215," in Tanner 1990, 267.

8. In this passage, Harvey is offering his own elaboration of the entry in Corominas 1954 that discusses *raza*.

9. For Torres, the history worth telling is one in which "purity of blood" becomes linked to the "stain of race." My argument is similar but slightly different, namely that the "stain of race," understood as a covert threat, becomes something for which one tests or screens by investigating "purity of blood." "Impurity of blood" is less a synonym for race than a sign of it. A concept of the stain of race must exist before someone's purity of blood can matter.

10. For a history of the crusading legacy of those wars, see O'Callaghan 2013.

11. This translation appears in section 7.24 of Dwayne Carpenter's edition of the *Siete partidas* (Carpenter 1986, 33). Alfonso the "Wise" was well known as a Christian ruler sympathetic to the Andalusian model of *convivencia*.

12. The word "Marrano" has a hotly debated etymology. It could mean "pig," connecting to the Jewish and Muslim prohibition on eating pork. It could allude to "error," or even a sense of "force," referring to the coerced nature of the conversion. See Malkiel 1948.

13. Father of the Likud prime minister of Israel Benjamin Netanyahu, Benzion Netanyahu held the theory that Jews were the first and fullest subjects of modern racism, implying for him that they deserved a national homeland where they could protect themselves. In this way, his book arguably serves his son's right-wing Zionist politics. In suggesting that it is the converso and not the Jew who was first racialized, I hope to show that what was actually at stake in early modern Spain was the emergence of a flexible politics of racial security that could transfer readily across changing populational targets (including, for that matter, Palestinians) and not a unique, stand-alone antisemitism.

14. This translation is taken from an unpublished paper by Isaac Salgado (2018). Sarmiento's original is as follows:

> es notorio que el dicho don Álvaro de Luna, vuestro condestable, públicamente á defendido e reçebtado e defiende e reçebta a los conversos de linaje de los judíos de vuestros señoríos e reinos, los quales por la mayor parte son fallados ser infieles e herejes, e han judaizado e judaizan, e han guardado e guardan los más d'ellos los ritos e cerimonias de los judíos, aspostatando la crisma e bautismo que reçevieron, demonstrando por obras e palabras que lo rescebieron en el cuero e non en los coraçones ni en las voluntades, a fin que so color e nonbre de cristianos, prebaricando, estroxesen las ánimas e cuerpos e faziendas de los cristianos viejos de la fee católica, según lo han fecho e fazen. (González Rolan, Saquero Suárez-Somonte, and Gonzáles Saquero 2012, 5–6)

15. Hereafter this work is simply referred to as the *Tratado*. The spelling can be either *alboraique* or *alborayque*, while the plural can be either *alboraiques* or *alboraycos*.

16. *Buraq* in fact derives from the Arabic word for "lightning." For details about al-Buraq and its uses here, see Carpenter 1999, 26.

17. In the original: "E las señales que dizen los Moros que el alboraique avia nonbranlas aqui por sus significaciones, e esas mesmas han los neofitos por condiciones" (Lazar 1997, 207–8).

18. Unlike the Jews, the Moors of Spain were primarily rural and more deeply embedded in the cultural distinctiveness of their own language, dress, music, and food. The insistence that they conform to Christian styles of life therefore generated a deeper kind of cultural conflict.

19. Although the Spanish crown blurred the line between church and state by presenting itself as Rome's temporal champion, we can already discern an emergent logic of "reason of state" that I will analyze in chapter 3. It took some time to mobilize a distinction between state and church as a mechanism of power in its own right. In a Westphalian context, states gradually came to present themselves as a neutral party managing a population suffused with religious strife. This important shift in the operation of security would give rise to what we now call the "security state." Although Spain was also subject to these changes, the development was more pronounced in Catholic France and Protestant Britain, both of whose monarchies placed themselves above their churches. I have pushed these issues into the background of this chapter so as to focus on the itinerary of the early technology of race, but with the full understanding that the development of monarchical power—even in Spain—overlaps with reason of state.

20. See the king and queen's written justification for the Spanish Inquisition in Ferdinand and Isabella's "Letter on the Inquisition" (Cowans 2003, 10–12). For the classic study of the Spanish Inquisition, see Kamen 1985.

21. This special *sambenito* designed for the impenitent was sometimes called a *samarra* or *zamarra* (Alfassa 2004, 8).

22. The *sambenito* was worn by all accused heretics. Its use for managing conversos, however, was a new phenomenon no longer explicable in pastoral power's terms alone. In the next few paragraphs, I begin to explain how the pastoral conception of heresy was modified, especially in its temporal registers.

23. I would suggest that the Ku Klux Klan's use of the hat symbolically employed the principle of Mardi Gras reversal to suggest the righteousness (as opposed to the sinfulness) of their defense of Southern white supremacy. For a brief discussion of this connection, see Beusterien 2012.

24. Robin Blackburn writes: "The term 'slave' in all western European languages refers simply to Slavs, who were seen as congenitally heretic or pagan. Between the tenth and the sixteenth centuries, the Slav lands furnished the Vikings and Italian traders with their main source of slaves, primarily from the eastern Adriatic and the Black Sea" (Blackburn 1997, 83).

25. Out of this huge corpus, I have found immensely useful for the specific purposes of this book Blackburn 1998; Lewis 2003; Martínez 2011; Palmer 2013; and Nemser 2017.

26. For a review of the turn to skin color as the basis for the caste distinctions, see Beltran 1945.

27. The *Requerimiento* was always to be read aloud to Native communities before commencing an attack, so it could be claimed that they had officially received the word of Christ, the authority of the Papacy, and the right of Spain's monarch to rule the New World. Any resistance to that rule and to being missionized therefore constituted a legal cause for a just war. The *Requerimiento* is translated in full in Hanke 1938.

28. See also Nájera (2011), who notes that Sepúlveda, a major champion of holy war against the Ottoman Empire, recycled his arguments to answer the question of the Indigenous.

29. For an account of this first known revolt, see Itman 2007. For one interpretation of Tupac Amaru II's revolt, see Szemiński 1974.

30. P. C. Emmer (1991) argues that the main difference between the first and second Atlantic system concerns the momentous invention of the plantation colony during the seventeenth century, which vastly expanded the slave trade on behalf of a specialized form of slave-capitalist mass production: the so-called triangular trade. Chapter 4 takes up the question of how race as a technology of power was reshaped by the liberal logic of plantocratic slave capitalism.

31. Around this same time in 1577, the English adventurer George Best similarly interpreted the African's blackness by way of Ham's disobedience of his father. According to Winthrop D. Jordan, Best wrote that "to punish this 'wicked and detestable fact': God willed that a sonne should bee born whose name was Chus, who not onely it selfe, but all his posteritie after him should bee so blacke and lothsome, that it might remain a spectacle of disobedience to all the worlde. And of this blacke and cursed Chus came all these blacke Moores which are in Africa" (Jordan 2013, 51).

32. Sandoval's original text, published in Seville in 1627, was the first book written by a European about the African slave trade. Sandoval wrote it as a kind of "missionary textbook" on how and why to convert the Africans. Goldenberg (2017) translates this passage from Sandoval's treatise, and also provides the original in a footnote on the same page. For the full text in the original Spanish, see Sandoval 1956.

33. Muhammad (2019) describes the sociological judgment of Blackness that was grounded in the use of crime statistics. The Noahide curse can be viewed as a prestatistical predecessor to this condemnation of Blackness.

34. In chapter 4 I will consider how this frame for anti-Blackness was rearticulated in the language of possessive individualism by the liberal discourse of plantocratic slavery.

35. For a sophisticated reflection on how the maroon's escape became a template for the political concept of freedom that would emerge in the age of revolution, see Neil Roberts, *Freedom as Marronage*, especially his setting out of the etymology of "marronage" (Roberts 2015, 4–5). See also Aronson and Budhos 2010, 56.

3. WESTPHALIAN REASON: THE POLITICAL THEOLOGY OF SEDITION

Epigraphs: The quote from Francis Bacon's "Of Unity in Religion" (1625) is drawn from Bacon 1996, 346–47. Hiram Wesley Evans, who served as grand wizard of the Ku Klux Klan, is quoted from Evans 1926. The lines by Judge Kaufman are taken from his 1951 statement issued upon sentencing Julius and Ethel Rosenberg to death for espionage (Kaufman 2021).

1. Historian Francois Soyer observes widespread fear in sixteenth and seventeenth century Spain that converso doctors were revenge-murdering their Christian patients. See Soyer 2019, 156–70. As Soyer notes, the converso doctor theory had a long prehistory back to the Middle Ages, including the alleged attempted murder of King Enrique III of Spain by his Jewish doctor.

2. For his definition of "geoculture," see Wallerstein 1991b, 139–99.

3. For Rawls's version of Westphalianism, see Rawls 1993. See also Stout 2009.

4. Skinner calls this "master concept" of the state an "impersonal form of political authority distinct from both rulers and ruled" (Skinner 1989, 120). Unlike Foucault, Skinner associates the state primarily with sovereign power (though one alienated from the people and that can never belong to any particular ruler). I conceive the state instead as a meeting ground between sovereign and governmental power, where the latter produces the need to identify populational enemies that threaten governability.

5. Foucault arrives at this analysis through a reading of Quesnay, de la Perriere, and other anti-Machiavellian thinkers of the time. Philip Bobbit describes in similar terms a transition from the "prince" to the "princely state" in sixteenth-century Italy and notes that the new princely states were distinguished by their use of standing apparatuses of governance such as "permanent bureaucracy, diplomatic corps, or armies" (Bobbit 2002, 89).

6. The text referenced here is Giovanni Antonio Palazzo's *Discorso del governo e della ragion vera di stato* (1606), whose claims are paraphrased by Foucault (2007, 255–59).

7. Theorists of "reason of state" were promoting the "interests" at least a century prior to the classical political economists.

8. "Interest, N., Sense II.9.b.," *Oxford English Dictionary*, Oxford UP, https://doi.org /10.1093/OED/7044247833, accessed December 16, 2023.

9. The Latin phrase *cuius regio, eius religio* does not actually appear in the Treaty of Augsburg but was coined later to explain its guiding principle. See Potz 2015. The Latin word *religio* does appear regularly in the treaty, however, as that which all the "estates and princes" shall be allowed to enjoy in peace (Reich 2004, 230–32).

10. Quoted from article V, paragraph 34, of the Osnabrück Treaty (one of two that make up the Treaty of Westphalia). See "The Westphalian Treaties from October 24th, 1648: Texts and Translations" n.d.; the English translation is taken from *A General Collection of Treatys* 1732. To use this source, visit http://pax-westphalica.de/ipmipo/index .html; for the Latin, select IPO at left, then the article number; for the English, select the translation language at the bottom of the Latin page.

11. Quoted from article V, paragraph 34, of the Osnabrück Treaty.

12. The key tract by Luther here is *Wider die mordischen und reubischen Rotten der Bawren* (1525), which usually translates into English as *Against the Murderous, Thieving Horde of Peasants*.

13. The Westphalian principle of *ratio status* effectively transubstantiated both the Catholic and Evangelical churches into versions of Christian religion or Christianity. Christianity differed from the church insofar as it was constituted not as a political authority in its own right, but rather a belief system that, in Talal Asad's precise words, "should be regarded by the political authorities with indifference as long as it remains within the private domain" (Asad 2003, 205). Robert J. Baird has similarly argued (by

analyzing David Hume's *The Natural History of Religion*) that to understand secularism we must "think our way through the modern vortex in which religion separated itself from Christendom and then in turn created Christianity and world religions as instances of itself" (Baird 2008, 167).

14. Some language on these pages is adapted from the introduction to Medovoi and Bentley 2021, esp. 5–7.

15. "Secular (*adj. & n.*)," *Oxford English Dictionary*, Oxford UP, https://doi.org/10 .1093/OED/9025843980, accessed July 15, 2018. See also Calhoun, Juergensmeyer, and Van Antwerpen 2011, 13, where the authors also observe this early idea of the "secular clergy."

16. Such specifically worldly forms of religious activity were called secular because they involved living within the *saeculum*, which in Latin simply named a lengthy unit of time, approximating a hundred years (thus the words *siècle* in French and *siglo* in Spanish). See also Calhoun 2010.

17. Cicero's speeches against Catiline (63 BCE), in which he accused the Roman senator of treacherously plotting to overthrow the Roman Republic, form one important basis for this classical figure of the traitor. A falsely attributed quotation from Cicero about this figure apparently circulates widely today in contemporary conspiracy theory circles, but is actually derived from a postwar novel by Taylor Caldwell.

18. Because of this heretical religious connection, treason was also often linked to black magic and the powers of the Devil. See Young 2018.

19. For a history of the political work of treason in sixteenth-century England, see Smith 1986. The evolving legal doctrine is reviewed in Bellamy 1979.

20. In the King James version of Mark 10:9, Jesus says regarding divorce, "What therefore God hath joined together let no man tear asunder." In comparing his rule to a marriage, James also draws upon a classic metaphor of the Hebrew prophets in which Israel is wedded to God, an image Paul echoes in his vision of the church as Christ's bride. See Jeremiah 3:6–20 and Ephesians 5:22–33. James's reference to the "whole island" alludes to his unifying status as king of both England and Scotland.

21. As Kantorowicz observes, the *corpus ecclesiae mysticum* was a surprisingly late concept developed by the papacy at the zenith of its aspiration to temporal authority, at a moment roughly contemporaneous with Lateran IV (Kantorowicz 2016, 194–210).

22. A tacitly antithetical relationship exists between two of Jean Bodin's books, *The Six Bookes on the Commonweal* from 1576 and *On the Demon-Mania of Witches* from 1580 (see Bodin 1995, 2014). For a discussion of this relationship, and its relation to the early heteronormative family, see O'Donnell 2020. King James adopted this antithesis.

23. Quoted from *The Charge of Sir Francis Bacon, Knight, His Majesty's Attorney-General, Touching Duels; Upon an Information in the Star-Chamber against Priest and Wright* (1614).

24. Sometimes *sedition* was also defined as a "concerted movement to overthrow an established government," a meaning that converged with treason. But increasingly it came to be associated with words that could incite the emergence of such a movement whether or not the individual in question had any treasonous plan. "Sedition, N., Sense 2.b.," *Oxford English Dictionary*, Oxford UP, https://doi.org/10.1093/OED/8437575397, accessed September 10, 2019.

25. "Sedition, N., Etymology.," *Oxford English Dictionary*, Oxford UP, https://doi.org/10.1093/OED/2917687778, accessed September 10, 2019.

26. According to Foucault, for example, "population" was slow to be invented, gathering momentum only in the mid-eighteenth century when the Physiocrats first established political economy as a distinctive discipline of knowledge. Before the Physiocrats, he claims, population was merely one more resource of the realm, like land or mineral wealth, so that the more of it one had, the richer one was (Foucault 2007, 67–79). This is an especially ironic mistake given that several lectures later in the same series Foucault himself analyzes Bacon's "Seditions and Troubles" (Foucault 2007, 267–72), a much earlier text where the technique of "population" already offers a great deal more.

27. "Population, N. (1), Sense I.1.," *Oxford English Dictionary*, Oxford UP, https://doi.org/10.1093/OED/3124160285, accessed December 8, 2023. The first use of the word "population" appears in Barlow's 1544 translation of Martín Fernandez de Encina's *Suma de geografia que trata de todas las partidas e provincias del mundo* (1520), an early review of Spain's geographical discoveries. The second use appears in T. Nicholas's 1578 translation of Francisco López de Gómara's 1553 history of the conquest, *Historia general de las Indias y todo lo acaescido en ellas dende que se ganaron hasta agora y La conquista de Mexico, y de la Nueva España*.

28. "Population, N. (1), Sense I.2.a.," *Oxford English Dictionary*, Oxford UP, https://doi.org/10.1093/OED/4719477532, accessed December 8, 2023.

29. "Statistics, N., Sense 1.a.," *Oxford English Dictionary*, Oxford UP, https://doi.org/10.1093/OED/1179806838, accessed December 8, 2023.

30. Bacon's comments here appear in "Certaine obseruations vppon a libel" (1592), quoted in Zeitlin 2018, 44.

31. Samuel Garrett Zeitlin notes that Bacon was a "member of Council for the Virginia Company of London from 1609, an incorporator of the Newfoundland Company in 1610 and of the Northwest Passage Company in 1612, and holding membership in the East India Company from 1618" (Zeitlin 2018, 48).

32. Bacon was not alone in this view. See also Richard Hakluyt's influential *A Discourse Concerning Western Planting* (1584).

33. On the origins of agrarian capitalism in the English countryside, see Wood 2002.

34. Bacon here merely echoes the view of Michel de Montaigne in "Of Ill Means Employed to a Good End," who observes that ill humors sicken the natural body, and "States are very often sick of the like repletion [of ill humors], and various sorts of purgations have commonly been applied" (Montaigne 1993, 902).

35. For the political uses of public opinion under Tudor rule, see Sharpe 2009.

36. Though focused on the Stuart era, see Clifton 1971 and Lake 1989. For the politics of antipopery in the period of the restoration, see Miller 1973.

37. See "The Papal Bull of Piux V, *Regnans in Excelsis*, 1570," in Bettenson and Maunder 2011, 267–68.

38. "Acts against Jesuits and Seminarists, 1585," in Bettenson and Maunder 2011, 268.

39. Libel also had origins in witty slanderous songs appealing to the illiterate. See Bellany 1994.

40. "Act Against Puritans, 1593," in Bettenson and Maunder 2011, 269–70.

41. The *Oxford English Dictionary* lists the first such use of *intelligence* as secretly obtained information in 1602. However, the use of *intelligencer* to mean a spy may date as early as 1542. "Intelligence, N., Sense 6.c.," *Oxford English Dictionary*, Oxford UP, September 2023, https://doi.org/10.1093/OED/1126472895, accessed December 8, 2023. For the connection of intelligence to risk management and "reason of state," see Hutchinson 2014.

42. Kevin Sharpe (2009, 453) attempts to intervene against forms of libelous slander.

43. One famous such case was the capturing of Edmund Campion, a Catholic missionary charged with having conspired with Rome to encourage sedition and overthrow the queen. After his execution in 1581, a series of pamphlets circulated indicting the government for its anti-Catholic violence, while others responded that the crown needed to defend itself against treasonous provocations by foreign agents (Lake 2016, 109–15). The Marprelate author was also hotly pursued by intelligencers.

44. "The Supremacy Act, 1559," in Bettenson and Maunder 2011, 260–61.

45. John Whitgift, the conservative high-church archbishop of Canterbury (and the young Bacon's teacher), described "Puritanism" as the name "very aptely giuen to these men," but "not because they be pure . . . but bicause they think them selues to be . . . more pure than others, as Cathari did, and seperate them selues from all other Churches and congregations as spotted and defyled." Quoted from "Puritanism," *Oxford English Dictionary*, Oxford UP, https://doi.org/10.1093/OED/8097341211, accessed December 11, 2023.

46. For a rich collection of documents and reflections on recusancy, see Crosignani, McCoog, and Questier 2010.

47. Because the feigning of conformity to Catholicism was seen as a threat to Mary Tudor's rule, anti-Nicodemite propaganda circulated widely during her reign (Overell 2000).

48. A wide range of intermediary positions likely existed between self-conscious Catholicism, quasi-separations from the Church of England, and residual forms of sacramentalism (Questier 2000).

49. Although the term *via media* did not actually appear until the nineteenth century, the idea of a middle path dates much further back. Especially in the Tudor period, the *via media* concerned charting a middle way *within* Protestantism between Lutheranism and Calvinism. In the Stuart period, however, it began connoting a middle path between Puritanism and Catholicism. King James I, for instance, expressed hope for a "general Christian union in religion, [as] laying wilfulness aside on both hands, we might meet in the midst, which is the centre and perfection of all things." But to find this middle way, "all the incendiaries and novelist firebrands on either side should be debarred, as well as Jesuits and puritans"' (White 1993, 221–22).

50. For an analogous history of pamphlets and reason of state in France, see Sawyer 1990.

51. Michael Heath provides multiple polemics on both sides of the confessional divide, but perhaps most vividly quotes the Protestant Phillipe de Mornay's reference to Muhammad and the pope as the Antichrists of the Orient and the Occident, respectively (Heath 1988, 291).

52. Balibar suggests that Islamophobic neo-racism in present-day Europe acts "from the formal point of view, *as a generalized anti-Semitism*" (Balibar 1991a, 24), in the sense

that antisemitism's lack of physical markers provides the model for the new racisms. I am suggesting here that Islamophobia (a political distrust of "Mahometans" as a threat to state authority) offers the general model for anti-Catholic and other religious racisms.

4. RACIAL LIBERALISM, RACIAL CAPITALISM: ENSOULING PROPERTY'S ADVERSARIES

Epigraphs: Edmund Burke's remarks (1790) are drawn from Burke 2014, 8. The 1898 editorial from the *Wilmington Messenger* is quoted in Wagner 2009, 19. The opening lines of the *Manifesto of the Communist Party* (1848) are drawn from Marx and Engels 2018, 473.

1. "Racial capitalism" was coined by South African communist activists who were analyzing their country's exceptionally paradoxical conditions (a thriving urban capitalist sector dependent upon apartheid's seemingly "noncapitalist" subsistence sector in the Black "homelands"). Robinson encountered the term through them.

2. Colleen Lye, for example, has shown how early twentieth-century anti-Asian racism was determined by the racialization of the threat of hyperexploited labor (Lye 2004).

3. Raine's response is to a shorter version of Fraser's argument. See Fraser 2019.

4. The key regulationist theorists are Michel Aglietta, Alain Lipietz, and Robert Boyer. Their analysis of capitalism has one important weakness: a nation-state frame of analysis that is apparently the byproduct of their focus on the Fordist regime of accumulation. They lose considerable purchase in the process on issues such as unequal exchange, the international division of labor, and issues of geopolitical power that Immanuel Wallerstein's tradition of world-system analysis is better at addressing. Elsewhere I have also criticized the regulation school for a kind of crypto-Keynesianism that can be avoided by integrating with it the Foucauldian analysis of power (Medovoi 2012b). Nonetheless, I find the basic heuristic distinction between the "mode of regulation" and the "regime of accumulation" to be immensely useful so long as these categories are not reified.

5. The distinction between regime of accumulation and mode of regulation should not be collapsed back into the traditional base/superstructure distinction. This is not an argument that the political, cultural, and ideological forms are the mere effects of economic processes. On the contrary, the regulationist argument presumes the mutual interdependence and overdetermination of these levels, while also acknowledging their contradictory relations. The regime of accumulation/mode of regulation distinction also would allow at least potentially for processes like expropriation to be understood at both levels: as economic processes as well as mechanisms for governance. Although the regulation school never considers expropriation as an element in modern phases of what they term the "regime of accumulation," we can consider how capitalism's successive regimes of accumulation have combined exploitation and expropriation in complex ways that fluctuate with each transition into a new phase, and through that process reorganize its racial formations.

6. The concept of "real abstraction," though implicit in Marx, is most rigorously worked out in Sohn-Rethel 1983, 20–22. See also the discussion of "real abstraction" and its kin in La Berge 2014, 99–100.

7. I should take some care to distinguish my usage of "racial liberalism" from that of Jodi Melamed (2011). Both of us are presenting racial liberalism as a political formation

that subtends, supports, governs, and rationalizes racial capitalism. However, the historical context and underlying meaning is quite different. Melamed uses "racial liberalism"
to describe a phenomenon of the postwar United States when Cold War political culture
moved from unvarnished white supremacy toward what she calls an "official antiracism"
that also served US international interests. Her racial liberalism is one that promised
gradual inclusion of Black Americans into liberal society while, in the process, maintaining its exalted conception of whiteness as that Cold War society's self-image. My version
of racial liberalism, by contrast, which runs from the seventeenth through at least the
early twentieth century, focuses on a racial logic that allowed liberalism to simultaneously
celebrate the free society of possessive individuals while explaining not only why certain
populations must be excluded from it, but also defended against them as its potential
enemies. One quick way to draw the distinction is this: Melamed considers how postwar
America became "liberal" about its racialism, while I am showing how capitalist Europe
and colonial America were always "racial" in their liberalism. I would argue that her racial
liberalism is a very late variant of the phenomenon I am describing, a Cold War version
that at a surface level sought to disavow its racialism in the face of fascism's defeat and
anticolonial victories against colonial racial rule.

8. The British (in contrast to continental Europeans) rarely used the term *police*, pre-
ferring the term *government*. For example, Francis Bacon, to the best of my knowledge,
only uses the term *police* once, in a footnote to "The Advancement of Learning," where
he translates the French words *martiale police* into English as "martial government"
(Bacon 1996, 589n126). Nevertheless, his use of "government" aligns with a conception
of police as the governance of people and things.

9. Harcourt (2011) presents this pattern as a racial counterpoint to the liberal market.
The flip side to laissez-faire, liberal penality targets those deemed as unnatural violators of
the market's natural order with its carceral system.

10. Foucault's final lecture of his 1975–76 series tacitly explores liberal biopolitical
racism insofar as it asks how the sovereign's right to kill is supplanted by the racial state's
right to use racism as a guideline for "letting die" in the name of its imperative to defend
society (Foucault 2003, 239–64). Yet somehow, Foucault had abandoned this account of
the liberal state by the time he delivered his 1977–78 lectures.

11. As secretary to three different colonial organizations during the 1660s and 1670s,
all in the business of expropriating Indigenous land to develop tobacco plantations, and
as an investor in the Royal African Company, which provided those plantations with
their supply of enslaved labor, Locke played a role in developing England's settlements
in the upper American South (Bernasconi and Mann 2005). He also helped to draft the
Fundamental Constitutions of the Carolinas, which provided an early legal framework for
racialized chattel slavery. For a study of how Locke's theory of property authorized settler
colonial dispossession, see Ince 2018.

12. Regardless of how Locke himself understood the relationship between his philosophical account of slavery and the early African slave trade he was part of, there is no
question that his writings gave rise to the influential proslavery argument that captive
Africans could be properly sold to slave traders because they had already lost a war to
their original captors. Robert Bernasconi and Anika Maaza Mann have further claimed

that this is how Locke effectively rationalized his *own* involvement in the slave trade (Bernasconi and Mann 2005). Either way, Locke's argument that slavery can result from just war establishes a superior realm of Europeans—the socially contractual victors of their own just wars (against Native peoples, for example)—by contrast to the vanquished Africans who have been plunged into social death as a consequence of their defeat.

13. Capital accumulation is thereby built into the very foundation of Locke's account of society. As Onur Ulas Ince observes, Locke's famous claim that once upon a time all the earth was "America" is braided with his account of money as a nonperishable token of value whose invention necessarily concludes America's history as nature's continent (Ince 2018). Because only money permits an individual to cultivate more goods than one person alone can use, it creates a moral imperative to enclose land so that it can be more intensively cultivated. For Locke, money eliminates the moral problem of natural spoilage (producing more of something than one can use) and replaces it with the moral problem of waste (inefficiency of production means the store of humanity through trade for money is decreased). Since more intensive cultivation increases the store and wealth of all mankind, which was God's command, money inaugurates a new era whose colonial morality of maximized accumulation justifies and necessitates both the seizure of Indigenous land as well as the enclosure of Britain's common land. Although Ince does not consider this directly, Locke's moral imperative to accumulate also creates a corollary imperative to employ wage labor since only in that way can production on large tracts of land be maximized. Such arguments could even be used to justify slave labor in the colonies, as one sees in the repeated declarations by colonial planters that slavery is a moral necessity given how without it the productive lands of America would other otherwise have been wasted.

14. The "liberalism" of Locke (and even more of Thomas Hobbes) is of course widely contested. Certainly, neither philosopher would not have called themselves a liberal (the term did not yet exist in its later political sense), and they are certainly operating in a very different political environment than the classical nineteenth-century liberals, who could situate themselves in a middle ground between conservatism and socialism. Nonetheless, I am treating them as early liberals in the sense that their accounts of the origin of society in the social contract sets in motion the concept of a market society grounded in possessive individuals that will gain increasing traction as a starting point for liberal governmental norms during the takeoff of capitalism.

15. For Hobbes, Beccaria, and Bentham alike, crime concerns a universal calculation that any rational person will make. Good government is all about creating conditions that will lead that calculation ineluctably to the conclusion that crime is not worth the risk of punishment. See Beccaria 1995; Bentham 2016; and Hobbes 1651.

16. Quesnay's term is referenced and usefully explored in Harcourt 2011.

17. Lombroso's typology of the criminal depends on physical markers—facial features, cranial size—that would be statistically linked with race, which, as he claimed, must be an influence on crime (Lombroso 2006, 115).

18. Most stories about the origins of capitalist production still tend to locate it in the metropole. See Wood 2002. This view grounded the claims of some Marxist historians of slavery like Eugene Genovese that the plantation system was a transitional form still mired in feudal relations. For classic debates within Marxism about the origins of capital-

ism, see Aston and Philpin 1987. For a vital exception to the "agrarian capital" argument that emerged from the Black radical tradition, see Williams 2021.

19. The *Oxford English Dictionary* indicates that the word "factorye" or "factorie" first indicated an "agency" or site that would represent a trading company abroad. The Portuguese slave companies would form *feitorias* or "factoryes" at the sites where slaves would be delivered. The second historical meaning (after agency or acting as a "factor" for someone else) first appears in 1582 under the heading "black trader factory" in a book that charts the history of the Portuguese voyages toward the East Indies. Sugar plantations also initially became "factories" of British companies, but at that point the term begins its steady migration toward signifying a site of production for the market. Tobacco plantations a bit further north in colonies such as Virginia and Carolina were only slightly less labor-intensive than sugar plantations. See "Factory, N., Sense 2.a.," *Oxford English Dictionary*, Oxford UP, December 2023, https://doi.org/10.1093/OED/9320047309, accessed December 16, 2023.

20. Andrew B. Liu agrees with Mintz that plantocratic slavery counts as a regime of capitalist production, but argues more specifically that in the absence of waged labor there was only a focus on absolute surplus value (through extending or intensifying the workday) rather than on relative surplus value (reducing labor time as an input via technological efficiency). As a result, Liu argues, plantocratic slavery never developed an industrial takeoff characterized by continuous technological innovations of the production process (Liu 2022). I am still reflecting on this sophisticated and interesting argument.

21. This historical process by which liberal freedom, chattel slavery, and colonial dispossession of land became not only compatible but mutually constitutive of a single game of power in the North American colonies is described in classic studies by Fields (1990) and Morgan (2003). Both observe that the mid-seventeenth-century Virginia colony, organized as a market society around tobacco export, sought at first to meet its labor needs on land seized from Native peoples by importing indigent men from England. Lacking personal property and legally positioned as indentured laborers, these destitute emigres were positioned paradigmatically as nonpossessive individuals. The colonial government associated their incapacity for freedom with various defects of the unpropertied: resistance to laboring (fleeing, idling, etc.), their tendency to disrupt the tobacco market, and most dramatically their willful participation in political tumults like Bacon's Rebellion, during which indigent Englishmen and other Europeans joined forces with similarly coerced African laborers. Bacon's Rebellion materialized for the propertied class the ultimate racial liberal nightmare: "criminals" of all origins and colors banding together to forcibly seize the tobacco, cattle, and land of their betters. The production of a "race" through a color line that separates those who shall be juridically treated as self-possessing (thus white) from those who may be enslaved (the issue of an African woman slave) guaranteed both the labor supply for the tobacco plantation system (a regime of accumulation) and a safeguarding of a political order governed by the planter society (a mode of regulation).

22. For Harris, especially, whiteness shares "critical characteristics of property," particularly a certain "common premise—a conceptual nucleus—of a right to exclude" (Harris 1993, 1714). Harris is right that whiteness functions with and as property to exclude those without it from liberal society, but it certainly does not exclude them from the laboring

population of racial capitalism. So, property and whiteness employ what I have been calling racial liberalism's "pincer action," excluding at a juridical level even while subjugating through a coerced inclusion at the level of commodity production.

23. Singh observes that even free Blacks were subjected to the colonial policing actions of these slave patrol (Singh 2014, 1094). For the classic history of the origins and development of the slave patrols, see Hadden 2001. For an account of police power as the central technology for demarcating the American color line, see Brucato 2014.

24. For a related argument that routes through the Indigenous rather than the slave, see Moreton-Robinson 2015.

25. This double-edged quality of whiteness among the poor deserves further reflection in leftist antiracist analysis. Too often their whiteness is seen as the granting of privilege tout court rather than as a strategic exposure to a highly precarious privilege. The recurring turn to racism by American white working classes should also be studied for its relation to fear and anxiety, specifically the apprehension of becoming subjected to a racially extended police power. For an interesting case study in the political complexities this could create in an example set in the antebellum South, see Johnson 2013, 46–72.

26. This is not because Locke was the first thinker to argue against enforcing religion by the sword. As I noted in chapter 3, a certain concept of toleration became both a premise and a rationale for reason of state. Francis Bacon, for instance, argued in the preceding century that religion should only be propagated through the arts of persuasion (Bacon 2012, 22). But Bacon favored this policy because it avoided stirring up unnecessary discontent and sedition against the state. Locke's argument for religious toleration, by contrast, concerned less its value for the state than its necessity for the civility of society. Wendy Brown characterizes this kind of tolerance as a "supplement" of liberal politics that completes the central principle of freedom (Brown 2009, 19). Here I will be discussing tolerance as completing instead what Mark Neocleous describes as liberalism's "supreme idea" to which even freedom is secondary: security (Neocleous 2007, 142).

27. For a rich discussion of Locke's public account of religion, see Pritchard 2013.

28. The "marketplace of ideas" metaphor can in fact be found even prior to Locke, in John Milton's 1644 essay *Areopagitica*, where he pleas for the lifting of restrictions on publishing (Milton 2013, 200–1). Though Milton's version is written at a revolutionary moment, its commercial metaphors will later be integrated into the antirevolutionary project of liberal democracy.

29. In a contemporary updating of this idea, Cécile Laborde argues that this toleration of religion and presumably certain other commitments must be grounded in their "ethical salience" for the liberal state (Laborde 2017). Understood this way, the redemption of souls is an ethical value that justifies the liberal state's special granting of protection to religious beliefs as opposed to the protection of any personal preference whatsoever.

30. Simon the Zealot was not Simon Peter, who is associated with the founding of the Roman Church. This is a different disciple of the same name who appears in Luke 6:15 and Acts 1:13.

31. See "Fanatic, Adj., Sense 2." *Oxford English Dictionary*, Oxford UP, September 2023, https://doi.org/10.1093/OED/1081973970, accessed December 16, 2023. This in fact is

why Locke, himself raised a Puritan, avoided calling members of disordered churches "fanatics." Locke, who sought tolerance for nonconformists outside the Church of England, did not want Puritans to be considered zealots.

32. According to the *Oxford English Dictionary*, the first appearance of "reactionary" in English appeared in a letter by Count Lazar Carnot, a French revolutionary who used it to describe as "villains" the "factious reactionaries" opposed to the revolution. In the same year, the word appeared in an English translation of a work by the Swiss lawyer Francois Divernois in which he discusses the crimes of the "the royal reactionaries" (*les réactionnaires royaux*). The "reactionary" figures right-wing extremism from the start. See "Reactionary, N.," *Oxford English Dictionary*, Oxford UP, https://doi.org/10.1093/OED /9282759650, accessed December 16, 2023.

33. Exemplary of this understanding of fanaticism was Voltaire's play *Mahomet, or Fanaticism* (Voltaire 2013), a drama in which the followers of Islam's founder appear as excessively passionate believers who will kill for their beliefs. Mahomet himself, however, is presented as a cynic who exploits the fanaticism of his followers for personal power. The play was widely presumed to be a veiled attack on the Catholic Church, with Mahomet a figure for the cynical uses of papal authority.

34. These in fact reflect the reasons why "Radical Republicans" and, looking ahead to the communist threat, even "Red Republicans" became the epithets of choice among antebellum slaveowners to describe abolitionists.

35. See "propaganda, (*n.*)," *Oxford English Dictionary*, Oxford UP, https://doi.org/10 .1093/OED/1010698303, accessed September 8, 2021. This sense of the word "propaganda" also migrates (like the "fanatic" themselves) from religion to politics. In the late seventeenth century, "propaganda" referred to a college of cardinals invested with responsibility for the Roman Catholic evangelical mission: the Vatican's so-called College of the Propaganda. Propaganda therefore referred to the propagation of religious ideas by what in England was deemed a religious extreme. By the late eighteenth century, however, the word had migrated to the political realm: "propaganda" would become an epithet for the improper (militarized) propagation of improper (dangerous) political ideas. The first such use of the word, according to the *Oxford English Dictionary*, apparently occurred in 1790, when an author named James Macpherson wrote in the immediate aftermath of the French Revolution that "all Kings have . . . a new race of Pretenders to contend with, the disciples of the propaganda at Paris or, as they call themselves, Les Ambassadeurs de genre humain." In calling the Jacobins "Pretenders," and presenting them in quasi-religious terms as the "disciples of the propaganda" for a false sovereign, Macpherson propounded yet another political theology. "Propaganda" too is extracted from the realm of religion, even while it continues to mimic the form of the theological enemy: it comes to represent the quasi-evangelical uses of ideas on behalf of a fanatical aim to destroy civil society in the name of humankind itself. By the 1870s, anarchists would embrace this military subtext in their own concept, "propaganda of the deed," which recommends educating the masses through symbolically freighted acts of public violence. See Fleming 1980; see also Bantman 2019.

36. See "party (*n.*)," *Oxford English Dictionary*, Oxford UP, https://doi.org/10.1093 /OED/5188443885, accessed September 8, 2021. An individual belonging to a party was

known as a "partisan," a derivative word that the *Oxford English Dictionary* indicates was originally inflected by the threat of fanaticism: a "devoted or zealous supporter; in early use *esp.* such a person used as a bodyguard. Also with unfavourable connotation: an unreasoning, prejudiced, or blindly fanatical adherent." In a revealing alternative meaning, a "partisan" was either literally a weapon (a kind of spear) used in military attacks or else a soldier who might use such a weapon. See "partisan (*n.2 & adj.*)," *Oxford English Dictionary*, Oxford UP, https://doi.org/10.1093/OED/6741329465, accessed September 9, 2021. Before liberalism, then, both "partisan" and "party" evoked a theologico-military adversary of the state and the population at large.

37. Susan Scarrow has noted that *party* only slowly became a nonperjorative term, and at first even in liberal democracies parties could be seen as antithetical to a broader public welfare. She notes for example that in the early American republic, "luminaries like President Washington warned against the 'baneful effects of the spirit of party'" (Scarrow 2006, 17).

38. This is the context in which Burke's affirmative account of the "party" occurs in "Thoughts on the Present Discontents" (Burke 1999b, 146).

39. Bhikhu Parekh's (1992) definition can be compared with Wendy Brown's (2003, 21–24) far briefer but helpful characterizations of liberal democracy. Stephen Holmes has argued that liberal democratic structures are set in place to contain the passions of individuals, which Hobbes believed otherwise led to the war of all against all (Holmes 1997).

40. Through this electoral game of power, liberal democracy effectively reordered the biopolitics of population. In the capitalist and colonialist context of the late eighteenth and nineteenth century, what liberal democracy established was an electoral strategy for managing conflicts within a ruling, *Herrenvolk* elite that governed the entire population, including the metropolitan and colonial lower "free" classes, slaves in the plantocratic colonies, women, and children. It was after all just one technique in the larger regulation of conduct, yet it was the part of the iceberg that stood above the water line, the visible part that confirmed the racial liberality and the republican (citizenship-based) character of the polity. The circular logic of liberal democracy's distinction between the possessively opinionated individual and his others are roughly equivalent to the tautology that concerns the ownership of "outward goods": only those proclaimed in full subjective possession of their political ideas may be enfranchised as voters, but it is through the act of voting that the possessive members of the electorate stage their self-ownership as political opinionated subjects.

41. Within the liberal democratic framework, a party's campaign becomes the selling of its candidates' proposals in the marketplace of political ideas. Parties publicly advertise their platform for the right path toward society's civil salvation in the hope that the electorate will "purchase" it in place of their competitors' wares. Democracy, governmentally contained by its liberal framework in this way, becomes reduced to a politico-commercial version of what Richard Tuck has called the figure of the "sleeping sovereign," a people who awake from their slumber periodically to select among competing magisterial candidates (Tuck 2016).

42. See "Declaration of the Rights of Man" 1789.

43. For a brilliant and thorough analysis of the sansculottes, not just as a social class but increasingly over the course of the revolution as an evolving Rousseauian political trope and a site of discursive struggle, see Sonenscher 2018.

44. For a history of "political police" in Britain, see Bunyan 1976. For a history set on the Continent, see Emerson 2013.

45. Burke supported slavery's gradual reform and eventual abolition via legal means, but was predictably horrified by the abrupt revolutionary abolition in Saint-Domingue. See Menon 2020.

46. Martin A. Miller shows how the state and insurgents battled throughout the nineteenth century over who had the capacity to instill "terror." See Miller 2013.

47. For a detailed account of Vesey's attempted revolt, see Robertson 1999.

48. Sally Hadden notes that Gabriel Prosser's revolt led then Virginia governor James Monroe to establish the Virginia Public Guard, while Walker's pamphlet led directly to the formation of "patrol committees" to oversee the slave patrols in North Carolina (Hadden 2001, 47–48, 57).

49. I am obviously using Harvey's notion of the "spatial fix" loosely, but the point here is that a crisis in the mode of political regulation (and not only in the regime of accumulation) may also require a spatial fix.

50. Jim Crow constituted a revised regime of legal and police power with which to distinguish the population subjected to wage labor exploitation from the one that faced the hyperexploitation of sharecropping, a labor system that Douglas Blackmon has characterized as "slavery by another name" (Blackmon 2009).

51. For a discussion of the explosive growth of incarceration in the 1980s and 1990s in relation to the social movement of the preceding decades, see Wacquant 2013. The unpropertied signification of Blackness evolved from a logic of what Orlando Patterson calls "social death" under slavery to one of "civil death" in the transition to Jim Crow, and recently to a surreptitious "new civil death" under the regime of mass incarceration. For a review of the legal doctrine of "civil death," see Chin 2011.

52. I will return to the antiracist strategy represented by abolition in the conclusion.

53. For a history of early nineteenth-century radical terminology, see Bestor 1948. Arthur E. Bestor Jr. writes, "The word 'communist,' as a matter of fact, was not created by any of the well-known schools—Fourierites, Saint-Simonians, or Owenites—but by certain relatively obscure leaders in the secret societies that grew up in Paris under the July Monarchy of Louis-Philippe (1830–1848)" (Bestor 1948, 279). Although the French word *communiste* was already in use by the 1830s, its English cognate is first attested when the utopian socialist John Goodwyn Barmby founded the London Communist Propaganda Society in 1841. By then, as I have already noted, communism had gained considerable notoriety on the continent. Barmby had previously been involved in the radical Chartist movement of 1830s and 1840s Britain, which sought economic power and universal suffrage for unpropertied working men. He apparently embraced the term after a visit to France, where he met activists who considered themselves to be contemporary "disciples of Babeuf," carrying the torch for a second revolution that would bring an end to private property. See "communist," *Online Etymology Dictionary*, https://www.etymonline.com/search?q=communist, accessed November 25, 2019.

54. For a reflection on communism's imagined and actual connections with Jacobinism, see Ingram 2018.

55. For a classic study of the June Days, see Tilly and Lees 1974.

56. The image appears in Morley 1985, 305–6, where it is discussed.

57. One might be tempted to see Karl Marx himself here, but that seems unlikely. Although the original pamphlets of the *Manifesto* were published in London in February 1848, the author remained anonymous, and the text appeared only in German. An English edition did not appear until 1850, and Marx's authorship was only revealed at that time.

58. Babeuf's *Manifesto of Equals* (1796), perhaps the first radical political declaration to call itself a manifesto, called for a second revolution to complete the work of 1789. For a history of Babeuf's movement, see Birchall 1997. By the early nineteenth century, Babeuf would come to be mythologized by the Italian revolutionary Filippo Buonarroti; see Buonarroti 1828. For more about Babeuf's standing as a protocommunist, see Rose 1978.

59. For a brief account of the Société des Saisons, see Carter 2009. For useful information about the entire post-Jacobin life of the secret society and the politics of conspiracy, see Levine 1989.

60. The League of the Just was largely composed of immigrant German artisans, many of whom were subsequently expelled from France after a failed revolt in 1839 and fled to London. It is there in 1847 that Karl Marx and Friedrich Engels merged their own Communist Correspondence Committee with the relocated League of the Just to form a new organization, the League of Communists, that became their home.

61. Political police date back to the 1790s, but grew rapidly after the 1848 revolutions. See Deflem 1996.

62. For Marx and Engels, these accusations are hypocritical in precisely the Proudhonian sense: the bourgeoisie cannot acknowledge that their property is nothing but theft. First they steal the sexuality of proletarian women by victimizing them as prostitutes or on the job, then they engage in sexual theft even from their own wives, whom they coerce through their material dependence. Marx and Engels were writing out of a complex socialist tradition in which gender equality but also free love were part of the vision of political emancipation, and although they did not fully share the agenda of that tradition, the manifesto responds to the accusations they inherited. For a careful reading of the *Manifesto*'s engagement with feminist issues of the day, see Tronto 2015.

63. The earliest phases of this history are addressed in Heale 1990.

64. This cartoon is discussed in Morley 1985, 307–8.

65. Figure 4.4 shows an English-language edition of the *Protocols*. The first English translation of the *Protocols* from the original Russian, attributed to Victor Marsden, was apparently published in 1923. Although I cannot absolutely confirm the date, the cover shown in figure 4.4 seems to be from a British edition of 1978.

CONCLUSION. THE MANY-HEADED HYDRA

1. For a discussion of Du Bois's concept of the global color line as a racial paradigm for Western imperialism, see Anievas, Manchanda, and Shilliam 2014. Immanuel Wallerstein's analysis of "race" as a coarse technology for distinguishing the populations of the world-

system along the axis that separates its core from its periphery is in many ways consistent with the Du Boisian account. See Wallerstein 1991a.

2. Sandro Mezzadra and Brett Neilson introduce their "border as method" approach with the example of the heterogeneous population of New York cab drivers, who can serve as emblems of how the proliferation of borders serves to create a heterogeneous labor force (Mezzadra and Neilson 2013, 1–25). I would suggest that their concept of "bordering" offers us a way to theorize the political technologies by means of which the "alien" figures a racialization process in its own right. The nation-state border proliferates to become the dividing line that sorts the population across residential, occupational, and legal zones.

3. In the United States, the term "dangerous classes" was first introduced by Charles Loring Brace (1876). Brace's concept was influenced by his work as a race theorist who in the preceding decade had published a full racial typology of the world's population (Brace 1863).

4. The Jubilee Plot was an alleged plan by Irish anticolonial nationalists to assassinate Queen Victoria on the date of her golden jubilee that appears to have been faked. For more information about it, as well as an overview of the politics of the "skirmishing" campaign in late nineteenth-century Britain, see Wenehand 2007.

5. For a canonical early study of America's xenophobic nativist tradition, see Higham 2002.

6. For the classic book about how the Irish came to *identify* as white, though not exactly how they were racially positioned, see Ignatiev 1996. See also Brodkin 1998; and Jacobson 1999. This body of work, largely from a moment when "whiteness studies" became a topic in American studies, now looks more complicated given the gap between the way that racial power worked through immigration law and the uses of "whiteness" in cultural representation, though obviously the two are linked.

7. As early as the 1790 Naturalization Act, US citizenship would be legally restricted only to those residents who were also a "free white person." The legally white alien therefore was eligible for US citizenship in a way that the nonwhite alien often was not. For the latter, the native/foreigner distinction persisted as a heritable racial threat. But at any given historical moment, it is important to see the work of this distinctive form of racial power so that its relationship to the color line can be properly traced. See Ngai 2014.

8. Middle-class German Jews, for example, in both Germany itself and the United States, would be racialized in this way.

9. For a careful analysis of this form of modern antisemitism, see also Bonefeld 2014.

10. One could argue that the fanatic as a secular enemy was, like the political sovereign he challenged, always a figure of political theology. While the sovereign models godlike divine authority that produces a rightful monopoly on violence and authority, the racial enemy analogizes a satanic resistance to that authority and a defiant source of violent action. The possessing specters of abolitionism, Jacobinism, or communism were figural effects of a modern technology of ensoulment through which new liberal threats had supplanted and displaced those of the insurrectional papist, the plotting converso, or the predatory heretic. Perhaps we should not be so surprised to encounter the Muslim terrorist in the twenty-first century given that they merely make explicit again the theme of religious war

that the political theology of the modern fanatical enemy of liberal society had always preserved in a secularized form.

11. Although I will be focusing on Islamophobic racism as a technique of government in South Asia, David Chidester has shown that religion was a category of knowledge/power that the British also brought to bear on governance in their African colonies. There too it worked with a similar logic of noncoevalness (Chidester 2014).

12. Said turned his attention to this variant of Orientalism in a later work, *Covering Islam* (1997). There, the theme of the security threat moves to the foreground. The Oriental is less a figure of passivity and instead one that defines danger.

13. In the famous popular version of the story, the revolt occurred because Hindu and Muslim fighters already in the employ of the British were provoked by false rumors that their new guns were greased with the taboo fat of cows and pigs. For Indian nationalists, these revolts are sometimes viewed as the first great moment of anticolonial insurgency in India, a moment that may be viewed as the earliest stirrings of a war for independence. Whether or not these revolts should really be interpreted in this national frame, what cannot be doubted is that, by throwing the British East India Company and its piecemeal approach to imperial policy on the defensive, they pushed the British to an entirely new political approach to empire.

14. According to Ilyse Morgenstein Fuerst, Lord Mayo asked the well-known Orientalist writer, scholar, and governor William Wilson Hunter to attempt an answer to this question (Morgenstein Fuerst 2017, 51). Ali Mohar has called this claim dubious (Mohar 1980). But there is no doubt that this question was one that concerned Lord Mayo, and that Hunter's book became a highly influential answer to it.

15. There is a paradoxical quality to the account of insurgency developed in this narrative form of knowledge/power. On the one hand, Guha suggests that British colonialist knowledge about peasant jacqueries in the Raj always read them as *spontaneous* actions aimed at "defying the authority of the state" and as "disturbing the publick tranquil(l)ity" (Guha 1994, 59). On the other hand, these improvised revolts were also always conceived as derivative of a religiosity that could be described as premeditated animosity. As Guha puts it, the religiosity that gave rise to the spontaneous revolt amounted to a "propagandistic ruse used by the leaders to sustain the morale of the rebels" (79). Whether aimed at Hindu or Muslim religiosity, therefore, the "prose of counterinsurgency" was a political language that formulated a technology of colonial warfare proactively responsive to the fomenting of fanatical violence among the colonized.

16. For a brief history of Pan-Africanism, including its connections with Third World communist thought, see Geiss 1969. For an overview of the Russian Revolution's powerful impact on revolutionary possibilities across the Global South, see Prashad 2019.

17. For an overview of US counterinsurgency campaigns throughout the era of Third World revolutions, see Westad 2011. For a reflection on the racial dimension of counterinsurgency, especially during the Cold War period, see Camp and Greenburg 2020.

18. In contrast to W. E. B. Du Bois, Paul Robeson, and Richard Wright, among others who adapted communism to their antiracist and anti-imperialist internationalist activism, Malcolm X made Islam into the basis of an antiracist and anti-imperialist (if not anticapitalist) Black solidaristic politics. By expressing support for Palestinian, Chinese, Vietnamese, Cuban, and other liberation movements, Malcolm X globalized the signifi-

cance of Black Islamism for the American security state. Sohail Daulatzai explores both the international ramifications of this and the work of the FBI's COINTELPRO projects to contain it (Daulatzai 2012).

19. The "fundamentalist" of the 1920s was thus a religious version of the political "reactionary" of the eighteenth century, someone who threatened liberalism through a wish to return to an irretrievable past.

20. I draw here and in several other instances on my short keyword essay on "fundamentalism" (Medovoi 2021).

21. For a crucial work on the revised American concept of the "fundamentalist," see Marty 1980. This highly influential piece of writing opened the floodgates to studies and discussions of the new fundamentalism as a revived religious fanaticism. The paradox of Marty's title, in which fundamentalism is "reborn" precisely by making its appearance in the non-Christian world, captures the move's complexities. At bottom, Marty feared that American Christian fundamentalism was spreading because it had been triggered by Soviet communist and Iranian Islamist fundamentalisms, both of which, it is worth noting, had seized control of what in his view should have been secular nation-states. For another far more neoconservative use that circulates around the communist/fundamentalist comparison, see Pipes 1986.

22. My understanding of racial neoliberalism owes debts to Goldberg 2009. David Goldberg carefully shows how, across different global regions, neoliberalism *militarizes* its racial processes. Its paradigm of politics, as I will discuss shortly, is grounded in war.

23. Gilles Kepel (2011) noted that Huntington had drawn on his work (Kepel 1994), but had somehow made use only of Kepel's chapter on Islam, ignoring his parallel discussions of the rise of political religion among Christians and Jews.

24. Barber's work expanded upon an earlier article that appeared in the *Atlantic* (Barber 1992).

25. Christophe Jaffrelot shows how Modi was elected to power in 2014 by transforming his party into a populist one that appealed to those disenchanted with the corruption of the Congress Party, as well as its tolerance of Islamic terrorism (Jaffrelot 2021, 74–111).

26. My tacit reference here is to the so-called race/class problematic in Marxist analyses of race. In more recent work, including Nancy Fraser's work, which I briefly discussed in chapter 4, race and class are brought together by marking different accumulation strategies under capitalism: exploitation versus expropriation for example. Sarika Chandra and Chris Chen have usefully reviewed this tradition, combining Fraser's analysis with Michael Dawson's discussion of "linked fate" as a way to incorporate the resistive uses of "race" by racialized populations (Chandra and Chen 2022). I find their reading tremendously generative, yet I suspect that it would be almost impossible to bring Islamophobia and antisemitism into a "race/class" frame precisely because they seem to represent practices of racialization that are not immediately tied to the problem of labor. For this reason, I have routed my work more around what could be called a "race/value/security" problematic that turns to political fetishizations. Color-line racism and nativist racism, for example, both tend to evoke what Hylton White has called a "fetishization of labor," by which he means the threat that is attached to a population insofar as they raise the danger of being reduced to the laboring body (White 2020). He reads the Black body, via Fanon's work, as evoking the unremunerated labor of Atlantic slavery and

producing thereby a threat of devaluation, whether or not the black bodies in question are working class. To understand other modes of racial power—anticommunism, with its threat of revolution; Islamophobia, with its threat of religiously inspired violence; and antisemitism, often alongside Sinophobia, evoking the threat of abstract domination by capital—requires that race/value/security be treated as the underlying problematic for an analytic of racial capitalism.

27. Moses argues that genocide has become an unenforceable crime against humanity precisely because so many regimes can plausibly deny any ethnic motive for their violence against populations, instead offering "declarations of national emergencies and proclamations of security threats" (Moses 2021, 17). Since the motivation is political rather than identity-based, the grounds for genocide vanish. Moses argues that international law should replace the crime of genocide with that of "permanent security." The problem, of course, is that since security currently sits at the heart of our definition of politics, liberal or otherwise, it is hard to imagine how "permanent security" could ever be declared a crime.

28. God, the monarchic sovereign modeled upon him, and the popular sovereignty of the people, in turn modeled upon the old monarchic sovereign—all of these have a purely positive moral valence. As Schmitt himself observes in his reading of Rousseauian political theory (even if he does not agree with it), "the will of the people is always good" (Schmitt 2005, 48).

29. Of course, Schmitt acknowledges that the enemy can change, a point that would seem to militate against a racial reading. But I would suggest that this is not really a contradiction because the racialization of populations does in fact change along with the politics. What racial power requires is not the permanent ascription of enmity to any *particular* population, but rather an ongoing designation of evil intentions to *whoever* serves as the enemy at any given historical moment.

30. Who, then, makes this political decision? The subject of politics is always presumed to be the liberal society, state, party, church, or commonwealth. But this subject of the political decision only comes into existence *through* the political act. The point here is the Nietzschean one that we retroactively posit an agent who exercises racial power, and for the same reason that "race" is always posited after the fact as the cause of racialization rather than its effect.

31. For his critique of "traditional Marxism," insofar as it adopts the "standpoint of labor," see Postone (1996, 62–70). See also Triekle 2014.

32. We saw this recently in the histrionic response to the Defund the Police campaign. Even as Republicans bought guns in anticipation of Black Lives Matter and antifa violence, they asserted that "defunding the police" was an insidious conspiracy to disarm society so it could be exposed to its internal enemies.

References

Ackrill, John L. 1972. "Aristotle's Definitions of 'Psuche.'" *Proceedings of the Aristotelian Society* 73: 119–33.

Agamben, Giorgio. 1998. *Homo Sacer: Sovereign Power and Bare Life*. Translated by Daniel Heller-Roazen. Stanford, CA: Stanford University Press.

Agulhon, Maurice. 1981. *Marianne into Battle: Republican Imagery and Symbolism in France 1789–1880*. Translated by Janet Lloyd. Cambridge: Cambridge University Press.

Ahmed, Sara. 2004. *The Cultural Politics of Emotion*. New York: Routledge.

Alfassa, Shelomo. 2004. "The Origins and Stigma of the Iberian Garment of Shame, the San Benito." *International Sephardic Journal* 1, no. 1: 5–18.

Alfonsi, Petrus. 2006. *Dialogue against the Jews*. Translated by Irven M. Resnick. Washington, DC: Catholic University of America Press.

Alsultany, Evelyn. 2012. *Arabs and Muslims in the Media: Race and Representation after 9/11*. New York: New York University Press.

Ames, Christine Caldwell. 2009. *Righteous Persecution: Inquisition, Dominicans, and Christianity in the Middle Ages*. Philadelphia: University of Pennsylvania Press.

Anidjar, Gil. 2003. *The Jew, the Arab: A History of the Enemy*. Stanford, CA: Stanford University Press.

Anidjar, Gil. 2008. *Semites: Race, Religion, Literature*. Stanford, CA: Stanford University Press.

Anievas, Alexander, Nivi Manchanda, and Robbie Shilliam. 2014. "Confronting the Global Colour Line: An Introduction." In *Race and Racism in International Relations: Confronting the Global Colour Line*, edited by Alexander Anievas, Nivi Manchanda, and Robbie Shilliam, 1–15. London: Routledge.

Anonymous. n.d. "The Marprelate Tracts: Tract 1." Edited by J. D. Lewis. Anglican Library. http://www.anglicanlibrary.org/marprelate/tract1m.htm.

Appadurai, Arjun. 2006. *Fear of Small Numbers*. Durham, NC: Duke University Press.

Arendt, Hannah. 1973. *The Origins of Totalitarianism*. New York: Harcourt, Brace.

Aronson, Marc, and Marina Budhos. 2010. *Sugar Changed the World*. New York: Clarion.

Asad, Talal. 1993. "Pain and Truth in Medieval Christian Ritual." In *Genealogies of Religion: Discipline and Reasons of Power in Christianity and Islam*, 83–125. Baltimore: Johns Hopkins University Press.

Asad, Talal. 2003. *Formations of the Secular*. Stanford, CA: Stanford University Press.

Aston, Trevor Henry, and Charles H. E. Philpin, eds. 1987. *The Brenner Debate: Agrarian Class Structure and Economic Development in Pre-Industrial Europe*. Cambridge: Cambridge University Press.

Attridge, Harold W., ed. 1989. *The HarperCollins Study Bible*. San Francisco: HarperCollins.

Bacon, Francis. 1996. *Francis Bacon*. Edited by Brian Vickers. Oxford: Oxford University Press.

Bacon, Francis. 2012. *The Oxford Francis Bacon I: Early Writings 1584–1596*. Edited by Alan Stuart and Harriet Knight. Oxford: Oxford University Press.

Baird, Robert J. 2008. "Late Secularism." In *Secularisms*, edited by Janet R. Jakobsen and Ann Pellegrini, 162–77. Durham, NC: Duke University Press.

Baldwin, James. 1995. *The Fire Next Time*. New York: Modern Library.

Balibar, Étienne. 1991a. "Is There a Neo-Racism?" In *Race, Nation, Class: Ambiguous Identities*, by Étienne Balibar and Immanuel Wallerstein, translated by Chris Turner, 17–28. London: Verso.

Balibar, Étienne. 1991b. "Racism and Nationalism." In *Race, Nation, Class: Ambiguous Identities*, by Étienne Balibar and Immanuel Wallerstein, translated by Chris Turner, 37–68. London: Verso.

Ball, Kirstie. 2009. "Exposure: Exploring the Subject of Surveillance." *Information, Communication and Society* 12, no. 5: 639–57.

Bantman, Constance. 2019. "The Era of Propaganda by the Deed." In *The Palgrave Handbook of Anarchism*, edited by Carl Levy and Matthew S. Adams, 371–87. Cham: Palgrave Macmillan.

Banton, Michael. 1979. *The Idea of Race*. London: Routledge.

Barber, Benjamin. 1992. "Jihad vs. McWorld." *Atlantic*, March, 53–65.

Barber, Benjamin R. 1994. *Jihad vs. McWorld: Terrorism's Challenge to Democracy*. New York: Random House.

Barnes, Thomas G. 1962. "Due Process and Slow Process in the Late Elizabethan-Early Stuart Star Chamber: Part II." *American Journal of Legal History* 6, no. 4: 315–46.

Barruel, Augustin. 1799. *Memoirs Illustrating the History of Jacobinism*. New York: Hartford.

Bartlett, Robert. 1994. *The Making of Europe: Conquest, Colonization and Cultural Change, 950–1350*. London: Penguin.

Bartlett, Robert. 2001. "Medieval and Modern Concepts of Race and Ethnicity." *Journal of Medieval and Early Modern Studies* 31, no. 1: 39–56.

Bayoumi, Moustafa. 2006. "Racing Religion." *New Centennial Review* 6, no. 2: 267–93.

Beccaria, Cesare. 1995. *On Crimes and Punishments and Other Writings*. Edited by Richard Bellamy. Cambridge: Cambridge University Press.

Beckert, Sven. 2015. *Empire of Cotton: A Global History*. New York: Vintage.

Bellamy, John. 1979. *The Tudor Law of Treason*. London: Routledge.

Bellany, Alastair. 1994. "'Raylinge Rymes and Vaunting Verse': Libellous Politics in Early Stuart England, 1603–1628." In *Culture and Politics in Early Stuart England*, edited by Kevin Sharpe, 285–310. Stanford, CA: Stanford University Press.

Beltran, Aguirre G. 1945. "Races in Seventeenth Century Mexico." *Phylon* 6, no. 3: 212–19.

Bentham, Jeremy. 2016. *An Introduction to the Principles of Morals and Legislation*. South Yarra, Victoria: Leopold Classic Library.

Bernasconi, Robert, and Anika Maaza Mann. 2005. "The Contradictions of Racism: Locke, Slavery, and the Two Treatises." In *Race and Racism in Modern Philosophy*, edited by Andrew Valls, 89–107. Ithaca, NY: Cornell University Press.

Best, Stephen M. 2004. *The Fugitive's Properties: Law and the Poetics of Possession*. Chicago: University of Chicago Press.

Bestor, Arthur E., Jr. 1948. "The Evolution of the Socialist Vocabulary." *Journal of the History of Ideas* 9, no. 3: 259–302.

Bettenson, Henry, and Chris Maunder, eds. 2011. *Documents of the Christian Church*. 4th ed. Oxford: Oxford University Press.

Beusterien, John. 2012. "The Celebratory Conical Hat of La Celestine." In *Crime and Punishment in the Middle Ages and Early Modern Age: Mental-Historical Investigations of Basic Human Problems and Social Responses*, edited by Albrecht Classen and Connie Scarborough, 403–14. Boston: De Gruyter.

Birchall, Ian H. 1997. *The Spectre of Babeuf*. New York: Springer.

Bird, Jessalyn Lea. 2004. "Crusade and Conversion after the Fourth Lateran Council (1215): Oliver of Paderborn's and James of Vitry's Missions to Muslims Reconsidered." *Essays in Medieval Studies* 21, no. 1: 23–47.

Birkett, Helen. 2006. "The Pastoral Application of the Lateran IV Reforms in the Northern Province, 1215–1348." *Northern History* 43, no. 2: 199–219.

Blackburn, Robin. 1997. "The Old World Background to European Colonial Slavery." *William and Mary Quarterly* 54, no. 1: 65–102.

Blackburn, Robin 1998. *The Making of New World Slavery: From the Baroque to the Modern, 1492–1800*. London: Verso.

Blackmon, Douglas. 2009. *Slavery by Another Name: The Reenslavement of Black Americans from the End of the Civil War until World War II*. New York: Anchor.

Bobbit, Philip. 2002. *The Shield of Achilles: War, Peace and the Course of History*. New York: Anchor.

Bodin, Jean. 1995. *On the Demon-Mania of Witches*. Translated by Randy A. Scott. Toronto: Centre for Reformation and Renaissance Studies.

Bodin, Jean. 2014. *The Six Bookes of a Commonweale*. Translated by Kenneth Douglas McRee. Cambridge, MA: Harvard University Press.

Bonefeld, Werner. 2014. "Antisemitism and the Power of Abstraction: From Political Economy to Critical Theory." In *Antisemitism and the Constitution of Sociology*, edited by Marcel Stoetzler, 314–32. Lincoln: University of Nebraska Press.

Botero, Giovanni. 2017. *The Reason of State*. Edited and translated by Robert Birely. Cambridge: Cambridge University Press.

Boyer, Robert. 1990. *The Regulation School: A Critical Introduction*. Translated by Craig Charney. New York: Columbia University Press.

Brace, Charles Loring. 1863. *Races of the Old World: A Manual of Ethnology*. New York: Scribner.

Brace, Charles Loring. 1876. *The Dangerous Classes of New York*. New York: Wynkoop and Hallenbeck.

Braude, Benjamin. 1997. "The Sons of Noah and the Construction of Ethnic and Geographical Identities in the Medieval and Early Modern Periods." *William and Mary Quarterly* 54, no. 1: 103–42.

Bray, Alan. 1982. *Homosexuality in Renaissance England*. New York: Columbia University Press.

Breight, Curtis. 1996. *Surveillance, Militarism and Drama in the Elizabethan Era*. New York: Springer.

Brodkin, Karen. 1998. *How Jews Became White Folks and What That Says about Race in America*. New Brunswick, NJ: Rutgers University Press.

Brown, Wendy. 2003. "Neo-Liberalism and the End of Liberal Democracy." *Theory and Event* 7, no. 1. https://doi.org/10.1353/tae.2003.0020.

Brown, Wendy. 2009. *Regulating Aversion*. Princeton, NJ: Princeton University Press.

Brown, Wendy. 2015. *Undoing the Demos: Neoliberalism's Stealth Revolution*. Cambridge, MA: MIT Press.

Browne, Simone. 2015. *Dark Matters: On the Surveillance of Blackness*. Durham, NC: Duke University Press.

Brucato, Ben. 2014. "Fabricating the Color Line in a White Democracy: From Slave Catchers to Petty Sovereigns." *Theoria* 61, no. 141: 30–54.

Buck-Morss, Susan. 2000. "Hegel and Haiti." *Critical Inquiry* 26, no. 4: 821–65.

Bunyan, Tony. 1976. *The History and Practice of the Political Police in Britain*. London: Julian Friedmann.

Buonarroti, Filippo. 1828. *Conspiration pour l'égalité dite de Babeuf*. Brussels: Librairie Romantique.

Burden-Stelly, Charisse. 2020. "Modern US Racial Capitalism." *Monthly Review*, July–August, 8–20.

Burke, Edmund. 1868. *The Works of the Right Honourable Edmund Burke*. Vol. 5. London: Bell and Daldy.

Burke, Edmund. 1999a. *Select Works of Edmund Burke*. Vol. 3, *Letters of a Regicide Peace*. Indianapolis, IN: Liberty Fund.

Burke, Edmund. 1999b. *The Portable Edmund Burke*. Edited by Isaac Kramnick. London: Penguin.

Burke, Edmund. 2014. *Revolutionary Writings: Reflections on the Revolution in France and the First Letter on a Regicide Peace*. Edited by Iain Hampshire-Monk. Cambridge: Cambridge University Press.

Burns, Kathryn. 2007. "Unfixing Race." In *Rereading the Black Legend: The Discourses of Religious and Racial Difference in the Renaissance Empires*, edited by Maureen Quiligan and Walter Mignolo, 188–202. Chicago: University of Chicago Press.

Bush, George W. 2001. "Address to Joint Session of Congress, September 20, 2001." American Rhetoric. https://www.americanrhetoric.com/speeches/gwbush911jointsessionspeech.htm.

Byrd, Jodi A. 2011. *The Transit of Empire: Indigenous Critiques of Colonialism*. Minneapolis: University of Minnesota Press.

Byrd, Jodi A., Alyosha Goldstein, Jodi Melamed, and Chandan Reddy. 2018. "Predatory Value: Economies of Dispossession and Disturbed Relationalities." *Social Text* 36, no. 2: 1–18.

Calhoun, Craig. 2010. "Rethinking Secularism." *Hedgehog Review* 12, no. 3: 35–48.

Calhoun, Craig, Mark Juergensmeyer, and Jonathan Van Antwerpen. 2011. "Introduction." In *Rethinking Secularism*, edited by Calhoun, Craig, Mark Juergensmeyer, and Jonathan Van Antwerpen, 3–30. Oxford: Oxford University Press.

Camp, Jordan, and Jennifer Greenburg. 2020. "Counterinsurgency Reexamined: Racism, Capitalism, and US Military Doctrine." *Antipode* 52, no. 2: 430–51.

Campos, Edmund Valentine. 2002. "Jews, Spaniards, and Portingales: Ambiguous Identities of Portuguese Marranos in Elizabethan England." *ELH* 69, no. 3: 599–616.

Carpenter, Dwayne. 1986. *Alfonso X and the Jews: An Edition of and Commentary on Siete Partidas 7.24 "De los judíos."* Berkeley: University of California Press.

Carpenter, Dwayne. 1999. "From Al-Burak to Alboraycos." In *Jews and Conversos at the Time of the Expulsion*, edited by Yom Tov Assis and Yosef Kaplan, 25–37. Jerusalem: Zalman Shazar Center for Jewish History.

Carter, J. Kameron. 2008. *Race: A Theological Account*. New York: Oxford University Press.

Carter, R. O'Brian. 2009. "Blanqui, Louis Auguste (1805–1881)." In *The International Encyclopedia of Revolution and Protest*, edited by Immanuel Ness, 1–4. Hoboken, NJ: Wiley-Blackwell.

Cavanaugh, William T. 1995. "A Fire Strong Enough to Consume the House: The Wars of Religion and the Rise of the State." *Modern Theology* 11, no. 4: 397–420.

Chakrabarty, Dipesh. 2008. *Provincializing Europe: Postcolonial Thought and Historical Difference*. Princeton, NJ: Princeton University Press.

Chandra, Sarika, and Chris Chen. 2022. "Remapping the Race/Class Problematic." In *Totality Inside Out: Rethinking Crisis and Conflict under Capital*, edited by Kevin Floyd, Jen Hedler Philis, and Sarika Chandra, 135–91. New York: Fordham University Press.

Chatterjee, Partha. 2019. *I Am the People: Reflections on Popular Sovereignty Today*. New York: Columbia University Press.

Chaudhary, Zahid R. 2020. "The Politics of Exposure: Truth after Post-Facts." *ELH* 87: 499–522.

Chidester, David. 2014. *Empire of Religion: Imperialism and Comparative Religion*. Chicago: University of Chicago Press.

Chin, Gabriel J. 2011. "The New Civil Death: Rethinking Punishment in the Era of Mass Conviction." *University of Pennsylvania Law Review* 160: 1789–1834.

Chua, Amy. 2004. *World on Fire: How Exporting Free Market Democracy Breeds Ethnic Hatred and Global Instability*. New York: Anchor.

Church, William F. 2015. *Richelieu and Reason of State*. Princeton, NJ: Princeton University Press.

Cicero. n.d. "First Speech against Catiline." Translated by Charles Duke Yonge. San Jose State University. https://www.sjsu.edu/people/cynthia.rostankowski/courses/HUM1AF14/s3/Lecture-26-Cicero-and-Caesar-Reading.pdf.

Clausewitz, Carl von. 1989. *On War*. Edited and translated by Michael Howard and Peter Pare. Princeton, NJ: Princeton University Press.

Clifton, Robin. 1971. "The Popular Fear of Catholics during the English Revolution." *Past and Present* 52: 23–55.

Cohen, Jeremy. 1997. "The Muslim Connection; or, On the Changing Role of the Jew in High Medieval Theology." In *From Witness to Witchcraft: Jews and Judaism in Medieval Christian Thought*, 141–63. Wiesbaden: Harrassowitz.

Cohen, Jeremy. 1999. *Living Letters of the Law: Ideas of the Jew in Medieval Christianity*. Berkeley: University of California Press.

Cooley, Mackenzie. 2022. *The Perfection of Nature: Animals, Breeding, and Race in the Renaissance*. Chicago: University of Chicago Press.

Cooper, John. 2011. *The Queen's Agent: Francis Walsingham at the Court of Elizabeth I*. London: Faber and Faber.

Corominas, Joan. 1954. *Diccionario crítico etimológico de la lengua Castellana*, Vol. 3. Berne, Switzerland: Editorial Francke.

Coulthard, Glen Sean. 2014. *Red Skin, White Masks: Rejecting the Colonial Politics of Recognition*. Minneapolis: University of Minnesota Press.

Covarrubias Orozco, Sebastián de. 1611. *Tesoro de la lengua Castellana, o Española*. Madrid: L. Sanchez. https://www.google.com/books/edition/Tesoro_de_la_lengua _castellana_o_espa%C3%B1o/qKm8nzelynUC?hl=en&gbpv=1&printsec=frontcover.

Cowans, Jon. 2003. *Early Modern Spain: A Documentary History*. Philadelphia: University of Pennsylvania Press.

Crosignani, Ginevra, Thomas M. McCoog, and Michael Questier, eds. 2010. *Recusancy and Conformity in Early Modern England: Manuscript and Printed Sources in Translation*. Toronto: Pontifical Institute of Mediaeval Studies.

Cruz, Moran, and Jo Ann Hoeppner. 1999. "Popular Attitudes toward Islam in Medieval Europe." In *Western Views of Islam in Medieval and Early Modern Europe*, edited by Michael Frassetto and David R Blanks, 55–81. New York: Palgrave Macmillan.

Cutler, Allan, and Helen Cutler. 1986. *The Jew as Ally of the Muslim: Medieval Roots of Anti-Semitism*. Notre Dame, IN: University of Notre Dame Press.

Das, Dilip K., and Arvind Verma. 1998. "The Armed Police in the British Colonial Tradition: The Indian Perspective." *Policing: An International Journal of Police Strategies and Management* 21, no. 2: 354–67.

Daulatzai, Sohail. 2012. *Black Star, Crescent Moon: The Muslim International and Black Freedom beyond America*. Minneapolis: University of Minnesota Press.

Davis, Angela Y. 2005. *Abolition Democracy: Beyond Empires, Prison, and Torture*. New York: Seven Stories Press.

Dawson, Michael C. 2016. "Hidden in Plain Sight: A Note on Legitimation Crises and the Racial Order." *Critical Historical Studies* 3, no. 1: 143–61.

Day, Iyko. 2016. *Alien Capital: Asian Racialization and the Logic of Settler Colonial Capitalism*. Durham, NC: Duke University Press.

DCAAP (DC African Archives Project). 2016. "Guide to the Oscar Brown Jr. Papers." Gelman Library, Howard University. https://dh.howard.edu/cgi/viewcontent.cgi ?article=1255&context=finaid_manu.

"Declaration of the Rights of Man." 1789. The Avalon Project: Documents in Law History and Diplomacy, Lillian Goldman Law Library, Yale Law School. https://avalon.law.yale.edu/18th_century/rightsof.asp.

Deflem, Mathieu. 1996. "International Policing in Nineteenth-Century Europe: The Police Union of German States, 1851–1866." *International Criminal Justice Review* 6, no. 1: 36–57.

de Miramon, Charles. 2009. "Noble Dogs, Noble Blood: The Invention of the Concept of Race in the Late Middle Ages." In *The Origins of Racism in the West*, edited by Miriam Eliav-Feldon, Benjamin Isaac, and Joseph Ziegler, 200–16. Cambridge: Cambridge University Press.

Diran, Ingrid. 2021. "Rethinking Biopower with Racial Capitalism." Paper presented at the annual meeting of the American Comparative Literature Association, Montreal, April 8–11.

Dubber, Markus Dirk. 2005. *The Police Power: Patriarchy and the Foundations of American Government*. New York: Columbia University Press.

Dubois, Laurent. 2005. *Avengers of the New World*. Cambridge, MA: Harvard University Press.

Du Bois, W. E. B. 1995. *The Philadelphia Negro*. Philadelphia: University of Pennsylvania Press.

Du Bois, W. E. B. 2007. *The Souls of Black Folk*. New York: Oxford University Press.

Du Bois, W. E. B. 2021. *Black Reconstruction*. New York: Library of America.

Egerton, Douglas R. 2000. *Gabriel's Rebellion: The Virginia Slave Conspiracies of 1800 and 1802*. Chapel Hill: University of North Carolina Press.

Emerson, Donald Eugene. 2013. *Metternich and the Political Police: Security and Subversion in the Hapsburg Monarchy (1815–1830)*. New York: Springer.

Emmer, P. C. 1991. "The Dutch and the Making of the Second Atlantic System." In *Slavery and the Rise of the Atlantic System*, edited by Barbara Solow, 75–96. New York: Cambridge University Press.

Evans, Hiram Wesley. 1926. "The Klan's Fight for Americanism." *North American Review* 223, no. 830: 33–63.

Fabian, Johannes. 2014. *Time and the Other: How Anthropology Makes Its Object*. New York: Columbia University Press.

Fanon, Frantz. 1952. *Peau noire, masques blancs*. Paris: Édition du Seuil.

Fanon, Frantz. 2004. "Algeria Unveiled." In *Decolonization: Perspectives from Now and Then*, edited by Prasenjit Duara, 42–55. London: Routledge.

Fanon, Frantz. 2008. *Black Skin, White Masks*. Translated by Richard Philcox. New York: Grove.

Federici, Silvia. 2004. *Caliban and the Witch*. New York: Autonomedia.

Fields, Barbara Jeane. 1990. "Slavery, Race, and Ideology in the United States." *New Left Review* 181, no. 1: 95–118.

Fields, Karen E., and Barbara J. Fields. 2012. *Racecraft: The Soul of Inequality in American Life*. London: Verso.

Fleming, Marie. 1980. "Propaganda by the Deed: Terrorism and Anarchist Theory in Late Nineteenth-Century Europe." *Studies in Conflict and Terrorism* 4. nos. 1–4: 1–23.

Foucault, Michel. 1986. "*Omnes et singulatim*: Vers une critique de la raison politique." *Le Débat* 41: 5–36.

Foucault, Michel. 1990. *The History of Sexuality: An Introduction*, Vol. 1. Translated by Robert Hurley. New York: Vintage.

Foucault, Michel. 2003. *Society Must Be Defended: Lectures at the Collège de France, 1975–1976*. Translated by David Macey. New York: Picador.

Foucault, Michel. 2007. *Security, Territory, Population: Lectures at the Collège de France, 1977–78*. Translated by Graham Burchell. New York: Picador.

Foucault, Michel. 2012. *Discipline and Punish: The Birth of the Prison*. Translated by Alan Sheridan. New York: Vintage.

Fraser, Nancy. 2016. "Expropriation and Exploitation in Racialized Capitalism: A Reply to Michael Dawson." *Critical Historical Studies* 3, no. 1: 163–78.

Fraser, Nancy. 2019. "Is Capitalism Necessarily Racist?" *Politics/Letters* 15. http://quarterly.politicsslashletters.org/is-capitalism-necessarily-racist/.

Fredrickson, George M. 2015. *Racism*. Princeton, NJ: Princeton University Press.

Friede, Juan. 1971. *Bartolomé de las Casas in History: Toward an Understanding of the Man and His Work*. DeKalb: Northern Illinois University Press.

Friedenreich, David N. 2011. "Muslims in Western Canon Law 1000–1500." In *Christian-Muslim Relations: A Bibliographical History*, Vol. 3, edited by David Thomas and Alex Mallett, 41–68. Leiden: Brill.

Fukuyama, Francis. 1989. "The End of History?" *National Interest*, Summer, 3–18.

Funkenstein, Amos. 1994. *Perceptions of Jewish History*. Berkeley: University of California Press.

Garrow, David J. 1981. *The FBI and Martin Luther King, Jr.: From "Solo" to Memphis*. New York: Norton.

Geiss, Immanuel. 1969. "Pan-Africanism." *Journal of Contemporary History* 4, no. 1: 187–200.

A General Collection of Treatys, Manifesto's, Contracts of Marriage, Renunciations, and other Publick Papers, from the 1495 to the Year 1712. Vol. 2. 2nd ed. 1732. London: J. J. and P. Knapton et al.

Gilmore, Ruth Wilson. 2007. *Golden Gulag: Prisons, Surplus, Crisis, and Opposition in Globalizing California*. Berkeley: University of California Press.

Gilmore, Ruth Wilson. 2022. *Abolition Geography: Essays toward Liberation*. London: Verso.

Gitlitz, David M. 1992. "Hybrid Conversos in the 'Libro llamado el Alboraique.'" *Hispanic Review* 60, no 1: 1–17.

Gitlitz, David M. 1993. "The Book Called Alboraique." *Mediterranean Language Review* 6: 121–43.

Given, James B. 1997. *Inquisition and Medieval Society: Power, Discipline, and Resistance in Languedoc*. Ithaca, NY: Cornell University Press.

Goldberg, David. 2009. *The Threat of Race*. New York: John Wiley and Sons.

Goldenberg, David M. 2017. *Black and Slave: The Origins and History of the Curse of Ham*. Boston: De Gruyter.

Goldsmith, Zachary Robert. 2019. "'An Oppressive Passion': Kant, Burke, Dostoevsky and the Problem of Fanaticism." PhD diss., Indiana University.

González Rolan, Tomás, Pilar Saquero Suárez-Somonte, and Pablo Gonzáles Saquero. 2012. *De la "Sentencia-Estatuto" de Pero Sarmiento a la "Instrucción" del Relator: Estudio introductorio, edición crítica y notas de los textos contrarios y favorables a los judeoconversos a raíz de la rebelión de Toledo de 1449.* Alcobendas: Aben Ezra.

Gordon, Linda. 2017. *The Second Coming of the KKK: The Ku Klux Klan of the 1920s and the American Political Tradition.* New York: Liveright.

Green, Dominic. 2003. *The Double Life of Doctor Lopez: Spies, Shakespeare and the Plot to Poison Elizabeth I.* London: Century.

Guha, Ranajit. 1994. "The Prose of Counter-Insurgency." In *Culture/Power/History: A Reader in Contemporary Social Theory*, edited by Nicholas B. Dirks, Geoff Eley, and Sherry Ortner, 336–71. Princeton, NJ: Princeton University Press.

Hadden, Sally E. 2001. *Slave Patrols: Law and Violence in Virginia and the Carolinas.* Cambridge, MA: Harvard University Press.

Hall, Stuart. 1996. "Race, Articulation and Societies Structured in Dominance." In *Black British Cultural Studies: A Reader*, edited by Houston Baker, Manthia Diawara, and Ruth Lindeborg, 16–60. Chicago: University of Chicago Press.

Hanke, Lewis. 1938. "The 'Requerimiento' and Its Interpreters." *Revista de Historia de América* 1: 25–34.

Harcourt, Bernard E. 2011. *The Illusion of Free Markets: Punishment and the Myth of Natural Order.* Cambridge, MA: Harvard University Press.

Harris, Cheryl I. 1993. "Whiteness as Property." *Harvard Law Review* 106, no. 8: 1707–91.

Hartman, Saidiya. 1997. *Scenes of Subjection: Terror, Slavery, and Self-Making in Nineteenth-Century America.* New York: Oxford University Press.

Harvey, David. 2001. "Globalization and the 'Spatial Fix.'" *Geographische Revue: Zeitschrift für Literatur und Diskussion* 3, no. 2: 23–30.

Harvey, L. P. 2006. *Muslims in Spain, 1500–1614.* Chicago: University of Chicago Press.

Heale, Michael J. 1990. *American Anti-Communism: Combating the Enemy Within, 1830–1970.* Baltimore: Johns Hopkins University Press.

Heath, Michael J. 1988. "Islamic Themes in Religious Polemic." *Bibliothèque d'Humanisme et Renaissance* 50, no. 2: 289–315.

Heng, Geraldine. 2018. *The Invention of Race in the European Middle Ages.* Cambridge: Cambridge University Press.

Higham, John. 2002. *Strangers in the Land: Patterns of American Nativism, 1860–1925.* New Brunswick, NJ: Rutgers University Press.

Hincks, Peter. 2006. *To Awaken My Afflicted Brethen: David Walker and the Problem of Antebellum Slave Resistance.* College Park: Pennsylvania University Press.

Hippler, Fritz, dir. 1940. *Der ewige Jude.* Deutsche Filmherstellungs-und-Verwertungs. Germany, 65 mins.

Hirschman, Albert O. 2013. *The Passions and the Interests: Political Arguments for Capitalism before Its Triumph.* Princeton, NJ: Princeton University Press.

Hobbes, Thomas. 1651. *Leviathan, or, The Matter, Forme, and Power of a Common-Wealth Ecclesiasticall and Civil.* London: Andrew Crooke.

Hobsbawm, Eric. 1996. *Age of Revolution: 1789–1848.* New York: Vintage.

Holland, Edwin C. ["A South-Carolinian," pseud.]. 1822. *A Refutation of the Calumnies Circulated against the Southern and Western States Respecting the Institution and Existence of Slavery among Them: To Which Is Added a Minute and Particular Account of the Actual State and Condition of Their Negro Population* [...]. Charleston, SC: A. E. Miller.

Holland, Sharon Patricia. 2012. *The Erotic Life of Racism.* Durham, NC: Duke University Press.

Holmes, Stephen. 1997. *Passions and Constraint: On the Theory of Liberal Democracy.* Chicago: University of Chicago Press.

Homeland. 2011–2020. *Homeland* . Showtime. United States, TV series, eight seasons.

Hörmann, Raphael. 2017. "Black Jacobins: Towards a Genealogy of a Transatlantic Trope." In *Transatlantic Revolutionary Cultures, 1789–1861*, edited by Charlotte A. Lerg and Heléna Tóth, 19–49 Leiden: Brill.

Hunt, Lynn. 1984. *Politics, Culture, and Class in the French Revolution.* Berkeley: University of California Press.

Hunter, William Wilson. 1876. *The Indian Musalmans.* London: Trübner.

Huntington, Samuel P. 1996. *The Clash of Civilizations and the Remaking of World Order.* New York: Simon and Schuster.

Hutchinson, Robert. 2007. *Elizabeth's Spy Master: Francis Walsingham and the Secret War that Saved England.* London: Weidenfeld and Nicolson.

Hutchinson, Steven. 2014. "Intelligence, Reason of State and the Art of Governing Risk and Opportunity in Early Modern Europe." *Economy and Society* 43, no. 3: 370–400.

Ignatiev, Noel. 1996. *How the Irish Became White.* New York: Routledge.

Ince, Onur Ulas. 2014. "Primitive Accumulation, New Enclosures, and Global Land Grabs: A Theoretical Intervention." *Rural Sociology* 79, no. 1: 104–31.

Ince, Onur Ulas. 2018. *Colonial Capitalism and the Dilemmas of Liberalism.* Oxford: Oxford University Press.

Ingram, James. 2018. "Jacobinism." *Krisis: Journal for Contemporary Philosophy* 2018, no. 2. https://krisis.eu/jacobinism.

Iogna-Prat, Dominique. 2003. *Order and Exclusion: Cluny and Christendom Face Heresy, Judaism, and Islam (1000–1150).* Translated by Graham Robert Edwards. Ithaca, NY: Cornell University Press.

Isaac, Benjamin. 2013. *The Invention of Racism in Classical Antiquity.* Princeton, NJ: Princeton University Press.

Itman, Ida. 2007. "The Revolt of Enriquillo and the Historiography of Early Spanish America." *Americas* 63, no. 4: 587–614.

Jacobson, Matthew Frye. 1999. *Whiteness of a Different Color.* Cambridge, MA: Harvard University Press.

Jaffrelot, Christophe. 2021. *Modi's India: Hindu Nationalism and the Rise of Ethnic Democracy.* Translated by Cynthia Schoch. Princeton, NJ: Princeton University Press.

James, C. L. R. 1989. *The Black Jacobins: Toussaint L'Ouverture and the San Domingo Revolution.* New York: Vintage.

Johnson, James Weldon. 1990. *The Autobiography of an Ex-Colored Man.* New York: Penguin.

Johnson, Jenna, and Abigail Hauslohner. 2017. "'I Think Islam Hates Us': A Timeline about Trump's Comments about Islam and Muslims." *Washington Post*, May 20.

Johnson, Walter. 2013. *River of Dark Dreams*. Cambridge, MA: Harvard University Press.

Johnstone, Monty. 1967. "Marx and Engels and the Concept of the Party." *Socialist Register* 4, no. 4: 121–58.

Jordan, Winthrop D. 2013. *White over Black: American Attitudes toward the Negro, 1550–1812*. Chapel Hill: University of North Carolina Press.

Judis, John B. 2016. *The Populist Explosion: How the Great Recession Transformed American and European Politics*. New York: Columbia Global Report.

Kalleberg, Arne L., and Till M. von Wachter. 2017. "The US Labor Market during and after the Great Recession: Continuities and Transformations." *RSF: The Russell Sage Foundation Journal of the Social Sciences* 3, no. 3: 1–19. https://doi.org/10.7758/rsf.2017.3.3.01.

Kalmar, Ivan Davidson. 2009. "Antisemitism and Islamophobia: The Formation of a Secret." *Human Architecture* 7, no. 2: 135–44.

Kamen, Henry. 1985. *Inquisition and Society in Spain in the Sixteenth and Seventeenth Centuries*. London: Weidenfeld and Nicolson.

Kantorowicz, Ernst. 2016. *The King's Two Bodies: A Study in Medieval Political Theology*. Princeton, NJ: Princeton University Press.

Karuka, Manu. 2019. *Empire's Tracks: Indigenous Nations, Chinese Workers, and the Transcontinental Railroad*. Berkeley: University of California Press.

Kaufman, Irving R. 2021. "Judge Kaufman's Statement upon Sentencing the Rosenbergs for Atomic Espionage—1951." Digital History. https://www.digitalhistory.uh.edu/disp_textbook.cfm?smtID=3&psid=1118.

Kedar, Benjamin Z. 1999. "On the Origins of the Earliest Laws of Frankish Jerusalem: The Canons of the Council of Nablus, 1120." *Speculum* 74, no. 2: 310–35.

Kepel, Gilles. 1994. *The Revenge of God: The Resurgence of Islam, Christianity and Judaism in the Modern World*. Translated by Alan Braley. Philadelphia: Penn State University Press.

Kepel, Gilles. 2011. "Beyond the Clash of Civilizations." *New York Times*, March 11.

King, Martin Luther, Jr. 1957. "Nonviolence and Racial Justice." *Christian Century* 74: 165–67.

Kisch, Guido. 1942. "The Yellow Badge in History." *Historia Judaica* 4, no. 2: 95–144.

Klotz, Marcia. 2005. "The Weimar Republic: A Postcolonial State in a Still-Colonial World." In *Germany's Colonial Pasts*, edited by Eric Ames, Marcia Klotz, and Lora Wildenthal, 135–47. Lincoln: University of Nebraska Press.

Knight, Frank Hyneman. 1921. *Risk, Uncertainty and Profit*. Boston: Houghton Mifflin.

Kofman, Sarah. 1994. *Nietzsche and Metaphor*. Translated by Duncan Large. Stanford, CA: Stanford University Press.

Kotsko, Adam. 2016. *The Prince of This World*. Stanford, CA: Stanford University Press.

Kundani, Arun. 2020. "What Is Racial Capitalism?" Talk delivered at Havens Wright Center for Social Justice, University of Wisconsin–Madison, October 15, 2020. https://www.kundnani.org/what-is-racial-capitalism/.

La Berge, Leigh Claire. 2014. "Rules of Abstraction." *Radical History Review* 118: 99–100.

Laborde, Cécile. 2017. *Liberalism's Religion*. Cambridge, MA: Harvard University Press.

Laclau, Ernesto. 2005. *On Populist Reason*. London: Verso.

Lake, Peter. 1989. "Anti-Popery: The Structure of a Prejudice." In *Conflict in Early Stuart England: Studies in Religion and Politics, 1603–1642*, edited by Richard Cust and Ann Hughes, 72–106. London: Longman.

Lake, Peter. 2016. *Bad Queen Bess: Libels, Secret Histories, and the Politics of Publicity in the Reign of Queen Elizabeth I*. Oxford: Oxford University Press.

Lampert, Lisa. 2004. "Race, Periodicity, and the (Neo-) Middle Ages." *Modern Language Quarterly* 65, no. 3: 391–21.

Larsen, Nella. 1986. *Quicksand and Passing*. New Brunswick, NJ: Rutgers University Press.

Lazar, Moshe. 1997. "Anti-Jewish and Anti-*Converso* Propaganda: *Confutatio libri talmud* and *Alboraique*." In *The Jews of Spain and the Expulsion of 1492*, edited by Moshe Lazar and Stephen Haliczer, 153–236. Lancaster, CA: Labyrinthos.

Lea, Henry Charles. 2010. *A History of the Inquisition in the Middle Ages*. Cambridge: Cambridge University Press.

Léglu, Catherine, Rebba Rist, and Claire Taylor, eds. 2013. *The Cathars and the Albigensian Crusade: A Sourcebook*. London: Routledge.

Lenin, Vladimir Ilich. 1920. *Imperialism, The Highest Stage of Capitalism: An Outline*. Translated by Institute of Marxism-Leninism. Moscow: Foreign Languages Publishing House. https://babel.hathitrust.org/cgi/pt?id=hvd.32044011474558&seq=11.

Levine, Norman. 1989. "Jacobinism and the European Revolutionary Tradition." *History of European Ideas* 11, nos. 1–6: 157–80.

Lewis, Laura A. 2003. *Hall of Mirrors: Power, Witchcraft, and Caste in Colonial Mexico*. Durham, NC: Duke University Press.

Linebaugh, Peter, and Marcus Rediker. 2013. *The Many-Headed Hydra: Sailors, Slaves, Commoners, and the Hidden History of the Revolutionary Atlantic*. Boston: Beacon.

Lipsitz, George. 2006. *The Possessive Investment in Whiteness: How White People Profit from Identity Politics*. Philadelphia: Temple University Press.

Liu, Andrew. 2022. "The Capitalist Epoch in the Rest of the World: Marx's Capital, History, Asia, and 'Levels of Abstraction.'" Paper presented at the annual meeting of the Institute for Culture and Society, Philadelphia, June 13–17.

Locke, John. 2016. *Second Treatise of Government and A Letter Concerning Toleration*. Edited by Mark Goldie. Oxford: Oxford University Press.

Lombroso, Cesare. 2006. *Criminal Man*. Translated by Mary Gibson and Nicole Hah Rafter. Durham, NC: Duke University Press.

Lombroso, Cesare, and Guglielmo Ferrero. 2004. *Criminal Woman, the Prostitute, and the Normal Woman*. Translated by Nicole Hah Rafter and Mary Gibson. Durham, NC: Duke University Press.

Loomba, Ania. 2009. "Race and the Possibility of Comparative Critique." *New Literary History* 40: 501–22.

Losurdo, Domenico. 2011. *Liberalism: A Counter-History*. Translated by Gregory Elliot. London: Verso.

Luxemburg, Rosa. 2015. *The Accumulation of Capital*. Translated by Agnes Schwarzschild. London: Routledge.

Lye, Colleen. 2004. *America's Asia: Racial Form and American Literature.* Princeton, NJ: Princeton University Press.

Macpherson, Crawford Brough. 1962. *The Political Theory of Possessive Individualism: Hobbes to Locke.* Oxford: Clarendon Press.

Malkiel, Yakov. 1948. "Hispano-Arabic *Marrano* and Its Hispano-Latin Homophone." *Journal of the American Oriental Society* 68, no. 4: 175–84.

Mamdani, Mahmood. 2005. *Good Muslim, Bad Muslim: America, the Cold War, and the Roots of Terror.* New York: Harmony.

Mann, Geoff. 2017. *In the Long Run We Are All Dead: Keynesianism, Political Economy, and Revolution.* London: Verso.

Manning, Roger B. 1980. "The Origins of the Doctrine of Sedition." *Albion* 12, no. 2: 99–121.

Martínez, María Elena. 2004. "The Black Blood of New Spain: *Limpieza de Sangre*, Racial Violence, and Gendered Power in Early Colonial Mexico." *William and Mary Quarterly* 61, no. 3: 479–520.

Martínez, María Elena. 2011. *Genealogical Fictions: Limpieza de Sangre, Religion, and Gender in Colonial Mexico.* Stanford, CA: Stanford University Press.

Marty, Martin E. 1980. "Fundamentalism Reborn: Faith and Fanaticism." *Saturday Review*, May, 37–38, 42.

Marx, Karl. 1977. *Capital: A Critique of Political Economy.* Vol. 1. Translated by Ben Fowkes. New York: Vintage.

Marx, Karl, and Friedrich Engels. 2018. *The Marx-Engels Reader.* Edited by Robert Tucker. New York: Norton.

Mastnak, Tomaž. 1994. "Fictions in Political Thought: Las Casas, Sepulveda, the Indians, and the Turks." *Filosfski Vestnik* 15, no. 2: 127–49.

Mastnak, Tomaž. 2001. *Crusading Peace: Christendom, the Muslim World, and Western Political Order.* Berkeley: University of California Press.

Mastnak, Tomaž. 2003. "Europe and the Muslims: A Permanent Crusade?" In *The New Crusades: Constructing the Muslim Enemy*, edited by Emran Qureshi and Michael A. Sells, 205–48. New York: Columbia University Press.

Medovoi, Leerom. 2002. "Globalization as Narrative and its Three Critiques." *Review of Education, Pedagogy, and Cultural Studies* 24. nos. 1–2: 63–75.

Medovoi, Leerom. 2007. "Global Society Must Be Defended: Biopolitics without Boundaries." *Social Text* 25, no. 2: 53–79.

Medovoi, Leerom. 2012a. "Dogma-Line Racism: Islamophobia and the Second Axis of Race." *Social Text* 30, no. 2: 43–74.

Medovoi, Leerom. 2012b. "Swords and Regulation." *Symplokē* 20, nos. 1–2: 21–34.

Medovoi, Leerom. 2021. "Fundamentalism." In *Religion, Secularism, and Political Belonging*, edited by Leerom Medovoi and Elizabeth Bentley, 147–54. Durham, NC: Duke University Press.

Medovoi, Leerom, and Elizabeth Bentley. 2021. "Introduction: Translated Secularisms, Global Humanities." In *Religion, Secularism, and Political Belonging*, edited by Leerom Medovoi and Elizabeth Bentley, 1–34. Durham, NC: Duke University Press.

Melamed, Jodi. 2011. *Represent and Destroy: Rationalizing Violence in the New Racial Capitalism*. Minneapolis: University of Minnesota Press.

Melley, Timothy. 2012. *The Covert Sphere: Secrecy, Fiction, and the National Security State*. Ithaca, NY: Cornell University Press.

Menocal, María Rosa. 2009. *The Ornament of the World: How Muslims, Jews, and Christians Created a Culture of Tolerance in Medieval Spain*. New York: Back Bay.

Menon, Parvathi. 2020. "Edmund Burke and the Ambivalence of Protection for Slaves: Between Humanity and Control." *Journal of the History of International Law* 22, nos. 2–3: 246–68.

Mezzadra, Sandro, and Brett Neilson. 2013. *Border as Method, or, the Multiplication of Labor*. Durham, NC: Duke University Press.

Miller, John. 1973. *Popery and Politics in England 1660–1688*. Cambridge: Cambridge University Press.

Miller, Martin A. 2013. *The Foundations of Modern Terrorism: State, Society and the Dynamics of Political Violence*. Cambridge: Cambridge University Press.

Milton, John. 2013. *Areopagitica; A Speech of Mr. John Milton*. In *John Milton's Prose: Major Writings on Liberty, Politics, Religion and Education*. Edited by David Loewenstein, 181–213. Hoboken, NJ: Blackwell.

Mintz, Sidney W. 1986. *Sweetness and Power: The Place of Sugar in Modern History*. New York: Penguin.

Mirpuri, Anoop. 2010. "Why Can't Kobe Pass (the Ball)? Race and the NBA in the Age of Neoliberalism." In *Commodified and Criminalized: New Racism and African Americans in Contemporary Sports*, edited by David J. Leonard and C. Richard King, 95–120. Lanham, MD: Rowman and Littlefield.

Mohar, Ali. 1980. "Hunter's *Indian Musalmans*: A Re-Examination of Its Background." *Journal of the Royal Asiatic Society of Great Britain and Ireland* 112, no. 1: 30–51.

Monahan, Torin. 2015. "The Right to Hide? Anti-Surveillance Camouflage and the Aestheticization of Resistance." *Communication and Critical/Cultural Studies* 12, no. 2: 159–78.

Montaigne, Michel de. 1993. *The Complete Essays*. Edited and translated by M. A. Screech. London: Penguin.

Moore, Robert I. 1996. "Heresy, Repression, and Social Change in the Age of Gregorian Reform." In *Christendom and Its Discontents: Exclusion, Persecution, and Rebellion, 1000–1500*, edited by Scott L. Waught and Peter Diehl, 19–46. Cambridge: Cambridge University Press.

Moore, Robert I. 2000. *The First European Revolution, c. 970–1215*. Hoboken, NJ: Wiley-Blackwell.

Moore, Robert I. 2008. *The Formation of a Persecuting Society: Authority and Deviance in Western Europe 950–1250*. Hoboken, NJ: John Wiley and Sons.

Moreton-Robinson, Aileen. 2015. *The White Possessive: Property, Power, and Indigenous Sovereignty*. Minneapolis: University of Minnesota Press.

Morgan, Edmund S. 2003. *American Slavery, American Freedom*. New York: Norton.

Morgenstein Fuerst, Ilyse R. 2017. *Indian Muslim Minorities and the 1857 Rebellion: Religion, Rebels and Jihad*. London: Bloomsbury.

Morley, T. P. 1985. "The Times and the Revolutionary Crisis of 1848." PhD diss., Thames Polytechnic, London.

Moses, A. Dirk. 2021. *The Problems of Genocide: Permanent Security and the Language of Transgression*. Cambridge: Cambridge University Press.

Mouffe, Chantal. 2005. "The 'End of Politics' and the Challenge of Right-Wing Populism." In *Populism and the Mirror of Democracy*, edited by Francisco Panizza, 50–71. London: Verso.

Muhammad, Khalil Gibran. 2019. *The Condemnation of Blackness: Race, Crime, and the Making of Modern Urban America*. Cambridge, MA: Harvard University Press.

Nájera, Luna. 2011. "Myth and Prophecy in Juan Ginés de Sepúlveda's Crusading 'Exhortación.'" *Bulletin for Spanish and Portuguese Historical Studies* 35, no. 1: art. 4. https://asphs.net/wp-content/uploads/2020/02/Myth-and-Prophecy-in-Sep%C3%BAlveda_s-Exhortaci%C3%B3n.pdf.

Nederman, Cary J. 2010. *Worlds of Difference: European Discourses of Toleration, c. 1100–c. 1550*. University Park, PA: Penn State Press.

Nemser, Daniel. 2017. *Infrastructures of Race: Concentration and Biopolitics in Colonial Mexico*. Austin: University of Texas Press.

Neocleous, Mark. 2007. "Security, Liberty and the Myth of Balance: Towards a Critique of Security Politics." *Contemporary Political Theory* 6, no. 2: 131–49.

Neocleous, Mark. 2021. *A Critical Theory of Police Power: The Fabrication of the Social Order*. London: Verso.

Netanyahu, Benzion. 1995. *The Origins of the Inquisition in Fifteenth-Century Spain*. New York: Random House.

Newman, Jane O. 2012. "Perpetual Oblivion? Remembering Westphalia in a Post-Secular Age." In *Forgetting Faith: Negotiating Confessional Conflict in Early Modern Europe*, edited by Isabel Kareman, Cornel Zwierlein, and Inga Mai Groote, 261–75. Boston: De Gruyter.

Ngai, Mae M. 2014. *Impossible Subjects: Illegal Aliens and the Making of Modern America*. Princeton, NJ: Princeton University Press.

Nichols, Robert. 2021. "Disaggregating Primitive Accumulation." In *Creolizing Rosa Luxemburg*, edited by Jane Anna Gordon and Drucilla Cornell, 247–68. Lanham, MD: Rowman & Littlefield.

Nilus, Sergiĕi Aleksandrovitch. 1965. *Protocols of the Meetings of the Learned Elders of Zion*. Translated by Victor E. Marsden. Ottawa: Canadian Publications.

Nirenberg, David. 1996. *Communities of Violence: Persecution of Minorities in the Middle Ages*. Princeton, NJ: Princeton University Press.

Nirenberg, David. 2007. "Race and the Middle Ages." In *Rereading the Black Legend: The Discourse of Religious and Racial Difference in the Renaissance Empires*, edited by Margaret R. Greet, Walter D. Mignolo, and Maureen Quilligan, 71–87. Chicago: University of Chicago Press.

Nirenberg, David. 2009. "Was There Race before Modernity? The Example of 'Jewish Blood' in Late Medieval Spain." In *The Origins of Racism in the West*, edited by Miriam Eliav-Feldon, Benjamin Isaac, and Joseph Ziegler, 232–64. Cambridge: Cambridge University Press.

Nirenberg, David. 2014. *Neighboring Faiths: Christianity, Islam, and Judaism in the Middle Ages and Today*. Chicago: University of Chicago Press.

Nygaard, Bertel. 2016. "The Specter of Communism: Denmark, 1848." *Contributions to the History of Concepts* 11, no. 1: 1–23.

O'Callaghan, Joseph F. 2013. *Reconquest and Crusade in Medieval Spain*. Philadelphia: University of Pennsylvania Press.

O'Donnell, S. Jonathon. 2020. "Witchcraft, Statecraft, Mancraft: On the Demonological Foundations of Sovereignty." *Political Theology* 21, no. 6: 530–49.

Ormerod, Paul, and A. P. Roach. 2004. "The Medieval Inquisition: Scale-Free Networks and the Suppression of Heresy." *Physica A: Statistical Mechanics and its Applications* 339, nos. 3–4: 645–52.

Osborne, Peter. 2000. *Philosophy in Cultural Theory*. London: Routledge.

Overell, M. Anne. 2000. "Vergerio's Anti-Nicodemite Propaganda and England, 1547–1558." *Journal of Ecclesiastical History* 51, no. 2: 296–318.

Pagels, Elaine. 1989. *Adam, Eve and the Serpent: Sex and Politics in Early Christianity*. New York: Vintage.

Palmer, Colin A. 2013. *Slaves of the White God: Blacks in Mexico, 1570–1650*. Cambridge, MA: Harvard University Press.

Parekh, Bhikhu. 1992. "The Cultural Particularity of Liberal Democracy." *Political Studies* 40: 160–75.

Peter the Venerable. 2016. *Writings against the Saracens*. Translated by Irven M. Resnick. Washington, DC: Catholic University of America Press.

Peter the Venerable. 2021. *Against the Inveterate Obduracy of the Jews*. Translated by Irven M. Resnick. Washington, DC: Catholic University of America Press.

Peters, Edward. 2006. "Moore's Eleventh and Twelfth Centuries: Travels in the Agro-Literate Polity." In *Heresy and the Persecuting Society in the Middle Ages: Essays on the Work of R. I. Moore*, edited by Michael Frassetto, 11–30. Leiden: Brill.

Pipes, Daniel. 1986. "Fundamentalist Muslims between America and Russia." *Foreign Affairs*, Summer, 939–59.

Postone, Moishe. 1980. "Anti-Semitism and National Socialism: Notes on the German Reaction to 'Holocaust.'" *New German Critique* 19, no. 1: 97–115.

Postone, Moishe. 1996. *Time, Labor and Social Domination: A Reinterpretation of Marx's Critical Theory*. Cambridge: Cambridge University Press.

Potz, Richard. 2015. "Cuius regio, eius religio." In *Encyclopedia of Early Modern History Online*, edited by Graeme Dunphy and Andrew Gow. Brill. https://referenceworks .brillonline.com/entries/encyclopedia-of-early-modern-history-online/cuius-regio -eius-religio-SIM_018148.

Prashad, Vijay. 2019. *Red Star over the Third World*. London: Pluto.

Pritchard, Elizabeth A. 2013. *Religion in Public: Locke's Political Theology*. Stanford, CA: Stanford University Press.

Proudhon, Pierre. 1993. *What Is Property?* Edited and translated by Donald R. Kelley and Bonnie M. Smith. Cambridge: Cambridge University Press.

Puar, Jasbir. 2011. "'The Turban Is Not a Hat': Queer Diaspora and Practices of Profiling." In *Beyond Biopolitics: Essays on the Governance of Life and Death*, edited by Patricia Ticineto Clough and Craig Willse, 65–105. Durham, NC: Duke University Press.

Puar, Jasbir, and Amit Rai. "Monster, Terrorist, Fag: The War on Terrorism and the Production of Docile Patriots." *Social Text* 20, no. 3 (2002): 117–48.

Questier, Michael C. 2000. "What Happened to English Catholicism after the English Reformation?" *History* 85, no. 277: 28–47.

Quijano, Aníbal. 1995 "Raza, etnia y nación en Mariátegui: Cuestiones abiertas." *Estudios Latinoamericanos* 2, no. 3: 3–19.

Quijano, Aníbal. 2000. "Coloniality of Power, Eurocentrism, and Latin America." *Nepantla: Views from South* 1, no. 3: 215–32.

Quijano, Aníbal, and Immanuel Wallerstein. 1992. "Americanity as a Concept, or the Americas in the Modern World." *International Social Science Journal* 44, no. 4: 549–57.

Raine, Barnaby. 2019. "Capitalism, Racism and Totality: A Response to Nancy Fraser." *Politics/Letters* 15. http://quarterly.politicsslashletters.org/capitalism-racism-and -totality-a-response-to-nancy-fraser/.

Rana, Junaid. 2007. "The Story of Islamophobia." *Souls* 9, no. 2: 148–61.

Rana, Junaid. 2011. *Terrifying Muslims: Race and Labor in the South Asian Diaspora*. Durham, NC: Duke University Press.

Rawls, John. 1993. "The Law of Peoples." *Critical Inquiry* 20, no. 1: 36–68.

Rawls, John. 2009. *A Theory of Justice*. Cambridge, MA: Harvard University Press.

Raymond, Joad. 2006. *Pamphlets and Pamphleteering in Early Modern Britain*. Cambridge: Cambridge University Press.

Reagan, Ronald. 1983. "Evil Empire Speech." Ronald Reagan Presidential Library and Museum. https://www.reaganlibrary.gov/archives/speech/remarks-annual-convention -national-association-evangelicals-orlando-fl.

Reich, Emil. 2004. *Select Documents Illustrating Mediæval and Modern History*. Sydney: Minerva Group.

Ricard, Robert. 1974. *The Spiritual Conquest of Mexico: An Essay on the Apostolate and the Evangelizing Methods of the Mendicant Orders in New Spain, 1523–1572*. Berkeley: University of California Press.

Ricoeur, Paul. 1977. *Freud and Philosophy: An Essay on Interpretation*. Translated by Denis Savage. New Haven, CT: Yale University Press.

Riley, Boots, dir. 2018. *Sorry to Bother You*. Significant Productions. United States, 112 mins.

Roberts, Neil. 2015. *Freedom as Marronage*. Chicago: University of Chicago Press.

Robertson, David. 1999. *Denmark Vesey: The Buried Story of America's Largest Slave Rebellion and the Man Who Led It*. New York: Vintage.

Robinson, Cedric J. 2020. *Black Marxism: The Making of the Black Radical Tradition*. Chapel Hill: University of North Carolina Press.

Robinson, I. S. 2008. "Church and Papacy." In *The Cambridge History of Medieval Political Thought, c. 350–c. 1450*, edited by J. H. Burns, 252–305. Cambridge: Cambridge University Press.

Robinson, William I., Salvador Rangel, and Hilbourne A. Watson. 2022. "The Cult of Cedric Robinson's *Black Marxism*: A Proletarian Critique." *Philosophical Salon*, October. https://thephilosophicalsalon.com/the-cult-of-cedric-robinsons-black-marxism-a -proletarian-critique/#_edn2.

Root, Deborah. 1988. "Speaking Christian: Orthodoxy and Difference in Sixteenth-Century Spain." *Representations* 23: 118–34.

Rose, R. B. 1978. *Gracchus Babeuf: The First Revolutionary Communist*. Stanford, CA: Stanford University Press.

Rosenberg, Yair. 2017. "Jews Will Not Replace Us: Why White Supremacists Go After Jews." *Washington Post*, August 14.

Rosenthal, Caitlin. 2019. *Accounting for Slavery: Masters and Management*. Cambridge, MA: Harvard University Press.

Rousseau, Jean-Jacques. 1983. *The Essential Rousseau*. Edited and translated by Lowell Bair. New York: Meridian.

Said, Edward. 1979. *Orientalism*. New York: Vintage.

Said, Edward. 1997. *Covering Islam: How the Media and the Experts Determine How We See the Rest of the World*. New York: Vintage.

Salaita, Steven. 2006. *Anti-Arab Racism in the USA: Where It Comes From and What It Means for Politics Today*. London: Pluto.

Salgado, Isaac. 2018. "From 1492 to 1449: Race, Religion, and Temporality." Paper presented at the Annual Meeting of the Western Political Science Association, San Francisco, 2018. www.wpsanet.org/papers/ . . . /1449%20-%20Race,%20Religion,%20 Temporality.docx.

Sandoval, Alonso de. 1956. *De instauranda Aethiopum salute*. Bogotá: Empresa Nacional de Publicaciones.

Sandoval, Alonso de. 2008. *Treatise on Slavery: Selections from* De instauranda Aethiopum salute. Edited and translated by Nicole von Germeten. Indianapolis, IN: Hackett.

Sawyer, Jeffrey K. 1990. *Printed Poison: Pamphlet Propaganda, Faction Politics, and the Public Sphere in Early Seventeenth-Century France*. Berkeley: University of California Press.

Scarrow, Susan. 2006. "The Nineteenth-Century Origins of Modern Political Parties: The Unwanted Emergence of Party-Based Politics." In *Handbook of Political Parties*, edited by Richard S. Katz and William Crotty, 16–24. London: Sage.

Schechter, Ronald. 2018. *A Genealogy of Terror in Eighteenth-Century France*. Chicago: University of Chicago Press.

Schmitt, Carl. 2003. *The Nomos of the Earth*. Translated by G. L. Ulmen. New York: Telos.

Schmitt, Carl. 2005. *Political Theology: Four Chapters on the Concept of Sovereignty*. Translated by George Schwab. Chicago: University of Chicago Press.

Schmitt, Carl. 2008. *The Concept of the Political*. Expanded ed. Translated by George Schwab. Chicago: University of Chicago Press.

Schumpeter, Joseph A. 2004. *Capitalism, Socialism and Democracy*. London: Routledge.

Sharp, Gene. 1973. *The Politics of Nonviolent Action*. 3 vols. Boston: Porter Sargent.

Sharpe, Kevin. 2009. *Selling the Tudor Monarchy: Authority and Image in Sixteenth-Century England*. New Haven, CT: Yale University Press.

Shirk, Mark. 2019. "The Universal Eye: Anarchist 'Propaganda of the Deed' and Development of the Modern Surveillance State." *International Studies Quarterly* 63, no. 2: 334–45.

Silverblatt, Irene. 2004. *Modern Inquisitions: Peru and the Colonial Origins of the Civilized World*. Durham, NC: Duke University Press.

Singh, Nikhil Pal. 2014. "The Whiteness of Police." *American Quarterly* 66,. no. 4: 1091–99.

Singh, Nikhil Pal. 2017. *Race and America's Long War*. Berkeley: University of California Press.

Skinner, Quentin. 1989. "The State." In *Political Innovation and Conceptual Change*, edited by Terrence Ball, James Farr, and L. Hanson, 90–131. Cambridge: Cambridge University Press.

Slobodian, Quinn. 2018. *Globalists: The End of Empire and the Birth of Neoliberalism*. Cambridge, MA: Harvard University Press.

Smedley, Audrey, and Brian D. Smedley. 2018. *Race in North America: Origin and Evolution of a Worldview*. London: Routledge.

Smith, Lacey Baldwin. 1986. *Treason in Tudor England: Politics and Paranoia*. London: Trinity.

Sohn-Rethel, Alfred. 1983. *Intellectual and Manual Labour: A Critique of Epistemology*. London: Humanities Press.

Sonenscher, Michael. 2018. *Sans-Culottes: An Eighteenth-Century Emblem in the French Revolution*. Princeton, NJ: Princeton University Press.

Soyer, François. 2014. "The Anti-Semitic Conspiracy Theory in Sixteenth-Century Spain and Portugal and the Origins of the *Carta de los judíos de Constantinopla*: New Evidence." *Sefarad: Revista de Estudios Hebraicos, Sefardíes y de Oriente Próximo* 74, no. 2: 369–88.

Soyer, François. 2017. "The Passion of Christ in the Church of San Cristóbal de Rapaz: An Example of Medieval Anti-Jewish Iconography in Colonial Peru?" *Journal of Iberian Studies* 5: 392–416.

Soyer, Francois. 2019. *Antisemitic Conspiracy Theories in the Early Modern Iberian World: Narratives of Fear and Hatred*. Leiden: Brill.

Stout, Jeffrey. 2009. *Democracy and Tradition*. Princeton, NJ: Princeton University Press.

Stover, Jennifer Lynn. 2016. *The Sonic Color Line: Race and the Cultural Politics of Listening*. New York: New York University Press.

Stuelke, Patricia. 2021. *The Ruse of Repair: US Neoliberal Empire and the Turn from Critique*. Durham, NC: Duke University Press.

Sweet, James H. 1997. "The Iberian Roots of American Racist Thought." *William and Mary Quarterly* 54, no. 1: 143–66.

Szemiński, Jan. 1974. "La Insurrección de Tupac Amaru II ¿Guerra de independencia o revolución?" *Estudios Latinoamericanos* 2: 9–60.

Táíwò, Olúfhemi O. 2022. *Reconsidering Reparations*. Oxford: Oxford University Press.

Tanner, Norman P, ed.. 1990. *Decrees of the Ecumenical Councils*. Vol. 1, *Nicaea I to Lateran V*. London: Sheed and Ward.

Tilly, Charles, and Lynn Lees. 1974. "Le peuple de Juin 1848." *Annales* 29, no. 5: 1061–91.

Tise, Larry E. 1990. *Proslavery: A History of the Defense of Slavery in America, 1701–1840*. Athens: University of Georgia Press.

Tolan, John. 2002. *Saracens: Islam in the European Medieval Imagination*. New York: Columbia University Press.

Torres, Max Sebastián Hering. 2003. "Limpieza de sangre ¿Racismo en la edad moderna?" *Revista Electrónica de Historia Moderna* 4, no. 9: 1–16.

Torres, Max Sebastián Hering. 2012. "Purity of Blood: Problems of Interpretation." In *Race and Blood in the Iberian World*, edited by Max S. Hering Torres, María Elena Martínez, and David Nirenberg, 11–38. Berlin: Lit Verlag.

Toscano, Arturo. 2017. *Fanaticism: On the Uses of an Idea*. London: Verso.

Toscano, Arturo. 2023. *Late Fascism: Race, Capitalism and the Politics of Crisis*. London: Verso.

Trachtenberg, Joshua. 1943. *The Devil and the Jews: The Medieval Conception of the Jew and Its Relation to Modern Antisemitism*. New Haven, CT: Yale University Press.

Traill, David A. 2006. "Philip the Chancellor and the Heresy Inquisition in Northern France, 1235–1236." *Viator* 37: 241–54.

Triekle, Norbert. 2014. "Struggle without Classes: Why There Is No Resurgence of the Proletariat in the Currently Unfolding Capitalist Crisis." In *Marxism and the Critique of Value*, edited by Neil Larsen, Mathias Nilges, Josh Robinson, and Nicholas Brown, 201–24. Chicago: MCM'.

Tronto, Joan C. 2015. "Hunting for Women, Haunted for Gender: The Rhetorical Limits of the Manifesto." In *The Cambridge Companion to The Communist Manifesto*, edited by Terrell Carver and James Farr, 134–52. Cambridge: Cambridge University Press.

Trump, Donald. 2015. "Here's Donald Trump's Presidential Announcement Speech." *Time*, June 16. https://time.com/3923128/donald-trump-announcement-speech/.

Trump, Donald. 2016. "Donald Trump's Argument for America." YouTube. https://www.youtube.com/watch?v=vST61W4bGm8.

Tuck, Richard. 2016. *The Sleeping Sovereign: The Invention of Modern Democracy*. Cambridge: Cambridge University Press.

Tyrer, David. 2013. *The Politics of Islamophobia: Race, Power and Fantasy*. London: Pluto.

Tyrer, David, and Salman Sayyid. 2012. "Governing Ghosts: Race, Incorporeality and Difference in Post-Political Times." *Current Sociology* 60, no. 3: 353–67.

Viroli, Maurizio. 2005. *From Politics to Reason of State: The Acquisition and Transformation of the Language of Politics 1250–1600*. Cambridge: Cambridge University Press.

Vogl, Joseph. 2014. *The Specter of Capital*. Translated by Joachim Redner and Robert Savage. Stanford, CA: Stanford University Press.

Voltaire. 2013. *Voltaire's Fanaticism, or Mahomet the Prophet : A New Translation*. Translated by Hanna Burton. Sacramento, CA: Litwin.

Wacquant, Loïc. 2013. "The Great Penal Leap Backward: Incarceration in America from Nixon to Clinton." In *The New Punitiveness: Trends, Theories, Perspectives*, edited by John Pratt, David Brown, Mark Brown, Simon Hallsworth, and Wayne Morrison, 29–52. London: Willan.

Wagner, Bryan. 2009. *Disturbing the Peace: Black Culture and the Police Power after Slavery*. Cambridge, MA: Harvard University Press.

Wakefield, Walter Leggett, and Austin Patterson Evans. 1991. *Heresies of the High Middle Ages*. New York: Columbia University Press.

Wald, Gayle. 2000. *Crossing the Line: Racial Passing in Twentieth-Century US Literature and Culture*. Durham, NC: Duke University Press.

Walker, David. 1830. *Walker's Appeal, in Four Articles, Together with a Preamble, to the Coloured Citizens of the World, But in Particular, and Very Expressly, To Those in the United States*. Boston: David Walker. https://docsouth.unc.edu/nc/walker/walker.html.

Wallerstein, Immanuel. 1991a. "The Construction of Peoplehood: Racism, Nationalism, Ethnicity." In *Race, Nation, Class: Ambiguous Identities*, by Étienne Balibar and Immanuel Wallerstein, 71–85. London: Verso.

Wallerstein, Immanuel. 1991b. *Geopolitics and Geoculture: Essays on the Changing World-System*. Cambridge: Cambridge University Press.

Webman, Esther. 2011. "Hate and Absurdity: The Impact of *The Protocols of the Elders of Zion*." In *The Global Impact of* The Protocols of the Elders of Zion: *A Century-Old Myth*, edited by Esther Webman, 1–23. London: Routledge.

Weis, René. 2002. *The Yellow Cross: The Story of the Last Cathars' Rebellion against the Inquisition, 1290–1329*. New York: Vintage.

Wenehand, Niall. 2007. "Skirmishing, *The Irish World*, and Empire, 1876–86." *Éire-Ireland* 42, nos. 1–2: 180–200.

Westad, Odd Arne. 2011. *The Global Cold War: Third World Interventions and the Making of Our Times*. Cambridge: Cambridge University Press.

"The Westphalian Treaties from October 24th, 1648: Texts and Translations." n.d. Acta Pacis Westphalicae, Supplementa electronica 1. http://www.pax-westphalica.de /ipmipo/indexen.html.

White, Hylton. 2020. "How Is Capitalism Racial? Fanon, Critical Theory and the Fetish of Antiblackness." *Social Dynamics* 46, no. 1: 22–35.

White, Peter. 1993. *The Early Stuart Church, 1603–1642*. London: Palgrave.

Williams, Eric. 2021. *Capitalism and Slavery*. Chapel Hill: University of North Carolina Press.

Williams, Kristian. 2011. "The Other Side of the Coin: Counterinsurgency and Community Policing." *Interface* 3, no. 1: 81–117.

Williams, Raymond. 2014. *Keywords: A Vocabulary of Culture and Society*. Oxford: Oxford University Press

Wolf, Kenneth Baxter. 2008. "Sentencia-Estatuto de Toledo, 1449." Medieval Texts in Translation. Claremont Colleges. https://scholarship.claremont.edu/cgi/viewcontent .cgi?article=1043&context=pomona_fac_pub.

Wood, Ellen Meiksins. 2002. *The Origin of Capitalism: A Longer View*. London: Verso.

Young, Francis. 2018. *Magic as a Political Crime in Medieval and Early Modern England: A History of Sorcery and Treason*. London: I. B. Taurus.

Yuran, Noam. 2014. *What Money Wants: An Economy of Desire*. Stanford, CA: Stanford University Press.

Zabin, Serena R. 2004. *The New York Conspiracy Trials of 1741: Daniel Horsmanden's Journal of the Proceedings with Related Documents*. New York: Bedford.

Zeitlin, Samuel Garrett. 2018. "War and Peace in the Political Thought of Francis Bacon." PhD diss., University of California, Berkeley.

Žižek, Slavoj. 2019. *The Sublime Object of Ideology*. London: Verso.

Index

Aberdeen Bestiary, 40–41

abolitionism: color line and, 171–74; crisis populism and, 210–16; proslavery ideology and, 168–71

abstract capital, 183–89

accumulation: carceral regime and, 173–74; industrialization and, 174–75; racial capitalism and, 135–39, 189–90; racial liberalism and, 141–42; regulationist theory and, 136–37, 230nn4–5; security for, 144–45

Actual State and Condition of Their Negro Population (Holland), 170

Africans: as colonial slaves, 126; Moorish enslavement of, 69, 79–82, 90–91; passing by, 94

Against the Inveterate Obduracy of the Jews (Peter the Venerable), 47–49

Agamben, Giorgio, 52–53, 108–9, 172

Aglietta, Michel, 230n4

agrarian capitalism, birth in England of, 115

Ahmed, Sara, 12

Albigensian Crusade, 44, 50

al-Buraq (magical steed), 70–71, 164–65.
    See also Libro del Alboraique

Alfonsi, Petrus, 46–48, 221n15

Alfonso X (King of Spain), 66, 223n11

Alien and Sedition Acts (US), 182

alien raciality, immigration politics and, 194

Aliens Act (Great Britain), 181–82

American Revolution, 167, 169

Angel, Salvador, 220n2

Anidjar, Gil, 21–22

animal breeding, language of race and, 61, 222n2

anti-Arab racism, 18–20; Crusades and, 45–47

anti-Asian racism, 136–37, 188–89; immigration politics and, 193–94; labor exploitation and, 230n2; neoliberalism and, 202–3; Orientalism and, 195–98

anti-Blackness: anticommunism and, 180–81; carceral regime and, 173–74; Hamitic curse and, 84–85; racial liberalism and, 151–52, 172–74; slavery and, 84–91

anticolonialism, counterinsurgency groups and, 198

anticommunism: Cold War and, 198–99; emergence of, 179–81, 235n34; French Revolution and, 133; liberalism and, 175–76; secret revolutionaries and, 177–78; state and role of, 128

anti-Indigeneity, colonialism and, 82–84, 87–91

anti-Islamism. *See* Islamophobia

antipopery: color line and, 125–28, 229n43; racial capitalism and, 138–39

antisemitism: conversos (Jewish converts) and history of, 66–73; ensoulment and, 20–23; history of, 32; Ku Klux Klan and, 127–28; *limpieza de sangre* (blood purity) statutes and, 66, 68; pastoral reformulation of, 47–49; *The Protocols of the Meetings of the Learned Elders of Zion* and, 187–88; racial capitalism and, 136–37, 185–88; racism and, 18–20. *See also* Jews

Appadurai, Arjun, 202–3

Appeal to the Coloured Citizens of the World, but in Particular and Expressly to Those of the United States of America (Walker), 168–69, 180

Arab Spring, racial neoliberalism and, 204

Areaopagitica (Milton), 234n28

Arendt, Hannah, 171

Arias, Diego, 73

Asad, Talal, 42–43, 53, 226n13

Atlantic slave trade, 29–30, 84–91, 225n30; possessive individualism and, 149–52

austerity campaigns, racial neoliberalism and, 201–3

auto-da-fé (act of faith), 77

Babeuf, François-Noël, 178, 237n54, 238n59

Babington Plot (1586), 121

Bacon, Francis, 97–98, 111–20, 122, 128–29, 139, 228n31, 231n8, 234n26

Bacon's Rebellion, 149, 233n21

badges, heresy identification with, 55

Baird, Robert J., 226n13

Baldwin, James, 59–60

Balibar, Étienne, 20–22, 130, 219n25, 229n52

Ball, Kirstie, 10–11

Banton, Michael, 32

Barber, Benjamin, 201–2

Barmby, John Godwyn, 237n54

Barruel, Augustin, 177, 187

Bartlett, Robert, 38–39

Bayoumi, Moustafa, 18

Beccaria, Cesare, 146

Beckert, Sven, 175

Bellay (Black Jacobin), 163–64

Benedictine Order, 42

Bentham, Jeremy, 139, 146

Bernard of Clairvaux, 40

Best, George, 225n31

Best, Stephen, 150–51

biopolitics: of anti-heresy, 38–44; body and soul and, 52–53; ensoulment and, 5–9; of population, 236n40

Birkett, Helen, 51–52

Black Jacobins: in America, 167–71; Haitian Revolution and, 161–67

Black Marxism (Robinson), 33–34, 134–35

Blackness: *casta* classification system and, 94–95; colonialist condemnation of, 14, 87–91, 225n33; depravity attributed to, 93–94; origins of race and, 60–61; passing and, 16–17; racial liberalism and condemnation of, 150–52; as statelessness, 171–74; surveillance and, 14–15; as threat, 171

Black radicals, communism and, 180–81

Blanqui, Louis, 178

Bobbit, Philip, 226n5

Bodin, Jean, 111, 227n22

border as method approach, 193, 239n2

border policing: emergence of, 181–83; immigration politics and, 192–93

Bosse, Abraham, 109

Botero, Giovanni, 104–5

Boyer, Robert, 230n4

Brace, Charles Loring, 239n3

Braude, Benjamin, 85

Bray, Alan, 110–11, 118

British East India Company, 195

Brown, Oscar, Jr., 1, 5, 191

Brown, Wendy, 200–201, 234n26

Browne, Simone, 14

Buck-Morss, Susan, 165

Burden-Stelly, Charisse, 180

Burke, Edmund: on abolitionism, 237n45; American Federalists and, 167; on French Revolution, 133, 157–61, 163, 172, 183–84; on Jacobins, 165–67, 172, 179; on money abstraction, 183–84, 186

Bush, George W., 202

Byrd, Jodi, 135

Camboulet, Simon, 163

campa de reconcentración, in Spanish colonies, 96

Campion, Edmund, 229n43

Canaanites, racial liberalism and, 141–42

Canon 16 (Council of Nablus), 54

Canon 21 "Omnis utriusque sexus" (Fourth Lateran Council), 51–52

Canon 68 (Fourth Lateran Council), 53–57

Canon 70 (Fourth Lateran Council), 56, 62

Capital (Marx), 139

capitalism: cotton and, 174–75; plantation system and, 232n18; regulationist theory and, 136–37, 230n4; sedition and birth of, 115. *See also* racial capitalism

Carbonari (Italy), 178
carceral regime, 237n51; racial capitalism and, 173–74, 231n9
Carnot, Lazar (Count), 235n32
Carta de los Judíos de Constantinopla (Letter of the Jews of Constantinople), 74–75, 84, 91–92, 98
casa de contratación (mercantile counting house), Peruvian Inquisition and, 92
casta (colonial caste system): classifications in, 94–96; race and, 91–92; whiteness and, 93–96
caste system, Spanish colonization and, 80–82
Castro, Americo, 222n4
Cathar movement, 41–44, 55, 63–64
Cavaliers (England), Catholic Church and, 118
Cavanaugh, William, 102–3, 105–7
Chakrabarty, Dipesh, 25, 134
Chambers, Whittaker, 200
Chandra, Sarika, 135
Charles V (King of Spain and Holy Roman Emperor), 101
Chartist movement (Great Britain), 177
Chatterjee, Partha, 205
Chaudhary, Zahid, 10
Chen, Christopher, 135
Chidester, David, 240n11
Chinese Exclusion Act (1882), 193
Chinese Revolution, 160
"chosen people," racial liberalism and, 141–42
Christiana gens (Christian peoplehood), 39, 45
Christianity: Crusades and, 44; heresy in, 41–44; Jewish status and significance in, 48–49; language of security and, 34–36; medieval universalist dream of, 101; origins of race and, 60–61. *See also* Roman Catholic Church
Chua, Amy, 188, 202–3
church, Locke's concept of, 152–55
Church of England: factionalism in, 123–25; Roman Catholicism and, 116–20, 229n48
Cicero, 109–10, 227n17
cimarrones (fugitive slaves), 89–91
citizenship: racial capitalism and, 138–39; US laws on, 239n7
civil society, Locke's concept of, 152–53
clash of civilizations thesis, 201

class: race and, 134–35, 241n26; whiteness and, 93–96, 234n25
clerical celibacy, 40
Cohen, Jeremy, 48–49
Coke, Edward (Sir), 99
Cold War: anticommunism and, 180; counterinsurgency groups and, 198; globalization and, 200–203; racial liberalism and, 230n7
colonialism: anti-Arab racism and, 18–20; anti-Blackness and, 84–91; anti-Indigeneity and, 82–84; Bacon's advocacy for, 114–15; Blackness and, 14; Catholic sedition and, 126–28; genealogy and, 86–91; geopolitics and, 91–92; Iberian empires and, 100–105; land dispossession and, 233n21; Locke's involvement in, 142–45, 231n11; Orientalism and, 195–98; population concepts and, 113; possessive individualism and, 149–52; racial capitalism and, 135–39; racism and, 24, 32, 80–82; religion and, 240n11; sedition and birth of, 115–20; Third World communism and, 181
color line: abolitionism and persistence of, 171–74; anticommunism and, 180–81; antipopery and, 125–28; *casta* and *raza* and, 94–96; colonialism and, 80–82, 149–52, 192–94; *conversos* (Jewish converts) and, 68–73; Du Bois on, 2, 192; embodiment and, 15–17; globalization of, 191–92; inner life of, 13–15; origins of race and, 60–61; passing as transgression of, 15–17; possessive individualism and, 149–52; racial capitalism and, 135–39; racism and, 18–20, 22–23; revolutions and, 164–67; Spanish colonialism and, 86–91
"Common Enemy," Locke's concept of, 146
communism: emergence of, 175, 237n54; European alarm over, 179–81; Jacobinism linked to, 177–78; Marx and Engels and, 179–81
concentration camps, colonial origins of, 96
Concept of the Political, The (Schmitt), 207–10
confession, Catholic institution of, 51–52
conspiracy groups: abstract capitalism and, 187–89; Jews linked to, 186–87; policing of, 178–79, 183–89
Conspiracy of the Equals (Conjuration des Égaux, 1796), 178, 238n59

Constantinople, Ottoman conquest of, 75
conversos (Jewish converts), 64–67; colonialism and, 81–82; depravity attributed to, 93–94; doctor theory, 226n1; in England, 98–100; Morisco threat and, 73–75; Peruvian *gran complicidad* and, 91–92; racialization of, 66–73, 223n13; Spanish Inquisition and, 77–79
convivencia (religious coexistence), in Spain, 64–67, 223n11
Corominas, Joan, 62
corpus ecclesiae mysticum (mystical body of the church), 110, 227n21
Cortez, Hernando, 80
cosmopolitanism, Jews linked to, 185, 194
Cota, Alonso, 67
Coulthard, Glen, 135
Council of Nablus, 54
counterinsurgency regimes, colonialism and, 197–98, 240n17
Counterintelligence Program (COINTELPRO), 180–81, 199
Court of Star Chamber, 112
Covarrubias, Sebastián de, 62–63
creative destruction, crisis populism and, 210–16
criminal threat: Blackness as, 150–51, 171–74; government and, 232n15; policing of, 144–45; of unpropertied, 145–49
crisis populism: origins of, 200, 203–5; solutions to, 210–16; top-down governance and, 203–5
Crusades: anti-Jewish discourse during, 49; apocalyptic imagination of, 221n14; heresy wars and, 44–47
crypto-Catholicism, Church of England and, 123–25
crypto-Jews, Spanish conversos as, 76–77, 92
crypto-Muslims, Spanish conversos as, 76–77
cuius regio, eius religio (whose realm, his religion), 101, 105–6, 226n9
cultural politics, globalization and, 202–3
cura animarum (care of souls), 36, 44
"Curse of Ham": colonial ideology concerning, 93–96; slavery justification and, 84–91, 225n31

Daemonologie (James I), 111
Daulatzai, Sohail, 199

Davis, Angela, 212
Dawson, Michael, 135–36
Day, Iyko, 188
Declaration of the Rights of Man and Citizen (1789), 158–59, 164
Defund the Police campaign, 242n32
De instauranda Aethiopum salute (How to restore the salvation of the Ethiopians) (Sandoval), 86–87
de la Cruz, Fray Francisco, 86–87
de Miramon, Charles, 61
demonic possession: crisis populism and, 207–10; racial liberalism and, 151
Der ewige Jude (*The Eternal Jew*) (film), 19–20, 22
Dialogi contra Iudaeos (Dialogue against the Jews) (Alfonsi), 46–48, 221n15
Diccionario crítico etimológico de la lengua Castellana (Corominas), 62
Diccionario Latino-Español (Nebrija), 62
Diran, Ingrid, 134
disarmament, crisis populism and, 214–16
discontentment, sedition linked to, 115–20
dogma-line racism, 22
Dogmatum falsas species (Philip the Chancellor), 31, 40
Dominic (Saint), 55
Dominican Order, 42
Donatists, 41
Dreyfus Affair, 187
"dual curse," colonialist use of, 86–91
Dubber, Markus Dirk, 140–41
Dubois, Laurent, 167–68
Du Bois, W. E. B., 173–74; on abolition, 211–212; on Blackness, 15; communism and, 180; double consciousness of, 16–17; on global color line, 2, 192, 198, 217n1
Dutch colonialism, Spanish fear of, 91–92

Eastern Greek Christians: Crusades and, 45–46; Fourth Lateran Council and, 51
economics, racial capitalism and, 137–39
elites, crisis populism and, 205
Elizabethan Religious Settlement, 117–20
Elizabeth I (Queen of England): Church of England and, 98–100, 117; papal excommunication of, 117–18; plots against, 121; Rising of the North (1569) against, 123

embodiment: biopolitics of the soul and, 52–53; heresy and persecution of, 42–43; passing and, 15–17; slavery as property and, 145–46, 150–51

Emmer, P. C., 84, 225n30

enclosure laws, land privatization through, 115

Engels, Friedrich, 133, 175, 179–81, 238n61

England: colonialism and, 114–15; Protestant Reformation in, 116–20; state structure and security in, 110–13

English Civil War, 118–20; fanaticism and, 156; political police and, 144–45

Enlightenment, slavery and, 165

enmity, theologization of, 208–10

Enrique III (King of Castile), 65

Enrique IV (King of Castile), 73

ensoulment: biopolitics and, 5–9; criminality and, 151; defined, 4; hermeneutics of suspicion and, 11–13; Jacobinism and, 161–67; racial capitalism and, 189–90; racial ensoulment, 170; racial power and, 20–23, 124–25; state and politics of, 100

Europe, geopolitical concept of, 129–31

Evans, Hiram Wesley, 97

exposure, politics of, racial truth and, 10–13

fanaticism: abstract capitalism and, 186; Burke's discussion of, 158–59; cultural representations of, 235n33; Locke's discussion of, 155–57; religious enemy framework and, 195–200, 239n10

Fanon, Frantz, 14, 219n24, 241n26

Fawkes, Guy, 118

FBI, COINTEL program of, 180–81, 199

fear, affective politics of, 12

Fear of Small Numbers, The (Appadurai), 203

Federalists, American Black Jacobins and, 167–68

Federici, Silvia, 41–42, 110–11

feudalism: capitalism and, 134–35; power and, 37; racism and, 28, 33–34, 134–35

fides catholica (catholic/universal faith), 47, 50–52

Field, Karen, 8

Fields, Barbara, 8

flocks: in Fourth Lateran Council agenda, 50–52; framing of heresy with, 43–44

Formation of a Persecuting Society, The (Moore), 39–40

Foucault, Michel: on biopolitics, 6, 52, 231n10; on embodiment, 4; on governmentality, 25, 104, 114–15, 220n6; on liberalism, 139–40; on pastoral power, 36–38, 51–52, 220n6; on politics as war, 13; on population, 113, 228n26; on racial power, 26–27, 231n10; on reason of state, 128–29, 226n5

Fourier, Charles, 175

Fourth Lateran Council, 35; body and soul and, 53–57; pastoral war and, 49–52; textile metaphor in, 62–63

France: abolition of slavery in, 166–68; communism in, 175; religious extremes and middle way in, 125; Westphalian system of states and, 103

Frankfurt school, 138

Fraser, Nancy, 136, 241n26

Fredrickson, George, 32

freedom, racial liberalism and, 141

Freemasons: antisemitism and, 187; communism and, 178; conspiracy groups and, 177; Jacobins and, 159; in The Protocols of the Meetings of the Learned Elders of Zion and, 187–88

French National Council, 168

French Revolution: American attitudes toward, 169–71; communism and, 176–77; fanaticism and, 156–60; Haitian Revolution and, 163–67; Jacobin ideology and, 160–67; Thermidorian reaction to, 178

friend/enemy distinction, antiracism and, 209–10

fugitivity, slavery and, 89–91

Fukuyama, Francis, 200

Fundamental Constitutions of the Carolinas, 231n11

fundamentalism, Islamic redefinition of, 199–200, 241n19, 241n21

Funkenstein, Amos, 49

genealogical etymology, 26; purity concepts and, 72–73

General Agreement on Tariffs and Trade (GATT), 200

Geneva school of neoliberalism, 200

genocide, denial of, 242n27

Genovese, Eugene, 232n18

geopolitics: capitalist world-systems and, 100–101; colonialism and, 91–92; Westphalian system of states and, 101–5

German Peasants' War (1525), 106–7

Germany: postwar antisemitism in, 186; Thirty Years War and, 103

Gespenst (specter), 179

Gilmore, Ruth Wilson, 173–74, 215

Gitlitz, David, 73

Gnostics, 41

Goldenberg, David Theo, 9, 86–87

Goldsmith, Zachary, 156–57

Goldstein, Alyosha, 135

Gospel of John, 31, 36–37, 40, 108

governmentality: Foucault's concept of, 27; liberalism and, 139–40; Locke's civil government philosophy and, 143–45; population and, 114–15; race and, 29; racial capitalism and, 25; racial neoliberalism and, 200–203; reason of state and, 104–5; secularism and, 107–9

gran complicidad (1631) (Peru), 91–92, 184

Great Recession, crisis populism and, 203–5

Greco-Roman ideology: police power and, 140; racism and, 33

Gregorian reforms, 39–40, 50, 220n8

Gregory VII (Pope), 39–40, 44, 220n8

Guha, Ranajit, 197

Gunpowder Plot, 118

Haitian Revolution, 160, 161–67; American slaves and, 168–71

Hall, Stuart, 135

Harcourt, Bruce, 140, 231n99

Harris, Cheryl, 149, 151, 233n22

Hartman, Saidiya, 150

Harvey, David, 173

Harvey, L. P., 63

Haymarket riots, 182

Hebrew Bible, Christian ambivalence concerning, 48

Hegel, G. F. W., 165

Heng, Geraldine, 32–34

Henry III (King of France), 116

Henry VIII (King of England), 116–20, 123

heresy: biopolitics of, 38–44; Crusades and, 44–47; Inquisition and, 42; Islam linked to, 46–47; origins of race and, 28; Protestant Reformation and, 101–5; sexuality linked to, 51–52

hermeneutics of suspicion: ant-Blackness and, 87–91; Black radicalism and, 180–81; racial power and, 11; racism and, 22–23; Spanish Inquisition and, 76–79

Hincks, Peter, 169

History of Sexuality, The (Foucault), 51–52

History 1 and History 2, Chakrabarty's concepts of, 25–26

Hobbes, Thomas, 108–9, 118, 144, 146–48, 232nn14–15

Hobsbawm, Eric, 178

Holland, Edwin C., 170–72

Holland, Sharon, 7

Holy Inquisition of New Spain, 88

Holy League (France), 125

Holy Roman Empire, 101, 103, 106, 125

holy war, Crusades characterized as, 44–47

Homeland (television series), 23–24

homme pervers, 155, 201; police power and, 147–48

Hörmann, Daniel, 161, 164

Horsmanden, David, 126–28

Huguenot Protestants (France), 125

Hume, David, 226n13

Hunter, W. W., 197, 240n14

Huntington, Samuel, 201, 241n25

immigration: police power and, 181–83; security technologies and, 192–93

Ince, Onur Ulas, 135, 232n13

indemnitas, Christian concept of, 35

India: British rule of, 196–98, 240nn13–15; far-right populism in, 204

Indian Mutiny (Sepoy Rebellion), 196–98, 240n13

India Police Act (1861), 196

Indigenous peoples: colonial genealogical claims about, 93–96; liberalism and enslavement of, 141–42; property seizure from, 142–45, 233n21; racial capitalism and, 135–39; Spanish colonialism and, 82–85

indiscernibility, racism and, 20–21

industrialization: capitalism and, 174–75; moneyed abstraction and, 184

infidel, etymology of, 221n18

Infrastructures of Race (Nemser), 95–96
Innocent III (Pope), 42–44, 49–50, 221n14
Inquisition: *casta* classification system and, 94–96; conversos and, 67; Fourth Lateran Council and, 50–51, 53; *persecutio* (prosecution) inquiry during, 42–44; in Peru, 91–92; technologies of security and, 76; tribunals and authorities for, 221n11. *See also* Spanish Inquisition
intelligence (state): covert technologies of, 120–21, 229n41; international and cross-border policing and, 178; Lopez's involvement in, 99–100; religion and, 122
interest of state, 105
internationalism: Jews linked to, 185; racial neoliberalism and, 200–203
International Monetary Fund (IMF), 200
inward possessions, Locke's discussion of, 152–53
Iogna-Prat, Dominique, 48
Iranian Revolution (1979), 199
Ireland, British colonialism in, 114–15, 193, 239n6
Isaac, Benjamin, 33–34
Isabella and Ferdinand (Spanish monarchs), 76
Islamophobia, 1–2; anti-Arab racism and, 18–20; biopolitics and, 6–7; Crusades and, 45–47, 221n16; ensoulment and, 20–23; fanaticism and, 235n33; neoliberal racism and, 200–203; Orientalism and, 195–98; postcolonial trends in, 198–200; post-9/11, 2, 22, 194; racial capitalism and, 136–37; religious enemy framework and, 194–200; state authority and, 128; Westphalian state and, 128–31, 229n51
ius publicum Europaeum (European public law), 129

Jacobinism, 128, 159–69, 197–98; conspiracy theories about, 177–79. *See also* Black Jacobins
James, C. L. R., 163, 180
James I (King of England), 110–11, 118, 227n20
Jesuits, threat in England of, 117–18
Jews: clothing requirements for, 53–57, 62–63, 77; as conversos, 64–67; Crusades and, 46–47; England's expulsion of, 98; etymology of racism and, 29; fanaticism and, 157;

Fourth Lateran Council on, 53–57, 222n26; language of race and, 62–63; medieval politics and, 64–65; in medieval Spain, 64–67; pastoral anti-Judaism and, 47–49; racialization of, 194; Spanish expulsion of, 74–75; Spanish Inquisition and, 76–79; state authority and, 128; status and significance in Christendom of, 48–49; witchcraft linked to, 111; yellow fabric for, 55, 63, 77. *See also* antisemitism
Jew of Malta, The (Marlowe), 98
Jihad vs. McWorld: Terrorism's Challenge to Democracy (Barber), 201–2
Joachim of Fiore, 221n14
"John Bull's Alien Act" (*Punch* cartoon), 182–83
Jubilee Plot, 193, 239n3
July Monarchy, 176, 237n54
June Days *(les journées de Juin)*, 176
justice, Locke on, 147

Kalmar, Ivan Davison, 21–22
Kantorowicz, Ernst, 107–9, 227n21
Kaufman, Irving, 97, 100
Keywords (Williams, Raymond), 26
King, Martin Luther, Jr., 128, 181
"Klan's Fight for Americanism, The" (Evans), 97
Knight, Frank, 9–10
knowledge, race and, 9–10
Kofman, Sarah, 26
Kotsko, Adam, 207–8
Ku Klux Klan, 78, 127–28, 224n23
Kundani, Arun, 134

labor: coerced, colonialism and, 149–52, 233n21; immigration and, 192–93; money and, 143–45; racial capitalism and, 135–39, 241n26
Laborde, Cécile, 234n28
labor theory of property, 142
Lacan, Jacques, 10
Laclau, Ernesto, 204
Lake, Peter, 98, 121
language of race: early definitions, 61–64; evolution of, 60–61
las Casas, Bartolomé de, 83, 86
Lateran IV. *See* Fourth Lateran Council

Law Report, 108

League of Communists (Great Britain), 179, 238n61

League of Outlaws, 178

League of the Just, 178, 238n61

Le Mans, Henry of, 40

Lenin, V. I., 135

Letter Concerning Toleration (Locke), 152, 156

"Letters on a Regicide Peace" (Burke), 159, 166

Levantine Christianity, Crusades and, 45–47

Leviathan (Hobbes), 108–9, 118

Lewis, Laura, 81–82

liberal democracy: definitions of, 236n39; party apparatus and, 158–60, 236n41; population biopolitics and, 236n40

liberalism: criminal threat and, 145–49; market theory and, 139–42; security and, 139–40, 142–45

Libro del Alboraique (*Book of the Alboraique*), 70–73, 93, 118, 224n15

Lima Inquisition (1571), 86

limpieza de sangre (blood purity) statutes, 66, 68, 72, 74, 77–80, 84, 93

Linebaugh, Peter, 149, 192

Lipietz, Alain, 230n4

Lipsitz, George, 149–50

Liu, Andrew B., 233n20

Locke, John: abstract capitalism and, 186; capitalism and, 232n13; colonialism and, 142–45, 231n11; on criminal threat of un-propertied, 145–49; liberalism and, 232n14; on money, 232n13; on religion, 152–55, 234n26; on securing society, 142–45; on slavery, 143, 231nn11–12; on state authority, 128–29; on threat of the improper, 152–55, 172–73; on zealotry and fanaticism, 155–57

Lombroso, Cesare, 148, 232n17

London Communist Propaganda Society, 237n54

Lopez, Roderigo (Dr.), 98–100, 111, 121

Losurdo, Domenico, 141

Louis-Phillipe (King of France), 175–76

L'Ouverture, Toussaint, 163, 166

Luther, Martin, 8, 101, 106

Luxemburg, Rosa, 135

lynching, 133, 171–74

Machiavelli, Niccolo, 104

Macpherson, C. B., 145–46

Macpherson, James, 235n35

Mahomet, or Fanaticism (Voltaire), 235n33

Mahometan: Locke's references to, 128–29, 154, 201–2; as Orientalist trope, 130, 195–96

Malcolm X, 198–99, 240n18

Manifesto of the Communist Party (Marx and Engels), 175, 179–80, 238n58, 238n63

Mann, Geoff, 160

Mardi Gras, race and, 78, 224n23

market theories: liberalism and, 139–42; police power and, 147–48; racial capitalism and, 137–39, 231n9

Marlowe, Christopher, 98

maroon communities, fugitivity and, 89–91, 225n35

"Marprelate" pamphlets, 120, 229n43

marrano (Spanish word), etymology of, 66, 223n12

Marranos, 66. *See also* conversos (Jewish converts)

Martínez, Ferrand, 65

Martínez, María Elena, 80, 89–91

Marty, Martin, 199, 241n21

Marx, Karl: capital formula (M-C-M') of, 149; on capitalism, 184; communism and, 175, 178–81, 238n61; French Revolution and, 133; on liberalism, 139; race and, 16; racial capitalism and, 25, 135–39; on security, 144; on utopian socialism, 214–15

Mary I (Queen of England), 99, 116–20, 229n47

Mary Queen of Scots, 123

Masonic lodges. *See* Freemasons

Mastnak, Tomaž, 44, 83, 130

Mayo (Lord), 196–97, 240n14

Melamed, Jodi, 135, 191–92, 230n7

Melley, Timothy, 13, 183

Menocal, María Rosa, 64

Merchant of Venice, The (Shakespeare), 98

Mexico, race and biopolitics in, 95–96

Mezzadra, Sandro, 193, 239n2

Middle Ages: Hamatic curse in, 84–91; pastoral warfare during, 38–44; racism in, 28, 32–34; slavery during, 69; Spanish life and religion during, 45–46, 64–67

milites Christi (soldiers of Christ), 44

millennialism, Crusades and, 45

Milton, John, 234n28

Mintz, Sidney, 149

Modi, Narendra, 197, 202, 241n25

monarchical authority: secularism and, 108–9; sedition against, 112–13; Spanish church-state relations and, 224n19; Spanish revolt against, 64–65, 67–68; treason and sedition against, 109–13

money: abstract capitalism and, 183–89; Jewish association with, 185–88, 194; Locke on, 232n13; racial liberalism and, 143–45

Montaigne, Michel de, 228n34

Moore, R. I., 39–40, 220n7

Moors: African slave trade and, 79–80; cultural distinctiveness of, 224n18; Spanish campaign against, 73–75; Spanish conversos and, 69–73. See also Moriscos

Moriscos: casta classification of, 94–96; Spanish Inquisition and, 76–79; threat in Spain of, 73–75, 90–91

Mormonism, demonization of, 195

Mornay, Phillipe de, 229n51

Mosaic law, 48

Moses, A. Dirk, 207, 242n27

Mouffe, Chantal, 204

Mudejares (Spanish Moors), 74–75

Muhammad: al-Buraq (magical steed) of, 70–71; Crusades and role of, 45–47, 221n15

Muhammad, Khalil Gibran, 88, 151–52, 225n33

mulattos: casta classification of, 94–96; Haitian Revolution and, 163

Muslims: Christian view of, 44–47; fanaticism and, 157; global movements by, 199–200; Jews linked to, 49; in medieval Spain, 64–67, 74–75; neoliberal racism and, 202–3; Trump's racialism of, 203–5. See also Moriscos

Nation of Islam (US), 199

nativism, 193–94

Naturalization Act (1790), 239n7

Nazi antisemitism, 21, 208–10

Nebrija, Elio Antonio de, 62, 222n4

nefesh (Hebrew word for soul), 52

Neilson, Brett, 193, 239n2

Nemser, Daniel, 95–96

Neocleous, Mark, 140–41, 234n26

neófitos (neophyte Christians), Spanish colonialism and, 82–84

neo-Marxist French regulation school, 137

Netanyahu, Benzion, 66, 223n13

Newman, Jane O., 106

New Testament, Jews in, 48

Newton, Richard, 161–65

Ngai, Mae M., 194

Nichols, Robert, 135

Nicodemites, 124, 229n47

9/11 attacks. See September 11, 2001, attacks

Nirenberg, David, 61–62, 64–65

Noahide legend, colonialism and, 84–91

Nygaard, Bertel, 175

Oath of Supremacy (England), 122

"Of Unity in Religion" (Bacon), 97

oikonomos (household law), 140

omnes et singulatim (all and one), paradox of, 107–9, 146–47

Oriental Christians, Crusades and, 45–46

Orientalism: colonialism and, 195–96, 240n12; Westphalian reason of state and, 130–31

Ormerod, Paul, 43

Ornament of the World, The (Menocal), 64

Osborne, Peter, 179

Ottoman Empire: Islamophobia and, 128–29; Spanish fear of, 74–75, 79; state formation and, 130–31

Oxford English Dictionary, 113

Palazzo, Giovanni Antonio, 104

Palestine Liberation Organization, 199

Palmer, Colin, 88–91

Palmer Raids, 180

pamphleteering: proliferation of, 119–20, 229n43; slave rebellions and, 168–70

Papists: antipopery and color line and, 125–28; emergence in England of, 120–25; Muslims and, 128

Paris Commune, 182

parties: far-right populism and, 204–5; possessive individualism and, 157–60, 235n36, 236n37, 236n41

passing: antisemitism and, 19–20; body/soul dialectics and, 15–17, 22–23; by conversos, Spanish fear of, 71–72, 91; sistema de las castas and, 94–96 pastoral power: anti-heresy biopolitics and, 38–44, 220n4, 220n7; anti-Judaism and, 47–49, 64–67; Crusades and, 44–47; Foucault on, 36–38, 40; Fourth Lateran Council and, 49–52; language of race and, 59–61; racism and, 28; secularism and reason of state, 107–9; sedition and, 112–13; slave fugitivity and, 89–91; state structures and, 105

Peace of Augsburg (1555), 101–2, 226n9

persecutio (prosecution) model of legal inquiry: Inquisition and, 42–44; Crusades and, 44–47

Peru: conversos in, 93–94; *gran complicidad* (1631) in, 91–92

Peter of Bruys, 40, 47

Peter the Venerable, 47–49

Philip II (King of France), 43–44, 50

Philip II (King of Spain), 99

Philip the Chancellor, 31, 40

Physiocrats, 228n26

pignus spiritus (spiritual guarantee), 34–36, 220n3

Pius V (Pope), 117

Pizarro, Francisco, 80

plantation ideology: capitalism and, 232n18; colonialism and, 114–15; factories and, 233n19; slavery and, 149–52, 163, 233nn19–20

police power: anticommunism and, 178–81; border policing and, 181–83, 192–93; Burke on, 159–60; carceral regime and, 173–74; colonialism and, 195–98; criminal threat and, 147–49; European terminology for, 231n8; international and cross-border policing and, 178; political police, 144–45, 160–67, 178, 180–81; politics of exposure and, 11, 218n8; in postbellum South, 171–74; racial liberalism and, 139–42; racial neoliberalism and, 201–3; slave patrols and, 168–71, 234n23; threat of the improper and, 152–55; whiteness of, 151–52

Police Union of German States, 178

politics: of exposure, racial truth and, 10–13; Jews in Middle Ages and, 64–65; modern ideological spectrum of, 156; monarchy and, 105–9; parties and, 157–60; racial enemies and, 205–10, 242n30; of racial threat, 2–3;

5–7, 151, 217n5; Schmitt on, 205–8; state and ensoulment of, 100

population: crisis populism and, 205; invention of, 113–15, 228n26; liberal democracy and biopolitics of, 236n40; seditions of discontentment and, 116–20

Portuguese conversos, 82; in England, 99

Portuguese slave trade, 69, 79, 84–86, 233n19

possessive individualism: abstract capitalism and, 186; churches and parties and, 157–60; colonialism and, 149–52; liberalism and, 145–49; Locke's civil society and, 153–55

Postone, Moishe, 21, 136, 138, 184–85, 188

power: Middle Ages mechanisms of, 37; racial capitalism and, 137–39; racial ensoulment and, 124–25; Westphalian system of states and, 102–5

preaching orders, 42–44, 51–52

primitive accumulation, racial capitalism and, 135

probanza (ancestry document), 94–95

propaganda, history of, 235n35

property: criminal threat of unpropertied and, 145–49; labor theory of, 142; liberal security and defense of, 142–45; policing and safeguarding of, 140; Proudhon on abolition of, 174–75; racial capitalism and seizure of, 135–39, 233n21; as theft, 174–75; wealth and, 148; whiteness as, 149–50, 233n22

propriety, property and, 145–49; threat of the improper and, 152–55

Prosser, Gabriel, 168–70, 237n48

Protestant Reformation: in England, 116–20; fanaticism and, 155–56; threat to Catholicism of, 101–5

Protocols of the Meetings of the Learned Elders of Zion, The, 31, 187–88

Proudhon, Pierre-Joseph, 174–75, 238n63

psuchē (Greek word for life), 52, 222n25

Puar, Jasbir, 22, 211

public opinion, seditions of discontentment and, 116–20

Punch magazine, 175–77, 181–83

Puritanism: emergence in England of, 120, 122–25, 229n45; fanaticism and, 157

Quesnay, François, 147–48

Quijano, Anibal, 32, 60–61, 100, 219n1

Qur'an, Christian criticism of, 47–49

Ra, Amur, 211

race and racism: abstract capitalism and, 184–86; anticommunism and, 180–81; antipopery and, 125–28; biopolitics and, 6; birth of whiteness and, 93–96; caste systems and, 81–82; class and, 134–35, 241n26; colonialism and, 80–82, 91–92, 101–5, 149–52; color line and, 13–15, 17; Crusades against Saracens and, 46–47; early definitions of, 61–64, 222n1; embodiment and, 3–4; emergence of concept, 24; European Medieval concepts of, 28, 32–34, 219n1; feudalism and, 134–35; Fourth Lateran Council canons and, 56–57; historical origins of, 32–34; Iberian sub-Saharan slave trade and, 79–80; Islamophobia and, 1–2; Jewish conversos and evolution of, 66–73; knowledge and risk and, 9–10; language of, 29, 59–61; Locke on property and slavery and, 143–45; neoliberal capitalism and, 30; politics and, 206–8; purity of blood and, 62–63, 223n9; reason of state and, 123–25; romantic anticapitalism and, 188–89; scholarship on, 217n3; slavery justifications and, 85–91; Spanish technologies of racial security, 76–79; truth and politics of exposure, 10–13; types of, 18–20. See also structural racism

racecraft, Fields' concept of, 8

racial capitalism: accumulation and, 135–39, 189–90; anti-Blackness and anticommunism and, 180–81; Atlantic trade triangle and, 29–30; biopolitics and, 24–26; carceral regime and, 173–74; in European Middle Ages, 33–34; evolution of, 134–39; globalization of, 191–92; immigration politics and, 193–94; liberalism and, 139–42; Nazi antisemitism and, 21; origins of, 230n1; present trends and, 192–94

racial dogma line, European state and, 130–31

racial formation, defined, 4

racial liberalism, 139–42; etymology of, 230n7

racial neoliberalism, 200–203; racial enemies and, 205–10

racial power: pincer action of, 23–24; Ricoeur's hermeneutics of suspicion and, 11

racial proliferation, right-wing populism and, 191–92

Racine, Barnaby, 136

raison d'état, French state sovereignty and, 125

ratio status principle, 226n13

Rawls, John, 23, 102

raza (raça) (Spanish concept of race): anti-Indigeneity and colonialism and, 82–84; antisemitism and, 74–82; *casta* and, 91–96; evolution of, 61–64, 100, 222n4, 223n6; whiteness and, 93–96, 149–52

reactionary, fanaticism and, 156–57, 235n32

Reagan, Ronald, 199–200

"Real San-Culotte, A" (cartoon), 161–66, 176–77

reason of state: antipopery and color line and, 125–28; emergence of, 103–5; English Civil War and, 118–20; fanaticism and, 155–56; Foucault on, 128–29; religion as technology of, 105–7; secularism and pastoralization of, 107–9; sedition and, 123–25; Spanish church-state relations and, 224n19; threat of the improper and, 152–55

Reconquista, 45–46, 64–67

recusants, in Elizabethan England, 123–25

Reddy, Chandan, 135

Rediker, Marcus, 149, 192

Red Scare, 180

Reflections on the Revolution in France (Burke), 133, 158–61

reflexivity, 13

Refutation of the Calumnies Circulated against the Southern and Western States Respecting the Institution and Existence of Slavery among Them, A (Holland), 170

regimes of accumulation, racial capitalism and, 137–39

regulationist theory, 136–37, 230nn4–5

Reign of Terror (France), 159

religious freedom and tolerance: colonialism and, 240n11; globalization and, 201; intelligence and security and, 122; Locke's discussion of, 152–55, 234n26; Orientalism and, 196–98; political spectrum of, 156, 234nn28–29; racism and, 24; reason of state and, 106–7; religious enemy framework and, 194–200; in Spain, 64; as state strategy, 122; as technology of reason of state, 105–7, 129–31; Westphalian system of states and, 102–5; zealotry and fanaticism and, 155–57 reparative approach, crisis populism and, 213–16

"Republican Medal, and Its Reverse, The" cartoon *(Punch)*, 175–77, 181–82

Requerimiento, Spanish colonialism and, 83–84, 225n27

"revolt of Enriquillo" (1519), 84

revolutions of 1848, 160, 176, 178

Reyna, Junaid, 18, 137

Reynal, Guillaume, 163

Ricoeur, Paul, 11

Ridolfi Plot (1571), 121

right-wing populism, global expansion of, 191–92

Riley, Boots, 17

Rising of the North (1569), 123

risk, race and, 9–10

Roach, Andrew, 43

Robinson, Cedric, 33–34, 134–35, 220n2

Robinson, William, 220n2

Roman Catholic Church: American criticism of, 97; anti-Catholicism and, 195; anti-heresy biopolitics and, 38–44; Church of England and, 98–100, 116–20, 123–25, 229n48; colonial slaves as part of, 126–28; Eastern Greek and Oriental Christians and, 45–46, 51; fanaticism and, 157; Fourth Lateran Council and, 49–52; Islamophobia and, 128–31; Ku Klux Klan denunciation of, 127–28; Oath of Supremacy (England) and, 122; pastoral warfare in, 38–44; *pignus spiritus* and, 35–36; preaching orders in, 42–44; propaganda of, 235n35; Protestant Reformation and, 101–5; racism and, 28; reformist initiatives in, 39–44; Spanish church-state relations and, 64–68, 224n19. *See also* Christianity

Romance languages, race in, 61–64

Root, Deborah, 76–79

Rosenberg, Julius and Ethel, 97, 100

Rousseau, Jean-Jacques, 147, 165

Royal African Company, 231n11

Russian Revolution, 160, 180

Said, Edward, 195–96, 240n12

Salaita, Steven, 18

"salutary and necessary coercion" (Fourth Lateran Council), 56–57

sambenito (penitential garment), 77–78, 118, 224n22

Sandoval, Alonso de, 86–88, 225n32

Sandoval, Prudencio (Bishop), 93–94

sansculottes, 159, 161, 164–66, 237n43. *See also* "Real San-Culotte, A" (cartoon)

Saracens: clothing restrictions for, 53–57, 62–63; Crusades against, 44–47; Fourth Lateran Council on, 53–57; Jews linked to, 49

Sarmiento, Pero, 59, 67–70, 223n14

Sayyid, Salman, 20–21

Schmitt, Carl, 108–9, 129, 205–8, 242nn28–30

Schulz, Wilhelm, 179

Schumpeter, Joseph, 185

Schechter, Ronald, 167

Scottsboro Boys, 172

Second Coming: Christian belief in, 45; colonialism and ideology of, 101; Jewish role in, 48

Second Treatise on Government (Locke), 142–45

secularism: Jewish subjugation to, 65; race and, 208–10; reason of state and, 107–9, 226n13, 227n16

security: birth of, 29; Black criminality and, 192; colonialism and, 86–91, 101–5; covert technologies of intelligence and, 120–21; crisis populism and, 205–16; Foucault on, 27, 37–38; Fourth Lateran Council agenda for, 50–52; hermeneutics of suspicion and, 12–13; history of, 24; Locke on society and, 142–45; Middle Ages language of, 34–35; police power and, 140–42; racial capitalism and, 138–39, 189–90; religion and, 122; slavery as threat to, 89–91; Spanish technologies of racial security, 76–82; state power and, 105

Security, Territory, Population (Foucault), 26, 36–38, 139

sedition: of the belly, 114–15, 138, 177; British Catholics linked to, 117–20; covert technologies of intelligence and, 120–21; defined, 227n24; enemies of the state and, 109, 111–13; papist versus Puritan seditions, 115–20

"Seditions and Troubles" (Bacon), 111–13

self-ownership, whiteness and, 149–50

Sentencia-Estatuto of Toledo, 68–70, 75

September 11, 2001, attacks: and Islamophobia, 2, 22, 194, 202; racial neoliberalism and, 202–3

Septuagint, 52

Sepúlveda, Juan Ginés de, 83, 225n28

sexuality: anticommunism and, 181, 238n63; antisemitism and, 70, 73; Fourth Lateran Council and, 53–57, 222n28; heresy and, 51–52; propertied and proprietary possession, 148; reason of state and, 110–11

Shakespeare, William, 98

sharecropping, 237n50

sheep and shepherding, heresy and images of, 40–44, 52, 220n4

Siete partidas (Spanish juridical code), 66, 223n11

Silverblatt, Irene, 92

Simon the Zealot, 155, 234n30

simony, abolition of, 39–40

Singh, Nikhil, 13, 151, 234n23

sistema de las castas (Spanish caste system), 80–82

skin color: colonial anti-Blackness and, 87–91; conversos (Jewish converts and), 68–73; Spanish colonialism and, 86–91

Skinner, Quentin, 103–4, 110, 226n4

slave patrols, 168–71, 234n23

slavery: anti-Blackness and, 84–91; Atlantic slave trade, 84–91, 225n30; capitalist production and, 149–52, 233nn19–20; colonialism justification of, 84–91; criminality and, 150–51; etymology of, 79, 224n24; of Indigenous peoples, 82–84; industrialization and, 233n19; liberalism and, 141–42; Locke and, 143, 231nn11–12; medieval division of labor and, 32–34, 220n2; Moorish participation in, 69; Ottoman Empire and growth of, 79; as property ownership, 145–46; racial capitalism and, 138–39; rebellions against, 30, 89–91, 144–45, 160–71; Spanish entry into, 79–82; surveillance and, 14; Western political philosophy and, 165

Slavs, slavery etymology and, 79, 224n24

Slobodian, Quinn, 200–201

Smedley, Audrey, 60–61

Smedley, Audrey and Brian, 32, 219n1

"Snake, The" (fable and song), 5–7, 23–24, 191–92

socialism, emergence of, 175

Social Contract, The (Rousseau), 165

Société des Saisons, 178

society, Locke's concept of, 152–55

Society Must Be Defended (Foucault), 26

sodomy: Jews linked to, 73; state security and, 110–11, 118

Sonthonax, Léger-Félicité, 163

Sorry to Bother You (film), 17

soul: biopolitics of, 52–53; Fourth Lateran Council and, 53–57; government of, 5–9; passing and, 15–17; racism and role of, 3–4; religious significance of, 7–8

South Africa, anti-apartheid activism in, 230n1

sovereignty: exceptionalism of, 108–9; sleeping sovereign, 236n41; Spanish struggle for, 64–65; Westphalian system of states and, 102–5, 226n4; witchcraft as threat to, 111

Soyer, Francois, 226n1

Spain: African slavery and, 79–82; church-state relations in, 64–68, 224n19; colonialism and, 80–82; Jews as conversos in, 64–67; in Middle Ages, 45–46, 64–67; technologies of racial security in, 76–82

Spanish Inquisition: colonial branch of, 86; language of race and, 61–62, 222n4; monarchical justification for, 224n20; Peruvian *gran complicidad* and, 92; technologies of security and, 76–79

spatial infrastructures: race and biopolitics and, 95–96; racial capitalism and, 173–74, 237n49

spiritual security, Locke's concept of, 153

state: Bacon on threats to, 116–20; Blackness as enemy of, 172–74; covert technologies of intelligence and, 120–21; early models of, 104–5; enemies of, 109–13; ensoulment and politics of, 100; international order and, 129–31; master concept of, 226n4; race and role of, 29, 100–105; religion as technology of, 105–7; sedition against, 111–13; Spanish church-state relations and, 64–68, 224n19; Westphalian model of, 100–105

State of Missouri v. Celia, a Slave, 150

St. Bartholomew's Day massacre, 125

Stout, Jeffrey, 102

structural racism, 4–5

Stuart political theology, 108–9, 128

Stuelke, Even, 215
Summa totius heresis Saracenorum (Summary
  of the entire heresy of Saracens) (Peter the
  Venerable), 47
surveillance: anti-Blackness and, 14; politics of
  exposure and, 10–11
suspicion, Ricoeur's hermeneutics of, 11–12
Sweet, James, 79–80

Táíwò, Olúfhemi O., 214
Talmud, Christian criticism of, 48–49
Tea Party (US), 204
technologies of security: immigration and,
  192–93; religion as, 105–7; in Spain, 76–82
terror: global war on, 202–3; political power
  and, 167; religious enemy framework and,
  194–95
Tesoro de la lengua Castellana o Española
  (Covarrubias), 62
theft, property as, 174–75
Third World communism, 181, 198
Third World Marxism, 135
Thirty Years' War, 103
threat, race as, 9–10
Tise, Larry E., 167
Toledan revolt (1447), 67
tolerance, Locke's civil society and, 152–55,
  234n26
Torres, Max Sebastian Hering, 62–63, 93,
  223n9
Toscano, Arturo: on fanaticism, 155–56,
  159–60, 186; on late fascism, 203
Trachtenberg, Joshua, 55, 222n29
Tractatus contra Petrubrussianos (Peter the
  Venerable), 47
traitor, Cicero's figure of, 109, 227n17
Tratado del Alboraique (*Treatise of the Alborai-
  que*). *See Libro del Alboraique* (*Book of the
  Alboraique*)
treason: Catholicism linked to, 126–28; evolution of, 109–13, 227n18
Treaty of Westphalia (1648), 102, 106
*True Report of the Detestable Treason Intended
  by Doctor Roderigo Lopez, A* (Bacon), 98
Trump, Donald, 70, 191; Muslim travel ban,
  203–5; racial threat politics of, 2–3, 5–7,
  172, 217n5
truth, racial, 10–13

truth effect, slave revolutions and, 89–91
Tudor political theology, 107–9
Tupac Amaru II, 84
Turkish despot, Orientalist stereotype of,
  130–31
Turner, Nat, 169–70
"two swords" doctrine: heresy and, 43–44;
  Jewish subjugation in Spain and, 64–65
Tyrer, David, 20–21

United States: Black Jacobins in, 167–71;
  Blackness and racial power in, 173–74;
  immigration control in, 182–83; nativism
  in, 193–94; racialized financial discourse in,
  186; right-wing populism in, 191–92
unpropertied: coalition of, 15–152; criminal
  threat of, 145–49
Ury, Jon, 126

veil of ignorance, Rawls's concept of, 23
Vesey, Denmark, 168–70
via media (middle way), Anglican tradition of,
  125, 229n49
Vietnam War, 197–98
violence, racial capitalism and, 136–39
Viroli, Maurizio, 103–4
Vogl, Joseph, 185
Voltaire, 235n33
von Stein, Lorenz, 179
Vulgate Bible, 35, 52–53, 155

Wagner, Bryan, 171–74
Wald, Gayle, 15
Waldensian movement, 41
Walker, David, 168–70, 180, 237n48
Wallerstein, Immanuel, 100, 230n4
Walsingham, Francis (Sir), 121
war: Locke's discussion of, 143–44; racism as,
  13–15
Wars of Religion, 102–3, 129
Watson, Hilbourne A., 220n2
Westphalian system of states: antipopery and
  color line and, 125–28; colonialism and,
  114–15; counterfeit worshippers in, 123–25;
  emergence of, 101–5; English Civil War and,
  118–20; fanaticism and, 155–56; Islamophobia and, 128–31; 229n51; parties in, 157–60;
  racial capitalism and, 138–39; racism and,

127–28; religion as technology of, 105–7, 226n13; religious enemy framework and, 195; security state and, 125; Spanish church-state relations and, 224n19; threat of the improper and, 152–55

What Is Property? (Proudhon), 174–75

White, Hylton, 241n26

whiteness: origins of, 93–96, 234n25; of policing, 151–52, 234n23; as property, 149–50, 233n22

white supremacy: anti-Arab racism, 18–20; as war, 13–15

Whitgift, John, 229n45

Williams, Kristin, 181

Williams, Raymond, 26

Wilmington Messenger newspaper (North Carolina) 133, 171–74

Wilson, Al, 5

witchcraft: racism and, 8; reason of state and, 110–11

wolf predators: epidermalization of, 55–57; heresy and images of, 40–44, 51–52; Jewish conversos as, 66–70

women, as criminal threat, 148, 238n63

World on Fire (Chua), 202–3

World Trade Organization (WTO), 200

World War I, 180

Wright, Richard, 180

Yuran, Noam, 185

zealotry, Locke's discussion of, 155–57

Žižek, Slavoj, 17